The renewal of post-war Manchester

Manchester University Press

The renewal of post-war Manchester

Planning, architecture and the state

Richard Brook

Manchester University Press

Copyright © Richard Brook 2025

The right of Richard Brook to be identified as the author of this work has been asserted in accordance with the Copyright, Designs and Patents Act 1988.

An electronic version of this book has been made freely available under a Creative Commons (CC BY-NC-ND) licence, thanks to the support of Lancaster University, which permits non-commercial use, distribution and reproduction provided the author(s) and Manchester University Press are fully cited and no modifications or adaptations are made. Details of the licence can be viewed at https://creativecommons.org/licenses/by-nc-nd/4.0/

Published by Manchester University Press
Oxford Road, Manchester M13 9PL

www.manchesteruniversitypress.co.uk

British Library Cataloguing-in-Publication Data
A catalogue record for this book is available from the British Library

ISBN 978 1 5261 5497 2 hardback

First published 2025

The publisher has no responsibility for the persistence or accuracy of URLs for any external or third-party internet websites referred to in this book, and does not guarantee that any content on such websites is, or will remain, accurate or appropriate.

EU authorised representative for GPSR:
Easy Access System Europe – Mustamäe tee 50, 10621 Tallinn, Estonia, gpsr.requests@easproject.com

Typeset in 10/12 Apolline Std by
Cheshire Typesetting Ltd, Cuddington, Cheshire

Contents

	Preface	*page* vi
	Acknowledgements	ix
	List of abbreviations	xi
	Introduction	1
1	The shape of the city: power and planning	9
2	Computing and the Cold War	63
3	In advance of progress: higher education and technology	123
4	Intractable investment: the Crown Agents and Central Station	193
5	Bookended by bombs and drawn out development: Market Place	233
6	The redoubtable resilience of the ring road	277
	Conclusion	313
	Bibliography	326
	List of illustrations	339
	Index	353

Preface

This book is about the relationships between planning, private architectural practice and the state, in post-war Britain. The genesis of this inquiry rests in two places: the first my role as a practising architect and the second in my work examining modern buildings designed and constructed in the twentieth century, predominantly those built after 1945.

As a practising architect, I was acutely aware of the role of architect as mediator. Design, as an exclusive artistic act, constitutes only a fraction of the working life of an architect; much more time is focused upon the interpretation of needs, desires, rules and guidance from a multitude of human and non-human actors and the two- and three-dimensional manifestations of these interpretations through drawings and models – thus, the architect as mediator. In one project, a Grade II* listed railway station, I had to interpret the demands and opinions of my client – Arriva Trains, who were the station operators, the owners of the infrastructure – Network Rail, four other train operating companies who had services using the station, the Rail Heritage Trust, Historic England, the county council, the city council and their Conservation Officer and Planning Department, the Rail Users Group, the building survey report, the ground conditions, the consultant engineer, the estate agent, the highways department, the named electrical sub-contractors for the display of information and the guidance in the building regulations. At different stages of the job, I used alternative modes of communication to describe and convince each party that our design was acting in response to their concerns or needs and met the statutory obligations in respect of safety, accessibility, durability and other performance factors. Models, photographic montage, drawings, sketches, spreadsheets, specifications and verbal presentations were all tools employed and all had their own agency in the processes of procurement and production. Amidst these acts of mediation I attempted to realise something unique and of myself, my contribution – the design.

This act of mediation may be conceived as one definition of design – working with form and material within a given set of parameters – but this precept effectively situates the architect at the top of a pyramidal hierarchy, evocative of the historic notion of the 'master builder'. Even carrying the title of Project Architect, did not mean that design was mine to dictate, though it was mine to control. In contemporary architectural practice only the traditional form of contract affords the architect such powers, as bestowed by the client.[1] However, the life of a building begins before its design; it begins as an idea or as a means to satisfy an objective. A practising architect is not always the first to imagine a scheme; other parties have usually been involved before an architect is commissioned; some form of government policy has most likely been read; for buildings of any scale a committee will have been formed; a planner may have been consulted, and so on. The architect is one of a number of human and non-human actors that have agency on the procurement and production of a building.

The addition to the railway station was not a hugely prestigious job, but nor was it everyday. I worked with much more mundane building types, including supermarkets, but even their production was not simple in terms of the numbers of factors influencing siting, mass, form, materials and internal arrangement. This led me to question how we understand the production of actual physical space and its constituents, and the impact this has on our experience of cities. This book aims to address this question and offers a model, or method, with which to unpack the forces acting on procurement and production and to ask what these forces have to say about the concomitant cultural, social, political and economic conditions.

I am interested in the architecture of the regions and in the quotidian. Building outside the capital city is often subject to more budgetary constraint and cost can be a major force in the determination of quality. Most buildings are not of the avant-garde and the easiest way to think of them is as stylistically derived from other precedents – the architectural firsts. I personally find this limiting in several ways, not least because such an approach discounts swathes of architectural production from analysis and understanding. The architecture of the regions may be characterised as derivative if one chooses to focus on style as a means of assessment, but I'm less interested in style than content. By this, I mean that the histories of the procurement and the production of buildings have much to say about society, in the broadest sense. As a teacher and as a practitioner of architecture I understand that design is as much about process as it is about product, and the processes of architecture are not simply bound by the limits of what we might narrowly define as design.

---

1 Since 1931 The Joint Contracts Tribunal has produced standard forms of construction contract, guidance notes and other standard forms of documentation for use by the construction industry in the UK. The standard, or traditional, form of contract means that the employer (client) is responsible for the design, and this is usually supplied to the contractor by the architect or design team working on the employer's behalf.

Concurrent to my architectural practice I developed an interest in the architecture and buildings of the mid-twentieth century. This began as a hobby and involved photography, but quickly became more as I travelled around the city region of Manchester to visit and record buildings as my spare time permitted. My interest in the mid-century was a form of 'architectural enthusiasm' driven by the aesthetic qualities of production, the apparent volume of buildings of the period in Manchester and the fact that many were being demolished or altered.[2] I had, up to that point, no overt passion for architectural history and many of the buildings I visited were relatively ordinary, even those attributed to well-known architects. To my mind they were special though and it was their collective ordinariness that made them so. The fact that much mid-century architecture was so popularly maligned, even that considered culturally significant by experts, made it more interesting to me. Why was it so disliked? Were we about to wipe out a whole swathe of the built environment before we had the chance to fully understand its role in society and society's role in its realisation? My mission was thus twofold, to try and record as much as I was physically capable of and to start to try and find ways of exploring meaning in everyday architecture.

These then are the main manifestations of my experience to date: a passion for the quotidian, a fascination with the region where I grew up, studied and worked and an understanding that the role of the architect is not limited to the conventional act of design. In the following pages I attempt to reconcile these interests, to situate the everyday and agency in their academic contexts and to apply a novel methodology to the study of architecture not viewed as high art. I also try to explain why I think these things are important to the study of architecture and cities more broadly.

---

[2] Craggs, R., Geoghegan, H., and Neate, H. (2013) 'Architectural Enthusiasm: Visiting Buildings with the Twentieth Century Society', *Environment and Planning D: Society and Space*, Vol. 31, No. 5, pp. 879–896.

Acknowledgements

This work would have been impossible were it not for the support of Nina. For more than a quarter of a century Nina has put up with all my idiosyncrasies in pursuit of knowledge about this wonderful city and region in which we reside. My former Head of School at the Manchester School of Architecture, Tom Jefferies, not only ignited my passion for the subject when I met him in 1995 as my teacher; he also unequivocally supported this research in many ways. Mark Crinson supervised my doctorate, much of which made its way into this manuscript. He was my first, and fiercest, critic as well as the interpreter of my abstract ramblings as we teased out what I wanted to say about architecture as a profession. Anthony Gerbino was my second supervisor and his gentle but deeply inquisitive questioning forced me to communicate with clarity and confidence. Michael Hebbert provided encouragement and generous academic citizenship throughout my research. Isabelle Doucet brought her expertise in architecture and in applied theory to the critique of my work and I am deeply indebted for her insight. Martin Dodge taught me how to use archives, how to never desist from seeking that last piece of the jigsaw and, even when it can't be found, to never give up on the idea. He is voracious in his appetite for knowledge and through our work together in other areas he has provided me with a skill set that I cherish.

Many others have been generous with their time and comments on my work: Jonathan Aylen, James Sumner, John Wilson, Simon Lavington, Simon Gunn, Otto Saumarez Smith, Elain Harwood and Robert Proctor. The 2013 Leicester conference, *The Transformation of Urban Britain Since 1945*, organised by Simon Gunn and Rebecca Magdin was instrumental in my thinking and where I first met John Gold, who examined my PhD and has always been kind and keen to share his own expertise. Peter Larkham convened the symposium where I first presented the work that became Chapter 6 of this volume and his drive and passion for planning history is infectious. I am indebted to Matthew Jarvis, a former student, who took on the ring road for his Masters dissertation and did a superb job. Several architects who worked for Cruickshank & Seward gave their time for conversations and interviews: Gordon Hodkinson, John Sheard, Eamonn O'Neill, Alan Morris, Peter Crummett, Frank Altmann and Denver Humphries. Gordon Hodkinson was an important designer for Cruickshank & Seward in the period I have studied, yet practised in the shadow of Arthur Gibbon. His modesty and humility belie an awesome talent and I was overwhelmed to receive his student work into the Special Collections of Manchester Metropolitan University. Sadly, Gordon passed away in January 2018 before he could see his work from the 1940s exhibited and appreciated by others. Gordon Broady helped me retrieve the remaining Cruickshank & Seward archive from packing cases in a warehouse in Trafford Park, so it too could be lodged with Manchester Metropolitan University's Special Collections. John Millar, Robert Maund and David Kaiserman shared their memories of Manchester's first planning department. John Whalley recollected his landscape designs for Central Station. David Govier, first of the County Record Office and latterly of Archives+, has been an avid supporter of my work in this area and has given access to areas of the collections closed to others.

Larysa Bolton and Sarah Hobbs at Archives+ have also been generous with their time and knowledge. Jan Shearsmith and Jan Hicks at the Museum of Science and Industry added to my visits by making further enquiries on my behalf. Ursula Mitchell at Queens University Belfast prepared all the material I needed on my flying visit. Whoever it is that takes care of the cataloguing at the RIBA Library has my utmost respect and gratitude. Jack Hale, Maureen Ward, Eddy Rhead, Ashiya Eastwood and Matt Retallick of The Modernist Society have given me the opportunity to share my work through public walks and talks over the last decade. All of my colleagues at the Manchester School of Architecture (MSA) have had something to do with this, whether as sounding boards, counsellors, or picking up the slack when I took on too much – thanks MSA. Finally, I wish to thank my parents for nurturing my love of the built environment, for all the visits to burial mounds, churches, cathedrals and stone circles across Britain, which may not be modern but were frequently monolithic.

The first draft of this manuscript was kindly supported by a Postdoctoral Fellowship award from the Paul Mellon Centre for Studies in British Art.

Abbreviations

BDP	Building Design Partnership
C&S	Cruickshank & Seward
CDA	Comprehensive Development Area
CPO	Compulsory Purchase Order
DSIR	Department of Scientific and Industrial Research
EE	English Electric
FE	Further Education
GM	General Motors
GMC	Greater Manchester Council
HE	Higher Education
HMSO	Her Majesty's Stationery Office
ICL	International Computers Limited
ICT	International Computers and Tabulators
IRC	Industrial Reorganisation Corporation
M&S	Marks & Spencer
MHLG	Ministry of Housing and Local Government
MIT	Massachusetts Institute of Technology
MoS	Ministry of Supply
MoW	Ministry of Works
MSI	Museum of Science and Industry
MTCP	Ministry of Town and Country Planning
NCC	National Computing Centre
NCP	National Car Parks Limited
NRDC	National Research Development Corporation
PAG	Planning Advisory Group
R&D	Research & Development
RIBA	Royal Institute of British Architects
SELNEC	South-East Lancashire North-East Cheshire
TRE	Telecommunications Research Establishment

LIST OF ABBREVIATIONS

UGC	University Grants Committee
UKAEA	United Kingdom Atomic Energy Authority
UMIST	University of Manchester Institute of Science and Technology
UoMA	University of Manchester Archives
WW	Wilson & Womersley

Introduction

Post-war planning and architecture were not always neatly packaged. Post-war plans, on the other hand, were often presented as sweeping and total solutions that promised new, modern cities, free from the grime and congestion of the industrial revolution. Some cities in the UK were reconstructed quickly – by 1955 most of Coventry's city centre was rebuilt. Many other cities, especially those in the Midlands, North and Scotland, did not begin their central area renewal until the early 1960s, yet had substantial plans drawn up and published in the immediate post-war period – Manchester presented its plans to the public in 1945. This was a golden era for planning. Lavish publications with full-colour illustrations, maps and diagrams made convincing cases for redevelopment that was modern, forward looking and promised social, cultural and commercial remedy to the horrors of the recent past. This investigation, of Manchester's post-war planning and architecture, began with its *1945 Plan* – a document so comprehensive and convincing that when I first encountered it in the downturn of the mid-1990s, I found myself asking why this fantastic vision had not come to be. The simple answer was that it was down to economics, Manchester Corporation did not have the money to realise its own plan. The real answers are more complex and have to do with land ownership, land assembly, shifting policy governing the environment, changing structures of government and the rise of personal mobility, as well as the global meta-narratives of the Cold War, decolonisation and the growth of consumerism in the West. Throughout this book, through a series of interlinked chapters, I show how all of these factors and more influenced and impacted on the Manchester's morphology in the messy assemblage that was the modern city.

Morphology looms large throughout this book. It is the shape of the city and the shape of its buildings with which I am concerned. This is a spatial account, a formal understanding of the forces acting on the making of urban space – an architectural view. However, this is not an architectural history in the conventional sense. I eschew notions of style in favour of an approach that accepts the agency of all sorts of actors, on plans and on construction. It is not always a biographical approach either – I accept that sometimes plans and policies had agency that was at least equivalent to that of people. Ideas involving the development of cities often run for decades and it can become the idea, not the author of the idea, that persists and prevails. This book is part urban history, part planning history and part architectural history. As such, I show how policy decisions, declared in Whitehall, were interpreted by the officials and officers of local government and, in turn, how architects were both informed by, and reacted to, policy and plan. In all of the empirical chapters I explore a perceptible set of relations from policy, to plan, to implementation. In so doing, I highlight the particular circumstances of a nationalised state with a burgeoning legislative landscape designed to control the development of town and country. The post-war period provided the policies, but it was the training of architect-planners that gave literal and metaphorical shape to statutory guidance.

Three-dimensional visions of entire cities were commonplace by the 1960s and, alongside certain powers vested in local authorities, planners were able to influence the shape of the city. Of course, existing topography, natural features and historic infrastructure had to be negotiated and the typical western European city was awash with layers of earlier development, also informed by mobility and exchange. Rivers, canals, railways, markets, warehouses and factories all left their own physical patterns on the city and Manchester was no exception. The first chapter explains Manchester's growth to become a regional capital and its form according to the operations that sustained its expansion.

Manchester is a case study here. While much of the detail is specific, the post-war setting was similar for places like Birmingham, Liverpool, Leeds, Sheffield, Newcastle, Glasgow and others – regional capitals of larger metropolitan areas, with strong traditions of local governance. These traditions met with the regional ministries of central government, making various tiers and hierarchies, within which types of political interplay had their own impact on urban form. Manchester, like many such cities, was a hub around which social, cultural, financial and technological forces coalesced and converged. Using a place-centred approach, each chapter addresses the variety and magnitude of forces acting upon a particular situation. What were the global circumstances that fostered certain industries and initiatives? In whose interest were decisions made? How was policy interpreted through the tiers of government into on-the-ground conditions? What impact did these complex associations between place, policy and personnel have on planning? And, in turn, how did planning affect construction? This book explores the nested, tiered and stacked networks at play in Manchester's post-war renewal that were exclusive to its outcomes, but also typical of the types of discourse around development that happened in similar cities.

For the most part, this group of renewal cities were post-industrial. For most too, their decline began before the outbreak of war in 1939. The conflict of the Second World War was merely an interruption to a period of transition away from industrial economies and not necessarily the catalyst to reconstruction, as is popularly held. In this sense, I use renewal not just to refer to central area 'urban renewal', which followed a particular North American model of development, but the wholesale renewal of the lifeblood of a city – how new economies were built and how they changed the built environment.[1] I explore the demands for development in a large provincial city that moved towards a service economy, but was intrinsically bound to a culture of innovation and manufacturing. The renewal cities of post-war Britain are much less explored in literature than the recovery cities as the forces acting on their development were manifold and occurred over extended time periods. Their complex narratives, which were bound with a period of rapid progressive change in political, cultural, social and economic contexts, have much to reveal about the state and its influence on urban and architectural form. A significant amount of scholarship uses the welfare state as a lens through which to view the post-war period. Of course, such an approach is essential in grasping the lived experiences of millions of citizens who were relocated to new homes, educated in new schools and treated in new hospitals. However, here I reveal a state wider than simply 'welfare', or even 'warfare', as one that touched almost every aspect of development and construction.[2] The state control of development after 1947 was at its zenith, yet waned under the rising pressures of a free-market economy from the late 1950s. This makes architecture and planning both suitable subjects and vehicles with which to understand the post-war development of post-industrial cities.

In terms of periodisation, the most substantial parts of the book address two decades, from the mid-1950s until the mid-1970s. It was an exciting time in the development of European cities, when capital flowed, energy was cheap and abundant, citizens were more mobile than ever before and a new optimism was embodied in popular culture. The earlier date marks the point at which the first new buildings were completed in Manchester city centre as well as the relaxation of building licensing. The later date captures the oil crisis, the ensuing economic shock and the massive upheaval of local government that saw the creation of the metropolitan counties, Greater Manchester included, in 1974. Each chapter spans a slightly different time frame, according to its subject.

The opening chapter presents a long history of planning in the city, which began even before city's incorporation in 1838, and attempts to map the spatial

---

1 The term 'urban renewal' refers to a specific form of urbanisation, comprehensive redevelopment, which was characterised by multi-level, mixed-use, shopping, office, gallery, museum and parking complexes that created pedestrian precincts, ramps, sunken inner-city dual carriageways, and a host of other distinctive urban conditions.
2 Historian David Edgerton has advanced the concept of the British warfare state in relation to the substantial resources deployed in service of rearmament in post-war Britain. See Edgerton, D. (2006) *Warfare State. Britain, 1920–1970* (Cambridge: Cambridge University Press).

and organisational relationships between the city and the city region. Chapter 2 deals with computing technology, backgrounded by the Cold War. It addresses the urgent need for independent British research following their exclusion from the US nuclear programme in 1946. Manchester became one centre in a north-west cluster of technologies related to the nuclear programme and the chapter closes with an account of the design and construction of the National Computing Centre that opened in 1975. Chapter 3 examines the expansion of the universities, beginning with a technical college that was awarded its chartered status in 1956. The conclusion of the chapter is signalled by the publication of the planners' review of their own proposals in 1974. In Chapter 4, decolonisation provides the financial context for the proposed development of Manchester's Central Station. Its closure was announced in 1965. There followed a drawn-out period of acquisitions and development proposals that led to naught and withered amidst political scandal in 1977. The penultimate chapter looks at a part of the central city that was subject to speculation on its future in the immediate post-war years and received a lot of attention from as early as 1947. Market Place, its development, was finally completed in 1972. Finally, the ambitious and influential plans for a central ring road are explored from the earliest drawings in 1945, their partial realisation through the 1960s and their eventual abandonment in 1976. These various time frames, which do not precisely coincide, nonetheless overlap. In this temporal overlapping certain policies and personnel emerge periodically and within the distinct chronology and narrative of each we see the actions of a strong local government and effective officers, albeit without the independent financial might to enact all of their aims.

As this account is not told via a linear chronology, the book is organised by geography. The opening chapter is as wide as it is long, the extended history of the metropolitan centre is mirrored by its geographical reach, which addresses the regional role of the city. The buildings associated with militarisation and computation in Chapter 2 form a network that spans the city and connects to the wider region. Closing in on the centre, the expansive university development of Chapter 3 takes a linear form of approximately 1½ miles (2km) along Manchester's Oxford Road. Central Station, in Chapter 4, is a contained site right on the edge of the central area and Market Place in Chapter 5 is, as its name suggests, in the heart of the city. The final chapter, on the central ring road, lassoes (some might say throttles) the city centre and connects its planning back to that of its region. Such ordering enables the various narratives to be punctuated by recurring decisions and to presence the voices of those who had interests wider than one particular site or building. Alongside the temporal overlaying, this geographical nesting also serves to illustrate the complex and interwoven nature of the forces at play in the shaping of a renewal city.

The architecture of renewal cities is largely under-explored as most of it falls under the umbrella term of 'mainstream modernism', is derided as 'gimcrack', or even 'crap', and, as such, has largely escaped the view of architectural historians

INTRODUCTION

to date.³ Mainstream modern architecture accounts for a considerable amount of the new construction realised across Europe in the post-war reconstruction process. This book offers a novel method for the examination of this type of development that understands the relationships between legislation, governance and the production of material space. Architectural history can be bound by notions of style, which is adequate when discussing the architectural firsts, elites, pioneers and avant-gardes, but can limit scholarship to these realms, which do not represent the majority of the built environment. This gap in representation is more acute when discussing the architectural cultures of cities outside the capital, where slender budgets impacted on construction quality. Of course, within this, architects used their ingenuity and skills as designers to help make the best possible outcomes. In Manchester, firms such as Cruickshank & Seward, H.S. Fairhurst & Sons, Building Design Partnership, Leach Rhodes Walker, Wilson & Womersley as well as the City Architect's Department made significant contributions to the modernisation of the city. It is the situation of their practice, amidst planning legislation and subsequently within the city, and understanding the forces influencing their architecture and its association with place, that offers new readings.

Using a place-centred approach to unpicking the forces acting on urbanisation presents a novel way of thinking about mainstream architectural production, work that was not explicitly modernist, but was ostensibly modern. Modern architecture did not really take hold in Britain until after 1945, save for private houses and a few notable schemes by émigré architects escaping from Nazi Germany and mostly en route to North America, where they also had considerable impact on architectural culture. Most architecture in Britain was, however, modern by the mid-1950s; the neo-Georgian and neo-Classical styles favoured in the inter-war period had faded from fashion. It was this version of modern architecture that came to be popularly derided and was unfairly cast as an agent of society's ills. Because of this, it has rarely been considered on its own merits, or as a subject with which to explore the wider contexts for its realisation. Throughout the following chapters, buildings *are* described and analysed in relation to their design and style – they have to be, it is inescapable – but I also want the reader to think of them as representative parts of much bigger stories, of the why and how they came to be commissioned and built. What was their role in the modernisation of Britain? How can mainstream modern architecture be used to narrate the development of the town and cities where it was realised? To answer these questions, I turn to architecture's relationship with post-war planning.

---

3 'Gimcrack' is used by Otto Saumarez Smith. He also refers to the books *Britain's Crap Towns* and Martin Parr's *Boring Postcards*, each of which cast development of the period negatively (albeit with some irony in Parr's case). Smith, O. Saumarez (2019) *Boom Cities: Architect-Planners and the Politics of Radical Urban Renewal in 1960s Britain* (Oxford: Oxford University Press), p. 2.

Several of the chapters examine, in detail, the relationships between planners and architects. This was a very particular period in British history, when a high proportion of planners had undergraduate degrees in architecture, and the connections between public and private sector colleagues were often negotiated using visual tools of models and drawings. It is this sense of negotiated practice that was especially apparent in the 1960s, as planners used the mechanisms of the planning system to interpret government advice and guidelines and to inform the decisions of architects and their clients. Tools like the statutory Development Plan, the designation of Comprehensive Development Areas (CDA), the use of Compulsory Purchase Orders (CPO), and slum clearance policies, were used to create real or proposed clean slates – large parcels of land that could be planned in totality. The powers invested in local authorities to be able to control development in this manner, combined with years of decline and the actual damage wrought by war, enabled the bold visions that characterised inner urban planning of the period. Manchester was no different. The comprehensive replanning of the city in the 1960s was as ambitious, if not more so, than that of the *1945 Plan*, but has received much less attention. In many ways it was this period of planning that left the biggest mark on the city, albeit informed by what had preceded it. In this book I trace these marks, starting with the analysis of the drawings and models of the planners and architects and following the parallel paths of decision making recorded in minutes and correspondence. Fully realised projects are presented with those only partially fulfilled and those that never came to be, in an attempt to show the influence of planning on architecture and the effects of both on the shape of the city.

This is not a full account of Manchester's post-war development. There are glaring omissions. There is little focus on housing, no investigation of healthcare provision, cursory mention of religious buildings and scant discussion of the massive Arndale shopping centre. Manchester's post-war housing was great in its scope and deserves a book of its own – its provision was equally wrapped up in the politics of the period. The hospitals closest to the city centre were the subject of a master plan by Fry & Drew (c.1965) that was on the edge of, and drawn into, that of the Education Precinct that encompassed the university and a number of colleges. Powell and Moya designed a new hospital (1965–73) on the southern edge of Manchester at Wythenshawe, a settlement founded on garden city principles and the subject of many existing studies. New churches were plentiful, but few were in the city centre. The most architecturally significant church, St Augustine's (Desmond Williams & Associates, 1968), was subsumed by the planning of the Education Precinct. The Arndale Centre was one of Manchester's largest developments and most symbolic of the rise of consumerism. Its monstruous qualities and considerable inward focus detached it from the city and allowed a suspension of reality for its occupants, the consumers. Its physical relationship with the city around it was muted, precious few of the shops it contained actually addressed the street. Instead, Market Place, the subject of Chapter 5, narrates the commercial change of the city and

INTRODUCTION

its drawn-out development reflects the diversity of interests negotiated in this period of transition.

Britain, on the threshold of the 1960s, was a very different place to Britain of 1945. This book is a deep study of a 'renewal city' and uses the planning and architecture of Manchester as a case through which to reveal shifts in politics, economics and culture in the post-war period. For the first time it uncovers the complex forces acting upon the production of space in the renewal cities of the 1960s and the close and direct relations between state legislation, planning policy definition and architectural production. I want the reader to take away this sense of architecture as a negotiated practice and to understand the array of influences acting on the decision making of design. As a regional capital, Manchester is typical of many other cities and here I attempt to argue for the productive qualities of such a spatial ordering. I view the city region as a productive unit around, within and across which rhizomatic networks of actors affect bounded space at a range of scales – the region, the city, the site, the built object, and the material details. In this book, each of these scales are used to reveal the interrelationships of actors and agents in the creation of buildings, public space and infrastructure. I seek to illustrate the palimpsestic qualities of our cities and to explain the physical traces of dreams, decisions, demolitions and developments that curiously linger and slowly fade.

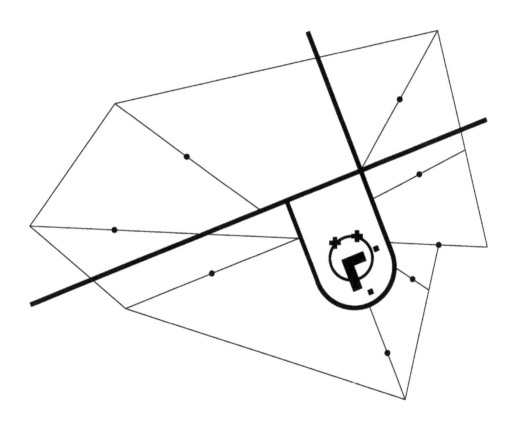

I

The shape of the city: power and planning

Introduction

The morphology of Manchester, as a city and as a city region, was created by its geography, its topography and, by virtue of these, its industry. In this opening chapter I draw together a history of planning with a history of the growth of the city and its region. The idea of the region is important in understanding the physical formation of the city and the influencing factors that informed the work of planners and architects. I deliberately prioritise planners as, from the mid-century onwards, theirs were often the first marks on paper and the first models of card and wood that suggested the form of the city to come. The work of, initially, borough surveyors or engineers, and then architect-planners was at a scale that addressed everything within the political boundary of the city, but also took account of much beyond its borders. This conception, of bounded territories and rhizomatic networks, is increasingly important and apparent in the proceeding empirical chapters, where the relationships between the abstract rationalities of legislation and concrete realities of construction are analysed. Much of this book relies on an examination of the statute designed to control the built environment, most of which did not exist until the twentieth century. Therefore, before we can examine the shape of the post-war city, a brief foray into Manchester's early expansion as an industrial city is a necessary diversion with which to provide some foundation.

Observations and Improvements

Prior to the formation of the Corporation of Manchester (1838) and before Engels had penned his treatise on the working class (1845), Sir William Fairbairn shared his *Observations and Improvements of the Town of Manchester* (1836).[1] Fairbairn was an entrepreneurial engineer of pedigree, both polymath and polyglot. His was one of the earliest texts concerning public space and civic life in the city. He recognised a discrepancy between the apparent wealth of the town and the quality of the built environment:

> As resident inhabitants of Manchester, we feel deep interest in its prosperity; not exclusively as a manufacturing town, but that it should stand conspicuous as a city, equally distinguished for the chaste form of its streets and buildings, as it does for its spirit of enterprise.[2]

Fairbairn's implication was that the mercantile classes had done little to improve the physical stature of the city despite their own acquisition of wealth. He wished to see improvements to the town not for the sake of some form of utopian vision, but for the purposes of commemoration and betterment. Understandably, as an engineer, he valued the influence of the pioneers who had shaped the industrial growth of the city. His intervention was predicated upon a proposal by Lord Francis Egerton to donate a bronze statue of the Duke of Bridgewater to the city, with the condition that the city would find a suitable site for its disposition.[3] Bridgewater was the owner and sponsor of the canal that bore his name and shuttled cheap coal to the burgeoning industrial heart of Manchester from 1761. Fairbairn's ideas were illustrated by another engineer, James Nasmyth, and were principally directed at the area around Piccadilly. The plans showed an 'elegant crescent' that curved between Tib Street and Port Street [Figure 1.01]. It would be called Bridgewater Place and would host statues of James Watt and Richard Arkwright, as well as the proposed figure of Bridgewater himself. Most of the proposals were neo-classical – reflective of Fairbairn's personal appreciation of the monuments of ancient Greece, as objects to which narrative and record could be ascribed with historical and allegorical means, to an almost moral end.[4]

> There is a feeling of liberal pride, in perceiving a progressive tendency to elegant proportion in public buildings and particularly in those large thoroughfares, where impressions are forcibly produced. In no part of Manchester is there a space so well adapted for the purpose as Piccadilly; by a slight curvature of the north-easterly side, an enlarged area may be formed, and in it the monuments would stand conspicuous in the heart of the city.[5]

---

1 Fairbairn, W. (1836) *Observations and Improvements of the Town of Manchester, particularly as regards the importance of blending in those improvements, the chaste and beautiful with the ornamental and useful* (Manchester: Robert Robinson, St Ann's Place).
2 Ibid., p. viii.
3 Ibid., p. iv.
4 Ibid., pp. 20–22.
5 Ibid., p. 25.

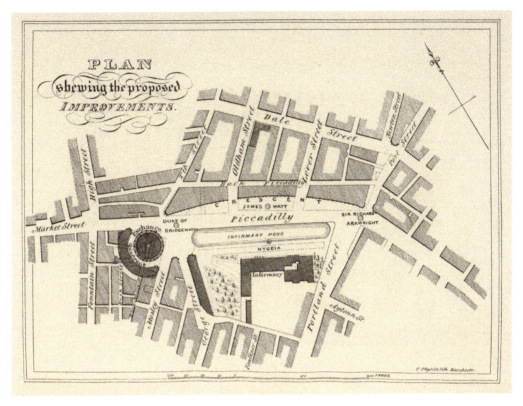

Figure 1.01 'Plan shewing the proposed Improvements', the first attempts at town planning in Manchester. Extract from Sir William Fairbairn's *Observations and Improvements of the Town of Manchester* (1836).

The pages contained discussion on the proportion, perspective and position of the proposed objects. Included was a new exchange or university building at the corner of Market Street and Mosley Street, with a circular plan and a domed roof [Figure 1.02]. A new exchange building was an existing idea, floated in the local press, that Fairbairn built upon. Behind his suggested site for a new exchange was an area to be known as The Quadrant, described as a civic and commercial quarter where the needs of business would be satisfied. Provision for a post office to house Foreign and Home Offices, an exchange, a register office and a hotel to provide access to archives and suitable accommodation for the travelling businessman, all formed part of the vision for the new district.

Inherent in Fairbairn's *Observations* are features of planning that are universal, which pre-empted contexts and situations to come. Fairbairn was reacting to the uncontrolled, unplanned development of the city. Planning, whilst attempting to control futures, is perennially bound by the demand to cure some existing ill. His mode for betterment encompassed three key strategies:

Figure 1.02 'Designs for a New Exchange and Quadrant'. Extract from Sir William Fairbairn's *Observations and Improvements of the Town of Manchester* (1836).

first, the promotion of civic pride; second, the organisation of the city by means of zoning (a tactic embedded in planning from its formal beginnings in the twentieth century); third, an attention to the circumstances for economic success. Fairbairn also anticipated objections from doubters and preservationists: 'The cry is still the same: enormous expense, wisdom of ancestors, innovation and relics of antiquity, are amongst a few of the weapons, with which the non-improvers make their attack.'[6]

However, it was not objections that curtailed Fairbairn's aims, the 'ambitious plan of joining civic improvement to the new industrial and scientific order' was set amidst shifting political sands.[7] The focus of Manchester's middle

---

6 Ibid., p. 22.
7 Wyke, T. (2012) 'Why is There No Statue to the Duke of Bridgewater in Manchester?' in Wyke, T and Nevell, M. (eds) *Bridgewater 250 The Archaeology of the World's First Industrial Canal* (Salford: Centre for Applied Archaeology, University of Salford), pp. 105–114.

classes was on local government reform and dealing with a period of economic uncertainty, characterised by the formation of the Anti-Corn Law League.[8] In the preceding years, the prevailing economic and social movements established in the city became known as the 'School of Manchester' and the ideas of free trade and laissez-faire capitalism were embedded in the corpus of civic society.[9] Of course, this book concerns the post-war city, and popular narratives would hold that under a Labour government, with strong local Labour authority, during a period of nationalisation, urban planning and development would follow socialist principles. As we will read, this was not necessarily the case, but the ideals propounded by Fairbairn – strong civic and economic provision, good quality public space and the zoning of distinct urban functions – prevailed, albeit in the face of constant commercial pressure.

Topography and the city shaped

Fairbairn was reacting to the city that had come to be, rather than a planned city – what Asa Briggs described as a 'shock city', where the priority was production.[10] Alongside Joseph Aston's description of 1804, Karl Friedrich Schinkel's views in 1826 and those of Leon Faucher and Friedrich Engels, published in 1845, he saw the cramped, disorganised and polluted conditions created by dense, industrial development.[11] Others too had noted that 'this famous great factory town.

---

8 Manchester was, at the time, the hub of the world's textile manufacturing industry and had a high population of factory workers who were disadvantaged by the Corn Laws, the protectionist policy that imposed tariffs on imported wheat and increased the price of food. The Corn Laws were supported by the land-owning aristocracy, because by reducing foreign competition they allowed landowners to keep grain prices high and therefore, as the population expanded, increase agricultural profits. The operation of the Corn Laws also meant that the factory workers in the industrial mills in the textile cities of northern England were faced with higher food costs. The mill owners, in turn, suffered higher wage bills and therefore higher finished-goods prices which restricted their foreign trade competitiveness. The League campaigned against the Corn Laws to reduce food prices and increase the competitiveness of manufactured goods abroad and Manchester Liberalism grew out of this movement.
9 Greenleaf, W.H. (1983) *The British Political Tradition. Volume Two: The Ideological Heritage* (London: Methuen), p. 41. In March 1848 Benjamin Disraeli, a Conservative, first used the term 'School of Manchester' to describe the edict of the Manchester Liberals that free trade would lead to a more equitable society, making essential products available to all.
10 Briggs, A. (1963) *Victorian Cities* (London: Odhams Press).
11 Canniffe, E. (2015) 'The Morphology of the Post-industrial City: the Manchester Mill as "symbolic form"', *Journal of Architecture and Urbanism*, Vol. 39, No. 1, pp. 70–78.

Dark and smoky from the coal vapours ... resembles a huge forge or workshop. Work, profit and greed seem to be the only thoughts here.'[12]

Prior to the industrial revolution Manchester was a market town. Its primary geography was attached to Deansgate, a street that ran almost in a straight line between the earliest Roman settlement and the medieval centre, flanked to the north-west by the River Irwell. According to planner R.H. Mattocks, 'even in Roman times Manchester was a regional centre with roads radiating in all directions. This radial system still exists, supplemented by other later roads, and all now pass through the centres of the many towns established on them'.[13] However, it was the climatic state of the city upon which its modern fortunes were founded. Manchester's situation, effectively in a bowl, ringed by the hills of the south Pennines, Dark Peak and White Peak, created a damp climate that was perfect for working textiles. Before its transformation into 'Cottonopolis', Manchester was already known for trading high quality cloth that was manufactured in the city. The navigation of the rivers, Irwell, Mersey and Weaver boosted trade and, before long, Bridgewater's canal and those that followed, would provide the mainstay for the transportation of fuel and goods. Manchester was portrayed as the geographic hub of navigable canals and waterways, and its status as the primary town in the region was established.[14]

As the canals grew, they were connected to one another. In the first decade of the nineteenth century, the joining of the Rochdale Canal, across the city centre in an east–west transect, to the Bridgewater Canal, meant that goods could be transported by barge between Leeds and Liverpool. The railways were less connected. Each of the railway undertakings was a private enterprise and, as such, built their own terminus as close to the centre of the city as possible [Figure 1.03]. The only cross-city connection was made in 1844 when the Leeds and Manchester Railway (1841) was joined to George Stephenson's Liverpool and Manchester Railway (1831) via a new station at Hunts Bank (now Victoria). Where once goods warehouses had surrounded the canal basins, they were now gathered around the railway stations. By the end of the nineteenth century four major passenger terminals, London Road, Victoria, Exchange and Central, as well as a host of goods yards covered large swathes of the central city. The railways altered the fabric of the city and the wider patterns of development. Each line arrived in the city via an elevated viaduct and these immutable brick-arched structures cut through the existing urban grain creating ochre cliffs and canyons. Commuting was enabled by the new lines and the suburban expansion of the

---

12 Schopenhauer, Johanna (1813) *A Lady Travels. Journeys in England and Scotland, the diaries of Johanna Schopenhauer.* Trans. Ruth Michaeliss-Jena and Willy Mersen (1988) (London: Routledge).
13 Mattocks, R.H. (1927) 'Review: Report of the Manchester and District Joint Town Planning Advisory Committee', *The Town Planning Review*, Vol. 12, No. 3 (June), pp. 226–228.
14 For a discussion of Bradshaw's map of Canals (c.1831) see Wyke, T., Robson, B., and Dodge, M. (2018) *Manchester: Mapping the City* (Edinburgh: Birlinn), pp. 13–18.

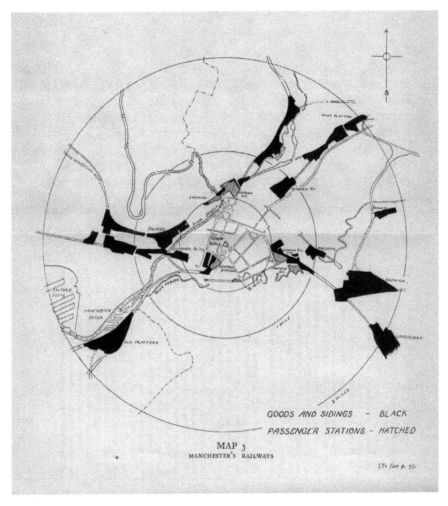

Figure 1.03 Manchester's railways, showing their termini at the edge of the city centre. Extract from *Manchester Made Over* (1936).

city was predicated upon such journeys. The radial pattern of development, established by the turnpikes and reinforced by the railways, preponderated upon the city and, connected or not, the centre was inevitably congested.

Cast in a particular light in 1943, the Royal Institute of British Architects phrased industrial urbanisation thus:

> As the nineteenth century wore on, those who had fled became engulfed again in the expanding city. Around them crept the sea of bricks and macadam ... The cities became choked, grossly overburdened with the weight of their humanity and transport; it took hours to get into them, hours to cross them, hours to

emerge at the other side. New roads were made around them, arteries sprouted from them away into the country; but here again came buildings, in seedy frills along the road.[15]

The industrial revolution set the agenda for planning in Manchester. As the economic might of manufacture and commerce helped to shape the city, it left in its wake insanitary living conditions, pollution and congestion. And, whilst the laissez-faire development climate prevailed, those in local government were first charged with, and then slowly handed the powers to deal with, housing, health and transportation. Manchester's role as a regional centre was founded and consolidated by its manufacturing base and its pre-eminence among the surrounding towns meant that its governance had implications beyond its geographic and political boundaries.

The 'Area'

In earlier days, and when the Region was less crowded, no doubt a considerable amount of general waste passed unnoticed. To-day conditions are different and there can no longer be afforded any waste, either in industry, or of the health or welfare of those engaged in it. Every acre of the Region must be put to its most productive use, and every possibility of communication provided.[16]

Established as the regional centre, Manchester had influence across the northwest of England and beyond. It was connected to the rest of the world via the Manchester Docks and the Ship Canal (opened in 1894). The geographic extents of Manchester's manufacturing and trade encompassed a much larger area of interdependent towns and cities, from the upland reservoirs of the Pennines to the port of Liverpool, a situation recognised by Patrick Geddes in 1915 when he made the first known reference to 'Greater Manchester'.[17] Geddes' work, more generally, acknowledged the association between environment and industry and the ensuing connections between towns, with historic functions built on their climate and topography. This grasp of the idea of the city region or conurbation was, at this stage, analytical – a recognition of a situation that had come to be, or, as in the Lord Mayor's view of Manchester, 'just happened'.[18] The statutory powers for local authorities to address development, which up to

---

15 RIBA (1943) *Rebuilding Britain* (London: Lund Humphries), p. 9. Published in February 1943 to accompany an exhibition of the same name at the National Gallery.

16 Manchester and District Joint Town Planning Advisory Committee (1924) *Report Upon the Regional Scheme* (Manchester: Manchester and District Joint Town Planning Advisory Committee), p. 9.

17 Geddes, P. (1915) *Cities in Evolution* (London: Association for Planning and Regional Reconstruction) New and revised edition, 1949, p. 15.

18 Ebenezer Howard quoting the Lord Mayor in correspondence, 'Town Planning for Manchester', *The Manchester Guardian*, 27 May 1920, p. 5.

this point was organic and piecemeal, was provided by the Town Planning Act (1919), which required the process of planning by all local authorities with a population of over 20,000.[19] The impetus for this legislation (also known as the Addison Act, after Dr Christopher Addison) was the construction of new homes in the wake of the First World War – it also enabled regional planning.

The Manchester and District Joint Town Planning Advisory Committee was formed in 1921 and composed of representatives from surrounding county boroughs.[20] The committee listed among its functions, 'To proceed with the preparation of a regional plan for the Area'.[21] However, the joint committees formed in Manchester and elsewhere had no executive powers and could not ensure implementation unless the participant authorities delegated their powers to the committee. The Manchester Committee addressed the prescient regional planning issues of the day, which have not fundamentally changed – transportation, communication, industry, agriculture and recreation, commerce and housing were all within their remit.[22] In 1922 Manchester hosted a town planning exhibition and conference at the Town Hall. As it approached, the event was reported with the headline 'Hundred years without planning', which signalled the popular view of the need for such work.[23] Also indicative of the recognised necessity was the subscription to the Committee and its aims by 'nearly all of the local authorities within a radius of fifteen miles of the city'. Where able, each authority was asked to provide town maps of 1820 and 1920, to speculate on what their respective townscape might have been if planning was implemented in the nineteenth century and what their town might look like in 2020! Although they lacked the assigned powers to necessarily design the future patterns, delegates and councillors were happy to ruminate over the possibilities attached to this new discipline and new modes of representation.[24]

---

19 Ashworth, W. (1954) *The Genesis of Modern British Town Planning. A Study in Economic and Social History of the Nineteenth and Twentieth Centuries* (London: Routledge & Kegan Paul), pp. 199–200.
20 Bolton, Bucklow, Glossop, Hyde, Manchester, Rochdale and Stretford.
21 Manchester and District Joint Town Planning Advisory Committee (1924) *Constitution And Functions* (Manchester: Manchester and District Joint Town Planning Advisory Committee). The area was defined in clause 2 as 'the Watershed Area of the Rivers Mersey and Irwell as coming within the jurisdiction of the Rivers Mersey and Irwell Watershed Joint Committee, and the Area shall also be deemed to include the area within the jurisdiction of any local authority which shall in accordance with Clause 4 hereof appoint a representative or representatives as the case may be on the Committee', p. 9.
22 Manchester and District Joint Town Planning Advisory Committee (1924), pp. 22–23; 26.
23 'Hundred Years without Planning. Manchester and District Exhibition', *The Manchester Guardian*, 30 June 1922, p. 16.
24 Heath, P.M., Manchester and District Joint Town Planning Advisory Committee, Manchester Society of Architects (1922) *A record of the town planning exhibition, held in the Town Hall, Manchester, Oct. 9th to 17th, 1922* (Manchester: Joint Town Planning Advisory Committee).

In 1926 the Committee published their *Report upon the Regional Scheme* accompanied by a comprehensive set of plans in twelve parts that, when assembled, showed the entire region's land-use patterns. The survey work was founded on that undertaken by architects directed by Patrick Abercrombie during the First World War.[25] The publication of this advisory plan is acknowledged as having provided 'an outline framework to improve communications and infrastructure and the zoning of future development', but also to have been without sufficient analytical insight to truly inform or direct such.[26] This lack of analytical projection, combined with the constrained powers available to local authorities at the time, meant that most early planning work was speculative, but nonetheless provided the background for discussions and decisions of the inter-war period.

It is a commonly held misconception that, after the Second World War, Britain launched itself headlong into massive reconstruction as a direct response to damage sustained during the Blitz. In fact, many towns and cities had identified the need for significant regeneration and planning in the immediate period before the outbreak of war – Manchester's *1945 Plan* was 'the intellectual ancestor of much planning work within the city for well over two decades'.[27] The Town and Country Planning Act (1932) enabled local government to determine the structure of urban areas, as it allowed authorities to consider planning comprehensively and to include proposals for land already built upon. The Housing Act (1930) also made provision for the demolition of slums. Ultimately, it was the publication of the *City of Manchester 1945 Plan* and subsequent regional plans that proposed the total reprogramming of the city by the authority. This admittedly complex task was more than significant in the history of the shape of the city, but certainly not isolated from its precedents. In his 1935 book, *The Rebuilding of Manchester*, Liberal politician and businessman Sir Ernest Simon decreed that, 'practically all the houses in the slum belt will have to be demolished ... This means there will be a splendid opportunity for planning the central area ... and for making a comprehensive plan for Manchester's whole future development.'[28] The impact of pre-war analysis on post-war planning is supported when considering the sheer number of comprehensive redevelopment plans published by various municipalities from 1943 to 1946.[29]

---

25 Mattocks, 'Review: Report of the Manchester and District Joint Town Planning Advisory Committee', pp. 226–228.
26 Williams, G. (1996) 'City Profile: Manchester' in *Cities*, Vol. 13, No. 3, pp. 203–212.
27 Kitchen, T. (1996) 'The Future of Development Plans: Reflections on Manchester's Experiences 1945–1995' in *Town Planning Review*, Vol. 67, No. 3 (July), pp. 331–353.
28 Ibid., p. 81.
29 Of 133 known plans published between 1941 and 1952, 85 were published between 1943 and 1946. Larkham P.J., and Lilley, K.D. (2001) *Planning the 'City of Tomorrow'. British Reconstruction Planning, 1939–1952: An Annotated Bibliography* (Pickering: Inch's Books), p. 6.

THE SHAPE OF THE CITY: POWER AND PLANNING

The architects, surveyors, engineers and planners employed by local authorities spent the war years, with precious few live building commissions, authoring these documents. Thomas Sharp's 1940 book, *Town Planning*, sold a quarter of a million copies in wartime, as inexperienced officers sought to learn and diversify their skills in the application of 'zoning' and other planning-led ideas.[30] Many towns and cities did not even sustain bomb damage, but took the opportunity to plan as an exercise in either slum clearance or civic development – as RIBA phrased it, 'September 1939 marked the beginning of a breathing space ... our towns stopped expanding.'[31] The powers granted to local authorities by acts of Parliament had slowly gathered pace through the 1930s and it was anticipated that these would only increase through new wider-reaching national policy.

Sir Ernest Simon was an astute self-publicist and politician. He was instrumental in the creation of Manchester's garden suburb at Wythenshawe and wrote widely on matters related to health and the built environment. He speculated about how the city should react to new local powers gifted by the various parliamentary acts of the 1930s. It may be argued that he foresaw the steady transfer of planning control and powers to the local authority and sought to plan and legislate for the common good at the head of this emerging discipline. As well as the aforementioned title, his other books included *How to Abolish the Slums* (1929) and *The Smokeless City* (1922) – the latter predating the Clean Air Act by some thirty-four years.[32] When Ernest Simon's *Rebuilding* is read alongside Alfred P. Simon's (no family relation) book *Manchester Made Over* (1936), it is impossible to not see the shape of the 1945 Plan emerging.[33]

Ernest Simon wrote with informed authority and a clear agenda about the improvement of quality of life through urban planning and legislation. In *Rebuilding* he dealt most specifically with the powers granted to local authorities during the first quarter of the century. One chapter, 'The Urgent Need for a Plan', could not have been more equivocal in its endorsement of a cohesive and comprehensive plan. He stated, 'The essential thing is that all the work which is done should be carried out as part of a unified scheme' and that 'the Town Planning Committee of the City Council is already busily at work ... but the

---

30 Sharp, T. (1940) *Town Planning* (London: Penguin); Cherry, G.E. (1974) *The Evolution of British Town Planning* (London: Leonard Hill), p. 130, refers to Sharp's book as 'the planning bestseller of our time'.
31 RIBA (1943) *Rebuilding Britain* (London: Lund Humphries), p. 10.
32 Simon, E.D. (1929) *How to Abolish the Slums* (London: Longmans, Green and Co.); Simon, E.D., and Fitzgerald, M. (1922) *The Smokeless City* (London: Longmans, Green and Co.). Salford first introduced smokeless zoning to the Fairhope and Ladywell districts in 1949, while the Manchester Corporation Act (1946) led directly to the first controlled zones in 1952, followed by 105 acres of central Manchester in 1956. Manchester Area Council for Clean Air and Noise Control (1984) *Twenty five year review: a review of some aspects of air pollution and noise control in the area of the Council 25 years after the Clean Air Act, 1956*.
33 Simon, A.P. (1936) *Manchester Made Over* (London: P.S. King & Son).

complete and detailed replanning of the city centre is a slow and complicated job.'[34] In typically forthright and optimistic style Ernest Simon concluded his imperious manifesto by expressing plainly his view of the deliverability of his proposal, 'Manchester can be rebuilt on the finest lines if the City Council fulfils two conditions: firstly that it proceeds forthwith to make really good plans for the redevelopment of the whole central area of the city; secondly, that it pursues the carrying out of these plans steadily and without faltering over the next fifty years.'[35]

Where Ernest Simon delivered a broad vision and a proposition for comprehensive planning in *Rebuilding*, in *Manchester Made Over*, Alfred P. Simon entered into specifics concerning the shape of the city, its problems and potential solutions. *Made Over* contains a foreword by urban planner Barry Parker who backed Alfred's insight as providing an unbiased view on the future of the city.[36] Alfred's proposals were temporally aligned with Ernest Simon's – they shared the long view of 'planning for fifty years'.[37] The issues identified in *Made Over* resonated with those espoused in the preceding decades – traffic congestion, the deprived inner ring of slum housing, the absence of an evening economy, a lack of public space and access to green space. The opportunities provided by the decentralisation of industry and understanding the importance of the knowledge economy were seen as vehicles by which to address some of the existing problems. Alfred was another advocate for the clean city and suggested that a remediated and replanned centre was key to its repopulation:

> When and if Manchester becomes city conscious and city proud, with clean streets, open spaces, clear unpolluted air, with the full use of existing amenities and the carefully planned provision of others, Manchester people will want to live in their city once more and not merely spend their working hours in it.[38]

Each of these observations and proposals were familiar and drew on the concerns of the established committees and earlier published treaties. The novel proposition found in *Made Over* affected what Alfred referred to as the 'Super-Centre'. In his description of what the city might be, he applied a liberal dose of imagination and put forward a number of speculations that were integrated in the *1945 Plan*. He believed in the agency of planning and wanted to enable 'the town planner to intervene so that life outside the workshop may be made easy and effective'.[39] Pre-emptive of 1950s ideas of travel he speculated:

---

34 Simon, E.D. and Inman, J. (1935) *The Rebuilding of Manchester* (London: Longmans, Green and Co.), pp. 81–82.
35 Ibid., p. 165.
36 Simon, A.P. (1936) *Manchester Made Over* (P.S. King & Son), p. v.
37 Ibid., p. xii.
38 Ibid., p. 33.
39 Ibid., p. 2.

For instance, if the principle of the helicopter were so far perfected as to allow of its practical use, our streets would be relieved of much congestion, but our buildings for transport purposes would have to be enlarged and entirely remodelled.[40]

Alfred's Super-Centre was to be formed of a civic core surrounded by shops and offices, then a belt of car parks and bus stations that fed the core, surrounded by a further belt of buildings 'facing outwards' toward the inner ring road.[41] The prose effectively outlined the shape of the *1945 Plan* – itself predicated on the organising device of a circulatory ring. These were not necessarily original demands, the City Surveyor under instruction from the City Council had been asked to develop plans for a ring road in 1932, but this was the first comprehensive vision for the centre and predicted much of the formal planning work to come.[42] Alfred's idea of a civic core built on a plan drawn up in 1934 by City Architect, G. Noel Hill. E. Vincent Harris's Central Library (1934) and Town Hall extension (1938) [Figure 1.04] and Hill's police headquarters on Bootle Street (1937) [Figure 1.05] were all approved and their disposition implied a developing quarter for civic life. To consolidate the group, Hill's proposal also included an extension to the art gallery and a processional route between Albert Square and the John Rylands Library (Basil Champneys, 1900) on Deansgate.[43] Seeing the Barton Arcade (Corbett, Raby and Sawyer, 1871) as inaugurating a trend for urban interior space, Alfred Simon argued that 'Manchester must some day realise the advantage of shops and sidewalks which can be visited under all conditions of weather'.[44] Manchester's Arndale Centre (Wilson & Womersley, 1979) brought this notion to a colossal conclusion!

The historic difficulties presented by Manchester's political geography were highlighted in *Made Over*, addressing the area around Victoria Bridge where the River Irwell divides Manchester and Salford: 'it is in the culverting of the Irwell and the creation of a noble square that the two cities can found a worthy monument to their first united effort for their common needs'.[45] Bound with this idea was a proposal to create a subterranean transport interchange that would redefine the gateway from south-east Lancashire and acknowledge the regional setting of the city. This too would emerge as a component of the *1945 Plan*, in the form of a substantial new development on the site of the existing Exchange Station. Alfred Simon's Super-Centre developed and synthesised much of the contemporary planning discourse, including that of the region. The proposals

---

40 Ibid., p. 41.
41 Ibid., pp. 42–43.
42 'Easing Manchester's Traffic Congestion Problem', *The Manchester Guardian*, 26 October 1932, p. 11.
43 'Manchester Civic Centre', *The Manchester Guardian*, 28 March 1934, p. 11.
44 Simon, *Manchester Made Over*, p. 47.
45 Ibid., p. 48.

Figure 1.04 Manchester Central Reference Library and Town Hall extension, part of the proposed civic core for the city centre.

were far reaching and it was the 1½-mile inner urban belt that, in his mind, held the key to unlocking the potential of the regional centre.

The 1930s city remained congested owing to its centripetal form. The morphological legacy of railway termini, ends of arterial roads and congested slums in a ring around the centre of Manchester was a product of industrialisation and reflective of the interdependence of settlements within the conurbation. In clearing this area Alfred Simon saw the opportunity to provide an inner ring road around which clusters of industries could be distributed to form their own 'character districts' with good access to transportation for the receipt and distribution of goods.[46] The existing difficulties of shipping goods across town from the docks in the west to the wholesale markets in the east illustrated how regional dynamics impacted centrally. In the pages of both *Rebuilding* and *Made Over*, Alfred Simon proposed inner and outer ring roads, civic areas free of traffic and new public space. Only *Rebuilding* contained suggested plans, despite the

---

46 Ibid., pp. 38–39.

Figure 1.05 Bootle Street Police Station seen from Southmill Street. The neo-Georgian style, in Portland stone, was typical for buildings of such stature in the inter-war period.

definition and physical descriptions in outlined in his prose in *Made Over*. The plans were 'prepared by Mr Max Tetlow ARIBA', but it is unclear who was the author of the scheme. It showed a reconfigured city centre with a new cathedral, two new public parks and a series of realignments to the roads to achieve a monumental boulevard, running south-west to north-east across the city, roughly along the path of Mosley Street [Figure 1.06]. The foundations of the

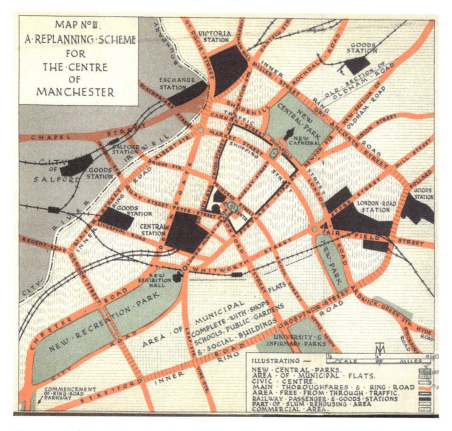

Figure 1.06 'Map III. A replanning scheme for the centre of Manchester'. The most significant proposal was the strengthening of the Mosley Street axis with a park at either end with a new cathedral and exhibition hall to act as termini for the vista from a central square flanked by the town hall and library.

1945 Plan were in the planning, reporting and writings, of officers, journalists and councillors, during the 1920s and 1930s.

Foundations

Alongside the wartime popular interest in planning, central government made a commitment to urban planning as part of the anticipated post-war reconstruction programme. In September 1940 responsibility for town and country planning was transferred from the Ministry of Health to the Ministry of Works (MoW), which became the Ministry of Works and Buildings (MoWB). In 1941, Sir John (later Lord) Reith, the first minister of the MoWB delivered his famous address which became the trope for reconstruction – 'to plan boldly and comprehensively'. Reith himself recorded this as his response to a delegation from Coventry, which had been devastated by sustained bombing, but it was a phrase he repeated at various assemblies and in the House of Lords.[47] Reith did not last long in post. In February 1942 MoWB was renamed the Ministry of Works and Planning (MoWP) and a fortnight later he was replaced by Lord Portal. The MoWP retained responsibility for planning until the creation of the new Ministry of Town and Country Planning (MTCP) and the appointment of its first minister, William S. Morrison, in February 1943.[48] Presaged by the outcomes of the Uthwatt Report, the new ministry was viewed as an essential part of the state planning machinery as 'the instrument by which to secure that the best use is made of the available land in the interests of the community as a whole'.[49] The Town and Country Planning Act (1944) gave local authorities constructive powers to prevent development, to assemble 'blitzed' or 'blighted' land through compulsory purchase and the right to control or direct almost all development within their boundaries. All of this was subject to the preparation and ministerial approval of a Development Plan. During and immediately after the war, a flurry of popular publications spun positivist propaganda about reconstruction being 'spectacular ... in its technical, sociological and economic character of intense interest' and mass participation ensuring that 'we can do it better than ever it has been done before'.[50] The popular mood, endorsed by Whitehall restructuring, was mirrored by local government activity in Manchester.

Manchester's post-war planning can be described in two epochs: the first from the early 1940s to the early 1960s and the second from the early 1960s to the mid-1970s. This periodisation is based on the appointments of key personnel with responsibilities towards the built environment and the statutory approvals of local plans by Whitehall. Rowland Nicholas, the principal author of the *1945 Plan*, was appointed as City Surveyor in June 1940.[51] He retired in 1963, whereupon the first Chief Planning Officer, John Millar, was announced as head of the newly formed planning department.[52] In April 1974, as the Local Government Act came into force, the entire structure of Manchester's municipal government was altered. The metaphorical distance between the 1940s and early 1960s was vast; all aspects of society had changed. The plan ratified in 1961

---

47 Reith, J.C.W. (1949) *Into the Wind* (London: Hodder & Stoughton), p. 424; HL Deb 17 July 1941 vol. 119 cc879.
48 See Cherry, G. (1982) *The Politics of Town Planning* (London: Addison-Wesley Longman) and Cullingworth, J.B. (1975) *Environmental Planning, 1939–69: Reconstruction and Land Use Planning, 1939–47, vol. 1* (London: HMSO).
49 The Uthwatt Report (1942) *The Final Report of the Expert Committee on Compensation and Betterment*. Cmd 6368 (London: HMSO), p. 12.
50 For example: Government Planning Department (1947) *Resurgam, Post War Reconstruction* (London); RIBA (1943) *Rebuilding Britain* (London: Lund Humphries); Casson, H. (1946) *Homes by the Million* (London: Penguin).
51 'Manchester's New Surveyor', *The Manchester Guardian*, 21 June 1940, p. 3.
52 'Three Officials to Replace Surveyor', *The Guardian*, 22 June 1963, p. 12.

came with the caveat that the central area planning should be revisited. As such, Nicholas and Millar each oversaw their own period of intense planning work. Nicholas's work was captured in the substantial *1945 Plan* [Figure 1.07] and Millar's proposals – no less substantial – were published as a series of reports in the 1960s, culminating in the *Manchester City Centre Map 1967*.[53] In the following section I explore the genesis and development of each epoch and their relation to one another, the city and the region.

The City of Manchester Plan 1945

Also known as the 'Nicholas Plan', the *1945 Plan* was part of a suite of three documents. Together, the plans and reports are acknowledged as being one of the most comprehensive studies of their type.[54] The other two concerned the regional planning of South Lancashire and North Cheshire and Manchester's role as the regional capital.[55] Despite its status as a recognised conurbation and a regional centre, until 1974 Manchester was a County Borough of Lancashire. As such, Manchester Corporation only governed within its city boundaries and regional planning still fell to established committees and relied upon the goodwill of the surrounding counties of Cheshire and Lancashire. The extensive surveys and research which were the basis of *1945 Plan* were 'carried out by an enthusiastic team of planners during the years 1942 to 1945' and, in Nicholas's view, were 'invaluable' in the preparation of the proceeding *Development Plan* that was submitted for approval in 1951.[56]

The distinction between the *1945 Plan* and the *Manchester Development Plan* lies in their role and jurisdiction. The *1945 Plan* was a wide-reaching speculative document, lavishly illustrated and responded to Lord Reith's assertions of bold and comprehensive planning.[57] The *Development Plan* of 1951 was a statutory planning document, directed by legislation contained in the 1947 Town and Country Planning Act.[58] The *Development Plan* was necessarily a framework, but the *1945 Plan* was more akin to a manifesto. While many of the architectural schemes illustrated in its pages were not realised, the impact and influence of

---

53 Nicholas, R.J. (1945a) *City of Manchester Plan 1945* (Norwich: Jarrold & Sons); Millar, J.S. (1967) *Manchester City Centre Map 1967* (Manchester: City and County Borough of Manchester).

54 Williams, G. (2003) *The Enterprising City Centre. Manchester's Development Challenge* (London: E. & F.N. Spon), p. 56.

55 Nicholas, R. (1945b) *The Manchester and District Regional Planning Committee Report on the Tentative Regional Planning Proposals* (Norwich: Jarrold & Sons); Nicholas R. and Hellier, M.J. (1947) *South Lancashire and North Cheshire Advisory Planning Committee: An Advisory Plan* (Manchester: Advisory Planning Committee).

56 Nicholas, R. (1967) 'Planning the City of the Future', in *Manchester and its Region*, p. 254.

57 Nicholas, *The Manchester and District Regional Planning Committee Report*, p. iii.

58 Nicholas, 'Planning the City of the Future', p. 254.

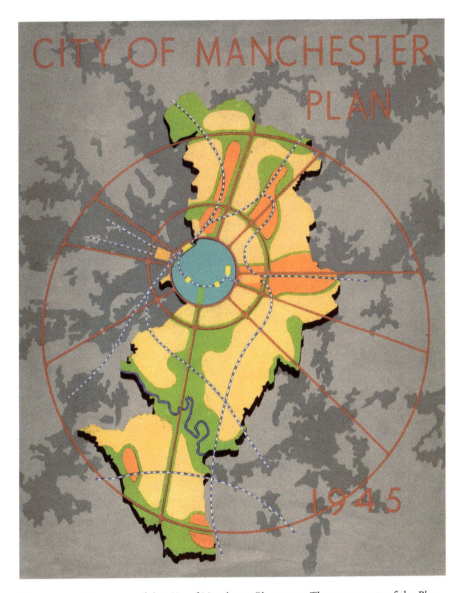

Figure 1.07 The cover of the *City of Manchester Plan, 1945*. The core tenets of the *Plan* were evident in this graphic – the elongated shape of the borough with green space, housing and industry and a core served by new radial and ring roads, while still reliant on rail transportation.

Figure 1.08   William Morrison and Rowland Nicholas looking over a model in the exhibition that heralded the publication of the *1945 Plan*.

the *1945 Plan* and its accompanying documents was wide reaching in popular society and planning culture.

Manchester's citizens, like those across the country, had more than a passing interest in planning proposals. More than 2,500 copies of the *1945 Plan* were published, distributed and sold. Its publication coincided with a large exhibition at the City Art Gallery that ran from June until September and, reflecting the popular interest in planning, attracted more than 155,000 visitors over seven weeks.[59] The show was officially opened by William Morrison, Minister of Town and Country Planning [Figure 1.08] and international visitors remarked on the advanced state of the sociological survey work underpinning the plan. It was by far the most viewed show of the year and the gallery's opening hours had to be extended to accommodate demand. The *Manchester Guardian* reported Rowland Nicholas's self-promoting view that it was 'the largest and most comprehensive planning exhibition ever held'.[60]

---

59   Manchester Art Galleries Committee, *1945 Annual Report*, p. 3.
60   'The Manchester Plan: "Largest and Most Comprehensive Exhibition Ever Held"', *The Manchester Guardian*, 26 June 1945, p. 3.

The exhibition took up all of the ten galleries, each room dedicated to a component of the *Plan*.[61] 'Housing', 'Neighbourhood Planning' and 'District Planning' took up a large proportion of the space, including a display of the proposed extension of the Wythenshawe estate. The most definitive aspects of the *Plan*, which were given resolute architectural form in illustrative plates, were the 'City Centre' and the 'Educational Centre' – conversely, they received less attention in the public exhibition, which was much more focused on residential development. Of course, housing was an immediate and urgent concern to Mancunians, many of whom still resided in homes that had been declared unfit during the 1930s. Nonetheless, the prevailing culture was one of future ambition, not shackled to the horrors of the war – a sentiment clearly elucidated on the cover of the exhibition pamphlet. The black and white illustration shows two children holding hands, a little girl looking behind to the ruins of war and an older boy looking forward to a new town hall rendered as a modern Scandinavian style building [Figure 1.09]. The pamphlet, costing 2d, sold 30,000 copies.

Other media was similarly forward facing. A 1946 film, *A City Speaks*, produced by the Corporation, showed footage of children at the planning exhibition, curiously narrated by adults discussing things like the reduction in the number of pubs in Miles Platting![62] The film did not dwell on the devastation of the war, instead it used a view of the worthy industrial history and entrepreneurial spirit of the city as the basic foundations for optimism and improvement. This gentle obviation of the impact of war was mirrored in Harper Cory's small publication, *Manchester: City of Achievements* published in 1947.[63] Cory did not use the word 'war' until the concluding chapter and, even then, he deployed it in a stereotypically British best-foot-forward manner. He acknowledged the pre-war decline in industry and described the war as an interruption of a controlled shift from a primarily cotton economy to a more diversified industrial base. This planned transition was, Cory argued, a sign of Mancunian ingenuity and one that would secure a continuing industrial economy in the region.

Planning the modern city was a complex task, one that became evident to the directing parties during the development of the *Plan* and its accompanying reports. The interrelationship of economic, transport, industrial and residential planning became clear in the survey work and predicated the form of the *Plan* as a holistic document that could be consumed by the lay observer.[64]

---

61 *Manchester and District Planning Exhibition – 1945*, pamphlet to accompany exhibition, printed by Henry Blacklock and Co. Ltd, Albert Square, Manchester.
62 Rotha, P. (Dir.) *A City Speaks* (1947); Wildman, C. (2012) '*A City Speaks*: The Projection of Civic Identity in Manchester', *20th Century British History*, Vol. 23, No. 1.
63 Cory, H. (1947) *Manchester: A City of Achievement* (Reprinted from *Canada's Weekly*).
64 Ibid., p. vi. Nicholas acknowledged the input of Derek Senior 'who has transformed a somewhat technical script into a book which the layman can appreciate.' Senior was a journalist trained as a planner.

Figure 1.09   Cover of leaflet for planning exhibition, 1945 alluding to past horrors and a future vision for the city.

The eighteen chapters of the *Plan* covered everything from history, population demographics, transportation, health, education, industry, pollution and even a digestible description of the survey methods. It was composed of a series of texts and supporting images in the form of photographs, maps, diagrams, tables and perspective illustrations. Despite the comprehensive and authoritative appearance of the *Plan* much of the regional and borough-scale planning was broad brush – necessitated by the structure of local government and the sheer number of authorities and committees involved. Indeed, in the regional plan (which included the word 'tentative' in its full title) Rowland Nicholas acknowledged that, '[t]he detailed proposals have not in all cases been discussed with the [local authority] surveyor for such a procedure might have necessitated their submission to his appropriate Committee'.[65] Contrastingly, certain local areas were presented with incredible detail.

However, there was a lack of information at the scales in between regional and local. Many chapters recited and interpreted generic best practice as informed by contemporary mantra and did not engage with the physical parameters of Manchester itself. The apparent breadth and depth of the *Plan* afforded it an air of realism, but local authorities lacked most of the powers to enact their visions. The documents were, however, an invaluable study and point of reference for those within the municipal departments of housing, education and engineering. A strong set of frameworks or guidelines was prevalent, with which to govern the distribution of new schools, social and health centres, amidst the urgent demand for new housing. It was these building types, of a less glamorous nature, that absorbed the office of the City Architect through the late 1940s and early 1950s, as the perfunctory occupation of the reconditioning of basic facilities took priority over the iconic reprogramming of the city centre.[66]

Nonetheless, it was the centre that loomed large in the colour plates of the *Plan*. A seemingly definitively zoned city centre, with a new ring road, railway station, bus stations, market, law courts, town hall and civic spaces was presented as a double-page fold-out [Figure 1.10]. It was accompanied by a series of architects' perspective renders that showed existing and new buildings in the same illustration and allowed the viewer to imagine what the future shape of the centre might be. The precise authorship of the proposals and their visualisation is unclear. The perspective drawings were produced by P.D. Hepworth and J.D.M. Harvey and various parts of the plan had input from others, but

---

65 Nicholas, 'Author's note', *The Manchester and District Regional Planning Committee Report*, p. vi.

66 Drawings held at Archives+ show a wave of primary and secondary schools in the immediate post-war period. Moss House, Newall Green, Brooklands, Crab Lane, Charlestown, Baguley Hall, Parkside, Oldwood, all under the direction of L.C. Howitt and within the post-war estates at the edge of the borough. In 1954 new designs for the airport at Ringway commenced. The civic centre of Wythenshawe was also on the drawing boards of the City Architects' Department.

Figure 1.10 'City of Manchester. Central Area'. Extract from *1945 Plan*. The medieval grid of the Victorian city rationalised according to prevailing modern ideals with undertones of beaux-arts planning.

Rowland Nicholas bore overall responsibility.[67] Stylistically, the plans and architectural visions were guided by beaux-arts thinking and neo-classical devices. The roads were imagined as boulevards, axial and symmetrical planning was used to bring some sort of order to the surviving, ad hoc, medieval street pattern

---

67 The City Architect, G. Noel Hill designed the Cultural Centre and appears to have had oversight of town planning for neighbourhoods and district centres. Whereas Housing Director Sir John Hughes oversaw the design of the dwellings that would populate the planned areas. Hubert Worthington was consultant architect for the Education Centre and Infirmary. Others included G. Sutton Brown, Arthur S. Hamilton, O. Lewis Abbott and Reginald Rowley. Derek Senior assisted with the prose.

of the existing centre. The 'Civic' and 'Historic' quarters identified in the plan around the Town Hall and Cathedral respectively would survive and reappear in later planning, but the 'distribution zone' intended to the fringe south of the city centre was short sighted.[68] Its proposed location was informed by proximity to the docks and railway goods stations, but distribution was set to move onto the roads in the second half of the twentieth century.

It seems remarkable, given the foresight of some of the planning, that the rise in motor transport and the decline of manufacturing trade were not really accounted for by the authors of the *Plan*. The manner of the detailed planning for the Education Centre, and the new Civic Centre was also distinctly traditional. The prominence of axial gestures terminated by significant buildings in the classical style defined the major inner-city proposals. The designs, prepared by G. Noel-Hill and Hubert Worthington for 'the centres of culture, education and medicine', were distinctly of this oeuvre (see Chapter 4). They were characterised by wide tree-lined boulevards and large institutional buildings including a new broadcasting house as well as a cultural centre and civic hall that would celebrate the achievements of urban industrial Manchester.[69] The 1945 *Plan*, like the cover of the exhibition pamphlet, had one foot in the past and another firmly forward. The surveys and planning ideals were advanced, but their material visualisations were stuck in inter-war aesthetics.

The 1930s had, however, set out the main tenets for physical reordering based on transportation. As with its precedents, the main feature of the central area was a 'city circle road' – it was one of a number of concentric ring roads in the regional proposal. Three new bus stations and a vast railway station, labelled as 'Trinity', would flank the circle road. Inside the circle many smaller streets were to be car free. The rendering of the plan implied the creation of new larger city blocks from the existing medieval grain. Despite claims that the Plan was 'no attempt to revolutionise the face of the city', the idea of wholesale change was endorsed by Nicholas's opinion of the city's architecture: 'the city's buildings, with few exceptions, are undistinguished'.[70] Not many existing buildings were viewed as important enough to schedule their preservation; even Waterhouse's fine neo-Gothic Town Hall (1868–78) was to be replaced by a building drawn to resemble Ragnar Östberg's Stockholm City Hall (1923). The Cathedral, Ryland's Library (Basil Champneys, 1900), Sunlight House (Joseph Sunlight 1932), Police Station (G. Noel Hill, 1937), Town Hall Extension and Library (E. Vincent Harris, 1930–38), and the Royal Exchange (Mills & Murgatroyd, 1867–74; extended Bradshaw Gass & Hope, 1914–31) were all shown as retained in the three-dimensional drawing of 'Manchester

---

68 Nicholas, *The Manchester and District Regional Planning Committee Report*, p. 194.
69 Ibid., p. 101. Noel-Hill is credited with the layout of the Cultural Centre and Worthington with the Infirmary and University elements of the combined proposals.
70 Ibid., Plate 79.

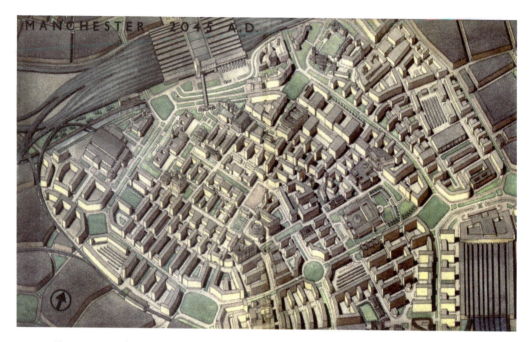

Figure 1.11 The endpiece of the *1945 Plan* that implicitly exposed an attitude to the built heritage of the Victorian city by virtue of the few buildings envisioned as surviving into the twenty-first century.

2045 AD' on the endpiece of the *Plan* [Figure 1.11]. The zoning and transport planning of the centre challenged the idea of the *Plan* as a framework that was 'sufficiently elastic to permit quite considerable alterations'.[71] The overriding sentiment, to cleanse the city of its redundant Victorian fabric, was prevalent across the pages. The idea of the city as 'unplanned' was a common trope. For 'unplanned', one might read 'insanitary', as the congested and polluted conditions were seen as concomitant with public health and the slum clearance policies of the 1930s.

Manchester was in decline before the outbreak of war in 1939. Recovery from the Great Depression was limited in the north-west and other heavily industrialised regions. Regardless of the necessarily optimistic rhetoric of the *Plan*, its exhibition, public information films and reporting, Manchester carried the spatial and social problems of earlier decades into its post-war condition. One legacy of private enterprise and personal wealth, unchecked by policy, was a dense urban landscape with precious little open space, save that which surrounded the many churches. It was speculated that, 'because of its strong laissez-faire tradition, the Council had not acquired large areas of land in the

---

71 Nicholas, *The Manchester and District Regional Planning Committee Report*, p. 1.

city centre – unlike, for example, Liverpool and Birmingham'.[72] Nicholas put it even more bluntly: 'land was considered far too valuable to be wasted on parks and gardens'.[73] The provision of public open space was also a priority of the *Plan*. High death rates in dense residential areas were attributed to the existing lack of parkland and green space at 'less than half the recognised minimum standard'.[74] The infrastructural capacity of the new city was also at odds with its historical development. The difficulty of crossing the city was still an issue in 1945. Two chapters of the *Plan* were dedicated to 'Highways' and 'Transport and Municipal Services'. Nineteen radial routes were identified as priority carriageways, fifteen of them in Manchester and the others partially routed through the adjacent boroughs of Salford and Stretford [Figure 1.12]. These would be linked by the aforementioned ring roads, at intervals radiating from the centre. As well as the City Circle, the 'Inner', 'Intermediate' and 'Outer' rings were proposed as a total system for the city region.[75] The highways planning would prevail as one of the primary organising devices for the city and the region in the following decades. However, the core work of the City Architect's and Housing departments in the immediate aftermath of war focused on addressing health, education and housing.

Comprehensive in its composition and ambitious in its undertaking, the *City of Manchester Plan 1945* had a lot of work to do. With historical distance it is easy to critique the lack of foresight about the decline of manufacturing and trade and the apparent ignorance of Victorian architectural heritage. The *Plan*, without statutory approval, served many masters – the City Council, the surrounding local authorities, the interests of citizens, businesses and rail companies, to name but a few. To negotiate the competing objectives of all of these parties and to present a suite of documents as substantial as they were, was undoubtedly a significant achievement. The shape of the city through the second half of the century would be variously informed by the ideas laid out and visualised in the *Plan*, but the immediate impact, in an era of severe austerity, was always likely to be piecemeal at best. Materials were in short supply and building was licensed until 1954.[76] Manchester Corporation was frustrated by its lack of jurisdiction in the physical control of the city. Pre-emptive of the sorts of powers contained in the 1947 Town and Country Planning Act, in 1944 it was pursuant to a private bill 'to extend … powers to control land usage'.[77]

---

72 Turner, G. (1967) *The North Country* (London: Eyre & Spottiswoode), p. 69.
73 Nicholas, *The Manchester and District Regional Planning Committee Report*, p. 184.
74 Ibid., p. 105.
75 Ibid., p. 58. The railways were also still viewed as essential to the city in 1945. The idea of an underground was mooted in the plan as was the expansion of the airport.
76 HC Deb 02 November 1954 vol 532 cc186–8.
77 NA: HLG 79/405. See Greenhalgh, J. (2017) *Reconstructing Modernity. Space, Power and Governance in Mid-Twentieth Century British Cities* (Manchester: Manchester University Press), p. 84.

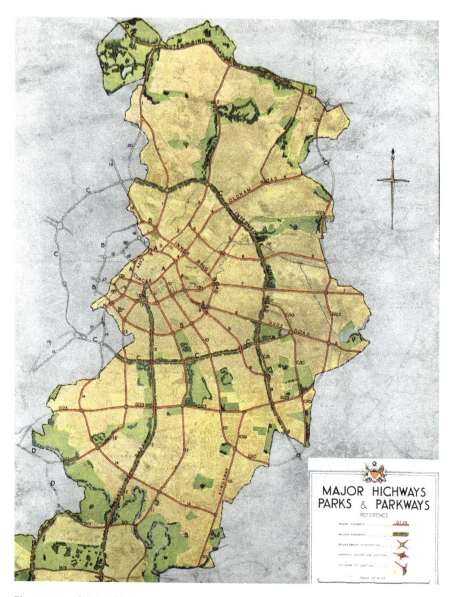

Figure 1.12 'Major highways, parks and parkways'. Showing the importance of transportation planning and the provision of green space. Extract from *1945 Plan*.

Dealing with the War Damage Commission and the regional and central offices of government amidst new legislative landscapes was not fast paced. Small matters took an age to agree and the comprehensive planning met with stultifying legal processes that presented another factor inhibiting physical recovery in the city centre for more than a decade.

The far-reaching powers of the 1947 Town and Country Planning Act gave local authorities the mechanisms by which to affect significant formal change. The production of a Development Plan and its statutory approval gave councils the rights to enact Compulsory Purchase Orders (CPO) and to create CDAs that allowed large portions of central cities to be redeveloped. Manchester's Development Plan was essentially faithful to the Nicholas plan and submitted to the Secretary of State in 1951; its approval took ten years. The original draft of the written statement was viewed by the Ministry of Housing and Local Government (MHLG) as 'unhelpful, vague and repetitive' and 'not a very good document'.[78] The amount of edits, corrections and redactions by the Ministry were substantial – (there is red pen and type all over the archived copy of the document) – it was torn apart. According to the Planning Advisory Group (1965) such delays were commonplace due to the sheer volume of plans submitted following the Town and Country Planning Act (1947).[79] Manchester's plan was the last in England to be approved, with much of the delay due to local politics.

A public inquiry into the Development Plan in 1952 was followed by protracted legal arguments and a further inquiry about overspill settlements at Mobberley and Lymm in 1957 – 'both of which came to nothing'.[80] Nicholas's adhesion to his vision of 1945 was seen as not detailed enough by objectors, but was deemed too detailed by MHLG for the legal status of a statutorily approved plan.[81] Furthermore, Nicholas and Town Clerk Philip B. Dingle implied in the draft version of the Written Statement that the document accounted for fifty years of planning, a proposal that was also allied to the contents of the *1945 Plan*. The Town and Country Planning Act (1947) made legal provision for a 'plan period' of twenty years. At a public inquiry in October 1952, lawyers acting on behalf of fifty-nine objectors argued that none of the proposals were valid due to this discrepancy and the Ministry in their edits made it explicit that the plan period was for twenty years and in fact to be reviewed by 1971.[82] Correspondence between the Corporation and the MHLG was characterised by its procedural tone and increasing legalese. There was clear frustration on the part of the Ministry that the approval had taken such a long time; every agreed alteration was tabulated and dated. The substantive heads of terms were agreed in March 1960, but it took until 29 November 1961 for statutory approval largely due to printing delays![83]

---

78 NA HLG 79/1422 *Manchester C.B. Development Plan*.
79 Planning Advisory Group (1965) *The Future of Development Plans* (London: HMSO).
80 NA: HLG 79/1422 *Manchester C.B. Development Plan*.
81 'Purpose Behind City's Plan: Objectors Answered', *The Manchester Guardian*, 17 October 1952, p. 12.
82 'Development Plan "Bad in Law": No Period Specified', *The Manchester Guardian*, 15 October 1952, p. 10; NA: HLG 79/1422 *Manchester C.B. Development Plan*.
83 NA: HLG 79/1422 *Manchester C.B. Development Plan*.

Figure 1.13 Manchester Reform Synagogue, Cummings & Levy, 1953, on Jackson's Row in the city centre.

The actual documentation of the *1951 Development Plan* was scant in comparison to the detail and information of the *1945 Plan*. It consisted of: [1] a *Town Map* with a broad outline plan for the entire city, [2] a *Programme Map* indicating periods of implementation over the coming twenty years, and [3] a *Written Statement* with descriptions and clarifications of the information contained in the two maps. Nicholas, writing in 1961 on the verge of retirement, was clearly proud of the longevity and legacy of his *1945 Plan*, but acknowledged the flexibility subsequently built into the approved version.[84] In many senses, the delays were inconsequential – the Corporation was able to go about the business of building new schools and houses outside the city centre using existing powers. Investment and development in the centre was piecemeal at best and no new buildings were completed until the mid-1950s.

The first new building was the Manchester Reform Synagogue on Jackson's Row (Cummings & Levy, 1953) [Figure 1.13]. Hot on its heels, though, and symbolic of the modernising to come in the following decade was the UK's first independent television studios, Granada Television, on Quay Street (realised in phases – Cruickshank & Seward, 1956; thereafter Ralph Tubbs, 1957–66).[85] In the absence of a statutorily approved plan the Town Planning Committee only had its framework and objectives with which to govern development.

---

84 GB127.Council Minutes/Town Planning and Buildings Committee/2/56, p. 902.
85 Tubbs, R. (1958) *Year One* (Manchester: Granada), p. 11.

In what John Millar referred to as 'the great non-planning era [...] with a Plan but little else, the city moved into the 1950s'.[86] The aim to consolidate nine 'war damaged areas' and the ambition to construct a city centre ring road were the guiding principles by which to approve or reject development.[87] As we shall read in the final chapter, the proposed route of the ring road was paramount to development approval until the mid-1970s. Buildings that did not interfere with either land assembly or the proposed route of the highways were favoured – the Reform Synagogue was on a central 'island' site and Granada TV HQ would flank the intended route of the ring road.

Britain in 1961 was a very different place from the Britain of 1945. It is therefore unsurprising that the approval of the Development Plan came with the caveat that the whole central area be subject to re-examination.[88] Short-term speculation characterised much development in the early 1960s, still dictated by the objectives for transport planning and, in line with prevailing thought, some form of comprehensive central scheme. The lack of detail and unprecedented delays in the *1951 Plan* were aligned to market forces as it wasn't until the late 1950s and early 1960s that pressure from the private sector began to bear upon provincial cities.[89] As journalist Graham Turner phrased it: 'The wave of property development, spreading from the south, shook many Northern councils out of their torpor.'[90]

The only constant is change – planning in a shifting landscape

The shape of the city was always attached to its transportation networks and these in turn related to its regional status. During the 1950s 'there was a growing realisation that the traffic problems of urban areas cannot be solved in isolation from consideration of the manner in which land is used and buildings are served'.[91] By the early 1960s 'understanding of the connection between land use planning was also accompanied ... by the growing acknowledgment that economic plans were required in order to provide the context for physical planning at both the national and regional scale'.[92] These attitudes presaged

---

86 Turner, *The North Country*, p. 69.
87 Nicholas, R., and Dingle, P.B. (1951) *Manchester Development Plan* (Manchester: City and County Borough of Manchester).
88 Kitchen, T. (1996) 'The Future of Development Plans: Reflections on Manchester's Experiences 1945–1995', in *Town Planning Review*, Vol. 67, No. 3 (July), pp. 331–353.
89 See Marriott, O. (1967) *The Property Boom* (London: Pan Books); Scott, P. (1996) *The Property Masters. A History of the British Commercial Property Sector* (London: E. & F.N. Spon).
90 Turner, *The North Country*, p. 69.
91 Colin Buchanan and Partners (1969) *The Conurbations* (London: British Road Federation), p. 15.
92 Ibid, p. 15.

the creation of Regional Economic Planning Councils by the Department of Economic Affairs and the Planning Advisory Group (PAG), directed by MHLG. The MHLG and Ministry of Transport also set up the Joint Urban Planning Group (JUPG), which published a series of *Planning Bulletins*, intended as guides to development.[93] Thus, the local planning environment was one contextualised amidst shifting Whitehall agendas. The Development Plan was one of the first planning mechanisms recommended for revision by the PAG and their 1965 report, *The Future of Development Plans*, suggested that 'sub-regional plans', 'structure plans' and 'local plans', were implemented as replacements, with an according revision to the statutory review processes. The PAG report was the basis for much of the legislation contained within the Town and Country Planning Act 1968. Set against these substantial changes to the national statute and approvals processes were those happening at a local level in Manchester.

Change was abundant in 1960s Manchester. In early 1961, the office of City Architect was transferred from the manicured civility promoted under Leonard Cecil Howitt's tenure, to a more direct, commercial style led by Sidney G. Besant-Roberts. Rowland Nicholas was coming to the end of his career and was appointed President of the Royal Town Planning Institute in 1960. Despite Nicholas 'profoundly' disagreeing with 'splitting the department up', on his retirement in 1963 the department was restructured and John Millar became the first City Planning Officer.[94]

Millar's earlier appointment as Assistant City Planning Officer, the most senior planning post in the former City Engineer and Surveyor's Department, coincided with the start of the property boom and the demand to revisit the planning of the central area. According to former deputy chief planner Robert Maund, 'the Planning Section had insufficient resources to be able to deal with this in anything like a comfortable manner. Politicians were persuaded that a properly staffed planning department was the only way to get a grip of this problem and hence John's appointment at the tender age of 39, as the first City Planning Officer.'[95] When Millar arrived in 1961 there were less than a dozen staff allocated to any aspect of planning and only one of these was technically qualified.[96] Millar set about building a team of capable planners, recruiting the

---

[93] For the PAG see Delafons, J. (1998) 'Reforming the British Planning System 1964–5: The Planning Advisory Group and the Genesis of the Planning Act of 1968', *Planning Perspectives*, 13(4), 373–387; For a view on the role of the JUPG see Smith, O.S., *Boom Cities*, pp. 51–57. For a contemporary view of land law in relation to changing planning policy see Moore, V. (1972) Planning in Britain: The Changing Scene. *Urb. L. Ann.*, 89.

[94] In conversation with John Millar. Wilmslow, 18 September 2013.

[95] Maund, R. (2015) *Aspects of Planning in Manchester and Greater Manchester 1960–1975*. Personal notes in correspondence with the author.

[96] Turner, *The North Country*, p. 69. Turner's recollected and cited versions of his interview with Millar is interspersed with opinion and fact. It is hard to discern which is the opinion of the author and which is that of the interviewee.

brightest graduates who were allied to the department through their studies. Between 1963 and 1968, the fledgling department dealt in detail with an area substantially larger than that of the 1945 *Plan*, yet their work remained largely hidden in a series of internal reports. The reports testify to the extents of the planning design work undertaken and, more than any preceding plan, informed the shape of the city into the twenty-first century. These were, however, set against the backdrop of changes to the Development Plan system and Millar had to be politically adept in addressing criticism about the seemingly languid pace of transformation whilst enabling his team to work productively in service of the city. In the following section I address the planning and architectural cultures of the city in the 1960s and show how the planners sought to control the comprehensive redevelopment of a rapidly changing city centre.

On this cusp of real post-war recovery, in 1960, Manchester hosted the British Architects' Conference. The theme of the event was Urban Renewal. At this point the 1951 Development Plan was yet to be ratified. Despite its thematic heading, the conference appeared to lack the targeted trajectory that an approved plan for Manchester's renewal may have provided and the lack of comprehensive renewal in Manchester itself seemed to stifle the discourse. Discussions were limited to acknowledging the piecemeal development visible in Manchester's recovery and making comparisons to wholesale reconstruction in Coventry and London. Otherwise, commentators were reduced to making observations about recently completed buildings in the city – of which there were few, and most were unspectacular. Actual discussion of urban renewal was limited to one session delivered by Sir Keith Joseph. It concerned the available powers at the hands of the local authority and debated their capacity to control large development; 'With something to get their teeth into, the session came to life', wrote the correspondent for *The Builder*.[97] Of course, legislation and its relationship to enabling changes to the built environment was not a new subject – in 1836 William Fairbairn recognised it as 'obvious that improvements ... could not be effected without the aid and assistance of legislature'.[98]

Regardless of the momentum of the proceedings, the organising committees resembled a roll call of Manchester architects. They included George Grenfell-Baines, the founding partner of Building Design Partnership (BDP), Reginald Cordingley, Professor of Architecture at Manchester University, Arthur Gibbon and John Seward from the firm of Cruickshank & Seward, F.L. Halliday of Halliday Meecham and L. Hugh Wilson, who went on to found Wilson & Womersley in Manchester.[99] Also present was the incumbent City Architect, Leonard Cecil Howitt, whose architectural production most epitomised the spirit of beaux-arts classicism and orthodoxy implied and illustrated in the

---

[97] *A Manchester Diary, The British Architects' Conference*, author cited as *From Our Own Representative*, The Builder, 24 June 1960, p. 1176.
[98] Fairbairn, *Observations and Improvements of the Town of Manchester*, p. 38.
[99] See p. 177.

THE RENEWAL OF POST-WAR MANCHESTER

Figure 1.14   Postcard view of the new Crown Courts, Crown Square. City Architect's Department, 1962.

1945 Plan. Howitt began in the office in 1911 and returned in 1937 as Deputy after working in Liverpool. He exemplified the role of the City Architect as one that encompassed civic pride, social responsibility and starched collars. Critics and historians have never really celebrated him or championed his oeuvre. However, Howitt, who did not eschew modern techniques, maintained a mannered and restrained order to his work and ought to be remembered for his final swathe of refined quality municipal buildings. Among these were the Crown Court [Figure 1.14], the reconstruction of the Free Trade Hall [see Figure 7.04], Heaton Park Inlet Valve House and Blackley Crematorium. Howitt, who was on the verge of his retirement and said to be of a self-deprecating nature at least had the opportunity to address the RIBA conference in his own city and was awarded the NW Branch Bronze Medal for the scheme at Blackley.[100] Also of note was Cecil Stewart's contribution – in an article that mirrored his conference address he supposed that the Victorian city of Manchester had 'not acquired the veneer of venerability', when compared to the Georgian city of Bath, medieval York and Roman Chester.[101] Stewart also made reference to the quality of the Victorian city, an unconventional opinion when compared to his peers.

---

100   Archer, John H.G. (1996) From a personal account of his time in the office of the City Architect; 'A Manchester Diary, The British Architects' Conference', author cited as 'From Our Own Representative', *The Builder*, 24 June 1960, p. 1175.
101   Stewart, C. (1960) 'Manchester 1960', *The Builder*, 10 June 1960, p. 1086.

He recalled the editor of *The Builder* 'a hundred years ago' comparing the city to Venice in its grandeur.[102] Here were the seeds of Manchester's conservation movement and the beginnings of viewing the Victorian city as heritage.

The absence of an approved Development Plan and a general lack of appreciation for Victorian buildings created particular conditions for new schemes. Until John Millar's team set to work in earnest in 1963, the principal organising device for new development was the proposed ring road. Eleven of the forty pages of the Written Statement of the 1951 Development Plan presented a table scheduling new road construction up to 1971.[103] The first sites to be developed through the late 1950s and early 1960s were often those that the council owned or those that did not interfere with the major ambitions of Rowland Nicholas's plans, despite their non-statutory status.[104] Derek Senior, a journalist with extensive knowledge of planning who was acknowledged by Nicholas for his contribution to the *1945 Plan*, suggested in 1960 that 'the corporation [was] content to see that [new buildings] conformed with its requirements in respect of access, car parking provisions, building lines, daylighting, density and the like', though this approach was said to have resulted in the new schemes being 'inevitably mixed in aesthetic quality'.[105] Commercial development was scant, the most notable schemes were Peter House (Amsell & Bailey, 1958) [Figure 1.15] and Pearl Assurance House (J.W. Beaumont & Sons, 1957).

Both of these buildings recalled Manchester's significant inter-war architecture in their use of Portland stone and were realised in a mild modern language with quasi-classical undertones, similar in some ways to those delivered by the City Architect's office in the period. Amendments to the Town and Country Planning Act in 1959 reinstated market values as the basis for any compensatory payments on the acquisition of land.[106] This had two principal effects; the first was to prevent local authorities from competing with private developers over the purchase of sites as they did not have sufficient funds to compete. The second was that many speculative developers had bought land in the immediate aftermath of the war and had maintained undeveloped plots until the first signs of recovery indicated that they could realise good rental returns on commercial property. The need to rapidly maximise returns led to the adoption of new manufacturing techniques that changed the material language of the built environment. Thus, the first wave of 1960s buildings co-opted the International

---

102 Ibid.
103 Nicholas and Dingle, *Manchester Development Plan. Written Statement.*
104 Ibid., p. 11. Section 7, Clause (45) states: 'In the meantime no development will be permitted which might reasonably be considered out of keeping with proposals for those parts of the central area which may merit special protection, such as the proposed "Processional Way" extending from the proposed Courts of Law to Albert Square.'
105 Senior, D. (1960) 'New Heart for Manchester', *The Manchester Guardian*, 15 June 1960, p. 18.
106 Parkinson-Bailey, J.J. (2000) *Manchester: An Architectural History* (Manchester: Manchester University Press), pp. 170–175.

Figure 1.15 Peter House viewed from beneath the canopy of the now demolished Odeon Cinema on Oxford Street.

Style and Manchester's first skyscrapers mushroomed in a ring around the central area on sites activated by the highway proposals. The best of these was undoubtedly the grouping of the Co-operative Insurance Society (CIS) and Co-operative Wholesale Society (CWS) towers (G.S. Hay of the CWS and Gordon Tait of Sir John Burnet, Tait & Partners, 1959–62), to which Henry Russell Hitchcock extended the accolade of Britain's finest tall buildings.[107] A new planning department could not arrest the pace of development, but it could provide new focus and frameworks to try and control it.

The birth of Manchester's City Planning Department came about not simply as a response to the growing legislative landscape, but also because of commercial pressures and as a direct result of the demand for restructuring of the City Architect's Department. Manchester appointed one of the first City Architects in 1902, Henry Price, and by 1961 over nearly sixty years and without any internal reorganisation, the department had steadily grown to a personnel of over three hundred with a raft of roles and responsibilities, and was physically dispersed across four separate divisions.[108]

---

107 *Architect & Building News*, 16 January 1963, p. 83.
108 Stafford, H.M. (1965) 'Manchester City Architect's Department: Management and Planning Following Reorganisation', *The Builder*, 28 May 1965, pp. 1187–1188. The

Following restructuring between 1961 and 1963, the City Architect's department had come to resemble a consortium composed of six divisions – two architectural, one quantity surveying, one building engineering, one management and planning and one town planning and building.[109] The structure and relationships of the department were represented in a less than straightforward diagram [Figure 1.16]. This structure was intended to reflect those of the private sector, with the monthly meeting of the heads of divisions being described as a 'partners' meeting'.[110] Millar's post was not formally recognised until the retirement of Rowland Nicholas in 1963. Nicholas held sway as Chief Engineer and Surveyor for the best part of two decades. Quite whether he retired or resigned is a little unclear, but the climate around development was shifting. Nicholas held on to his vision of comprehensive redevelopment with the municipality at the helm, but was under significant pressure from a burgeoning private sector that inundated the department with planning applications. According to Millar, 'we had two architect planners available, one of whom was me, but there were no less than one hundred working for them [the private developers]. It was absurd.'[111] By 1967 Millar's department had grown to also employ a staff of about 100, which he regarded as 'reasonable'.[112]

Between 1963 and 1967 Millar's department revisited the major components of the inner-city proposals. They produced a series of reports for six newly designated CDAs that acted as outline frameworks for developers. The outline status did not have set national parameters about how it should be communicated and various authorities gave their CDA frameworks different levels of definition. Some relied exclusively on text; others made drawings and models. Millar recruited a bunch of young architect-planners, many of whom were educated at the School of Architecture and Town Planning at the University of Manchester. Thus, Manchester's CDAs were well defined, perhaps over-specified, and had very clear three-dimensional visions that were interconnected at a city scale. Millar's view was that 'design was useful in many respects'.[113]

Up to 1963, a host of commercial developments had already changed the landscape of the city and it was the free market rather than the authority that was shaping the streets. Prior to the formal publication of any reports by the

---

article contains extracts from an address given by Stafford to the Manchester branch of the Incorporated Association of Architects and Surveyors (now Association of Building Engineers) at the Engineer's Club, 6 April 1965.
109 Stafford, 'Manchester City Architect's Department: Management and Planning Following Reorganisation', p. 1188.
110 Ibid.
111 Turner, *The North Country*, p. 70.
112 Ibid., p. 70.
113 Interview with John Millar, 18 September 2013.

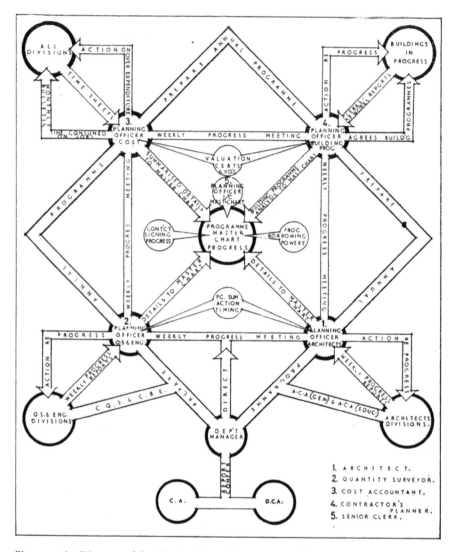

Figure 1.16 Diagram of the City Architect's Department following a restructure in the early 1960s.

planning department, certain provisional CDA schemes were published in the architectural press, including that of the *Cathedral Area* and the *Civic Area*[114] [Figure 1.17]. They received provisional endorsement on the basis of the general descriptive nature of the articles, and little in the way of analytical critique.

---

114 *Interbuild*, February 1963, pp. 40–41; *Architectural Review*, August 1962.

THE SHAPE OF THE CITY: POWER AND PLANNING

Figure 1.17 Drawings by David Gosling of a sequential journey through the proposed Civic Area. Playing on the image of 'Townscape', the illustrations were supposed to show the variety of spatial encounters as a rich succession, with objects to draw the eye as one moved from square to square.

Most of the CDAs were subject to various forms of speculation by the private sector, in advance of their designation by the local authority. In this sense, the developers were attempting to determine the extents of their own plots, though ultimately the legal boundaries were negotiated by multiple stakeholders. One such speculative scheme was designed by W.S. Hattrell and Partners in 1962 for the Cathedral Area, which proposed the demolition of Manchester's Corn Exchange (Ball & Elce, 1889–90 and Potts, Son & Pickup, 1904–14). In extracts from the architects' report reprinted in the regional journal of the RIBA, *Architecture North West*, only lip service was paid to the historic context – the loss of the Corn Exchange was not acknowledged in the copy. Typically, more attention was given to the proposed highway infrastructure and the need for any scheme to integrate with the wider aims of the planning department. The scale and nature of this mixed-use multi-level proposal was indicative of the pending priority afforded to comprehensive development, which superseded the previous promotion of island and gap sites. However, the measured critique of the *Architects' Journal* foresaw the generic failings of commercially led comprehensive development and criticised its lack of real connectivity and its aspect and contribution to the streetscape.[115] Nonetheless, this negative assessment was not enough to derail the expansive replanning of the central area in similar formal arrangements.

The CDA guidelines authored by Millar's department were intended as frameworks for developers and their architects. For more general consumption, by politicians, officers of the authority and other interested parties, a series of reports through the mid-1960s provided updates on development and insight into the scale and scope of planning and construction in the city. These were not published as widely as the *1945 Plan*, but were accompanied by a 'permanent' exhibition in the former gas showroom of the Town Hall extension from September 1965 that included a huge scale model of the entire city centre [Figure 1.18].[116] The 1964–65 report referred to the prescient issues affecting the city and the department in policy and organisational terms and emphasised the need for 'collaboration between the City Engineer and Surveyor's and Town Planning Departments', especially in transport and parking matters.[117] The opening sentence of the *Review of Work* placed the emphasis on the 'need to rid the city of the image of grime and obsolescence inherited from the first industrial revolution' – a prevailing sentiment since the 1930s.[118] However, Millar's use of the word 'image' implied civic boosterism and city

---

115 'Manchester. Corn Exchange Project', *Architect's Journal*, 24 October 1962, p. 947.
116 'Permanent Display of the Changing Manchester', *The Guardian*, 20 September 1965, p. 5.
117 Ibid., p. 22.
118 Millar, J.S. (1965) *Manchester Corporation. City Planning Department 1964–65* (Manchester: City of Manchester), p. 7.

Figure 1.18 Model showing the comprehensive redevelopment of the city centre on display in Manchester Town Hall extension in the 1960s. In the foreground is Hulme (left) and the University (right). The noticeboard to the right proclaims that, 'A 3 dimensional approach is essential in evolving a strategy and structure for the city.'

marketing more aligned with the need to attract inward private investment. Public–private partnerships were essential to the renewal of town and city centres in the post-war period. Levels of entrepreneurialism and involvement varied between local authorities; some entered as full partners in specially formed limited companies, others simply acted as landlords and earned income from rent and rates. Manchester's Labour council worked with developers but, with a strong tradition of local government and talented leaders and officers, was also able to negotiate terms. The three-dimensional frameworks of the CDAs were one tool for such negotiations.

It wasn't just the central area that was addressed by Millar's team, huge swathes of the inner-urban districts formed residential redevelopment areas [Figure 1.19]. Twelve such sites had been identified by 1967 for which planning briefs were prepared. Ultimately these briefing documents authorised the demolition of 110,000 dwellings considered unfit for habitation and displaced many poorer communities to the overspill estates at the edge of the city and within

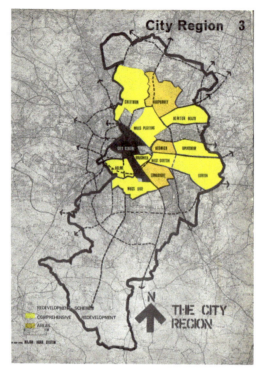

Figure 1.19   Map showing the full extents of areas being planned under John Millar's direction in the mid-1960s. Vast parts of the city were being redrawn and rebuilt as the local authority sought to address decaying Victorian housing, declared as slums in the 1930s.

other counties.[119] Although, by 1970, the Corporation had only secured 50% of the 40,000 homes required as overspill.[120] The quality of the housing stock that replaced the terraced streets was questionable and much of it was built using new and untested systems. The government, through the Building Subsidies Act 1956, endorsed system-built homes owing to the speed with which they could be erected.[121] In Manchester low-rise deck access slab blocks were preferred to

---

119   Rodgers, H.B. (1980) 'Manchester Revisited: A Profile of Urban Change', in White, H.P. (ed.) *The Continuing Conurbation. Change and Development in Greater Manchester* (Farnborough: Gower Publishing Co.), p. 27.

120   Shapely, Dr P. (2004) 'The Press and the System Built Developments of Inner City Manchester, 1960s–1980s', *Manchester Region History Review*, 2004. Cited in C. Raiswell, Housing Information Unit, Manchester City Council Housing Department, email 25 September 2002.

121   Joseph Rowntree Foundation (1991) *Views from the Crescents* (Hulme Manchester: Hulme Views Project) [no pagination].

THE SHAPE OF THE CITY: POWER AND PLANNING

Figure 1.20 Photograph for *Urban Renewal Manchester* showing Lego models of mass housing schemes. This particular model was Gibson Street, which gained the nickname 'Fort Ardwick' due to its barrier-like qualities.

high-rise point blocks. This was, in part, a legacy of the inter-war policy promulgated by politicians, who favoured low density developments, like those of the garden suburbs at Wythenshawe and Burnage.[122] Chief Assistant Architect, Robert Stones set up a 'semi-autonomous Housing Development Group' with the help of John Millar. The only scheme built to their designs was at Gibson Street in Longsight, constructed by Bison (Concrete Northern), in 1968.[123] This generally disliked, and rapidly to fail, development was known with an ironic affection as 'Fort Longsight' and was arguably no more complicated in its assembly than the upturned Lego bricks which had been used to represent it in early massing studies [Figure 1.20]: it was completed in 1966 and demolished in 1992.

However, the most infamous and iconic Manchester housing blocks were the Crescents in Hulme (1972), designed by Wilson & Womersley and named after English classical architects, John Nash, William Kent, Charles Barry and Robert Adam [Figure 1.21]. The story of Manchester's slum clearances and its forays into experimental housing on a massive scale is one that warrants its own study. Suffice to say that alongside the city centre redevelopments, the actual area of the city of Manchester that was under consideration for replanning during this period was extensive.

---

[122] Shapely, 'The Press and the System Built Developments of Inner City Manchester, 1960s–1980s', p. 31. Cited in *Minutes of Housing Committee*, Vol. 26, p. 568.

[123] Shapely, Dr P. (2004) 'The Press and the System Built Developments of Inner City Manchester, 1960s–1980s', *Manchester Region History Review*, p. 31.

Figure 1.21 The 'brutalist playground' in front of Charles Barry Crescent – one of the four infamous Hulme Crescents.

Albeit that the work of the municipal planners in the 1960s was built upon the *1945 Plan*, it ultimately had more impact on the shape of the city. Rather than leaping from broad-brush to detailed design, the various reports, briefs and development guidelines produced in the 1960s addressed a sequence of scales that led to reasonably flexible frameworks for architects to design within. The comprehensive planning proposals were attached to the generally held principle that wholesale redevelopment was necessary and that schemes should be of sufficient scale to be integrated with one another and with the city as a whole. The piecemeal development of the 1950s and early 1960s was viewed as undesirable and not contributing to the overall advancement of the city. This sentiment was so widely accepted that, in the Manchester Corporation Act (1965), the Corporation obtained temporary powers to force CPOs on obstructive parties who held minority interests that impeded development.[124] Up to this point, this type of power could only be legally executed in the context of housing provision and a few other statutory purposes. With defined CDAs and extended CPO powers, a confident and able department prepared a central area plan, arguably more ambitious than that produced in 1945.

In legislative terms, the planning work was stuck between the development plan system instituted in the Town and Country Planning Act 1947 and the

---

124 Millar, *Manchester City Centre Map 1967*, p. 75.

new advice of the PAG for sub-regional, structure and local plans. Development plans were subject to quinquennial review. Manchester's 1961 approval was based on a document authored in 1951 based on surveys from the 1940s. When, in 1966, John Millar broached the subject of a development plan review with MHLG, it was met with some consternation over its status, the need for such a review in light of PAG guidelines and subsequent pending changes to the Town and Country Planning Act. Millar's view was that 'everything these days should be regarded as interim and subject to a process of constant review'.[125] In respect of a statutory quinquennial review he simply wished to avoid being 'cast to the dungeon for failing in [his] responsibility to the lawyers!'[126] This really signals Millar's grasp of the reality of planning in a shifting landscape and some of the absurdities created by cycles of change in central government. Ultimately, Millar was sanctioned to proceed in a manner that was fit for the local situation. This in-between position, negotiated by Millar, in some way accounts for both the form of development proposed and the level of definition in the proposals for central Manchester.

The PAG endorsed the recommendations of *Traffic in Towns*[127] that advocated the separation of traffic and pedestrians and the creation of 'environmental areas', likened to 'urban rooms'. and the planning bulletin on town centre renewal called for a non-statutory 'Town Centre Map' that incorporated more detailed proposals than the Development Plan technique allowed. Millar was also clear about the relationships between planning, land use and transportation. He worked closely with John Hayes, City Engineer, to produce separate reports on car parking and the revised route of the ring road.[128] MHLG were of the opinion that Manchester seemed 'to be doing the best that is possible to reconcile the requirements of current legislation with new style thinking'.[129] Millar navigated the legislative situation to act in the best interests of the city and his skills in so doing were laid out explicitly in the publication of the *City Centre Map 1967*.

The *City Centre Map* laid out in words, drawings and photographs the comprehensive vision developed through Millar's direction and negotiation. It was intended to 'form the basis for further consultation with those interested in the planning of the Central Area of Manchester'.[130] At this point, all of the advisory schemes for the six CDAs were approved in principle by the City Council and

---

125 NA: HLG 144/86.
126 Ibid.
127 Buchanan, C. (1963) *Traffic in Towns: A Study of the Long-term Problems of Traffic in Urban Areas* (London: HMSO).
128 Hayes, J., City Engineer (1968) *Manchester City Centre Road* (Manchester: City of Manchester Corporation); Manchester Corporation (1967) *Joint Report on Car Parking in Central Manchester* (Manchester: City of Manchester).
129 NA: HLG 144/86.
130 Millar, *Manchester City Centre Map 1967*, p. 1.

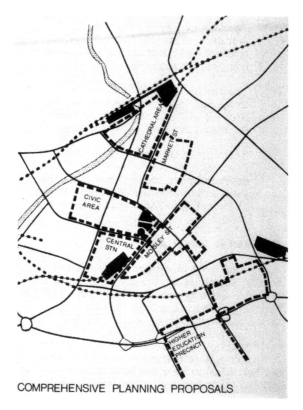

Figure 1.22 The Comprehensive Development Areas as set out in the *City Centre Map, 1967*. Whilst not all were realised, and none in their totality, this schematic set the spatial framework for development into the twenty-first century.

the need for 'public and private interests' to be 'working together as a team' was seen as vital to realising the objectives of the plan [Figure 1.22].[131] The five central CDAs related to the ring road and to one another, the sixth CDA was Manchester Education Precinct (MEP) and slightly autonomous. It was being designed by Wilson & Womersley under the supervision of a joint committee (see Chapter 3). The Market Street Area included land that would become the Arndale Centre (Wilson & Womersley, 1972–79) and was predicated on the pedestrianisation of Market Street itself. The creation of a 'really fine shopping centre' which maximised returns, had 'the character of a permanent exhibition' and removed traffic from the centre was viewed as a necessary provision to 'induce people into making special expeditions to the regional centre'.[132]

---

131   Ibid.
132   Ibid., pp. 56–59.

Scheduled to adjoin the Market Street Area was The Cathedral Area. It was presented as the historic quarter of the city and was one of the few instances where concessions were made to built heritage. It did not, however, escape the precinctual treatment so beloved of mid-century urban designers. According to the planners, the successful completion of the ring road would create a 'precinct to contain the Cathedral and Chetham's Hospital'.[133]

The perpetual icons of medieval Mancunian culture, namely the public houses the Old Wellington Inn and Sinclair's Oyster Bar, were referred to as being of 'special architectural or historic interest'. The stated aim of their retention and integration 'in a sympathetic way with the renewal of the surrounding area' was ultimately questionable and is addressed in Chapter 5.[134] The proposals acknowledged that 'the best [architectural] work of the Victorian era is coming to be appreciated' and that the Civic Amenities Act 1967 offered the powers to protect 'areas of distinctive scale and character'.[135] Albert Square and its connection to Deansgate and John Rylands Library was one such case. It was captured in proposals for The Civic Area.

Of all the CDAs, the Civic Area had closest links to the *1945 Plan*. A ceremonial axis, or processional route, was designed to connect the Town Hall to the Crown Court and the associated new buildings were intended for 'local government' occupancy.[136] The release of land for speculative commercial uses led to the development of Brazennose House (Leach Rhodes Walker, 1964) and the 'processional' vehicular boulevard [see Figure 7.03] was modified to become a pedestrian space 'precinctual in character' and of a more 'intimate human scale'.[137] The opportunities for framing vistas and for 'continuously changing views' were illustrated in architects' perspectives prepared during the consultation period [Figure 1.17].[138] In reality, much of the design for the Civic Area was well anticipated by 1967. Models for both the Crown Square development (Leach Rhodes Walker, 1970) and the Magistrate's Court (Yorke Rosenberg Mardell with City Architect S.G. Besant Roberts, 1971) [Figure 1.23] were presented in the *City Centre Map*. Most of this area was developed in line with the approved 1961 Plan and few additional powers were necessary to secure land. The composition of streets and small squares in conjunction with comprehensive renewal 'simultaneously displayed elements of the brutal and the redemptive', a common contradiction in the boom cities.[139]

This dual approach was exemplified in the proposals for Mosley Street as a cultural and entertainment centre. The Advisory Planning Scheme for the CDA

---

133 Ibid., p. 61.
134 Ibid.
135 Ibid., p. 42.
136 Ibid., p. 63.
137 Ibid., p. 64.
138 Ibid.
139 Smith, O.S. *Boom Cities*, p. 8.

Figure 1.23 Viewed from Quay Street, the white gridded exoskeleton of the Magistrates' Court (Yorke Rosenberg Mardell with City Architect S.G. Besant Roberts, 1971) is on the left of this image. In the background can be seen the squat tower of Manchester House (Leach Rhodes Walker, 1965) and behind that, the Portland stone clad home of the inland revenue, Albert Bridge House (E.H. Banks, Ministry of Works, 1959).

covered some thirty-five acres from Piccadilly to Central Station and promoted an upper-level pedestrian system, an extension to the City Art Gallery and a new Opera House. The area around Piccadilly had been bombed at Christmas 1940 [Figure 1.24] and was home to Victorian warehouses which were regarded as obsolete and valueless. At the western end of the area was a cluster of existing cinemas and bars, near to the junction of Oxford Street and Portland Street. Mosley Street was already developing without the intervention of the planners. In 1961, the fledgling Building Design Partnership (BDP – formerly Grenfell Baines & Hargreaves) prepared a master plan for the south-western portion at Lower Mosley Street on behalf of developers Donald Shearer and Company. Touted as Manchester's 'West End', 'pedestrians would be separated from traffic on platforms raised above street level, and there would be a new public square, a mall, courts and arcades' with 'a new bus station, air terminal, hotel, offices,

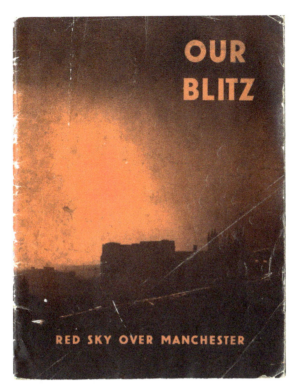

Figure 1.24   Cover of the fundraising publication *Our Blitz*.

restaurants and entertainment centres'.[140] The scheme was to be 'financed privately but with support, though not necessarily financial, from Manchester Corporation'. This type of speculation was typical of the manner in which developers engaged and influenced the planning agenda. By 1967 a host of new commercial developments had already been built or were approved. The majority of them were on bomb-damaged sites and remained aligned to the historic street pattern and existing legal boundaries.[141] Several schemes in the Mosley Street Area made concessions to the pending master plan (see Chapter 6), but the overall project faltered and the connected and comprehensive vision was never realised. The site at Lower Mosley Street was much more contained and continued to attract speculation throughout the 1960s and 1970s. Adjacent was the last of the central area CDAs, Central Station.

Central Station was still operational as a railway station when the *City Centre Map* was published in 1967. However, its planned closure was public

---

140   'Big Development Plan for Manchester', *The Guardian*, 13 April 1961, p. 22.
141   Millar, *Manchester City Centre Map 1967*, p. 83.

knowledge and the opportunity for the Department to pre-emptively plan for its future contrasted to the other CDAs, where private developers led the conversation. Nonetheless, this did not prevent speculation and a consortium led by Taylor Woodrow made a proposal in 1968 that was designed by BDP and published in a lavish, boxed brochure. This was used to lobby the Corporation to promote a joint venture. Millar's team imagined the site to be based on Copenhagen's Tivoli Gardens and saw it as a great opportunity to create a public space provision as yet unrealised in Manchester.[142] The laissez-faire nature of the mercantile city and the legacy of public space as a host for popular protest meant that the city centre had always been devoid of parks and gardens.[143] Eventually, a huge scheme designed by (C&S) was given outline planning approval in 1974 following an extended period of design studies by the practice. The principal features of the plans were the retention of at least some part of Central Station, the demolition of the railway warehouses, the construction of a new tower and the creation of public gardens. The scheme was dramatically halted amidst the post-colonial Crown Agents affair of the 1970s, of which the full story of this site is narrated in Chapter 4.

Like the *1945 Plan*, much contained within the *City Centre Map* was not realised in the form imagined and presented by the planners. The complexity of site ownership in the centre of the city was obstructive to 'comprehensive treatment of a complete area' and the CDA processes tended to be lengthy.[144] The lack of sites owned by the Corporation was also blamed for the pace at which they could bring sites to market. Even with judicious application of the temporary powers endowed by the Manchester Corporation Act 1965, progress was perceived as slow and behind that of other major urban centres.[145] However, the shape given to the city by the work of the planners in the 1960s prevailed and is recognisable in the twenty-first century centre. The city centre of the *1945 Plan* was effectively a zoning exercise and infill process predicated on the existing street pattern, mixed with a beaux-arts approach. That of the 1960s planners, while still idealistic, was local and specific and took account of the existing city and its merits. They acknowledged the complexities and demands of integrated approaches to circulation, transportation, recreation and commerce and the appreciation of Victorian built heritage was raised. Both plans were contingent upon a central area ring road (the full impact is explored in Chapter 6). A public inquiry halted the most intense section of proposed multi-level carriageways

---

142 Ibid., p. 69.
143 In St Peter's Fields 'on 16 August 1819 a peaceful rally of 60,000 pro-democracy reformers, men, women and children, was attacked by armed cavalry resulting in 15 deaths and over 600 injuries'. The event came to be known as the Peterloo Massacre and had significant effect with regard the ability to gather in public and the lack of provision of public space as a means of preventing such.
144 Turner, *The North Country*, p. 71.
145 Waterhouse, R. 'Eternity Ring', *The Guardian*, 17 September 1974, p. 16.

along Portland Street in 1973. This, combined with general economic malaise and the huge changes to local governance brought about by the creation of Greater Manchester in April 1974, meant that development slowed and the scale and type of planning activity shifted to regional economic planning, aligned with Whitehall guidance.

In these terms, planning and the region finally coalesced in political and spatial realms. The Greater Manchester County Council had the power to plan in a way that had formerly been inhibited and its formation indicated an alternative geography to that of the county palatines of Lancashire and Cheshire – one informed by more recent industrial economics. Of course, its structure mimicked that of the various inter-borough committees established since the 1920s as a means to govern space. However, the term region is one that is expansive as it is contained, as networked as it is delineated. In Chapter 2 I explore the national and international contexts around the development of the computer and the growth of the computer industry in Manchester.

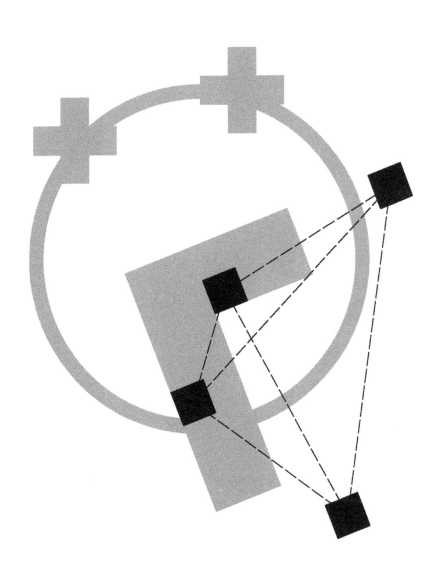

2

Computing and the Cold War

Introduction

In geographic terms, this chapter concerns networks – a regional military industrial network attached to the British nuclear programme and a network of buildings in Manchester related to computing and defence. Defence and military research during the war, by both Allied and German scientists, had all but captured the knowledge that would define the global political landscape for the rest of the century and beyond – the nuclear bomb, the rocket and the computer. The first controlled nuclear explosion by the Soviet Union in 1949 and the outbreak of war in Korea in 1950 made the rearmament programme and civil defence central to government activity. Welfare expenditure shrank and defence spending grew, feeding what David Edgerton has termed the 'Warfare State'.[1] The birth of computing and its government sponsorship was predominantly attached to military aims, in missile trajectory calculations and nuclear fuel production. The relationship between militarism, computing and British architecture is little examined to date. Here, I wish to explore the history and networks that centred much of this industry in the region and the personnel, policy and plans that enabled the architecture that supported it.

Against a background of a continuous state of preparedness for military engagement, but within a period noted for fiscal austerity, I show how military objectives bypassed development norms. I describe how the interplay between central policy and funding, local interpretation and implementation affected construction. The close relation between research, funding and expertise in academic, governmental and industrial–commercial settings is examined to show how people, policy and place acted in the operative networks of the region. Through the histories of acquisitions, procurement and transformation

---

[1] Edgerton, *Warfare State*.

of sites, existing buildings and new construction I argue that these contexts each impacted upon the architectural production – of the world's first building for the computer at the University of Manchester, a laboratory and missile factory for Ferranti (an electrical engineering firm), an R&D and production facility for International Computers Limited (ICL) and the headquarters for the National Computing Centre (NCC).

British architecture and the state of the nation state

From a much stronger economic base, the United States undertook the majority of Western post-war investment in military technologies. The first significant sponsorships of computing were predominantly attached to military objectives.[2] In Europe, as France, England and Germany realised that they had fallen behind in an important technological race, crash programmes and rapidly developed policies were deployed to close the gap. Discussing the computer industry, economist Kenneth Flamm acutely captured a relation that is central to the tenet of this chapter: 'private firms and their commercial technologies [were] closely linked to public investment in computer technology'.[3] Each of the buildings discussed in this chapter was funded by the state and the state also supplied the contracts for the services and products housed and manufactured in them.

It is common to view the architecture of the state through particular building types – schools, hospitals, social housing and suchlike – but these private sector enterprises involved significant state intervention as well. Historians typically examine buildings of the welfare state using political binaries, typologies or through the biographies of their architects – often a combination of these three approaches.[4] The types of schemes in this chapter do not lend themselves readily

---

2 Flamm, K. (1988) *Creating the Computer. Government, Industry and High Technology* (Washington DC: The Brookings Institution), pp. 29–27; p. 5.
3 Ibid, p. 6.
4 For example the story of the race to build new homes and the political rhetoric around the numbers produced each year by successive Conservative and Labour governments. See Esher, L. (1981) *A Broken Wave: The Rebuilding of England 1940–1980* (London: Viking); Bullock, N. (2002) *Building the Post-War World* (London: Routledge); Gold, J.R. (2007) *The Practice of Modernism: Modern Architects and Urban Transformation, 1954–1972* (London: Routledge); Powers, A. (2007) *Britain: Modern Architectures in History* (London: Reaktion Books); Glendinning, M., and Muthesius, S. (1994) *Tower Block: Modern Public Housing in England, Scotland, Wales, and Northern Ireland* (London: Paul Mellon Centre for Studies in British Art); Saint, A. (1987) *Towards a Social Architecture: The Role of School-building in Post-war England* (London: Yale University Press); Muthesius, S. (2000) *The Postwar University – Utopian Campus and College* (London: Yale University Press); Fair, A. (2018) '"Modernization of Our Hospital System": The National Health Service, the Hospital Plan, and the "Harness" Programme, 1962–77', *Twentieth Century British History*, Vol. 29, Issue 4, pp. 547–575. Biographical – Glendinning, M. (2008) *Modern Architect: The*

to an investigation of political bias in the party system; they were realised under different administrations. The economic consensus of Butskellism was seen in both military and modernisation agendas of successive administrations during the post-war period.[5] The overarching political culture and its underlying value system was a shared territory, between left and right, overshadowed by the end of the Second World War and the beginning of the Cold War.[6] The rearmament programme and the civil defence programme were 'inseparable' and technological culture of Britain was underpinned by investment in military contracts.[7] Policy drove commissions for weaponry, the forced mergers of the Industrial Reorganisation Corporation (IRC) and the institution of new public–private partnerships.[8] The Ministry of Supply (MoS) became the de facto sponsor of these contracts, but, as David Edgerton notes, there was 'a powerful, potentially commercially exploitable, overlap between new military and civil technologies, notably in aviation and nuclear power' and 'these were also seen as the key civilian technologies of the future, to be used by nationalised electricity providers and airlines'.[9] The development of buildings for new technologies in Britain was intrinsically tied to the state and the civil implementation of science that had its genesis in defence expenditure.

Reinhold Martin referred to the 'aesthetic and technological extension' of the military industrial complex in post-war US architecture as 'the organizational complex'.[10] Within the 'organizational complex' the individuality of the new consumer was defined by a series of choices 'made within a system that was

---

Life and Times of Robert Matthew (London: RIBA Publishing); Curtis, W.J.R. (1994) *Denys Lasdun. Architecture, City, Landscape* (London: Phaidon); Rodger, J. (2007) *Gillespie, Kidd & Coia: Architecture 1956–1987* (Glasgow: Lighthouse). Titles among the recent Twentieth Century Architects series published by the RIBA and English Heritage also take a biographical approach to the works of Ryder & Yates, Powell & Moya, Ahrends, Burton & Koralek and others.

5 The political consensus in economic policy terms was labelled in 1954 as 'Butskellism', to describe the similarities in the administration of the office of Chancellor of the Exchequer by Rab Butler (Conservative) and Hugh Gaitskell (Labour). An article in the *Economist* by Norman Macrae dramatised the convergence and referred to a fictitious Mr Butskell. 'Mr Butskell's Dilemma', *Economist*, 13 February 1954, p. 439; Kelly, S. (2002) *The Myth of Mr. Butskell: The Politics of British Economic Policy, 1950–55* (London: Ashgate).
6 Edgerton, *Warfare State*.
7 Grant, M. (2009) *After the Bomb: Civil Defence and Nuclear War in Cold War Britain, 1945–68* (London: Palgrave Macmillan).
8 The IRC's main function was to promote the efficiency and international competitiveness of British industry by encouraging firms to merge into larger units where this was judged to be in the national interest. Hague, D.C. (1983) *The IRC: An Experiment in Industrial Intervention: A History of the Industrial Reorganisation Corporation* (London: Unwin Hyman).
9 Edgerton, *Warfare State*, p. 105.
10 Martin, R. (2003) *The Organizational Complex: Architecture, Media and Corporate Space* (Cambridge, MA: MIT Press).

designed to offer variety by providing interchangeable elements in standardized formats. Architects would call these elements *modules*'.[11] It is this modularity that Martin calls upon as he draws a strand through the post-war, science derived, aesthetics to the birth of the networked paradigm and its affect upon architecture – the cessation of mechanisation to organisation. In the 1940s and 1950s large US corporations in the technology sector, General Motors (GM), IBM and Bell Laboratories, employed architects and designers like Eliel and Eero Saarinen, Eliot Noyes and Skidmore, Owings & Merrill to deploy networked logic in the design and assembly of their buildings, visual identities and products. The association between client and architect in the case of GM was so close that it was a collaborative effort between the car manufacturer and architect Eero Saarinen that developed the neoprene gasket for the curtain wall of GM's Technical Centre in 1953.[12] The comparative opportunities for architecture in Britain did not attract an equivalent level of capital and, amidst the diminished economic and material resources of the immediate post-war period, buildings for new technologies were primarily vessels for the activity contained within. The luxury of expressing commercial identity through built form was restricted by scarcity and modes of procurement in a resource starved, nationalised state.

The post-war British context for development was an inherited bureaucratic structure, itself shaped by conflict, combined with scarce resources and capital. This meant that the drive to advance society and develop new technologies was curtailed and forced to optimise existing situations, particularly in construction. The desire to progress, despite adverse conditions is captured by the idea of 'defiant modernism', but this was accompanied in manufacturing towns by a further sense of pride, attached to notions of authenticity.[13] Traditional engineering skills and the design of bespoke components prevailed, even in perceptibly hi-tech products. In certain sectors, new technologies were perceived as being of inferior quality if they were assembled from parts made elsewhere. Within Ferranti's computer division in Manchester, a city known for its engineering manufacturing tradition, each component was made on site, just as earlier electrical technologies had been, to maintain a quality standard. It is conceivable that this type of nostalgic pride was a necessary diversion in a society that longed to be modern but was compelled to function amidst Victorian infrastructure.

The re-use of everything in post-war Britain extended to buildings too. Both new construction and existing sites have their own place in this account that

---

11 Ibid., p. 5.
12 Ibid., p. 161.
13 See Bud, R. (1998) 'Penicillin and the New Elizabethans', *The British Journal for the History of Science*, Vol. 31, No. 3, pp. 305–333. The term 'defiant modernism' was first deployed by Bud in this article but has since been used by other historians of technology. See Sumner, J. (2014) 'Defiance to Compliance: Visions of the Computer in Postwar Britain', *History and Technology*, Vol. 30, No. 4, pp. 309–333.

will show how high-technology and architecture in Britain missed meeting one another until the late 1960s. The cases studied here reveal architecture's value in relation to technology, at the birth of the Cold War in the 1950s, during the height of 1960s optimism and at the brink of economic collapse in the 1970s.

Computing and Manchester: network building

Despite burgeoning building control legislation, design bulletins did not exist for weapons production facilities and computer manufacturing centres. Novel technologies demanded unique and specialised approaches. Buildings procured by the MoS were not subject to local planning processes and were comparatively well funded. Invariably, much discussion and planning took place before an architect was appointed and, in this sense, it is the biographies and networks of other individuals that had more influence on the early procurement phases of projects. In Manchester this was exemplified by the presence of a single actor amidst multiple networks over time – Bertram Vivian Bowden.

Bowden was educated at Chesterfield Grammar School and Emmanuel College, Cambridge. He worked with Ernest Rutherford in the 1930s, with whom he co-authored papers on the properties of gamma radiation.[14] During the war he was posted to Washington DC and Massachusetts Institute of Technology (MIT) to work on the development of radar. He led a British team in his role as principal scientific advisor to the MoS Telecommunications Research Establishment (TRE).[15] On return to the United Kingdom, Bowden joined the Atomic Energy Authority (UKAEA).[16] His experience of military technological research in well-funded higher education institutions proved a dramatic influence and shaped his collaborative approach in the future – including his stewardship of technological education in the city. Bowden was 42 and leading the computer sales division at Ferranti when he was appointed as Principal of the Manchester Municipal College of Technology (later University of Manchester Institute of Science and Technology – UMIST) in 1953.[17]

---

14 Rutherford, Ernest, and Bowden, B.V. (1932) 'The γ-rays from Actinium Emanation and their Origin'. *Proc. R. Soc. Lond. A*, 136, no. 829, pp. 407–412; Rutherford, Ernest, Wynn-Williams, C.E., Lewis, Wilfrid Bennett, and Bowden, B.V. (1933) 'Analysis of α-rays by an Annular Magnetic Field', *Proc. R. Soc. Lond. A*, 139, no. 839, pp. 617–637; Ernest Rutherford, Wilfrid Bennett Lewis, and B.V. Bowden (1933) 'Analysis of the long range α-particles from radium C' by the magnetic focussing method'. *Proc. R. Soc. Lond. A*, 142, no. 846, pp. 347–361.

15 'Proposed talks on future of College of Technology: Dr B.V. Bowden to be New Principal', *The Manchester Guardian*, 27 June 1953, p. 3.

16 Tweedale, Geoffrey, 'Bertram Vivian Bowden', *Ann. Hist. Comp* 12, no. 2 (1990), pp. 138–140.

17 'Proposed talks on future of College of Technology: Dr B.V. Bowden to be New Principal', p. 3.

In 1964–65 Bowden served in Harold Wilson's Labour government as minister of state at the Department of Education and Science. Here, Bowden, and others, are actors in a narrative that illustrates policy, personnel, finance and technology and their agency, converging upon a fixed location – Manchester.

The development of the computer has its own histories written with various accents – on the mathematics, on the engineering and on the critical theory attached to its evolution.[18] Here it is the networks of personnel, their genesis and their location in Manchester that are most relevant. Bowden worked with Freddie Williams, Tom Kilburn and Peter Hall at the TRE during the Second World War.[19] Williams and his assistant Kilburn were electronic engineers who found themselves rapidly without purpose in August 1945 as hostilities drew to a close.[20] They gravitated towards the University of Manchester where Max Newman, a Cambridge mathematician, took a post as Professor of Pure Mathematics in 1945. Williams was appointed by Newman as Chair of Electrical Engineering in November 1946 and Kilburn was 'on loan' from the MoS.[21] By June 1948 the assembled group of mathematicians and electrical engineers achieved a global first in realising Alan Turing's 'stored programme' computing principle in the machine now popularly known as *Baby*.[22] Shortly afterwards Bowden and Hall took positions with Ferranti, also in Manchester.

Atomic warfare was a powerful force shaping the government agenda in the late 1940s.[23] The political elite, in the face of diminishing global power, wanted to restate Britain's international authority. In the United States the McMahon Act (1946) denied Britain any further collaborative role in the development of

---

18 Lavington, Simon, *Early British Computers: The Story of Vintage Computers and the People Who Built Them* (Manchester: Manchester University Press, 1980); Lavington, Simon, *The Pegasus Story. A History of a Vintage British Computer* (London: The Science Museum, 2000); Lavington, Simon, *Moving Targets – Elliott-Automation and the Dawn of the Computer Age in Britain, 1947–67* (London: Springer-Verlag, 2011); Lavington, Simon, *A History of Manchester Computers* (Manchester: The National Computing Centre, 1975); Flamm, *Creating the Computer*; Campbell-Kelly Michael, and Aspray, William, *Computer. A History of the Information Machine* (New York: Basic Books, 1996); Hendry, John, *Innovating for Failure: Government Policy and the Early British Computer Industry* (Cambridge, MA: MIT Press, 1989); Bowden, Bertram Vivian (ed.) *Faster Than Thought. A Symposium on Digital Computing Machines* (London: Sir Isaac Pitman & Sons, 1953); John F. Wilson, *Government and the electronic components industry: the case of Ferranti, 1953–1973* (Manchester: University of Manchester, Department of History, 1991) Working paper No. 7.
19 Johnson, D. 'What Manchester did Yesterday', *The Guardian*, 15 December 1975, p. 5.
20 Interview with Freddie Williams by Paul Drath, 29 June 1972. See Drath, Paul, *The Relationship Between Science and Technology: University Research and the Computer Industry 1945–1962* (PhD diss., University of Manchester, 1973). Library ref: Th3452.
21 Professor Newman, report to the Buildings Committee, 15 October 1948, Minutes of the Building Committee, vol. 1, 1946–1958, 90. UoMA: GB 133 USC/4/1.
22 Lavington, *A History of Manchester Computers*.
23 As well as Edgerton's treatise on warfare and the state see, Grant, *After The Bomb*.

the atomic bomb, despite the significant contribution by British scientists in pioneering its research. The Berlin Blockade coincided directly with the successful operation of *Baby* and, as the Cold War began in earnest, the government prioritised the development of the computational power necessary to calculate atomic bomb implosions. The 'control and funding' in the fields of aviation, nuclear power and the related technologies in military and civil contexts fell to the MoS, which became the largest single funder of research in both domains.[24] In October 1948 the MoS asked Ferranti to help to build a computer, to designs by Williams, Kilburn and Newman, funded by the Ministry of Defence and given technical support from the TRE. The government paid Ferranti approximately £175,000 over five years to build this machine.[25] Bowden was involved in matters of funding with representatives of various government ministries during his time at Ferranti.[26] His skills in canvassing were evident as he aimed to secure further research monies for 'a number of worthwhile research contracts' that were peripheral to the development of the computer, if the advisory committee to the National Research Development Corporation (NRDC) found it to be 'in the national interest'.[27]

Science and technology were not only at the heart of the government's interests, but were widely embraced by the nation long before the White Heat of Wilson-era politics. In 1951 The Festival of Britain positively heralded the 'atomic age'; its buildings, exhibits and visual identity all resonated with the buzz and hum, the whizz, click and whirr of modernity at the same time as they disavowed the recent effects of such warfare.[28] On the South Bank, as well as the comparatively restrained Festival Hall realised under the direction of Leslie Martin, fantastic temporary structures exploited new construction technologies and explored new architectural possibilities.[29] When considered in terms of defiant modernism and the cultural rhetoric of innovation in Britain, it is noteworthy that the Design Group of the Festival rejected modular construction in favour of unique, bespoke contributions that would emulate the themes of the Festival – scientific endeavour and innovation. The gravity defying Skylon,

---

24 Edgerton, *Warfare State*, p. 106.
25 Lavington, *Early British Computers*, p. 26.
26 Correspondence from the NRDC to Prof. Sir David Brunt of Imperial College, member of the Research Advisory Committee on computing. NA: DSIR 10/343.
27 Ibid.
28 For an account of the use of science and the imagery of science in the festival of Britain see Forgan, S. (1998) 'Festivals of Science and the Two Cultures: Science, Design and Display in the Festival of Britain, 1951', *British Journal for the History of Science*, Vol. 31, No. 2, pp. 17–240.
29 Glendinning, M. (2003) 'Teamwork or Masterwork? The Design and Reception of the Royal Festival Hall', *Architectural History*, Vol. 46, pp. 277–319; Glendinning, M. (2005) 'The Royal Festival Hall: A Postscript', *Architectural History*, Vol. 48, pp. 323–326.

Figure 2.01 The Ferranti Nimrod Digital Computer on show at the Science Museum Festival of Britain Exhibition (1951). Postcard collected by Malcom Shifrin after his having beaten Nimrod at the game of Nim.

designed by Powell and Moya, and Ralph Tubb's Dome of Discovery created the embryo of British hi-tech architecture.[30]

Away from the river, at the Science Museum in Kensington, was an Exhibition of Science that largely focused on basic concepts under the banner, 'Inside the Atom'.[31] Amidst the exhibits was a simplified version of the Ferranti Mark 1 computer, named Nimrod, which invited visitors to participate in the strategy game of Nim [Figure 2.01]. The aim of the exhibit was exposure – there was no market for the computer, its commercial applications were relatively

---

30 Norman Foster was influenced from an early age by illustrations in the comic, *The Eagle*, among which, in 1951, was an exploded view of the Dome of Discovery. See Sudjic, D. (2010) *Norman Foster: A Life in Architecture* (London: Weidenfeld & Nicolson). For Festival architecture see Goodden, H. (2011) *The Lion and the Unicorn: Symbolic Architecture for the Festival of Britain* (Norwich: Unicorn Press); Powell, K. (2009) *Powell & Moya* (London: RIBA Publishing); Leventhal, F.M. (1995) '"A Tonic to the Nation": The Festival of Britain, 1951', *Albion: A Quarterly Journal Concerned with British Studies*, Vol. 27, No. 3, Autumn, pp. 445–453; Banham, M., and Hillier, B. (1976) *A Tonic to the Nation: The Festival of Britain in 1951* (London: Thames & Hudson); Conekin, B. (2003) *The Autobiography of a Nation: The 1951 Exhibition of Britain, Representing Britain in the Post-War World* (Manchester: Manchester University Press).

31 Sumner, 'Defiance to Compliance'.

unknown in 1951. Bowden was appointed as chief salesman of Ferranti's computer in the same year and continued to champion science and technology, in the interests of the nation, for the rest of his career.[32]

Bowden constructed strong narratives to support his broadly socialist agenda. His 1953 book, *Faster Than Thought*, took its title from the Nimrod brochure and established the historiography that situated Britain at the centre of computer development.[33] His interests in centring new technologies in Manchester specifically were both public spirited and privately endorsed as they would provide foundation for the growth of education and commerce in the city; Bowden understood the connection between the two. The geography of the networks with which Bowden was engaged varied over time. His work with Rutherford at Cambridge associated him with Newman and Patrick Blackett in the 1930s;[34] his role at the TRE with Williams and Kilburn took him to Washington and MIT in the 1940s; his local industrial networks in the 1950s connected these earlier encounters, forged his path as an educationalist and ultimately led to his ministerial post in the 1960s. As an actor in this complex networked model, Bowden was not only able to influence histories but also had the capability and inclination to lobby government for support.

Whether the planned objectives for the computer were civil or military, research was mostly situated in universities.[35] Newman's assembled experts at Manchester were one such group. Parallel projects existed at Cambridge (Electronic Delay Storage Automatic Computer) and at Birkbeck College,

---

32 Bowden liked to think of himself as the 'world's first computer salesman', http://history.computer.org/pioneers/bowden.html [Accessed 12 April 2017].

33 Bowden, B.V. (1953). *Faster Than Thought* was a deliberate attempt to write US competitors out of the history of computers and the first to pen a biography of Charles Babbage as the forefather of computation. Sumner, 'Defiance to Compliance'.

34 Blackett, a physicist and government and military advisor, 'was a forceful advocate of university expansion and government funding of research and development. He was a member of the Barlow committee (1945–6), the council and the research grants committee of the Department of Scientific and Industrial Research (1956–1960), and the National Research Development Corporation (1949–64), where he pushed for the development of the computer industry. He was dean of the faculty of science (1948–50) and pro-vice-chancellor (1950–52) at Manchester.' ODNB, www.oxforddnb.com/view/article/30822?docPos=1 [Accessed 8 January 2015]. His role in the Wilson administration and the creation of the IRC is explored in Kirby, M.W. (1999) 'Blackett in the "White Heat" of the Scientific Revolution: Industrial Modernisation under the Labour Governments, 1964–1970', *The Journal of the Operational Research Society*, Vol. 50, No. 10 (October), pp. 985–993.

35 By the late 1960s there was a plethora of other research establishments including the National Physical Laboratory, the Atomic Energy Authority research and reactor groups, and others to study water, hydraulics, fire, engineering, armament, rocket propulsion etc. For a full list see Table 6.1 in Edgerton, *Warfare State*, p. 248.

London (Automatic Relay Computer).[36] There was some urgency in the development of the computer, a fact reflected in the commitment by the University of Manchester to construct a 'temporary' building for the Computing Machine Laboratory. The Laboratory was instituted in 1946, following an award from the Royal Society. Newman received a grant of '£3000 a year for five years for salaries, together with the sum of £20,000 to be spent on construction during the same period'.[37]

The new building, designed by the office of J.W. Beaumont & Sons, was hurriedly erected as soon as it became apparent that Williams's memory solution was ahead of the substantially resourced research team at Princeton.[38] Thus, the world's first building (1951) designed for the computer was a simple two-storey form of loadbearing brick, sparingly detailed across three structural bays [Figure 2.02]. The urgency was for the development of the technology – the container simply had to be fit for purpose. The TRE and MoS were in full support of the research project, but it was still a struggle to secure the use of steel as a building material for the temporary accommodation.[39] Despite being designed as a temporary measure, the building still stands on Coupland Street in the heart of the University of Manchester campus. The eventual permanent home for the computing laboratories was the Electrical Engineering Building (1953) also designed by Beaumont within the 'Science Centre', which was planned by Sir Hubert Worthington as part of the *1945 Plan* (see Chapter 3) [Figure 2.03].[40]

Compared to the United States, Britain struggled to grasp the commercial possibilities of the computer and, because of this, investment in the design of products, branding and architecture was comparatively slow. At the University of Manchester, tradition, scarcity and a lack of vision combined to create architecture that was unremarkable and even out of date – Mies van der Rohe completed his first building on the Illinois Institute of Technology (IIT) campus in 1943. The Armour Research Foundation Metals Building (now Minerals and Metals Building) was part of the US war effort and Mies's first major construction in the United States. Exposed steel structure and curtain wall glazing lent

---

36 Lavington, *A History of Manchester Computers*, p. 5.
37 Royal Society, Minutes of the Council, 1945–48, Vol. 17. As quoted by Lavington, *A History of Manchester Computers*, p. 4.
38 Williams's method of using cathode ray tubes to store information in effect creating the first Random Access Memory (RAM) storage device. Drath, 'The Relationship Between Science and Technology'; Report by Professor Newman to the Buildings Committee, 15 October 1948. Minutes of the Building Committee, Vol. 1, 1946–1958, p. 90. UoMA: GB 133 USC/4/1.
39 TRE & MoS information from Report by Professor Newman to the Buildings Committee, 15 October 1948. Minutes of the Building Committee, Vol. 1, 1946–1958, p. 90. UoMA: GB 133 USC/4/1; Lack of steel information from per. comms Lavington, S., 20 August 2014.
40 Nicholas, *City of Manchester Plan 1945*.

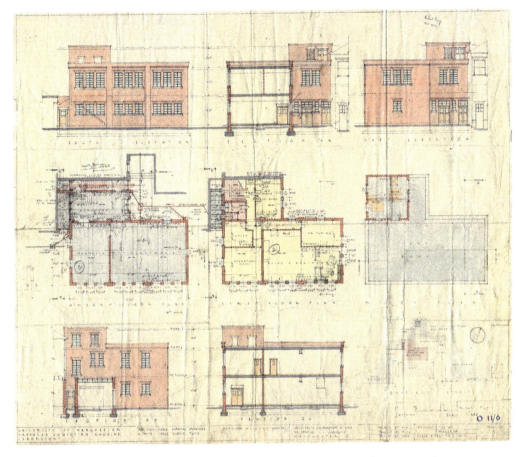

Figure 2.02 Architect's drawing of the scheme for a computing laboratory at the University of Manchester, the world's first building for the computer.

the building an industrial aesthetic and set the tone for the modernist master plan and buildings that were to follow. Mies was latterly conscious of the relationship between his buildings and technology and was popularly cited as having 'tried to make an architecture for a technological society'.[41] Mies's IIT campus was well known and widely published in European architectural journals but its influence was not evident in the schemes by the offices of Beaumont, Worthington or Fairhurst for the University of Manchester.[42]

Not all US architecture for new technologies was technologically driven, though. There were contrasts to Mies and Saarinen's prominent productions.

---

41 *Time Magazine*, Vol. 87, 1966, p. xlviii.
42 *Architectural Design*, October 1951, p. 287; *Architecture d'Aujourd'hui*, 1953, No. 50–51, pp. 26–27; *Casabella* 1957, No. 214, pp. 5–19; *Bauen & Wohnen*, 1959, No. 9, pp. 317–319.

Figure 2.03   Photograph showing the Electrical Engineering (Zochonis) Building (right, J.S. Beaumont, 1953) and the more modern Chemistry Building (left, H.S. Fairhurst & Sons, 1964) on Brunswick Street. Beaumont's building is more in the spirit of Worthington's master plan for the 'Science Centre'. Its clumsy neo-Georgian style was seen as dated by certain stakeholders (see Chapter 3).

Philip Johnson's Computer Laboratory (1961) for Brown University was 'conceived as a *porticus* – a porch – to emphasize its importance as a technical center ... Neo-classical in concept'.[43] Nonetheless, this was a distinctively modern building of 'plate glass' and 'precast stone', albeit with exposed aggregate of red granite chips to 'harmonize the new center with the 19th Century [sic] which surrounds it'.[44] However, by 1964 the *Architectural Record* asked: 'The Computer Centre: New Building Type?' in an article on Eliot Noyes's 'building for machines' for Westinghouse near Pittsburgh.[45] Noyes's scheme set the typological standard of situating the computer rooms at the centre of the plan and, owing to their size and weight, on the ground floor.

---

43   'Recent work of Philip Johnson. Computer Laboratory for Brown's University, Providence, R.I.' *Architectural Record*, July 1962, pp. 124–125.
44   Ibid.
45   'The Computer Centre: New Building Type?' in *Architectural Record*, November 1964, pp. 153–155.

Spaces for computers were heavily serviced and situating the computer hall centrally made the environmental control of temperature and humidity more efficient. Most early applications were forms of advanced calculations, often related to payroll and other information that might be commercially sensitive, so the enclosed nature of computer rooms, surrounded by other spaces and often with no natural light, also offered enhanced security. The Westinghouse facility was not the component-led modularity of Saarinen's work for IBM, it was an extension of Noyes's complete corporate design package for Westinghouse. The primary aim of the low, serrated form was to advertise Westinghouse; it was part of the company's branding, enhanced by a sign designed by Noyes, with a logo by Paul Rand. The architects wanted a 'vigorous exterior, which would be seen and identified by cars passing by on the highway'.[46]

It was IBM who brought technology and marketing together in their European commissions too. Marcel Breuer designed the French IBM headquarters (1957–62) at La Gaude. It took the dynamic form of a double Y-shaped plan and two of its wings were raised on piloti above the sloping site. The precast concrete façade was the first use of the Breuer-Beckhard system, later deployed across the United States.[47] IBM's first UK commission went to Farmer & Dark, who designed a building for laboratories and offices (1963) in a rather squat eight-storey tower and adjoining single-storey block set in the kitchen garden of a Georgian mansion outside Winchester.[48] The façade was a curtain wall with projecting toughened glass fins and described as having a 'mechanistic elegance'. Here was the explicit association of architecture and technology in the UK. In the slightly crude manner of Johnson at Brown University, the architects also chose to use a local stone, in this case, flint, pressed into the concrete of the gable walls of the lower block to give a 'rough, masculine and chunky' appearance. Nevertheless, this was an innovative use of glazing technology and the first explicitly modern building for the computer in the UK. The application of new material technologies and modernity as a reflection of new technology and branded identity was somewhat arrested in Britain and not truly realised until Norman Foster built at Cosham for IBM in 1971.[49]

---

46 Ibid.
47 Beckhard, H. 'The Breuer-Backhard Precast Facades', in Donaldson, B. (ed.) (1991) *Exterior Wall Systems: Glass and Concrete Technology, Design and Construction* (Philadelphia, PA: American Society for Testing and Materials), pp. 154–169.
48 IBM had a policy to situate their 'brainpower' outside large centres of population. 'Laboratories and Offices', *The Architects' Journal Information Library*, 12 February 1964, pp. 371–382.
49 See Knight, F. 'Designing for Computers', *Building*, 11 October 1968, pp. 87–92; 'IBM Pilot Head Office, Cosham, Hants.; Architects: Foster Associates', *Architectural Design*, August 1971, pp. 474–478; 'Two office buildings: (1) IBM pilot head office building, Cosham; (2) Computer Technology, Hemel Hempstead; Architects: Foster Associates', *Design*, October 1971, pp. 54–61; 'Two IBM office buildings. 1, Offices and factory,

There were other buildings in the UK for computers in the late-1960s. Fry and Drew designed a computer centre for Rolls-Royce (1967) at their site in Derby.[50] The largest adopter of early computation in British industry was the National Coal Board who built a great number of computer centres from as early as 1962.[51] Cedric Price also designed a computer centre for the British Transport Docks Board at Southall (1969) that assumed the typological standard set by Noyes and set the main suite centrally in the plan.[52] The nuclear industry also required computers and their use in civil and military applications was wide and varied. Research and application went hand in hand. The connections between civil and military research were blurred and the outcomes of one could affect the other. It was not only civil and military research that was blurred; the associations between research and commercial application were similarly interconnected. The University of Manchester ran a research reactor at the UKAEA site at Risley, where the National Computing Centre had its first base. The *Argus* computer, built by Ferranti, came from their research into control computers for guided weapons in the garden suburb of Wythenshawe in the south of Manchester.

The work of Ferranti at Wythenshawe was an intrinsic part of the technological culture focused upon the region. Through this culture, civil and defence applications were interwoven, relationships underpinned by personnel who held military positions during wartime and parliamentary posts in the post-war period. Whilst directed from Whitehall, it was the regional military industrial structures that influenced the focus of nuclear and computing cultures in the north-west of England. The geography of regionally clustered nuclear R&D was a product of war. From as early as 1935, Cabinet discussed the flight range of Luftwaffe bombers and the location of munitions factories.[53] Sites in the north-west of England were preferred owing to their distance from mainland Europe. Of 44 Royal Ordnance Factories (ROF), 19 were retained after 1945 for the

---

Havant, Hants; Architects: Arup Associates. 2, Offices, Cosham, Hants; Architects: Foster Associates', *Architectural Review*, January 1972, pp. 4–24.

50   Rolls-Royce Computer Centre, Derby, designed (1966) by Fry Drew & Partners / [photographed by] John Maltby Ltd. RIBA Photographs Collection: 5215–5215/29; Knight, F. 'Designing for Computers', *Building*, 11 October 1968, pp. 87–92; Jackson, I., and Holland, J. (2014) *The Architecture of Edwin Maxwell Fry and Jane Drew. Twentieth Century Architecture, Pioneer Modernism and the Tropics* (Farnham: Ashgate).

51   A search of the NA catalogue reveals a great number of computer centres across the UK built for the divisions of the National Coal Board. These buildings were not published in the architectural press.

52   *Architectural Design*, October 1969, pp. 547–552; *Architectural Design*, January 1971, p. 25; Price, C. (1984) *The Square Book* (London: Wiley Academy), 2003 edition, pp. 82–83; www.cca.qc.ca/en/search/details/collection/object/407028 [Accessed 2 August 2017].

53   Cabinet papers. National Archives (hereafter NA): CAB 24-/55/82.

peace-time production of arms, including the nuclear programme.[54] For atomic production facilities, 'a certain separation from centres of population had to be balanced against the accessibility of local labour. Within these constraints it was the proximity of industrial and academic organisations ... that led to the selection of North West England as the key location.'[55]

As well as the development of the computer, pioneering nuclear research was undertaken by the UKAEA at Risley near Warrington and an array of defence contracts were awarded to companies in the north-west, most notably sites at Warton and Samlesbury near Preston operated by English Electric (later British Aerospace).[56] At Wythenshawe, Ferranti, in partnership with the Bristol Aeroplane Company, developed the most successful guided weapon project of the period, Bloodhound, though the factory and laboratories were originally designed for the manufacture of gyroscopes for the control of missiles.[57] The choice to develop a computer that could make calculations for missiles with the same industry partner and in the same city as the missile guidance system was not an accident.

Wythenshawe is a suburb to the south of Manchester, on the edge of Cheshire and has had several distinct periods of development. It was originally conceived as a Garden Suburb and planned by Barry Parker, who also planned the first Garden City at Letchworth. It was built after 1927 on land that the Corporation purchased from the Tatton Estate.[58] Its primary political sponsor, Ernest Simon, lauded the first wave of new homes and amenities as a success, but complete development was halted by the outbreak of the Second World War.[59] During the war parts of the undeveloped suburb were used as airfields, adopting the recently completed airport at Ringway (1938). Following the cessation of hostilities there was a desperate shortage of housing in the city and

---

54 Gary Willis, *Fields into Factories: The Impact on the Post-war Rural Landscape of Britain's Second World War, 1936–1946*. Paper presented at *Rural Modernism* conference, Northumbria University, 1–2 August 2019.
55 Julian Garratt, 'Atomic Spaces North West England 1945 to 1957' (MSc diss., University of Manchester, 2016).
56 English Electric first moved to the site at Warton in 1948. Keil, C.G. (1960) 'Supersonic Wind Tunnels: Details of the Two New High-Speed Tunnels Operated by English Electric Aviation Ltd. at Wharton', *Aircraft Engineering and Aerospace Technology*, Vol. 32, No. 11, p. 338.
57 Letter from Dr N. Searby, Chief Engineer, Ferranti to W.W. Abson of the Ministry of Supply, 24 August 1951. NA: AVIA 54/1274. For the story of automated control see Aylen, J. (2012) 'Bloodhound on my Trail: Building the Ferranti Argus Process Control Computer', *International Journal for the History of Engineering & Technology*, Vol. 82, No. 1, January, pp. 1–36.
58 Deakin, D. (1989) *Wythenshawe; The Story of a Garden City* (Chichester: Phillimore & Co.), pp. 33–35.
59 Simon and Inman, *The Rebuilding of Manchester*, p. 165.

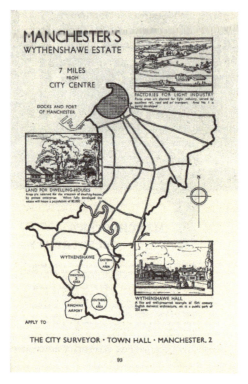

Figure 2.04 Municipal advert to encourage businesses to relocate to the growing Wythenshawe area, 1947.

Wythenshawe was a prime location for the creation of an overspill estate. The Corporation was not sufficiently solvent to build new houses until the 1950s, but they were able to provide incentives for new industries to locate themselves on greenfield sites with good road links and access to both blue- and white-collar workforces [Figure 2.04]. Among the first of the new buildings in the early 1950s was Ferranti's R&D and production facility for guided weapons research and manufacture, designed by C&S.

C&S worked for Ferranti prior to the Wythenshawe commission. They designed the extension to the factory at the Hollinwood site in Oldham, opened in 1950.[60] Hollinwood was acquired by Ferranti in 1895 and was a former ironworks, not necessarily the obvious choice for the electrical industry that

---

60 *Oldham Evening Chronicle*, 31 May 1950. File of general arrangement building and floor-plans, and architect sketches of the proposed interior scheme of the Company Archives at the new computer building, Hollinwood. MSIM: [no title] 1996.10/2/4/1243.

might be considered as a cleaner manufacturing process.[61] This adaption and appropriation of existing premises for new technological purposes is typical of how industrial technologies evolved in Britain. Sites were often palimpsests, each layer added only when necessity dictated and new technologies were conceived and built in old premises – a situation repeated when Ferranti computing bought a former foundry in West Gorton for the production of their Argus Computer.[62] This was not the case at Wythenshawe though. The design and construction of this site, vital to the defence industry and rearmament programme, was bespoke and brand new.

New development at Wythenshawe offered new opportunities for Ferranti. The site, the roads, the industries and the houses of this second wave of development were all new. Whilst the prospect of available labour was touted as a good reason to locate business in Wythenshawe, Ferranti were keen to ensure that appropriate housing stock was provided.[63] The company contemplated creating their own housing association under the provisions of the Housing Act (1936) that allowed industrial firms to do so.[64] The Corporation Finance Committee rejected Ferranti's request for assistance towards the construction of fifty houses in view of the firm's financial standing. It was a bold demand on the part of Ferranti who had the buildings, all of their contents and its future phases fully funded by the MoS.[65] Nor did they pay for the site – it was the MoS who took the lease on that too![66] Sir Vincent Ferranti was known to insist that 'the state should provide most of the funds for developing and making the products it required'.[67] Such an attitude had proven results as, 'by 1952 [Ferranti] had reached the stage of being Britain's only commercial computer manufacturer, with six firm orders, without having taken any risks and without having invested any significant resources of its own in the venture'.[68] The financing opportunities from local and national state sources were fully exploited at Wythenshawe.

As a ministry-sponsored project, the scheme was not subject to usual planning processes and no record of an application exists among the minutes of the

---

61 Wilson, J.F. (1999) *Ferranti: A History. Building a Family Business, 1882–1975* (Lancaster: Carnegie Publishing), p. 115.
62 The West Gorton site and its history is explored in detail later in this chapter.
63 Harper, C. (1947) *Manchester – City of Achievement* (London: Thomas Skinner).
64 'Houses for Workers at New Factory. No Corporation Loan', *The Manchester Guardian*, 4 November 1952, p. 9.
65 Estimate for the Erection and Completion of the Proposed New Buildings at Wythenshawe, Manchester for Messrs Ferranti Ltd acting as agents for The Ministry of Supply under 6/Agreements/854 (C.F.14A). 1951. MSIM: YA1996.10/6/14/2.
66 Draft of letter from Major Abate, MoS, to Mr Shaw, Treasury, 13 February 1952. NA: AVIA 54/1284.
67 Wilson, *Ferranti: A History*, p. 400.
68 Hendry (1990), p. 91.

Town Planning Committee.[69] The buildings were ostensibly without context, on a level greenfield site at the edge of the city. The only definitive marks on the verdant surface were those of the new roads and existing runways of RAF Ringway. Planning for the organisation of the buildings on site began in 1947.[70] The proximity of the airport limited the height of the development and its anticipated mass was approved under the Ministry of Civil Aviation Airport Safeguarding Direction, 1949.[71] Four options were prepared, none of which were much more than proximity diagrams, shown with scale and orientation, to assess the feasibility of the site and define the required floor area. Each was drawn in a simple orthogonal arrangement and with few formal constraints.[72] Instead of responding to context, the arrangement of the buildings on site was dependent upon operational demands.

Of the feasibility studies, 'Scheme B' was the most resolved and reflected the need to exercise secure control over space and personnel by presenting a series of discrete buildings arranged along a connecting corridor [Figure 2.05]. It was not always essential that groups of engineers knew what others were up to and sometimes it was in the national security interest that they didn't. Access and egress was important, as was the capacity to engineer building services as required by the internal function of each block. The design team had to respond to the programmatic demands of research groupings and the production and handling of missiles. The architects were instructed that 'complete functional efficiency in the laboratories should be their first priority'.[73] Despite the overtly functional nature of the brief and a site, apparently without context, there was one short reference to style amidst the largely quantitative feasibility studies: the arrangement of option B was described, in positive terms, as 'more modern'.[74] The buildings had to be flexible, 'owing to the rapidly developing research programme' and designed to be extended from the earliest briefs.[75] A framed

---

69 A full search of the Minutes of the Town Planning & Buildings Committee between 1945 and 1954 yielded no evidence to suggest that the development was ever presented to the Committee. Archives+: GB127.Council Minutes/Town Planning and Buildings Committee/2/23–43.

70 'Proposed Development at Wythenshawe Southern Industrial Estate', Confidential memo, 1 December 1947. A1-sized folded paper among 'Cost Estimate Reports (Wythenshawe Project)', MSIM: YA1996 10/2/4/903.

71 City Surveyor with reference to later addition. Drawing among plan nos 38195. Orange card folder. Archives+.

72 Ibid.

73 Wilson, *Ferranti: A History*, p. 410.

74 Estimate for the Erection and Completion of the Proposed New Buildings at Wythenshawe, Manchester for Messrs.Ferranti Ltd acting as agents for The Ministry of Supply under 6/Agreements/854 (C.F.14A). 1951. MSIM: YA1996.10/6/14/2.

75 'Research laboratories & workshops for Ferranti Ltd at Wythenshawe, Manchester; Architects: Cruickshank & Seward', *Architect & Building News*, 10 March 1955, pp. 293–297.

COMPUTING AND THE COLD WAR

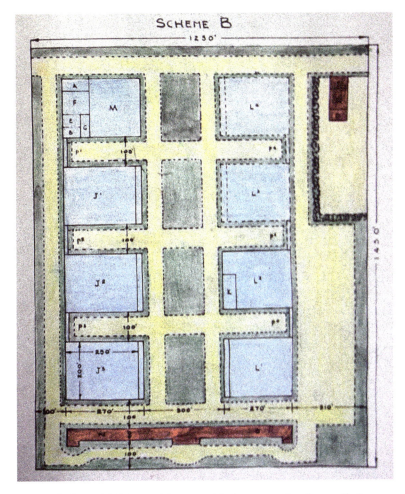

Figure 2.05 'Scheme B'. Discrete laboratory blocks arranged orthogonally in groups of four with connecting corridors to the outside edges. These drawings are without context, but it is assumed that the bottom of the image would have run parallel to Simonsway. The author of this drawing is unknown.

structural solution permitted both internal flexibility and the potential to add bays in the future. In this case, the frame was steel; the external columns were clad in concrete. Steel was not readily available in the immediate post-war years but ministerial support, backed by huge defence expenditure, meant that issues such as the supply of materials rarely featured in project records.[76]

---

76 Loose bundle of cost estimate reports, and correspondence re together with general arrangement building and floor plans re the Wythenshawe development of a laboratory and factory site for the manufacture of Guided Weapons 1947–1953. MSIM: 1996.10/2/4/903.

As a part of the post-war rearmament strategy the development of a guided missile system was of some urgency. This was reflected in correspondence between Dr N. Searby, Chief Engineer, Ferranti and the MoS, where the exact specification for the buildings changed as construction was under way. The design testing of the gyroscopes began at Ferranti's works in Moston, but soon outgrew its home and was housed in temporary quarters on site at Wythenshawe until the laboratories proper were established. Research trips by Ferranti also influenced the demand for space, particularly for the testing of missiles; the practice and methods for this were informed by a visit to the United States.[77] Ferranti were also keen to see other sub-contracts for missile components developed at Wythenshawe. Here, state technopolitics met with the regional convergence of knowledge, expertise and policy. The state enabled the use of the site – owned by Manchester City Council and leased by the MoS on behalf of Ferranti. The national security situation influenced the buildings' organisation and ensured the supply of steel that was difficult to obtain for ordinary construction purposes. Work began on detailed design in October 1950 and construction in 1951.[78]

Ferranti Wythenshawe was the second explicitly modern building designed by Arthur Gibbon and his team at C&S; the first was a new company headquarters for Renold Chains at a nearby site that won an award from the RIBA in 1954 [Figure 2.06].[79] Several of the details were adopted from the earlier scheme and the modern language of C&S evolved through such adaptations. One of these was the articulated concrete frame with flush jointed brick spandrel panel infill, another, the use of structural concrete to achieve cantilevers.[80] The buildings were relatively simple, but Gibbon knew how to deploy resources to maximum effect. The volume that formed the main entrance to the facility was a little taller than the rest and supported a curtain wall extending over the full two-storey height. A slender, sculpted concrete canopy neatly hid the rainwater pipe

---

[77] 'Until our US, tour in April 1951 we had not fully appreciated the large amount of space required for various types of pre-flight testing of full-sized missiles' Item 1.5, 'Extension of Wythenshawe Workshops', Secret report attached to letter from Dr N. Searby, Chief Engineer, Ferranti to Major A.T. Abate of the Ministry of Supply, 11 February 1952. NA: AVIA 54/1284.

[78] Wilson, *Ferranti: A History*, p. 410; 'Electronic Research', *The Manchester Guardian*, 3 July 1951, p. 10.

[79] 'Administrative Office Building for the Renold and Coventry Chain Co. Ltd. at Wythenshawe, Manchester; Architects: Cruickshank & Seward', *The Builder*, 10 December 1954, pp. 937–941; *Architectural Review*, December 1954, pp. 374–379; *Architects' Journal*, 9 December 1954, pp. 702–705; *Architect & Building News*, 9 December 1954, pp. 715–722.

[80] 'Research Laboratories & Workshops for Ferranti Ltd. at Wythenshawe, Manchester; Architects: Cruickshank & Seward', *Architects' Journal*, 10 March 1955, pp. 330–331.

Figure 2.06   Renold Chain Company headquarters, Renold House, Ringway, Manchester, 1954.

in its cast depth and its soffit formed a continuous surface from outside to inside [Figure 2.07].[81] Within, a robust, but elegant, cantilevered concrete staircase connected the two floors, itself illuminated by the expansive glazing. Many of the details seen in later C&S buildings had their first iterations in this, and the nearby office for Renold Chains, and were drawn by Gordon Hodkinson, Gibbon's assistant for most of his career. Whilst these were not hi-tech they were undoubtedly modern and the beginnings of C&S's post-war revival, which included a rapid increase in workload and a stylistic shift to modern architecture [Figure 2.08].

Architecturally, Gibbon and his team drew on continental and North American influences. Gibbon was known, for example, to ask his assistants to 'add a bit of a Nervi canopy' and other calculated borrowing of elements.[82] He used the widely known titles *Switzerland Builds* and *Sweden Builds* as source

---

81   Ibid.
82   Interview with Gordon Hodkinson. Hale, 1 October 2012.

Figure 2.07   Entrance canopy to the Ferranti facility. The simple concrete frame with brick infill panels was common to several early buildings designed by Arthur Gibbon for Cruickshank & Seward.

material.[83] In the buildings at Wythenshawe for Ferranti the influence of Mies's work at IIT was apparent in the rationally gridded facades and the curtain wall glazing.[84] The scheme was realised in phases; the first, research laboratories and workshops, was opened by Duncan Sandys, Minister of Supply, in June 1954. The buildings were described in the popular press as making 'lavish use of glass'.[85] They were steel framed, with external columns and beams encased in concrete. Infill panels were of a typical northern dark red brick. Most of the adjoining blocks were two-storey although some single-storey elements housed 'special laboratories'. The laboratory buildings themselves were portal framed so that there were no columns internally and the space was easily adaptable as technology and machining advanced. Internal walls were simply formed from a bespoke

---

83   Kidder Smith, G.E. (1950a) *Sweden Builds. Its Modern Architecture and Land Policy Background Development and Contribution* (London: The Architectural Press); Kidder Smith, G.E. (1950b) *Switzerland Builds – Its Native and Modern Architecture* (London: The Architectural Press).
84   'Metals and Minerals Research Building for Illinois Institute of Technology', *Architects' Journal*, 3 January 1946, pp. 7–10.
85   'Mr Sandys Opens Laboratories: Growth of Electronics', *The Guardian*, 26 June 1954, p. 3.

Figure 2.08   The modern architectural language in the Ferranti facility extended to the gatehouse.

sectional timber partitioning in the offices, and steel partitions in workshops and laboratories. Much of the servicing was integrated into the construction of the scheme, either within raised floor voids or within the wall or floor build-up. The site was designed to accommodate future extensions and the internal circulation routes and spaces between the first phases of construction facilitated such.

The earlier notion of discrete blocks arranged along a spine corridor served operational security needs, created good conditions for research and development and allowed for expansion. Each of the six wings of laboratories was organised according to the size of the research teams and sub-divided into a further six sections with space for five engineers. Dedicated lab and office space permitted concentrated research and communal refreshment areas in each wing allowed for the exchange of ideas and the sharing of technical problems. Every wing had a group leader who reported to the chief engineer on a monthly basis. The hierarchical structure of the organisation was reflected in the ordering of space and, according to Ferranti's official history, this arrangement 'proved to be a great success, both in encouraging small group work and effective communication through informal and formal channels'.[86] The canteen for the site was

---

86   Wilson, *Ferranti: A History*, p. 410.

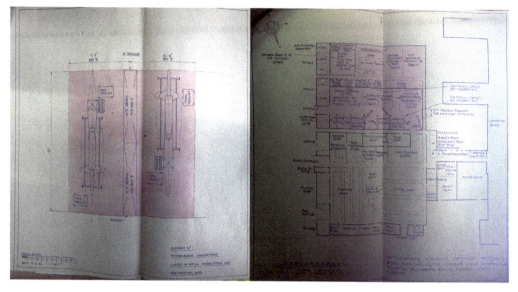

Figure 2.09 Option studies for extension to missile testing facility at Wythenshawe.

a standalone building and its interior furnished in a manner befitting of the atomic age with suspended lamps and stylised graphic prints on the curtains.

Whilst early archival documents and correspondence were labelled 'secret', the activity on site did not remain so, the expansion of the testing facility was publicly reported under the headline 'Two New Bays for Rocket Factory. Guided Missile Research'.[87] Where the laboratory buildings were organised by the structure of the research teams, the factory was designed specifically around the missile testing bays and the production of gyroscopes [Figure 2.09]. In the engineering tradition, specialist components for the guidance systems were designed and engineered on site – US-style subcontracting and outsourcing were seen as cheapening the product. This was true at Wythenshawe and also later at ICL.[88] C&S's services were retained by Ferranti for the extension and for a number of smaller buildings through to the late 1950s – these additions were subject to planning regulations and recorded through building control processes.[89] The client remained as the MoS and, regardless of the information published in the press, the planning applications recorded the 'intended use of the building and each floor' as 'Experimental work. Exact nature of work not disclosed'.[90]

---

87 'Two New Bays for Rocket Factory. Guided Missile Research' *The Guardian*, 3 February 1955, p. 4.
88 Wilson, *Ferranti: A History*, p. 116.
89 Plan nos 38195, 43941, refer to 'experimental building'. Archives+.
90 Plan nos 38195. Orange card folder. Archives+.

Wythenshawe was part of the Corporation's post-war rebuilding plans and, as such, the perceptibly hi-tech and clean manufacturing processes of Ferranti fitted perfectly with the city's ambitions. The government demand for weapons projects dovetailed with the site and skills available. The only formal context for the scale and appearance of the building was the height restriction imposed due to the proximity of the airport. The laboratories and testing facilities were really determined by the functional and operational demands of very specific working practices. In this sense the policy objective of missile production had its impact on form, while the local conditions at Wythenshawe informed the buildings' scale and materiality.

Computers at West Gorton: palimpsest of production

Unlike at Wythenshawe, the site that would eventually accommodate new buildings for International Computers Limited at West Gorton was not greenfield; it was a former iron foundry rooted in the eastern industrial area of Manchester. The history of this site, before its transformation, provides a good lens through which to explore the relationship between new technologies and architecture in post-war Britain. In the following I unfold a sequence of events and constructions that tally directly with post-war 'make-do-and-mend' mentalities and the engineering and manufacturing traditions of the north of England.[91]

Making machines

The early history of attempts to forge a computer industry from the research pioneered in Manchester is peppered with mergers in the race for control of the domestic market and in the face of stiff imports from the United States [Figure 2.10]. In one such coalition English Electric merged with unlikely computer developers J. Lyons & Co., the caterers! Lyons & Co. catering company were able to imagine the commercial applications of the new technology and ordered one of the first business computing machines in the UK. Computer manufacturing at West Gorton began with Ferranti and was consolidated through government-sponsored mergers to form International Computers and Tabulators (ICT) and International Computers Limited (ICL), but ultimately failed to survive against strong US competition.

The route to production for Ferranti was not a straight course from the successful research at the University. Political happenstance and a number of resilient and resourceful individuals all had their impact on the bumpy road to

---

91 *Make Do and Mend* was a pamphlet issued by the British Ministry of Information in the midst of the Second World War. It was intended to provide housewives with useful tips on how to be both frugal and stylish in times of harsh rationing. The slogan became a mantra for all sorts of activities in the period following the cessation of conflict but whilst goods were still rationed.

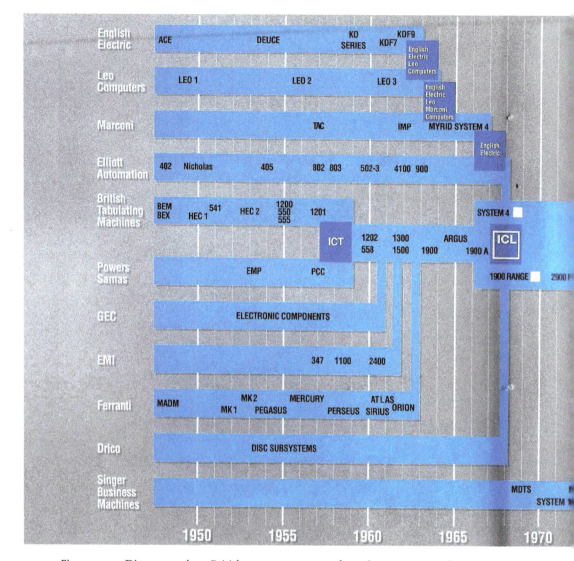

Figure 2.10 Diagram to show British computer mergers from the 1940s onwards in the creation of ICT/ICL.

realisation. Among them was the divisional manager at Moston, Eric Grundy, who, despite managerial direction to the contrary, pursued the development of a computer project. In October 1948 Patrick Blackett arranged for Sir Ben Lockspeiser to observe *Baby* in action at the University.[92] Lockspeiser noted:

---

92 Blackett saw the appraisal groups of the Ministry of Technology as 'analogous to wartime operational research teams'. Edgerton, *Warfare State*, p. 247.

COMPUTING AND THE COLD WAR

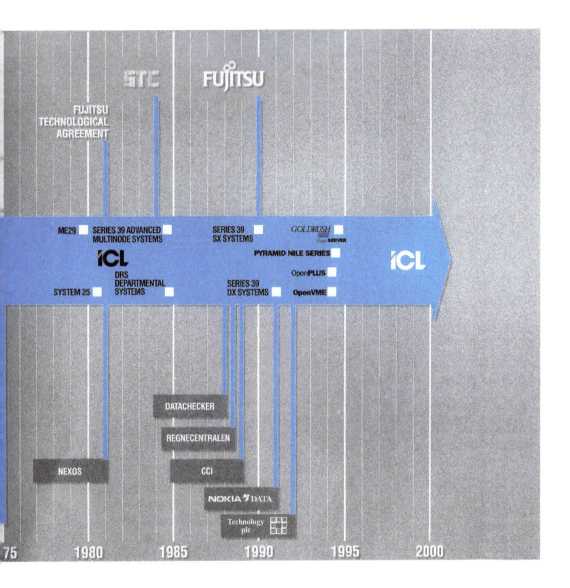

I was alerted by Blackett to Freddie [Williams]'s computer when I was struggling with the problems of control and stability of guided missiles in the early days. We were firing experimental rockets and telemetering the results to the ground, but the processing of the data took so long that I jumped at the chance of drastically shortening the time involved.[93]

---

93 As quoted in Edwards, E.P.J. (1994) 'Ben Lockspeiser. 9 March 1891–18 October 1990', *Biographical Memoirs of the Fellows of the Royal Society*, No. 39 (1 February), pp. 246–261.

Shortly afterwards, Grundy was informally instructed to proceed with the construction of 'an electronic calculating machine to the instructions of Professor F.C. Williams' and appointed Dr Dietrich Prinz to research the viability of the technology.[94]

On return from a US visit, Prinz declared that Williams and Kilburn were 'far ahead of anything the Americans had achieved with stored programme computers'.[95] At this point Lockspeiser made a formal approach to chairman and managing director Sir Vincent de Ferranti about forging a link with the university team, though Ferranti had provided informal support and components for some years prior. Grundy's instrument department was not the natural home for the computer, nor was he the best candidate to collaborate with Williams, but it was the conditions of expertise and capability that drew funding to Manchester.[96] The award of this money by Lockspeiser 'broke many of the rules of government contracting',[97] and Lockspeiser's intervention is one indicator of the difficulty of researching Cold War history. Shrouded in secrecy, his actions may have been cavalier, but could equally have been clandestine – Prime Minister Clement Atlee ploughed ahead in secret with the British rocket programme in January 1947 without seeking parliamentary approval. Some of this activity was eventually disclosed in Parliament in January 1951.[98] Dependent upon the focus of research and development, contracts were awarded by the NRDC and the Department of Scientific and Industrial Research (DSIR) under direction of the MoS. To add further complexity, contracts usually included a commitment from the government to purchase an agreed number of the completed computers!

Within this tale of innovation and ad hoc approvals it is easy to recognise the traits of the 'British Problem' and a sense of defiant modernism in a declinist context.[99] In technopolitical terms the precise aims of the state and its agents

---

94 Lockspeiser's roles are told by Hendry and his motives suggested by Lavington. Hendry, J. (1989) *Innovating for Failure: Government Policy and the Early British Computer Industry* (Cambridge, MA: MIT Press), po. 42, 51, 71, 89; Lavington, *A History of Manchester Computers*; Drath, 'The Relationship between Science and Technology.

95 Swann, B.B. (1974) 'The Ferranti Computer Department' pp. 1–4. As cited by Wilson, *Ferranti: A History*, p. 347.

96 It has been suggested that Williams would have preferred to work with former colleagues from the TRE employed by Ferranti, among them Dr N. Searby, who, as we have seen, was charged with other projects. Wilson, *Ferranti: A History*, p. 347.

97 Hendry, *Innovating for Failure*, p. 89.

98 Stocker, J. (2004) *Britain and Ballistic Missile Defence, 1942–2002* (Abingdon: Psychology Press); Ovendale, R. (1994) *British Defence Policy Since 1945* (Manchester: Manchester University Press).

99 Historians have adopted the British Problem across a range of disciplines. Brian Harrison's examination of post-war Britain provides a number of perspectives from which to consider this particular concept. Harrison, B. (2009) *Seeking a Role: The United Kingdom 1951–1970* (New Oxford History of England) (Oxford: Oxford University Press).

remain unclear – the computer and its attendant military applications were shrouded with cover stories and the realisation of both civil and military applications served the interests of successive post-war governments. The complex organisation, funded and procured by the state, and its regional networks across higher education and industry, impacted on the built environment as existing facilities were adapted and new ones constructed in service of the computing and nuclear cluster.

The development of the Mark I computer was funded by the NRDC and its formal commissioning took place on 9 July 1951. Despite its pioneering status, only seven Mark I machines were made and Williams's team had very little to do with the production; they had moved on to work on Mark II (Meg), which would become the Ferranti Mercury model.[100] The Mark I machines were built at the factory in Moston and at Gem Mill in Chadderton; neither was designed for the manufacture of computers, and the latter was cotton factory until 1937. This typifies the approach to new technologies and particularly civil technological development in Britain – new premises were not built until market viability was established. Sir Vincent's attitude to computing was observed thus: 'if Sir Vincent were looking for a new enterprise to invest Ferranti money in, he would not himself pick computers. He has, however, no objection to a Government agency picking computers for him provided that he is fully compensated for the use of Ferranti facilities.'[101] Bowden, however, was unequivocal in his support for the development of the computer, he wrote: 'I feel ... that Ferranti's stake in this new enterprise is a very large one and that the possibilities are unlimited.'[102] Ferranti struggled to gain funding for the development of the Mark II, but the move of a team of engineers from Elliott Brothers to Ferranti led to the transfer of project funds and the development of their Pegasus computer [Figure 2.11]. It was this development that necessitated the acquisition of premises at West Gorton [Figure 2.12].[103]

Ferranti built computers on the site at West Gorton from the late 1950s onwards. They purchased the former ironworks from Brooks and Doxey in 1956 for £250,000. Brooks and Doxey manufactured textile machinery on the 11.5 acre site from the 1850s, latterly in buildings constructed between 1939 and 1945. The site allowed for rapid occupation and expansion and Ferranti were reported in March 1956 as 'likely to begin [production] in about a month or six

---

100 Ferranti also built the MUSE and ATLAS machines in collaboration with the university.
101 Notes made by Lord Halsbury, NRDC. As quoted by Tweedale, G. (1992) 'Marketing in the Second Industrial Revolution: A Case Study of the Ferranti Computer Group, 1949–63', *Business History*, Vol. 34, No. 1, pp. 96–127.
102 Letter from B.V. Bowden to V. de Ferranti, 15 July 1953. Wilson, *Ferranti: A History*, p. 353.
103 This paragraph is an extremely compressed account of the beginnings of computer production by Ferranti. For a detailed history see Wilson, *Ferranti: A History*, pp. 341–398.

Figure 2.11　Production of the Pegasus computer inside a former ironworks and textile factory in east Manchester c.1957. More of a workshop than a cleanroom.

weeks'.[104] By October the facility had been operational for four months and was already Europe's largest computer manufacturer. They had built five machines in four months and had orders for thirty-four more, valued at £2m.[105] Despite being heavily insulated against losses by virtue of their government funding, Ferranti invested very little on physical alterations to the ironworks site. From a marketing perspective it seems peculiar that a company at the vanguard of a technology that would change the world had no built manifestation of this, a new headquarters or factory, like their US competitors. Regardless of American

---

104　'Ferranti Expansion. Purchase of Manchester Ironworks', *The Times*, 20 March 1956.
105　'Europe's Largest Computer Factory: Ferranti Development', *The Manchester Guardian*, 2 October 1956, p. 16.

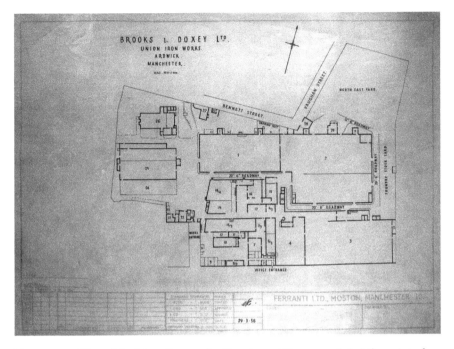

Figure 2.12 Plan of the West Gorton site (Brooks and Doxey works) at the point of acquisition by Ferranti in 1956.

attitudes, in West Gorton in 1956, the machines were new and the buildings were simply adapted for re-use.

Adaptation to the existing buildings at West Gorton was minimal. When considered in light of Sir Vincent's view on the compensatory nature of government research funding, the lack of investment in new buildings makes more sense. A lack of commercial interest and failure to grasp the potential of the computer within political sectors meant that there was no drive for new buildings to act as marketing tools. Archive images of West Gorton from the 1960s show ICT logos mounted upon two of the remodelled site entrances [Figures 2.13 and 2.14]. It is unclear whether this remodelling was commissioned by Ferranti or by ICT. The styling of the entrance from Thomas Street appears to be from the 1950s – one might assume Ferranti made it after 1956. In any event, neither recorded intervention speaks of high technology. The site itself can be viewed as a palimpsest of production – from its earliest day as an ironworks to the manufacture of textile machinery and then computers, new layers of built fabric were not constructed until new processes were commercially established. New building for the research and manufacture of computers did not arrive on site until 1967, eleven years after computing machine manufacturing had commenced.

Figure 2.13 Gorton, ICT offices, Thomas Street, from Hoyland Street, facing south, 1964. Minimal intervention on the part of ICT to alter the fabric of the existing site.

Acquisition, mergers and reorganisation

From the mid-1950s Ferranti had serious discussions with ICT about the merging of their computer interests. It was not until September 1963 that the two companies came together.[106] ICT was originally formed from the merging of British Tabulating Machine Company and Vickers.[107] According to historian Martin Campbell-Kelly it was the R&D and manufacturing capacity of Ferranti's operation that was attractive to ICT; as well as being the largest in Europe, the R&D division was known for its innovation in software programming.[108] ICT acquired all of Ferranti's mainframe computers and the manufacturing plant at West Gorton.[109] Several Ferranti personnel were given senior positions in ICT,

---

106 Campbell-Kelly, M. (1989) *ICL. A Business and Technical History* (Oxford University Press: Oxford), p. 221.
107 Ibid., pp. 171–190.
108 Ibid., pp. 219–220.
109 'ICT Moves to Meet Stronger Competition', *The Guardian*, 8 August 1963, p. 21; Campbell-Kelly, *ICL. A Business and Technical History*, p. 223.

Figure 2.14 Rebranded 'factory gate' to the ICT site. 'Gorton, Kelsall Street from Thomas Street, facing South', 1964.

most notably Basil de Ferranti, who soon became managing director, but also Peter Hall – manager of the Ferranti computer department – who became a deputy director.[110]

ICT's chairman, Sir Cecil Weir was not in business for 'fun' (as Sir Vincent de Ferranti was accused). His vision was for the firm to become the 'dominant British supplier of data-processing equipment, and eventually the leading European company'.[111] As such, their public profile in the industry was much higher than that of Ferranti. Their logo was produced in a clean sans-serif font, with the kerning compressed, implying a tight efficiency. One of their adverts won the first prize in the Premio Europeo Rizzoli competition in Milan.[112] Their desired dominance would require 'one of the largest computer rooms in Europe' as well as new offices, a cinema and presentation suite.[113] Prospects were promising as the company was reported as receiving £100m investment, under

---

110 Ibid., p. 221.
111 Campbell-Kelly, *ICL. A Business and Technical History*, p. 195.
112 Ibid. Caption to illustration in second glossy insert between pp. 276–277.
113 'ICT Expansion in Manchester', *The Guardian*, 17 January 1967, p. 9.

'arrangements made with the help of Morgan Grenfell and the Ministry of Technology'.[114] The commercial business of computers in Britain faced serious competition from US rivals. Labour Prime Minister Harold Wilson knew this; on his first day in office he formed the Ministry of Technology and told Frank Cousins, the (first) Minister of Technology, that he had 'a month to save the British computer industry'.[115] The Flowers Report, *Computers for Research*, was commissioned to determine (and create a case for) the number of machines required by higher education and research councils.[116] The conclusions of the report highlighted the strengths and weaknesses of the domestic industry and pointed to a particular gap in the provision of large-scale computers.

The creation of the Ministry of Technology had vastly expanded the scale of the NRDC and one of Cousins's first actions was to award ICT £5m for their 1900 series computers in May 1965.[117] An energised company with grand ambitions required new facilities to realise their potential and it was ICT who commissioned Cruickshank & Seward to develop the West Gorton site in 1966 – Peter Hall was a friend of John Seward.[118] In Peter Sainsbury's perspective painting of the tower and adjacent two-storey block designed in 1966 [Figure 2.15], the buildings' profiles sharply cut the Mancunian skies. The sky was rendered to a vanishing point, giving the impression that the bright-white buildings were moving forwards. Following Wilson's re-election in March 1966, the Ministry of Technology and the newly formed IRC were the two main instruments for continued attempts to revitalise British industry.[119] The electrical and electronics industries were the IRC's first focus. Among its early directives was the merger of English Electric and Elliott-Automation; this would ultimately lead to the creation of ICL and, in turn, promised a more secure outlook.[120]

The secure outlook provided by ICL was, like Ferranti before it, topped and tailed by government support. ICL was formed in March 1968 by the

---

114 'City Providing £50m to Support ICT Leasings', *The Guardian*, 26 September 1967, p. 10.
115 Wilson, H. (1971) *The Labour Government 1964–1979* (London: Weidenfeld & Nicolson and Michael Joseph), p. 8.
116 The committee was chaired by Prof. Brian Flowers, Chair of Physics at Manchester University and had significant input from Bowden in his role as Minister of State for Education and Science. Agar, J. (1996) 'The Provision of Digital Computers to British Universities up to the Flowers Report (1966)', *The Computer Journal*, Vol. 39, No. 7, pp. 630–642.
117 Campbell-Kelly, *ICL. A Business and Technical History*, p. 247.
118 In conversation with Peter Crummett, architect with C&S. Manchester School of Art, 20 August 2014; In conversation with Gordon Hodkinson. Hale, 21 August 2014.
119 So virulent were the activities of the short lived IRC, it was reported that '[a]nyone who charted the monthly value of assets absorbed during this period (1967–68) and plotted the curve into the next decade would find that the final merger takes place in November 1978 ... There would ... be only one company left in the United Kingdom.' *The Times*, 27 April 1972, p. 23.
120 'IRC Intervention could Lead to £100m Contracts', *The Guardian*, 23 May 1968, p. 11.

Figure 2.15 Watercolour perspective by Peter Sainsbury of the proposed tower for ICT at West Gorton. The old Victorian buildings are shown as swept away and the existing brick buildings to be retained on site are deliberately hidden by soft landscaping.

merging of the computer interests of ICT and Plessey English Electric.[121] It was reported as an initiative to create a British commercial competitor for the US computer giants IBM and Honeywell.[122] The Ministry of Technology provided funding of £13.5m and took up 10.5 per cent of the equity. Its equity share was the first use of the Industrial Expansion Act (1968).[123] In central government in the late 1960s the procurement policy for 'large computers' favoured ICL in an almost exclusive contract. Other British machines were said to have a '25% preference'.[124] However, in many respects, the impetus and perhaps the advantage had already been lost to the United States. In 1968 Professor Stanley Gill was ready to resign his role as advisor to the Ministry on the basis that they were not moving fast enough to protect the interests of the British

---

121 The merger had been discussed as early as 1960, but it was reportedly an invitation from the Ministry of Technology, in October 1967, that convened a group of 'technical experts' in 'close secret' from each of the three companies in The Cavendish Hotel, Pall Mall, London; 'IRC Intervention could Lead to £100m contracts'.
122 Lee, J.M., 'Britain to Finance Computer Merger', New York Times, 12 June 1968, p. 61.
123 The Act received Royal Assent in mid-June and ICL was vested in early July 1968.
124 Letter from C.R. Walker, Private Secretary for the attention of the PM, 2 July 1970. NA: PREM 15/412.

Figure 2.16   The research building with tower behind.

computer industry.[125] The consensus between government advisors was that IBM had stolen the march and was developing fast machines – in sleek new buildings.

Construction caught up

Almost the entire site at West Gorton was eventually reconfigured in phases to replace the repurposed buildings with bespoke construction, directed by John Seward of C&S. The first part of the site to be developed was outside of the curtilage of that owned by Ferranti and was leased from the Corporation. Phase I of the construction programme was the Research Department Building, a two-storey slab at the foot of the Phase II tower – they were conceived together [Figure 2.16]. C&S's original commission, by ICT, was approved by Corporation planners in October 1966 but, presumably due to the mergers and creation of ICL, construction did not commence until June 1969.[126] Following

---

125 Correspondence between S. Gill and Tony Benn (Minister of Technology), 20 May 1968, 19 June 1968. NA: FV 49/2.

126 Planning approval date from *Report on the proposed research and development building at International Computer and tabulators Ltd., Thomas Street, West Gorton, Manchester 12.* Cruickshank & Seward archive (uncatalogued), Manchester Metropolitan University Special Collections. Building Control Plans were deposited 6 December 1966 and

Figure 2.17 Internal screening within the research building, for security and overlook.

the typological standard set by Noyes, the computer hall in the Phase I building was surrounded on all sides by other rooms and had no windows to the outside. For security purposes there was a direct visual link from the ground floor offices across the computer hall and into the tape rooms – the three spaces were separated by glazed screens [Figure 2.17]. A lecture hall was designed to share new knowledge in the field or to introduce prospective clients to the new machines. Product promotion was still important, even in an established market.

The offices on the first floor were sited above the computer hall and had external courts that allowed light into the deeper areas of the plan. The interiors of office and administration areas had a partition system on a grid that could be moved and adapted according to need; the ceiling lighting plan permitted the same. Each space had very specific humidity and temperature requirements and the building was serviced by four different plant rooms, for the hall, tape rooms, offices and lecture hall respectively. As such, the building had its own substation. This heavy mechanical engineering demand had its impact on the appearance of the building, with long lines of louvres provided for the venting of the various served spaces. Externally, these banks of louvres were complemented by concrete cladding panels, faced in a light-grey mosaic tile,

---

approval granted 10 January 1967. Construction commenced 23 June 1969. Engineer was Ove Arup & Partners. Contractor was Laing; Plan nos 67077. Orange card folder, Archives+.

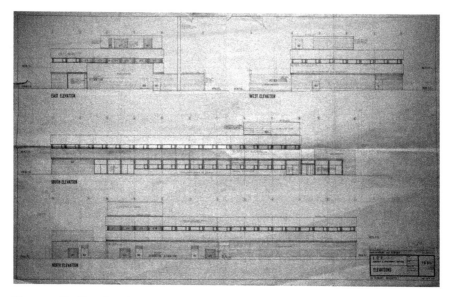

Figure 2.18 Drawing showing the elevations of the research building. A strong horizontal emphasis is accentuated by the brick ground floor and cladding panels with ribbon windows above.

and contrasted against Blockley's black facing brick with black mortar.[127] The robust and secure masonry at ground floor level gave way to the punctuated lightwells and ventilated plant rooms of the upper floor and provided an architectural language for the rest of the site – a securitised, serviced and sleek aesthetic [Figure 2.18].

The eleven-storey tower was the most prominent building on site and the second to be constructed. The material palette was the same as the research block and used the contrasting tones of dark brick and light mosaic panel to good effect in the articulation of function. The dark brick was used to face the vertical circulation core and the light-grey tiles deployed on the outside of each office floor. The ribbon window, as opposed to floor to ceiling curtain walling (by this time a sign of commercial office space), mimicked the fenestration of the lower block, but had residual benefits. Writing about the tower, Peter Hall recalled, 'glass walls are fine if the occupants keep things tidy inside. Development people never do. Hence the Tower Block has what I regard as rather sensible windows.'[128]

---

127 Architectural specification notes from drawings found on site, 3 July 2012 and 17 August 2014.
128 *Another ICL Anthology* www.bitsandbytes.shedlandz.co.uk/anotherICL_anthology.pdf [Accessed 8 August 2014].

Figure 2.19 Gorton, Wenlock Way off Clover Street, ICL in view, flats. The brave new world of late 1960s Manchester and the reinvestment in east Manchester is evident in this composition that appears to deliberately situate new housing and industry side by side – the new terrace. The low block to the left of the image housed the research department.

The development of the site by ICL was in line with the Corporation's objectives for the area. West Gorton was a former industrial zone characterised by heavy industry. Like the ironworks and nearby locomotive works, much of the workforce had been housed in back-to-back terraced housing. The demolition of the terraces as part of the post-war clearance made way for new social housing in cul-de-sac estates and tower blocks [Figure 2.19]. The arrival of a new and cleaner industry with the prospect of employment and residual benefits to a reconfigured community in east Manchester was very welcome, but not officially a component of a master plan or Corporation initiative. The ICL tower sat as a counterpoint to the adjacent blocks designed by the local authority and was a sentinel to change in society at large:

> We moved into the Tower Block in the first week of February 1971. The vending machines were for decimal currency only as it was not thought worthwhile

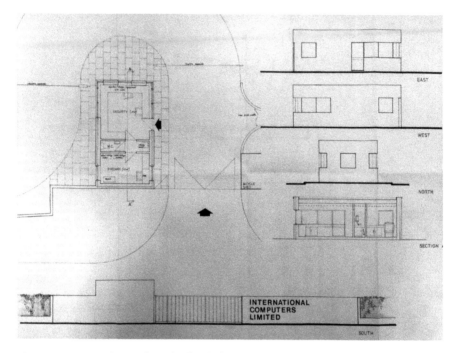

Figure 2.20 Drawing to show the familial nature of the satellite buildings on the growing campus. The small gatehouse adopted the architectural language of the earlier major phases.

buying dual-currency machines for a week. The vending machine man had some decimal currency, but it was embargoed until 15th February 1971. We had a week with the machines filled with an odd assortment of food such that each slot had two or three items adding up to one shilling.[129]

ICT was buoyant before ICL was created and continued success led to on site expansion in the 1970s. The next major building was a second computer hall, an expanded and value engineered version of the original research building. A PVC-coated, steel cladding panel, still in light grey, replaced the mosaic tile. The dark brick was again deployed at ground floor and the ribbon windows were now a feature of the growing family of objects. As the main computer hall was designed, so were a series of peripheral buildings, to serve and support the plant. A restaurant, telephone exchange and security booth, all single storey, adopted the simple black brick and black mortar scheme in a group of small buildings that were like components to the whole [Figure 2.20]; only the restaurant was constructed. The master plan for the full scheme shows the suite of buildings connected by a narrow circulatory band, an external covered

---

129 Per. comms with Brian M. Russell, ICL, 9 August 2014.

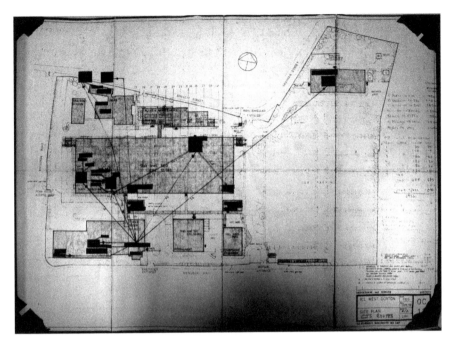

Figure 2.21 ICL West Gorton. Proposed site plan October 1979. The buildings are 'plugged' together by connecting covered walkways and tie neatly into the gridded 'motherboard' of the master plan. The buildings to the north of the main site were built during 1939–45 and never demolished. The remote Sun Microsystems building (top right) also configured to the same orthogonal projection.

walkway [Figure 2.21]. The site can be read as a motherboard, a rational gridded landscape into which buildings were inserted as demanded and connected to the rest of the machine. The final addition was a small building on an adjoining site for SUN Microsystems, a US manufacturer, to develop computer-aided engineering solutions.[130]

A deal with an American firm was contradictory to the aims of the Ministry of Technology in first sponsoring ICL, but emblematic of the change in market conditions and government. The Common Market of the European Economic Community was well established and international trade had grown significantly, Margaret Thatcher was Prime Minister and Conservative economic policy opened the British industrial sector to foreign competition and investment. In the preceding decades the support, predominantly financial, of central government had ultimately fostered (some have said 'saved') the British computer

---

130   Reeves, E.A. (ed.) (1992) *Newnes Electrical Pocket Book* (Oxford: Butterworth-Heinemann), p. 116.

industry. Like the case of Ferranti at Wythenshawe, for ICL the central state provided the funds for construction and contracts. Furthermore, the Ministry of Technology and the IRC had actually formed the company and taken an equity share! Up to May 1970 ICL had £13.5m of government grants to establish the manufacturing and R&D at West Gorton and other sites. In the same period it received over £8m of orders from central government departments.[131]

This history of the site at West Gorton illustrates how investment in new technologies was directed by the whims and will of high-ranking civil servants and ministers. The fluctuating conviction of various administrations, from the earliest days of the Mark I machine, was reflected in the way the site evolved according to the grants and loans from the various government departments that sponsored such activity – mirrored in the piecemeal additions to the existing buildings and the slow transformation of the site. Ferranti manipulated the advantages gained in their sponsorship of early computation at the university. Much like the factory at Wythenshawe, the interests of the local authority did not play a significant part in the development of the site, other than a broad alignment with renewal objectives. The pace and form of architectural production was a signifier of the levels of state investment – ICL's state sponsorship was manifest in the quick construction of the most significant building on the site, whereas Ferranti's earlier minor adaptations testified to the uncertainty around the future of computing. In the case of the computer as machine, central government administrations were generally in favour of policy that developed research and manufacturing in the interests of the British economy. In the case of computing as an application, there was less clarity or consensus in the realisation of Britain's first National Computing Centre, also founded in Manchester. Its procurement phases ran parallel to the sponsored mergers that created ICL and reinforced Manchester's position as the home of computing in the UK. It was also a story of political urgency and boosterism that lasted for almost a decade.

The National Computing Centre

Frank Cousins publicly announced the creation of the NCC in Parliament in March 1965.[132] Its functions were described as to 'set up a national library of computer programmes and to carry out research on the development of new programmes'.[133] Manchester was announced as the preferred location in December 1965, though the exact details of the site were not revealed until

---

131 Select Committee on Science and Technology (Sub-Committee D). Minutes of evidence, 6 May 1970, p. 422, para. 2071. NA: PREM 15/412.
132 HC Deb 01 March 1965 vol 707 cc924-30; D'Agapeyeff, A., 'A Programme for British Computers', *The Guardian*, 16 March 1965, p. 6.
133 'Plans for computer centre', *The Guardian*, 13 November 1965, p. 14.

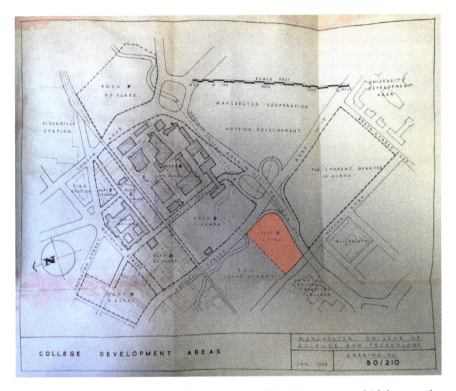

Figure 2.22 Plan showing 'Area G' of the proposed UMIST campus, which became the site for the National Computing Centre.

January 1966.[134] The proximity to existing centres of expertise at the University and UMIST was one reason for its selection – situated next the new urban motorway, Link Road 17/7 (Mancunian Way), and the site for the British Broadcasting Corporation's new northern headquarters on Oxford Road. Its physical position was sandwiched between machines of communication and mobility, which, like the computing centre, epitomised post-war modernity.

In the Corporation's Approved Development Plan the 2.6-acre site was originally intended to form part of the Higher Education Precinct and provisionally reserved in 1964 for development by the Institute of Science and Technology [Figure 2.22].[135] Following a direct request from Ministry of Technology, the

---

134 HC Deb 07 December 1965 vol 722 cc245–51.
135 Millar, J. 'Proposed erection of the Second Phase of the National Computing Centre, Oxford Road and Mancunian Way', Appendix 7 to *Town Planning and Building Committee Minutes*, 29 May 1969. Minute book no. 71, pp. 940–941. Archives+: GB127.Council Minutes/Town Planning and Buildings Committee/2/71.

City and the Institute agreed that the location was 'ideally situated for this important national project'.[136] The Ministry did not purchase the site; instead, as with Ferranti at Wythenshawe, it was leased from the Corporation by central government.[137] Again, the mechanisms of government created their own specific contractual circumstances in service of modernisation, be it for civil or military aims. Similarly, the procurement and delivery of the first phase of NCC construction was forged from a set of existing relationships, in personnel and in geography, which also emerged from state structures.

Professor Gordon Black was appointed as the first director of the NCC.[138] At the time of his selection he held two posts, one as professor of automatic data at UMIST, and another as technical manager (computing) at the UKAEA site at Risley near to Warrington. At Risley, in collaboration with the university, Britain's first fully transistorised nuclear reactor was commissioned in July 1964.[139] The governing council of the NCC was convened in May 1966.[140] It comprised representatives from government and industry. Among those chosen were Peter Hall (colleague of Bowden, Williams and Turing at the TRE and a director at ICT, later ICL), Andrew St Johnston (joint managing director of Elliott-Automation), W.E. Scott (managing director of English Electric-Leo-Marconi Computers) and F.J.M. Laver (director of the computer division of the Ministry of Technology).[141] This grouping reflected the public–private enterprise envisaged by Ministry of Technology as one established with central government funding but ultimately intended to attract its own revenue from the services provided. As such, the NCC was founded as a limited company.[142]

Surprisingly, ICT, who had developed their hardware from Ferranti's Pegasus and Atlas machines at works in nearby West Gorton, were not the preferred provider of computers for the NCC. Instead, Professor Black chose to procure an English Electric KDF9. The reasons for this were manifold, not least the difficulties experienced in programming early Ferranti and ICT machines, but also that Ferranti and ICT had effectively enjoyed a commercial monopoly in Manchester and Black was keen to encourage market competition, in line with the objectives of the Ministry of Technology, the NCC's main sponsor.[143]

---

136 Ibid.
137 Whiteley, G., 'Computer Capital of Europe', *The Guardian*, 19 January 1966, p. 1.
138 'A Man of Energy to Put Drive into Computers', *The Times*, 9 December 1965, p. 5.
139 Razey, M. (1964) 'The Universities Research Reactor', *Electronics and Power*, Vol. 10, Issue 10 (October), pp. 372–373.
140 'National Computing Centre Gets Under Way', *The Times*, 26 May 1966, p. 19.
141 Ibid.
142 Hawthorne, G., 'Setting up Company to Run National Computer Centre', *The Guardian*, 24 May 1966, p. 4.
143 Correspondence between J. Cooper, Contracts and Purchasing Section Officer, UKAEA and F.A. Ticehurst, Director of Contracts and Stores, UKAEA. UKAEA green folder marked, *Construction of national Computing Centre (Manchester)*. NA: AB 42/38.

The contractual arrangements for the construction of the first phase were indicative of the urgency to establish the NCC. In January 1966 before the council was convened or the limited company formed, the Ministry of Technology proposed that the UKAEA architects acted as agents on their behalf.[144] The design of the Computer Building, the first component of the centre, was 'virtually a replica of that at Culham' and delivered under the direction of R.S. Brocklesby, ARIBA on behalf of the Ministry of Technology.[145] Brocklesby was also charged with negotiating the position of the Corporation and the University Grants Committee (UGC) over the lease agreements for the site.[146] Architects from UKAEA designed the first phase 'under considerable pressure'. It was such a rapid decision to construct that there was not really a design brief and the interior plan for the main building, proposed as a tower, was said to be 'left until the new board can be consulted'.[147] For its first few months the NCC was actually based at Risley within the UKAEA estate.[148] Quay House on Quay Street in Manchester was the next address and would remain so for years afterwards.[149] The initial urgency for the creation of the Centre was not manifested as a desire to build the entire headquarters.

A computer centre without a computer would have been disastrous, and the first phase emerged rapidly. The building itself was a spartan grey box with minimal amounts of fenestration [Figure 2.23]. It was clad in 'dark grey PVC coated sheeting' onto a precast Bison concrete frame. It was essentially a two-storey building, with offices and plant room on the ground floor and the computer hall, tape rooms and operator rooms on the first floor. A further volume, equivalent to a second floor, or third storey, had large trusses, which afforded space for wide plenum ducts to move big volumes of air. Like its precedents, the computer hall was surrounded by other spaces and had no visual connection to outside. The supervisor's office had windows into the computer hall, much like that at ICL. The value of the computer and computation was such that industrial espionage was a perceived threat and there was a sense of an inverted panopticon in the building type.

---

144 Letter from R.A. Thompson, Ministry of Technology to A.E. Drake, UKAEA, 12 January 1966. UKAEA green folder marked, *Construction of national Computing Centre (Manchester)*. NA: AB 42/38.

145 Culham is a UKAEA site south of Oxford and was the site of a purpose built fusion laboratory established in 1960, www.ccfe.ac.uk/CCFE.aspx [Accessed 8 August 2014]. Building Control plans were deposited on 2 July 1966 and approved on 12 July 1966. Plan nos 65124. Orange card folder, Archives+.

146 Correspondence between J. Cooper, Contracts and Purchasing Section Officer, UKAEA and F.A. Ticehurst, Director of Contracts and Stores, UKAEA. UKAEA green folder marked, *Construction of National Computing Centre (Manchester)*. NA: AB 42/38.

147 Hawthorne, 'Setting up Company to run National Computer Centre'.

148 Information taken from letterhead in UKAEA green folder marked, *Construction of National Computing Centre (Manchester)*. NA: AB 42/38.

149 'Computer Jobs Play Hard to Get', *The Guardian*, 22 September 1968, p. 35.

Figure 2.23   The spartan grey box of the first incarnation of the National Computing Centre, R.S. Brocklesby ARIBA, UKAEA Architects, c.1967.

The site for the NCC was, literally, pivotal in the reconstruction of Manchester in the second half of the twentieth century. It was at the physical junction of two major Corporation planning initiatives, the Education Precinct running north–south and the east–west aerial motorway, Link Road 17/7 (later Mancunian Way). The Education Centre was part of the ambitious *1945 Plan* and recognised the value of the university to the economy of the city. Mancunian Way was a component of post-war highway planning, its purpose being to connect the manufacturing centres of the east of the city with the docks to the west. As television grew as a medium an adjacent site was allocated to the BBC for their new northern headquarters. Additionally, the focus on higher education at UMIST drove the growth of further education at the municipal technical college across Oxford Road and directly opposite the site (Figure 2.24).[150] The prominence of the NCC site in both policy and physical terms situated it firmly in the new Manchester – it was seen to be technological and on the move.

The first scheme conceived by UKAEA was for an administration building that could be extended at a later date.[151] The initial phases of construction (the spartan grey box) were under way as phase two was reported as 'a tower

---

150 In the UK further education typically refers to that undertaken at a college, after high school and before university, normally between the ages of 16 and 18. Higher education refers to degree-level qualification at university.

151 Letter from J. Coper to Mr. F.A. Tatford, UKAEA. (n.d.) Green folder, UKAEA file. NA: AB 42/38.

COMPUTING AND THE COLD WAR

Figure 2.24 Photograph taken from between the National Computing Centre, Cruickshank & Seward, 1967–74 (left) and the BBC North headquarters, R.A. Sparkes, 1971–75 (right), looking across Oxford Road to the recently completed Phase II of the Municipal College of Technology (later Manchester Polytechnic), W.B. Heppell, City Architect, 1974.

building to take offices, computing libraries and conference rooms ... At first it will be five storeys high. Later it will be extended to 20 storeys.' This, as the reporter observed, would 'make it the tallest building in the educational precinct' and it was 'being designed as one of the focal points on Oxford Road next to Mancunian Way'. The facade was to be formed from precast units 'modelled to give the building an interesting facade'.[152] Conversely, the City Planning Officer, John Millar, viewed the outline planning application, submitted by C&S in May 1969, as having 'adopted a deliberately reticent architectural approach to avoid [the] building competing with the BBC Regional Headquarters immediately to the north'.[153] It is similarly difficult to know to which BBC scheme Millar referred. The multidisciplinary practice Building Design Partnership (BDP) were appointed as architects and prepared a design that was included in

---

152 Hawthorne, 'Setting up Company to run National Computer Centre'.
153 It is impossible to ascertain exactly what the visual qualities were of this scheme at this time as no drawings are appended to the minutes. Millar, 'Proposed erection of the Second Phase of the National Computing Centre, Oxford Road and Mancunian Way'.

Figure 2.25 Early drawings by BDP for the BBC North HQ. This scheme was incorporated into Wilson & Womersley's proposals for the Education Precinct.

Wilson & Womersley's Education Precinct master plan (1967) [Figure 2.25].[154] It featured an upper floor that cantilevered over those below to form an exaggerated colonnade to Oxford Road, the underside of which was anticipated as the soffit of a first-floor pedestrian walkway, part of the vertically separated vision of the planners [Figure 2.26]. This building was not constructed and BDP eventually provided only mechanical engineering services to a design prepared by in-house BBC architect, R.A. Sparkes.

The twenty-storey tower [Figure 2.27] proposed by the UKAEA Architects' Department, without a real programme or design brief, can be seen as satisfying the national ambition of Wilson and his pet project, Ministry of Technology, but also responding to the local prestige assigned to the site by the Corporation – the tower would have been the tallest building on Oxford Road, which was undergoing significant change at the time. It would have been a new symbol in a new district of new policy and signified the commitment of the government to new technology as well as the Corporation's support for new industries in the knowledge and service sector, as manufacturing continued to shrink. Ultimately, though, the true forces of capital and the financial control exerted by the Treasury made short work of dismissing the proposals for a

---

154 The 1967 document shows a yellow hatched area across the front of a building whose footprint mimics that of the building shown in this model and accompanying drawings. The yellow is a key to first floor pedestrian walkways. Wilson, H. and Womersley, L. (1967) *Manchester Education Precinct: The Final Report of the Planning Consultants 1967* (Manchester: Corporation of Manchester).

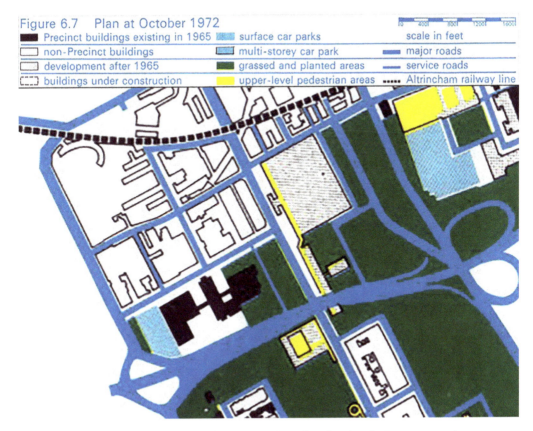

Figure 2.26   Extract from the Education Precinct plan showing the interconnected upper-level pedestrian walkways in yellow.

tower block largely due to the lack of certainty over the operational functions of the NCC.[155] The notion of a more substantial building on site, which would achieve the aims of politicians as well as the needs of the organisation, became drawn out.

Arguments persisted over the scale of the scheme and the accommodation required for the fledgling organisation, which struggled to justify its purpose. The Corporation pressed the NCC for resolution about when the headquarters would be built, but the rate and type of expansion of services and employees was never explicit and became the subject of extended correspondence between

---

155   At one point the prospect of also including the Data Processing Centre of the Office for Scientific and Technical Information (OSTI) within the NCC building was seriously considered. Letter from R.D. Alyward, Ministry of Technology, to H.S. Lee, Treasury, 23 July 1968. NA: T224/1946.

Figure 2.27 Model by BDP that included the UKAEA Architect's proposal for a twenty-storey tower to house the NCC.

the Ministry of Technology and the Treasury.[156] Treasury officials questioned the logic of a building that appeared to be too big for its programme and were of the opinion that Manchester Corporation had put too much focus on 'prestige'.[157] They wrote to the Ministry of Technology to warn them that the project was a 'possible candidate for savings in 1968–69 and 1969–70'.[158] The building eventually delivered by C&S can be read with direct reference to these discussions and the anomalies between the figurative representation and actual programmatic requirements. The building had to be sufficiently substantial in its stature and appearance to fulfil the vision of a national flagship project, yet modest enough to avoid being a white elephant.

Exactly how C&S were appointed to design the NCC is subject to speculation. Harold Wilson visited Manchester in May 1967 to open Phase 1 of the NCC and Mancunian Way on the same day. He made a speech in the Renold Building at UMIST.[159] The Renold Building was the best of Arthur Gibbon's work for C&S, had state of the art acoustics designed by Hope Bagenal and top quality Rank projectors. It was technologically superior to other spaces in Manchester and perfect for a piece of political propaganda about progress. If the directors of the NCC,

---

156 Letter from T.H. Stables, Ministry of Technology, to W.G.E. Morton, Treasury, 1 April 1969. NA: T224/1946.
157 Letter from H.S. Lee, Treasury to F.J.M. Laver, Ministry of Technology, 26 April 1968. NA: T224/1946.
158 Ibid.
159 'Premier to open Mancunian Way', *The Guardian*, 16 March 1967, p. 18.

Figure 2.28 Perspective painting by Peter Sainsbury of the proposed NCC building, March 1967.

including Peter Hall, had been asked for a recommendation for 'an architect who can prepare a dazzling drawing as the backdrop to a speech by the PM', they would most likely have pointed in the direction of C&S – Peter Hall was a friend of John Seward, and Bowden, who held his ministerial post in 1966, was effectively Arthur Gibbon's main patron. C&S were considered a safe pair of hands by Ministry of Technology as they had plenty of public-sector experience in university projects.[160] Like the first building for the NCC, this scheme was also prepared hurriedly overnight by John Seward and Peter Sainsbury, architect and perspective artist. By all accounts the plans were retrospectively composed, by John Seward and Stan Barker, with reference to the watercolour painting [Figure 2.28].[161]

The NCC was never large enough to have filled the twenty-storey tower, but a building with some physical presence as a national centre was necessary. To the Ministry of Technology in 1967 'the NCC [was] an important element in the Government's declared policy of seeking to promote a rapid increase in the use of computers'.[162] In these terms two of the buildings' formal characteristics begin to make sense – the plan and the inverted ziggurat section. In the earliest plans by C&S the cruciform geometry created a lateral extension to the site

---

[160] Letter from R.D. Alyward, Ministry of Technology, to P.L. Dyer, Treasury, 28 February 1968. NA: T224/1946.

[161] An account by John Sheard in conversation, 5 August 2012 and recorded in Parkinson-Bailey, *Manchester: An Architectural History*.

[162] Letter from F.J.M. Laver, Director of Computer Division, Ministry of Technology to 'Leo', 15 June 1967. NA: T224/1418.

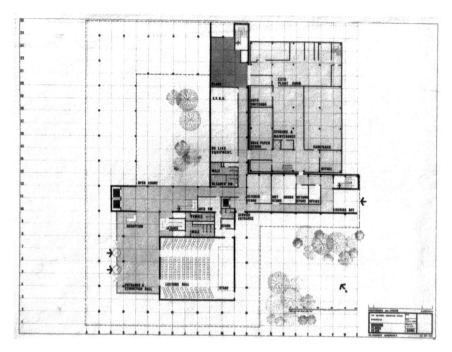

Figure 2.29 Early iteration of the ground-floor plan for the NCC, 1967. Mancunian Way would appear to the right of this sheet if included on the drawing. The discernibly separate section of the plan to the top right is the original UKAEA computer building.

edges without making too much floor space [Figure 2.29]. The new building encompassed the original UKAEA grey box and its exterior was reclad with a dark brick to match the C&S scheme [Figure 2.30]. Most of the new ground floor comprised circulation or service space; the only real piece of programmed space was the lecture theatre. The scheme as built had a further wing to the NW corner which created an internal courtyard with a landscape plan by Derek Lovejoy and Partners [Figure 2.31]. The design of the building in section also helped the mass to overstate its presence. This formal gesture increased the footprint of the upper floors and created an exaggerated colonnade, similar to that proposed by BDP for the BBC next door. The inverted ziggurat form afforded the building an almost overbearing muscular stature that belied its spatial provision.

The adjacent aerial motorway and emerging northern television headquarters meant that the scheme also had to assume a particular height for simple contextual massing – it could not really be any lower than either of these flanking edifices [Figure 2.32]. The cantilevered upper floors were a reaction to the Education Precinct master plan and would allow the insertion of first-floor walkways and connect to the planned wider pedestrian aerial domain. In formal terms the NCC building was a negotiation between central government

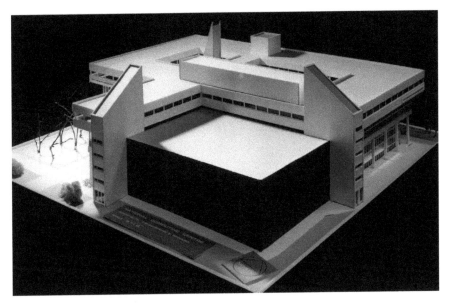

Figure 2.30 Photograph of model with SW aspect. The dark cuboid form is the original NCC building (spartan grey box). Not only is it flanked by the wings of the new scheme, but the stairwells also step out to further camouflage the rudimentary genesis of the institution.

objectives (intangible) and local government projects (tangible). It was also a piece of technopolitics, big enough for the site, big enough for the Corporation and big enough for the Ministry of Technology to appear credible as the building was finally completed in 1975, ten years after the NCC had been set up.

The white tiled façade of the upper sections of the NCC made clear reference to computer-age motifs and futuristic aesthetics.[163] The neutrality of the grid could be seen as a visual tool to carry messages about societal freedoms and controls in other media – though this seems more relevant with historical distance than it probably did to the architects at the time. The grid also implied network and both network and control were in the minds of the Ministry of Technology as they conceived the NCC and sponsored the computer industry. The Ministry understood that one of the 'social consequences' of the computer would be 'the much greater possibilities ... for government surveillance of the individual'.[164] The use of white can be viewed in the context of C&S's works,

---

163 Superstudio's *Continuous Monument* (1969) and Stanley Kubrick's *2001, A Space Odyssey* (1968) both made dramatic use of pristine white gridded landscapes in their visions.
164 Ministry of Technology Computer Policy based on Minister's statement to the House 1 March 1965. NA: FV 49/2.

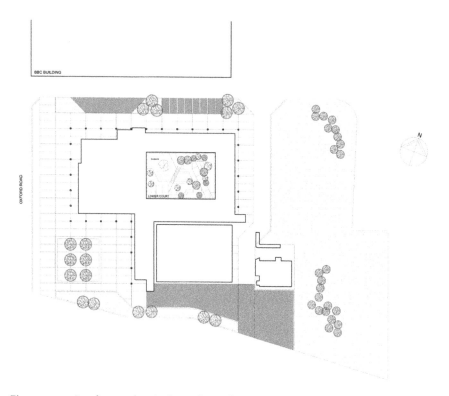

Figure 2.31 Landscape plan (redrawn by author).

from the faience of the Ritz Ballroom (1928), through Arthur Gibbon's use of Snowcrete in the 1960s and in John Seward's palette for ICL (1969) and other commercial projects.

Structurally, the NCC was conventional, formed from reinforced concrete. An orthogonal square grid extended across the entire ground plan and columns were spaced on the nodes of the grid as required. The logic extended to the hard landscaping – cobbled setts picked out the column line of the structure and extended this line from the face of the building to the back of the pavement where trees were planted in an aligned cluster [Figure 2.33]. To the north façade the car parking spaces were similarly picked out in cobbled setts and aligned with the columns. Much of the ground-floor plan was arranged using the same grid, though the upper floors were less rigidly organised and walls were mostly partitions. The only deviation from the square grid and 90 degree angles was the landscape plan for the internal courtyard that used diagonal geometry in contrast. The internal court was echoed by another internal water garden, above the lecture theatre. The courtyard was really the only spatially remarkable image that the building could project. Other than the lecture theatre, most other space was given to conventional office accommodation so the marketing

Figure 2.32 NCC under construction. The shadow of Mancunian Way fills the frame on the right. The left foreground is the edge of the John Dalton Building, and in the background is the BBC.

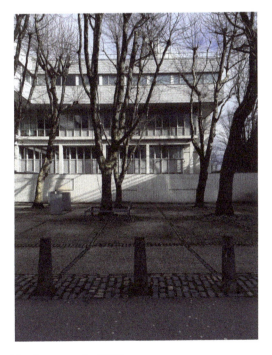

Figure 2.33 Hard landscape at the NCC.

Figure 2.34 Promotional brochure for the NCC.

brochures of the NCC prominently featured a photograph of employees enjoying the sunshine and water [Figure 2.34]. In this sense, the skin of the building was the branded identity of the NCC. Its drama was all on show and disguised a conventional interior – the logic of the grid aligned with this convention.

In technopolitical terms, the NCC was a manifestation of central government policy. However, its location in Manchester was a product of regional structures. Whilst the majority of government buildings directly related to rearmament were built before 1960, here I have shown how interconnected civil and military R&D were centred in one region, through sites, personnel and organisations over more than a decade. The site itself was a piece of Manchester Corporation's post-war jigsaw, requisitioned for national interests. Both the form and material of the building were influenced by interplay between national and local policy objectives and infrastructure. The orbit of agents and the orientation of their networks towards Manchester began in the TRE during the war. The NCC was given a home in Manchester because of the legacy of Turing, Williams, Newman and Kilburn that was, in turn, mythologised by Bowden, who perpetuated the idea of Manchester as the birthplace of the computer. If the building was a metaphor for the competencies and power of the Ministry of Technology and the rhetoric of White Heat, then its over-amplified physical stature would be hot air, the drawn-out process to completion would reflect the gestural nature of policy and the cloaking of the original building would be papering over the cracks. So, while the shining white form stood prominently against a new horizon and signified investment in technology, the long development of the institution, and the eventual construction of its headquarters, reveals an alternative picture of post-war architecture and its relation to policy and political objectives.

Computing, a conclusion

New technology in post-war Britain and the perceived explosion of modernity, in the form of motorways, nuclear power, urban renewal and computation, was not without its idiosyncratic conditions. The generally held expansionist view of the period does not always reveal the ad hoc, best-fit and ingenious approaches to activities like R&D amidst scarce material and capital resources. In this chapter, through the detailed examination of a series of interconnected sites and buildings, I have tried to address several key ideas and their impact upon the production of architecture. Primarily, the notion of a continuous state of preparedness for war has provided a context to explore issues attached to finance and procurement in relation to policy definition by central and local government.

This approach has also enabled an exploration of the relationship between military research and the civil applications of knowledge over three decades. The commission, design and construction of these buildings, all sponsored by central government, were not delivered under the direction of a particular political party – indeed, they survived the traditional cull of projects by successive incoming administrations. This serves to reinforce Edgerton's premise of the *Warfare State* and the underlying interests in the continuing defence of Britain. It also points to political consensus towards infrastructural modernisation and the fact that Wilson's government built on ideas and policy fostered by Macmillan and the Conservatives during the 1950s.[165] However, this book is concerned with the ways in which policy was interpreted, rather than the party political motivations that drove its definition. The regional networks of industry, knowledge and research that were created by, or grew from, conflict, influenced where development would take place. Local planning and administrative conditions impacted on the selection of particular sites and existing master plans informed

---

165 '[T]he Conservative government embraced a rhetoric of modernisation' and "the cabinets of both Macmillan and Douglas-Home contained a number of ministers with strong modernising tendencies. In fact, the policy objectives of the outgoing Conservative administration formed much of the intellectual agenda of Wilson's own campaign and Cabinet. See Tomlinson, Jim (1997) 'Conservative Modernisation, 1960–64: Too Little, Too Late?', *Contemporary British History* 11:3, pp. 18–38; Sharr, *Demolishing Whitehall*, 9.

spatial and material decisions. Vivian Bowden and Peter Hall had some association with each of the buildings discussed in this chapter and, whilst Bowden served as a minister in the Labour government and had a clear socialist agenda, his passion for technology and education were the main driving force behind his advice and intervention. The regional networks of people, policies and plans affected the form of the city and its buildings in very particular ways.

The regional scale helps to reveal latent contexts within which mainstream architecture can be considered. These contexts are invisible through conventional modes of measure, survey, observation and comparison. The form and material of the NCC offers the best example of this – its strongly gridded, shining white assembly is easily and conventionallyunderstood as a product of the twentieth century, with rationalist and sci-fi undertones. Describing its design, as related to the planning policy objectives of the local authority (its situation in the city) and as a response to central government agenda (its need to be significant), demonstrates how the regional scale reveals relationships between policy and form and the types of policy and interplay that an architect must negotiate. The clients were diverse in their composition of state, industry and academic representatives and each had their own influence at the various stages of procurement, design and construction. In all three cases, particularly that of the NCC, the needs of central government effectively overrode demands of the local authority. It could be argued that Ferranti, both at Wythenshawe and West Gorton, capitalised on prioritised governmental objectives and had as much influence as Whitehall in terms of the forces acting upon procurement, but that Manchester Corporation was a silent partner. In the final two chapters I explore the Development Plan and two of the central area CDAs – where the local authority exercised strong vision and influence in a period of rapid urban renewal. Before moving to the renewal of the central area, the following chapter addresses another CDA, a piece of linear city – the Higher Education Precinct.

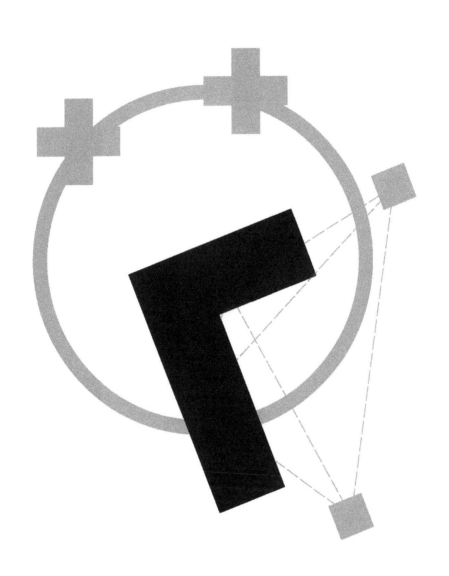

3

In advance of progress: higher education and technology

The demolition of Scherrer and Hicks's Maths Tower (1967–68) [Figure 3.01] at the University of Manchester was a lamentable loss of one of the city's most striking modern buildings. Purportedly not fit for purpose, the tower was sadly brought down within months following the death of Emil Scherrer in 2006. The tower was one of the most significant commissions made by the University in the post-war years; certainly, it was the most elegant, the obvious influence of Alvar Aalto and James Stirling was cleverly balanced in a solid versus transparent counterpoint of the key formal elements. It was designed, and acted as, a landmark. The Maths Tower was not only significant in its form and expression, but also knitted with other elements, including the Precinct Centre to form the first wave of the brave new world of aerial pedestrian runways that were scheduled to connect the Victorian University to All Saints, the site of the Polytechnic (now Manchester Metropolitan University) and onwards.

This extended area of 280 acres, bounded by Upper Brook Street and Cambridge Street, over a mile in length north to south, was designated as Manchester Education Precinct (MEP) in the 1960s and previously identified as the Educational Centre in the *1945 Plan*. This Comprehensive Development Area (CDA) also included the University of Manchester Institute of Science and Technology (UMIST), a former municipal technical college (hereafter referred to as 'the College') that became a chartered university in its own right from 1956, and of which Vivian Bowden was the principal from 1953. The College was developed from the mid-1950s, in advance of most other higher education institutes in Britain. Of the six CDAs defined in the *City Centre Map 1967*, MEP was the only one not under the direct control of John Millar's planning department – it was designed by the fledgling partnership of Wilson & Womersley. It is these two anomalies – the College's accelerated expansion, and the circumstances for the appointment of an external planning consultant for the entire university area – that are explored in this chapter to reveal the locally nuanced conditions for university expansion in a distinctly urban context. In so

THE RENEWAL OF POST-WAR MANCHESTER

Figure 3.01   The Maths Tower viewed from the head of the ramp to the Precinct Centre.

doing, the relationships between another group of government ministries, policies and local actors and their influence on the built environment are revealed.

The rapid expansion of British universities in the 1960s is more typically exemplified by the 'plate glass universities' – East Anglia, Exeter, Kent, Lancaster, Sussex, Warwick and York – instituted following decisions made by the UGC in the late 1950s and early 1960s. Manchester's higher education institutions also saw rapid growth at this time, albeit within existing streets and districts as opposed to the utopian enclaves of the self-contained new universities. The legacy of the *1945 Plan* specifically identified the education sector as a growth industry and proposed Hubert Worthington's imagined Educational Centre as the template for development.[1] Manchester's lacklustre period of construction in the 1950s was met head-on by the vigorous recovery of the 1960s and by this time beaux-arts visions like Worthington's were eclipsed by schemes like James

---

[1] Hubert Worthington, son of Thomas, of the established Manchester architectural firm Thomas Worthington and Sons.

Stirling's Engineering Building at Leicester (1959) and Chamberlin Powell & Bonn's proposals for the University of Leeds (1960).

The College's development was well under way by 1960 and its envisaged southward expansion moved closer and closer to the northern edges of areas for which the University had their own plans. This prospective clash over land was one motivating factor for the promotion of a joint development plan.[2] Its principal sponsors were Vivian Bowden (Principal of the Manchester College of Science and Technology), Sir Charles Renold (Vice-President of the Manchester College of Science and Technology), Sir Maurice Pariser (Chair of the Board of Governors and local leader of the Labour Party) and Sir William Mansfield Cooper (Vice-Chancellor of the University of Manchester, 1956–70). Bowden described the land around Oxford Road as 'some of the worst slums I have ever seen; they must in fact be amongst the worst in England'.[3] The urban context had to account for the wider ambitions of the city and the plans for the university were also bound with the concentric series of ring roads first proposed in the 1940s.

By 1960, as Bowden penned his indictment, houses near the university, like other designated slums in the city, were generally past their useful life as homes. Their demolition was part of the plan for an expanded education and cultural precinct in 1945. As with so much of the *1945 Plan*, the expansion was dependent on complicated land acquisitions for which the University did not have the necessary powers. To make matters more complex, funding for development involved numerous government departments, each of which required consultation before local authorities could enact compulsory purchases. Against this background, the University developed a range of 'neo-Georgian' buildings during the 1950s in a similar and unified style by H.S. Fairhurst & Sons on Brunswick Street [Figure 2.03], broadly aligned with the beaux-arts vision of Worthington's Plan in 1945 [Figure 3.02].[4] The architectural qualities of the Brunswick Street ensemble were unpopular with certain politicians; the visual appearance of the new buildings was regarded as antiquated. In contrast, the first new buildings at the College of Science and Technology were distinctly modern. Nonetheless, the preceding master plans for the College had classical undertones and were initially also prepared by Worthington. The majority of the site to be cleared for the College was former industrial land and represented

---

2 Other needs were in the mind of interested parties too. Referring to shared residential accommodation for students, in a letter to Mansfield Cooper, Sir Charles Renold stated, 'I think that the case for the College and the University getting together and making a global assessment of the problem emerges clearly.' 28 April 1960. Held at Manchester University Archives. Ref: VCA/7/386 Folder 1.

3 Letter from B.V. Bowden, Principal of the Manchester College of Science and Technology to R. Nicholas, City Surveyor. 10 May 1960. Held at Manchester University Archives. Ref: VCA/7/386 Folder 1.

4 Hartwell, C. (2001) *Manchester* (London: Penguin Books), p. 118.

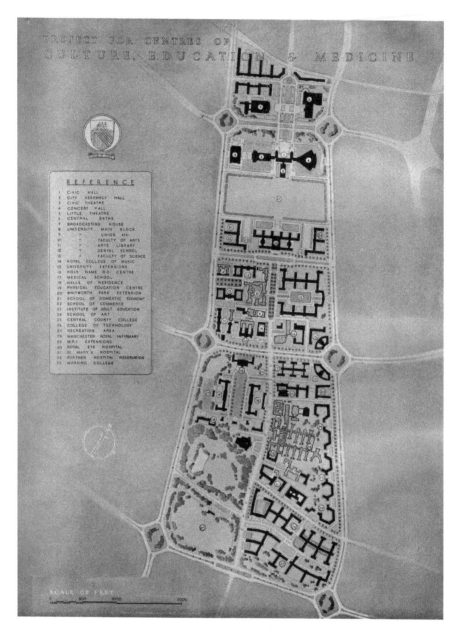

Figure 3.02 Hubert Worthington's plan for the Centre of Education, Culture and Medicine from Manchester's *1945 Plan*. The strong axial and symmetrical planning was used to organise the buildings of the 1950s and 1960s along Brunswick Street (labelled '15' on the plan).

a significant engineering challenge. The campus was to be built south of the Manchester to Liverpool railway viaduct in an area that was one of the oldest industrial sectors of the city and had the River Medlock running through it. The culverting and redirection of the river was key to releasing the land.

In tandem with the industrial expansion of technology, the teaching of science and technology expanded too and needed new buildings to grow into. The origins of the College can be traced back to the foundation of the Manchester Mechanics Institute in 1824 in the Bridgewater public house. In 1902 the Institute relocated to a new home on Sackville Street, designed for them by Spalding and Cross, latterly extended to designs by Bradshaw, Gass and Hope [Figure 3.03] that took thirty years to complete (1927–57). The Institute became the School of Technology (1902) and later the Municipal College of Technology (1918).

Figure 3.03 The Sackville Street Building viewed from the top floor of the Renold Building. The original building is to the left and the extension to the right.

The college gained its own charter in 1956, meaning more focus on degree-level academic courses (it was not until 1966 that the name UMIST was adopted).

The College makes an interesting case study for several reasons, the most obvious of which is its transition from locally resourced further education (FE) college to a nationally funded higher education (HE) facility. It was one of the first institutions to make this move and its development predated the wider expansion programme for British universities. The processes for approval and funding provided a point of reference for the development of future government policy. The site dedicated for the expansion of the institute combined with Manchester's post-war plans entangled it with the ambitions of the Corporation – its southern edge was bounded by a proposed aerial motorway that cut a swathe through existing, but condemned, dense terraced housing. Whilst the earliest plans were drawn by Worthington's office, the development of the campus was a collaborative exercise where a committee arrived at a consensus view that informed architectural decisions. In the ten years from 1959 to 1969, thirteen new buildings were realised on the complicated inner city site, their design distributed between three local practices, Thomas Worthington & Sons, H.S. Fairhurst & Sons and Cruickshank & Seward. C&S's suite of white concrete buildings, set amidst the lawns of a well-organised campus [Figure 3.04], are broadly considered to be among the best post-war architecture in the city.[5]

Manchester's College, with Imperial College London, was one of the first significant investments in the expansion of higher education after 1945. As such, it does not exist comfortably within the now established histories of university development in the UK. The *Old Universities* fall into three descriptive classifications: *Ancient* (Oxford, Cambridge, St Andrews, Glasgow, Aberdeen, Edinburgh and Durham), *Redbrick* (Birmingham, Liverpool, Leeds, Sheffield, Bristol and Manchester) and *Plate Glass* (East Anglia, Essex, Kent, Lancaster, Sussex, Warwick and York).[6] The College was not any of these, though it may be seen as at the vanguard of the College of Advanced Technology programme that was instituted in 1956 and applied special status to ten colleges, which later became universities.[7] The idiosyncratic situation of the institution lies in its creation and the prevailing British attitude towards higher technical education. In his treatise for the expansion of the College in 1956, Bowden described the innovations of

---

5 Manchester Modernist Society celebrated the campus with 'Campus Day', http://umist campus.wordpress.com/2012/06/26/manchester-modernist-society-designate-conserva tion-area-status-to-the-umist-campus/ [Accessed 15 March 2014]; Hartwell, *Manchester*, pp. 123–125.
6 Also known as the 'Shakespearian Seven' – Attributed to the officers of the University Grants Committee. Birks, T. (1972) *Building the New Universities* (Newton Abbot: David & Charles), p. 15.
7 Simmons, R. (2020) 'Science and Technology in England and Wales: The Lost Opportunity of the Colleges of Advanced Technology', *British Journal of Educational Studies*.

Figure 3.04 Aerial view of the UMIST campus c.1973.

the industrial revolution as having been made by 'self-taught men'.[8] He believed it was the societies, founded by industrialists, that were largely responsible for the development of scientific and technical education in Britain.[9] The College made the unusual provision of both further and higher education in science and technology subjects.

A concordat with the University of Manchester underwrote the awarding of higher degrees.[10] The College itself retained its funding structure from the Ministry of Education and Manchester Corporation (universities were funded solely by the UGC and under direct control of the Treasury).[11] As early as 1936

---

8   Bowden, B.V. (1956) *Proposals for the Development of the Manchester College of Science and Technology* (Manchester: Manchester College of Science and Technology), p. 5.
9   A view endorsed by Venables, P. (1978) *Higher Education Developments: the Technological Universities 1956–76* (London: Faber & Faber), p. 15.
10 The 1905 agreement situated the University Faculty of Technology within the College.
11 The relevance of the funding regime is discussed further in this chapter. Bowden, *Proposals for the Development of the Manchester College of Science and Technology*, p. 31.

and perhaps pre-empting the post-war organisational demands, logistical planning at a regional scale was required to 'organise a more rational use of equipment' (at the College), and to transfer less specialist courses to other local institutions.[12] The local understanding of the regional, if not national, importance of the College was reinforced in the years following 1945 and, as the extension to the Sackville Street building neared completion in the mid-1950s, discussions between the University of Manchester, the City of Manchester Education Committee and the UGC were under way as to how best to develop the institution.[13] Part of this preparation involved the construction of new technical colleges by Manchester Corporation that would divert some of the more vocational courses from the College and thus permit greater focus on higher technological education.[14]

The UGC was historically able to 'propagate without interference' from the Treasury and the Board of Education and, up to 1939, it was the universities that set the ideological tone within which their development took place.[15] At this time the accepted consensus was that the state should be the 'subordinate partner' in this relationship.[16] The outbreak of war changed this situation as buildings were requisitioned for alternative purposes, young men were enlisted and institutions were evacuated in their entirety. The study of science was subject to particular intervention 'directly related to the various and developing needs of the war machine'.[17] The legacy of this type of direct instruction from the state, combined with the numerous reports produced in the mid-1940s that examined the

---

12 The University of Manchester Institute of Science and Technology (1974) *1824–1974, 150 Years of Progress at UMIST* (Manchester: University of Manchester/UMIST), p. 9.

13 University Grants Committee, *Higher technological education – Development of Manchester College of Technology*. NA: UGC 7/895.

14 In Manchester, the first phase of Openshaw Technical College (Halliday and Agate, 1954) was among the first post-war buildings in the city and would later be joined by the College of Building (1957), West Wythenshawe College of Further Education (1958), the Domestic and Trades College (1960), Moston College (1962) and John Dalton College (1964). See Steele M. (2014) 'The Making of Manchester's Technical Colleges (1954 1964)' [MRes Thesis, MMU]; Manchester Municipal College of Technology, *Application to the University Grants Committee for the years 1952–1957*, supplementary statement. NA: UGC 7/895.

15 Salter, B., and Tapper, T. (1994) *The State and Higher Education* (Ilford: The Woburn Press), p. 107. See also Bocock, J., and Taylor, R. (2003) 'The Labour Party and Higher Education: 1945–51', *Higher Education Quarterly*, Vol. 57, No. 3, July, pp. 249–265; Shattock, M. (1994) *The UGC and the Management of British Universities* (Buckingham: SRHE & Open University Press) for a good account of the UGC's changing relationship with the government in the post-war period.

16 Salter and Tapper, *The State and Higher Education*, p. 107.

17 University Grants Committee (1948) *University Development 1935 to 1946* (London: HMSO), Para. 6. In the period 1939–45 the College was put to use as a research and training facility for the British and US military, during which the Textile Technology Department produced a thread for use with 'sticky bombs'.

educational needs of a range of professions, was a strengthening of the UGC's 'machinery'.[18] It seems unusual now that the Ministry of Education was not involved in either the advice or funding allocation in HE provision: it was not until 1964 that responsibility for the UGC was transferred from the Treasury to the newly formed Department of Education and Science.[19] Thus, the College was in a position to inform the policy of the UGC as it developed new and unique building types and the type of cost control exerted on the new universities was developed through the analysis of these prototypes in Manchester and elsewhere. Effectively a generous budget was available to the College, if it was able to justify its demands. The College also secured an annual review of its construction budget and was not subject to the quinquennial system applied elsewhere.[20] Due, in part, to the lack of input from the Ministry of Education, the unprecedented new technological institutions had much more control of their own planning and building programmes than the new universities that would follow.

The autonomy of the College in determining its built future can also be attributed to the national policy landscape. In 1944 Ernest Bevin, Minister of Labour in the wartime Cabinet, brought attention to the lack of technically skilled workers. This was underlined by a series of reports, which would consider the demand for retraining and scientific manpower and the role of colleges and universities in this provision.[21] The Hankey committee (1945) 'identified the extent of Britain's (re)training needs', the Percy committee (1945) looked at higher technological education and the Barlow committee (1946) examined the demand for educated workers in the future.[22] Collectively, the outcome was a

---

18 The professions were served by the Goodenough Report (medicine), the Teviot Report (dentistry) and the Loveday Report (agriculture). The term 'machinery' is utilised in the Barlow Report. Barlow Report, Lord President of the Council (1946) *Scientific Manpower* (London: HMSO) Cmnd. 6824, Para. 33.

19 Bocock and Taylor (2003) describe the 'furious lobbying' by both the universities and the UGC against any transfer of power to the Education Ministry as suggested in the Barlow Report. See also Shattock, *The UGC and the Management of British Universities*, p. 8.

20 In a letter to Sir John Wolfenden, Bowden acknowledged the 'unusual' financing provision that the UGC had made to the College and that he hoped it could continue. He made clear that the situation had allowed the construction of buildings 'which cost considerably more than a single year's allocation: which take three years to complete'. Correspondence, 12 October 1964. Minutes of the Planning and Development Committee, p. 204. UoMA: TGB/2/1/3.

21 For a detailed description of the Labour Government's policy and response to these reports see Bocock and Taylor,'The Labour Party and Higher Education: 1945–51'.

22 Hankey, Lord (1945) *Higher Appointments: Report of the Committee Appointed by the Minister of Labour and National Service in July 1943 (Chairman Lord Hankey)* (London: HMSO) Cmnd. 6576; Percy Report (1945) Ministry of Education, *Higher Technological Education. Report of a Special Committee* (London: HMSO); Barlow Report, Lord President of the Council (1946) *Scientific Manpower* (London: HMSO) Cmnd. 6824, Para. 33. Quote from Bocock and Taylor, 'The Labour Party and Higher Education: 1945–51'.

recommendation for a significant increase in student numbers, particularly in technological education. The Percy Report made the distinction between the provision of technological education in universities and colleges – Manchester was unusual in its delivery of both FE and HE courses in one institution. It also established the need for technical colleges to underpin the immediate expansion, as the universities were not in a position to do so.[23] Technical colleges also needed investment and it was this dual purpose of expansion and improvement that drove the initiative for the first wave of new colleges of technology, among which was Manchester.

As well as recommending expansion in science and technological higher education, the Barlow Report proposed that certain existing university colleges should become universities in their own right *and* that a number of Institutes of Technology should also be established. It advocated for the increased involvement of the UGC in planning for the development of the universities and proposed that at least one new university was founded.[24] These factors, and the extant situation of the College in an industrial city with a history of innovation already delivering HE courses, combined to make Manchester a prominent candidate for investment and growth. However, despite the recommendations, the Labour Government was slow to act and did not consolidate its views until its 1951 pre-election statement on *Higher Technological Education*.[25] Labour lost the general election, but the case for the expansion was clear and the incoming Conservative administration had to address demand. Their policy response was not implemented until the White Paper on Technical Education (1956). In the meantime, necessity being the mother of invention, the plans for the College, its transition to exclusively HE provision and its full charter as a university, progressed, despite there being no agreed national framework.[26]

---

23 Bocock and Taylor, 'The Labour Party and Higher Education: 1945–51'.
24 Which was eventually realised in Keele in 1949. Keele was in many ways an anomaly rather than a test case and is discussed further in this chapter. See also Bocock and Taylor, 'The Labour Party and Higher Education: 1945–51' (2003), pp. 260–261.
25 *Higher Technological Education: Statement of Government Policy* (1951) (London: HMSO), Cmnd. 8357. Bocock and Taylor (2003) argue that there was no strong tradition of Labour policy on universities and that they also fought entrenched elite liberal views of what an English university should be that didn't include technological or eminently vocational study. They also describe the existing universities as 'reluctant expansionists'.
26 The awarding of a separate independent charter to the College was championed by the Vice Chancellor of the University, John Stopford, in November 1951, only one month after the general election. Stopford was a physician and a leading member of the Joint Research Council that studied the relationships between industry and science. His primary concern was the continuing provision of HE level technological teaching in Manchester and his fear was that the Ministry of Education would push the College 'right down to the level of one of these colleges in neighbouring towns'. Letter from John Stopford to Sir Arthur Trueman, Chair of the UGC, 26 November 1951 and Letter from John Stopford to Sir Arthur Trueman, Chair of the UGC, 24 January 1952. NA:

Early discussions concerning how the College might serve regional and national objectives involved the University, the Manchester Education Committee and the UGC. Each of the parties saw the appointment of a Principal as pivotal to the transformation of the College. The selection of a candidate with 'the vision, the qualities of leadership and the knowledge' to drive the expansion was viewed as crucial.[27] Equally important were networks between education and industry and how this would inform the evolution of the institution. After some searching and extended discourse between the interested agents of the state, Bertram Vivian Bowden was appointed. As outlined in Chapter 2, Bowden was well connected with both academic and industrial organisations in the region.[28] He was vocal in his promotion of technological education in Manchester, writing that, '[t]he college will perform a vitally important service for the industry of the country as a whole and of this district in particular' and that '[i]t is our responsibility and privilege to pioneer.'[29] Bowden was aware of the progress being made by American business in the use of computing and conscious that the advantages gained from work at Bletchley Park and other research institutes during the war were at risk, as Britain failed to capitalise on the commercial possibilities of its innovation.[30] America was not just Bowden's point of comparison, but also his precedent and he referred frequently to the US structures of research funding and the amount of scientific research done in US universities. He had spent some time at the Massachusetts Institute of Technology (MIT) during the war. Bowden's industry connections, strong research pedigree and his international experience influenced his personal aspirations for the College.

Manchester Corporation was an active partner in the transition from college to university. Following a statement in the House of Lords in June 1952, they established a general and parliamentary committee.[31] The committee concluded that 'it

---

UGC 7/895; Manchester Joint Research Council (1954) *Industry and Science. A study of their relationship based on a survey of firms in the Greater Manchester area carried out by the Manchester Joint Research Council, 1950–1953* (Manchester: Manchester University Press); Letter from John Stopford to Sir Arthur Trueman, Chair of the UGC, 30 November 1951. NA: UGC 7/895.

27 Ibid.
28 Johnson, D., 'What Manchester did Yesterday', *The Guardian*, 15 December 1975, p. 5.
29 Bowden, *Proposals for the Development of the Manchester College of Science and Technology*, Preface.
30 Ibid., p. 126.
31 'The Government consider that a most important means of increasing productivity in industry is to improve facilities for higher technological education. They are convinced that this can best be done by building up at least one institution of university rank devoted predominantly to the teaching and study of the various forms of technology.' Statement made by Lord Woolton. Woolton was born in Salford and was Conservative Party Chairman between 1946 and 1955. *Science and Industry*. HL Deb 11 June 1952, Vol. 177 cc35–114.

would be in the national interest if a technological university were established in Manchester'.[32] The proposal for the transition of the College to University, by the grant of a Royal Charter, was publicly disclosed in March 1954 by Lord Woolton on a visit to Manchester and roundly endorsed by Bowden and Maurice Pariser.[33] The Charter was formally announced on 1 August 1955.[34] Bowden was reported to believe that the variety of industries in the region offered a unique opportunity to develop the teaching of technology alongside commercial research interests.[35] Following the Royal Assent of the Manchester Corporation Act, the transfer of the College was formalised and on 1 August 1956 the new governing body took control of the institution, replacing the Education Committee of the City Council who had been administrative guardians since 1892.[36]

Such a complex process required trust and strong working relations between central and local government. The land reserved for expansion was agreed in 1955 and the provision of new FE colleges to free up the College for HE was made by the local authority.[37] The new institution needed a new vision and Bowden wrote, in politically charged prose, his *Proposals for the Development of the Manchester College of Science and Technology*. The 1956 treaty envisioned the plans for the College as a ten-year undertaking.[38] His belief in the worth of technology was a strong driving force and his post as Principal gave him the vehicle to promote and test his convictions. His method of publishing as propaganda, successfully deployed in the expansion of the College, had precedent in his earlier career at Ferranti.[39] As well as reading as something of a manifesto, the short book was populated with comments intended to reinforce the gravitas of the endeavour to interested parties. He frequently used Imperial College London to contextualise the proposals for Manchester. One comparison referred directly

---

32 The report suggests a concerted and coordinated effort by the City, the College and the University in the promotion of the idea. *City of Manchester. Proposed University of Technology. Report of the General and Parliamentary Committee.* Council Circular, Item No. IX (b). 21 November 1952. NA: UGC 7/895.
33 'Independence for College "Government Policy"', *The Manchester Guardian*, 13 March 1954, p. 2.
34 'Grant of Royal Charter to College of Technology: Changes planned in Manchester', *The Manchester Guardian*, 1 August 1955, p. 8.
35 Ibid.
36 Bowden, *Proposals for the Development of the Manchester College of Science and Technology*, Preface.
37 Ibid., p. 135; Copy of letter from Chief Education Officer to the Principal of the College, 2 July 1956. Appended to Minutes of Council of Municipal College of Technology. 27 July 1956, pp. 115–116. UoMA: TGB/2/1/1.
38 Bowden, *Proposals for the Development of the Manchester College of Science and Technology*, Preface.
39 Bowden had adopted the tagline from the brochure for Nimrod, the world's first computer gaming machine and used it to reinforce the narrative of Manchester as the birthplace of the computer in his 1953 publication. See Chapter 2.

to the act of building: 'The difficulties of expansion that we have to face are as nothing compared with those which must have confronted the authorities who had to pull down half South Kensington in order to expand the Imperial College.'[40] Bowden's description of the land contracts implied that a great deal of faith was required by the respective parties; that each would adhere and support implicit agreements concerning the sources of funding for various acts of land assembly and purchase.[41]

The interrelationship of the various actors was highlighted by delays in the approval of the Manchester Corporation Bill that followed in 1958. The Bill was designed to facilitate the diversion and culverting of the River Medlock, vital to facilitating construction on site, and its slow passage through Parliament impacted directly on the construction schedule. This in turn required an 'exceptional' transfer of funds by the UGC, from one year's programme into another.[42] As building projects were delayed, costs began to rise and placed phasing possibilities at odds with funding streams.[43] The UGC did not wish to be consulted on the design of buildings until the schemes reached a particular submission status, where proposed buildings could be costed in relation to other buildings of a similar type procured by the UGC.[44] This was problematic in terms of the first major building on site, the lecture room block, as it was a 'new departure in educational building' and seen as risky to significantly develop without consultation.[45] During the emergence of the master plan and the buildings the UGC were, in effect, finding their feet with regard to cost. As the UGC gained experience costs would become much tighter, but in 1957 there was no indication that they would apply standardisation to the building models and subsequent expenditure on the Manchester campus. Indeed any 'unimaginative cheeseparing' was deemed 'undesirable' if it limited the quality of new

---

40 Bowden, *Proposals for the Development of the Manchester College of Science and Technology*, p. 135.
41 This sentiment was mirrored by the Leader of the House of Commons: 'The House will be interested to hear that the Corporation of Manchester, which has shown the utmost forward-looking patriotism the whole way, is prepared to reserve an area of seventeen and a half acres for the development of Manchester College of Science and Technology, which recently received a Royal Charter as an autonomous institution.' 'Technical Education' House of Commons Debate, 21 June 1956, vol. 554 cc1639–767.
42 Letter from H.J. Oram of the UGC to Mr Davies of the College, 4 July 1958. Transcript Minutes of the Planning and Development Committee, p. 256. UoMA: TGB/2/5/1.
43 Universities were obliged to submit five-year plans to the UGC that indicated their capital expenditure on buildings, staff and equipment. Minutes of the Planning and Development Committee, 7 August 1958, Item 2, p. 258. UoMA: TGB/2/5/1.
44 'Schedule 1' was a set of key indicators in relation to areas and costs associated with conventional laboratory style education buildings.
45 Minutes of the Planning and Development Committee, 19 September 1957, Item 6, p. 78. UoMA: TGB/2/5/1.

buildings.[46] Generally, the UGC viewed the College's committee structures favourably and valued their advice in design and procurement protocols.[47] The building programme itself was under constant adjustment in line with parliamentary decisions that impacted upon the work of the UGC and ultimately the development of the College.

The inner city campus steadily took shape. Sir Hubert Worthington was appointed as Site Architect in July 1955.[48] He had some relevant experience through his completed buildings for Merton College, Oxford (1939–40).[49] The new campus was to be built to the south of the Manchester, South Junction and Altrincham railway, extending into Chorlton-upon-Medlock, in an area that was one of the oldest industrial sectors of the city. The dark curves of the polluted River Medlock wound their way through the allotted land and carved through the brick mass of the railway viaduct, which itself cut a divisive east–west transect across the site. The culverting and re-routing of the river was key to releasing the land and initial plans envisioned exclusively new buildings on the site. The new Link Road, 17/7, would form the southernmost boundary. The site was subdivided into Areas A, B and C for the purposes of phased development [Figure 3.05]. It is Areas A and C that are explored in this chapter.[50]

Worthington was not the only architect retained as the College grew. In July 1956 the Site Architect was proposed as being joined by 'two or three Project Architects, every project for a building to be given to one or other member of the panel'.[51] The appointed firms were H.S. Fairhurst & Sons and Cruickshank &

---

46 Three years later, as the new universities were in development, following the creation of an architects' department at the UGC to filter and disseminate construction and cost information, the tone began to change. The publication of *Methods used by Universities of Contracting and of Recording and Controlling Expenditure* (UGC, December 1960) built upon the Gater Report on the financial control exercised by the UGC. The language used indicated a tightening of budgetary controls and the methods used to establish such. Minutes of the Planning and Development Committee, Memorandum of Joint Meeting, 9 July, 1957, p. 72. UoMA: TGB/2/5/1.

47 Report on UGC letter dated 13 June 1960. p. 571. Refers to suggested prices for new science buildings. UoMA: TGB/2/5/1.

48 A series of plans by Worthington from 1956 to 1961 are held in the files of Lord Bowden. UoMA: BVB papers. See also Minutes of the Planning and Development Committee, 21 January 1957, Item 6(b)(i), p. 10. UoMA: TGB/2/5/1; and letter from Bowden to Mansfield Cooper, 10 May 1960. UoMA: VCA/7/386 Folder 1.

49 Whyte, W. (2013) 'Introduction: "A Pastiche or a Packing Case" Building in Twentieth-Century Oxford', *Twentieth Century Architecture*, No. 11 (London: The Twentieth Century Society), p. 24.

50 Area B was not subject to significant development until the late 1960s and was not fully occupied until 2006. As shown in Chapter 2, Area G was leased to the Ministry of Technology for the National Computing Centre.

51 Minutes of Council of Municipal College of Technology, 10 July 1956, p. 78. UoMA: TGB/2/1/1.

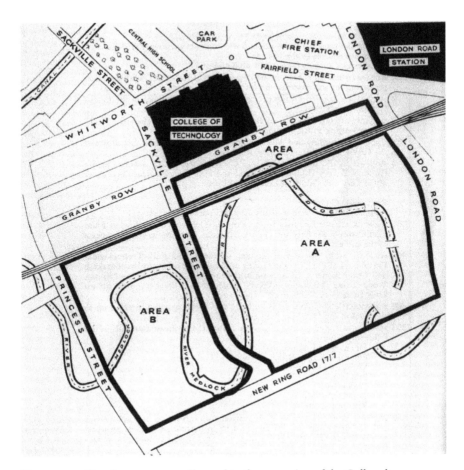

Figure 3.05 Development areas allocated to the expansion of the College by Manchester Corporation in 1955. This chapter deals specifically with Areas A and C. Not labelled on this plan is Altrincham Street, which runs adjacent and parallel to the south face of the railway viaduct seen here as a set of four lines running diagonally across the centre of the image. The black mass of the existing college also incorporates the extension of 1927–57 (see Figure 3.03).

Seward (C&S). Possibly owing to the death of Sir Hubert Worthington in 1963, the major share of the new buildings were designed by Fairhurst and C&S. Representatives from all three practices were regularly in attendance at the Planning Committee meetings of the institute. This association of the Mancunian architectural establishment of the day was extremely significant and perhaps one of the reasons for the considerable strength of the master plan and the capacity to carve out a campus from the carcass of a knotted and crumbling part of the city [Figure 3.06]. In the drawing produced by the office of the City Surveyor in 1949, the majority of the existing buildings contained in the loop of

Figure 3.06   A survey of the anticipated lifespan of existing buildings around Temple Street and the River Medlock.

the river between Altrincham Street and Mount Street were shown to have an expected lifespan of less than twenty years. The notable exception was the large L-shaped block coloured orange, estimated to have a further forty years. This building, Jackson's Mill, became a central component of the ensuing campus, albeit by necessity rather than design.

In 1956 a representative of the UGC suggested that there was no 'established procedure' for the assessment of 'long-term development of [university] sites and buildings' – essentially, the design of the campus in Britain had no real cost yardsticks.[52] Hence, the proposals for the College in the 1950s were at the forefront of large-scale university development. Other universities were growing at the time; Keele was founded in 1949 and was a forerunner of greenfield campus development in Britain, but its architecture was called into question.[53] At Liverpool University buildings for Veterinary Science and

---

52   Minutes of Council of Municipal College of Technology, 11 May 1956, p. 31. UoMA: TGB/2/1/1.
53   Birks, *Building the New Universities*, p. 10–11; Muthesius, *The Postwar University*, p. 105. Keele was the brainchild of A.D. Lindsay, former Master of Balliol College, Oxford and

Civil Engineering designed by Edwin Maxwell Fry and realised between 1955 and 1960 demonstrated a 'concern for context within a functional vernacular tradition'.[54] These were situated within a master plan by William Holford, first outlined in 1949.[55] Fry's buildings were overlooked by Lionel Brett in his 1957 assessment of university architecture, possibly due to their relatively unremarkable appearance. Brett referred broadly to the 'monumental record of the failure of nerve in academic patronage' in the earliest assessment of university master plans and post-war architecture in the British architectural press.[56] Generally scathing, his article did, however, acknowledge the success of Gollins, Melvin and Ward's (1953) winning entry to the competition for the expansion of Sheffield University – C&S placed third and the site and their scheme were similar to the problems and solutions encountered in Manchester.[57]

Whilst the master plan for the Manchester site was officially in the hands of Worthington, C&S, particularly Arthur Gibbon, had a strong influence in the early stages and were charged with the design of the later stages of the campus organisation. In Manchester the 'long-term development' of the site and buildings was a collaborative experiment. Its status as such would feed into and inform the UGC's policies for development and the evolution of the New Universities.[58] When the first one, Sussex, was founded in 1958, the appointment of a consultant architect was regarded as essential.[59] Thus, the College's appointment of a professional team in 1956 was in advance of most

---

ardent Labour supporter. He had been interested in establishing a university in the Potteries since 1925 and saw the advice of the Barlow Report as an opportunity to test his ideas. See Bocock and Taylor, 'The Labour Party and Higher Education: 1945–51', pp. 260–261.

54 Jackson, I. (2011) 'Post-War Modernism: Maxwell Fry's buildings at the University of Liverpool', *The Journal of Architecture*, Vol. 16, No. 5, p. 676.

55 Holford, W.G. (1949) *Proposals for the Development of a Site for the University of Liverpool* (Liverpool: Liverpool University Press); Holford, W.G. (1955) *The Report of the Development Committee to the Council and Senate of the University on Building Progress 1949–1954* (The First Quinquennial Review of the Post-War development plan) (Liverpool: Liverpool University Press).

56 'Universities. 1, Yesterday. 2, Today', *Architectural Review*, October 1957, pp. 234–251.

57 Sheffield University was on the edge of the city centre, close to the route of post-war ring and radial roads and on a sloping site. 'First Three Prize Winning Designs for New University Buildings at Sheffield: Winners Gollins, Melvin, Ward & Partners', *Architect & Building News*, 3 December 1953, pp. 689–698; *Architects' Journal*, 10 December 1953, pp. 718–732; *The Builder*, 27 November 1953, pp. 827–835.

58 The UGC was inexperienced in procuring large buildings as there had been no similar period of expansion. In the post-war years as well as appointing their own architects to assess work, they also began to collect and tabulate cost information that eventually led to standardisation of budgets for particular building types.

59 Birks, *Building the New Universities*, p. 11. Sir Basil Spence was invited to submit a plan for the new university in 1959.

national programmes. This could be partly attributed to the experience of the city of Manchester in promoting such ideas and in their comprehensive approach led by City Surveyor Rowland Nicholas in 1945. Indeed, in October 1956 Nicholas was also co-opted to the Planning and Development Committee of the College.[60]

As the Robbins Report was published in 1963 the expansion of the College was predominantly planned and already under construction.[61] It was unlike any campus, other than its immediate predecessor, Imperial College London.[62] It predated almost all of the redbrick university post-war development plans and each of the new universities.

In a series of master plan studies, produced between 1955 and 1961, Worthington and the assembled group designed for the site that was viewed as on the edge of 'an abomination of desolation'.[63] A total of five plans were drawn and presented to the Planning and Building Committee for approval, but copies of the earliest drawings have not survived. However, it is recorded in a photograph of Tom Warburton, a senior technician, making the first model [Figure 3.07]. 'Scheme Two' [Figure 3.08] is exemplary of the approach taken by Worthington prior to the appointment of Fairhurst and C&S. This early iteration of the master plan was similar to the approach Worthington applied in the proposals for the Education Centre in the *1945 Plan*. A strong central axis aligned with the edge of the Sackville Street building and perpendicular to the dominant railway viaduct. The axial symmetry was not absolute, but the footprints of the proposed buildings were comparable to one another in size and organisation. The north–south axis in the early master plans implied a neo-classical approach to the formal organisation of the site. From the elevated position of Altrincham Street, parallel to the viaduct, a split, symmetrical stair led down to a pair of square gardens, which in turn led to an elongated lawn, more suggestive of the formal landscapes of stately homes than any existing

---

60 Minutes of Council of Municipal College of Technology, 23 October 1956, p. 193. UoMA: TGB/2/1/1.

61 The Robbins Report recommended immediate expansion of universities, and that all Colleges of Advanced Technology should be given the status of universities. Committee on Higher Education (1963) *Higher Education. Report of the Committee appointed by the Prime Minister under the Chairmanship of Lord Robbins 1961–63* (London: HMSO).

62 The growth of Imperial College was only slightly in advance of UMIST and also involved Worthington. The master plan by Norman and Dawbarn was published in 1956. 'Imperial College', *Survey of London: volume 38: South Kensington Museums Area* (1975), pp. 233–247, www.british-history.ac.uk/report.aspx?compid=47532 [accessed 18 March 2014].

63 Lord Bowden of Chesterfield (1974) 'The Present Situation', in Cardwell, D.S.L. (ed.) (1974) *Artisan to Graduate. Essays to Commemorate the Foundation in 1824 of the Manchester Mechanics' Institution, now in 1974 the University of Manchester Institute of Science and Technology* (Manchester: Manchester University Press), pp. 248–257, p. 250.

Figure 3.07   Tom Warburton. Pictured making adjustments to the first architectural model of the proposed developments.

precedent for university master plans. Two centrally placed blocks closed vistas and defined the limit of the lawn. One block was more precisely drawn and it is easy to read this as having a lecture theatre attached – the trapezoidal plan shape was an implicit sign for such. The building heights are not referred to on the drawing but a photograph of a study model shows the two central buildings as slab blocks of approximately nine storeys and the rest of the buildings much lower in profile. The tall buildings would have enclosed their own axial vista in an east–west orientation. This was quite a contained organisational structure to impose upon the site and contrasts with the eventual permeable grain of the completed group of buildings. As each building was allocated to one of the architectural team, its mass and form were determined and they replaced the generic blocks on Worthington's drawings. Worthington, the experienced practitioner, remained as Site Architect, but it is clear from the records that many decisions were by consensus.

Consensual agreements between architects and client were not the only decisions affecting the architecture and planning of the College. There were local and national interests in a complex relational structure that continued to influence development. Discussions about the precise alignment of Link Road 17/7 were intertwined with the land to be released for the expansion of the Technical College which, in turn, had ramifications for the proposed alignment

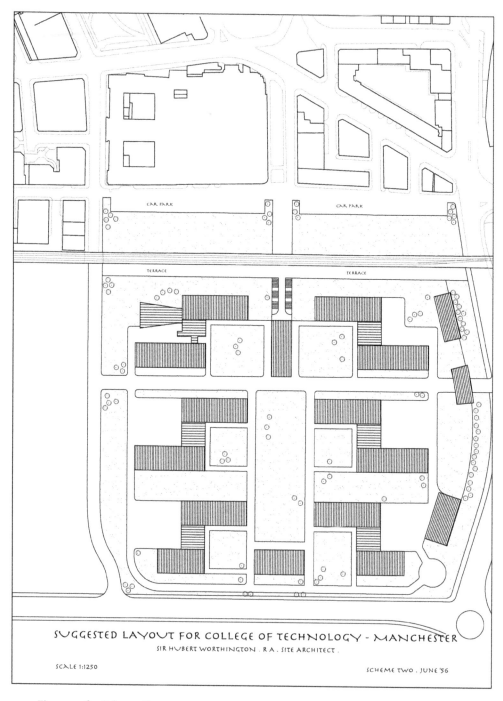

Figure 3.08 Scheme Two.

of the River Medlock culvert and the overall master plan.[64] Representatives of the Corporation were often in attendance at Committee meetings and frequently proposed amendments.[65] The College's association with the wider aims of the city complicated the purchase of property for the expansion programme and ensuing statutory processes. The Manchester Corporation Bill of 1957 was designed to achieve the major objectives of permission for the alignment of Link Road 17/7 and the culverting of the River Medlock, both of which had a bearing on the plans for the College, but equally could be achieved independently. While many sites were procured by agreement, a number of owners steadfastly refused to sell their property, owing to widely differing values ascribed by agents. Under CPO powers the price was likely to increase further and site owners knew this.[66] A decision was made between the College and the Corporation to defer the application for CPO powers from the 1957 Bill.[67] The cost of culverting the River Medlock was eventually shared between the local authority and the UGC.[68]

In this instance we see the relations between local and national government that planning historian Gordon Cherry reconciled as a dual system of 'shared responsibilities' and John Davis explained as expanding the activities of local government whilst progressively determining their financing.[69] It was the conflicts of the twentieth century that created the regional offices of government departments, yet increasingly, in the post-war period, local government was in direct communication with Whitehall, rather than relying on regional offices as a conduit. Thus, some of the powers invested in the regional ministerial offices were diminished and local government responsibilities intensified. This was not necessarily accompanied by increased budgets or financial autonomy and, as in the case of the Medlock culvert, the funding of these physical alterations

---

64 Minutes of the Planning and Development Committee, 5 March, 1957, Item 5, p. 20. UoMA: TGB/2/5/1.

65 For example, City Surveyor Rowland Nicholas advised as to the location of the main service road. Sub-committee meeting to consider Revision of Layout Scheme 3, 28 April 1958. Minutes of the Planning and Development Committee, p. 213. UoMA: TGB/2/5/1.

66 A CPO is a legal function in the United Kingdom that allows certain bodies that need to obtain land or property to do so without the consent of the owner. It may be enforced if a proposed development is considered one for public betterment.

67 Note attached to Minutes of the Planning and Development Committee, 17 January 1958, p. 162. UoMA: TGB/2/5/1.

68 Report of meeting held 6 January 1959. Transcript. Minutes of the Planning and Development Committee, p. 331. UoMA: TGB/2/5/1.

69 As quoted by Shapely, 'The Entrepreneurial City, pp. 498–520; from Cherry, G.E. (1996) *Town Planning in Britain Since 1900. The Rise and Fall of the Planning Ideal* (Oxford: Wiley-Blackwell), p. 16; Davis, J. (2001) 'Central Government and the Towns', in Daunton, M. (2001) *The Cambridge Urban History of Britain* (Cambridge: Cambridge University Press), pp. 261–286.

to the city was shared and agreed by negotiation – a concrete manifestation of transitional political contexts informing the physical environment.

The relational networks of the region were also at play in the development of the campus form. As well as Bowden, the locally convened master plan sub-committee included City Engineer and Surveyor, Rowland Nicholas, Sir Charles Renold (for whose company C&S had designed an HQ building), Councillor Maurice Pariser, Sir Hubert Worthington, H.T. Seward, Arthur Gibbon and Harry S. Fairhurst.[70] This grouping initially came together to consider 'Scheme 3', effectively the point at which the formal relationship of each of the buildings around a series of interlocking quads emerged [Figure 3.09]. Bowden was concerned with the site organisation in terms of its open space. His was a vision where buildings should 'be sited with dignity and propriety, and in such a way that the sun and air can penetrate the buildings and the spaces between them'.[71] He specifically requested certain ratios between floor space and ground area and that 'there must be large courts, trees and lawns allowing vistas of the buildings'.[72] Scheme 3 was presented on 4 June 1957 and approved by the Committee at their next meeting.[73]

The UGC also insisted on a campus type development for the College that encompassed the social life of the student body in a way that the old universities did not.[74] The provision of high quality conferencing space that could be used by industry was seen as central to the purpose of the College. This direction and advice was simply borne of the assembled structures and reports made by various sub-committees and synthesised by Bowden himself in treatise and correspondence. The systematic association of curriculum and building programme developed in the New Universities programme and presented as 'socio-diagrams' in development plans was not yet general visual currency or part of design processes.[75] At the College, the content and the organisation of the master plan was subject to both national advice and local interpretation.

The most significant adjustment to this third iteration of the master plan was the retention of Jackson's Mill. The mill, in the heart of the site, was not

---

70 Sub-committee meeting to consider Revision of Layout Scheme 3, 28 April 1958. Minutes of the Planning and Development Committee, p. 212. UoMA: TGB/2/5/1.
71 Bowden, *Proposals for the Development of the Manchester College of Science and Technology*, p. 134.
72 Minutes of the Planning and Development Committee, 7 May 1957, Item 8, p. 53. UoMA: TGB/2/5/1; Bowden, *Proposals for the Development of the Manchester College of Science and Technology*, p. 134.
73 Minutes of the Planning and Development Committee, 4 June 1957, Item 2, p. 54; Minutes of the Planning and Development Committee, 16 July, 1957, Item 2, p. 60. UoMA: TGB/2/5/1.
74 *Concentration of Lecture Room Accommodation*. Note attached to Minutes of the Planning and Development Committee, 17 January 1958, p. 156. UoMA: TGB/2/5/1.
75 Muthesius, *The Postwar University*, pp. 88–89.

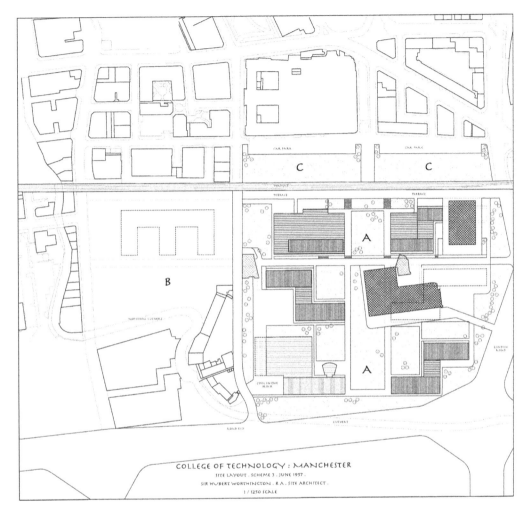

Figure 3.09 Scheme Three.

protected as a heritage asset as one might expect today; it was simply perceived as a stopgap solution to rapidly find accommodation for the expansion of the Chemical Engineering department which, it was felt, could not wait for a new building. The conversion was anticipated to have a useful life of about 'ten or fifteen years'; it is still in use today.[76] The interruption of the north–south axis by the retention of the mill had the effect of implying a series of quads rather than the linear parade of the previous plan. An addition to the mill (Staff

---

76 Bowden, *Proposals for the Development of the Manchester College of Science and Technology*, p. 114.

House) would further define the sequence of quads and reinforce the idea of campus as a social and recreational environment.[77]

The production of the master plans continued through 1960 and 1961, but without any new contribution by Worthington. The drawings simply reflected the detailed design work undertaken by project architects at H.S. Fairhurst and C&S. It was important to keep the master plan up to date as it accompanied the 'unusual' annual submissions to the UGC. Following Sir Hubert Worthington's death in July 1963, Thomas Worthington & Sons were retained as Site Architects, but their responsibilities were limited to the supervision of external works and keeping the master plan drawings up to date.[78]

Strangely, it was the death of Sir Hubert Worthington that prompted the Committee to note his intentions in relation to the campus organisation and the performative aspects of external finishes. The separation of pedestrians and service vehicles by means of an 'outer ring', the planning of an interconnected series of squares and the site layout as the 'agent' to unite the buildings into a cohesive campus were the three guiding principles. 'Floorscape', street furniture, planting, lettering, water and sculpture were designated as coordinated, designed specifically for purpose and intended to 'produce that intangible element, atmosphere, which will leave its mark on the students'.[79] The planting strategy adopted an approach where trees should be 'grouped naturally and should be forest varieties rather than ornamental types' and areas of lawn for recreation were maximised.[80] The job of planning the rest of the campus was handed to Arthur Gibbon who had already overseen the design phases of three new buildings for the College. The architecture of these will be discussed in the following section of this chapter. Before doing so it is worth reflecting on the ultimate campus form, its influences and the degree to which various actors and their relations affected it.

The master plan for the campus created a modern urban park from the ad hoc industrial grain that had grown up around the river. Whilst adopting the word 'quad' when describing external spaces, these were not the enclosed courts of Oxford colleges. The campus was a new modern imposition, as if a clean slate, delimited by existing and proposed infrastructures. Its design did not take account of the existing grain of the streets, but instead sought to address the new and to adjust the existing to suit. The progressive sweep included the re-ordering of nature, as the river was diverted into a concrete culvert, moulding the city through pours and assemblies. The series of towers defined the new

---

77 The events that led to the commission and design of Staff House are discussed further in this chapter.
78 Minutes of the Planning and Development Committee, 10 October 1963, p. 744. UoMA: TGB/2/5/2.
79 Area 'C' Development sub-committee, 14 November 1963. Minutes of the Planning and Development Committee, pp. 846–848. UoMA: TGB/2/5/2.
80 Ibid., p. 848. UoMA: TGB/2/5/2.

formal logic of the site. Gibbon was responsible for the design of four of these and the siting of the fifth. There must be an assertion here that Gibbon, more than Worthington, designed the campus. Gibbon had a good relationship with Bowden and referred to him privately as his 'patron'.[81] They knew one another from C&S's work on the Ferranti factory at Wythenshawe.[82] Most of the architectural precedent for the new buildings came from continental Europe but the precedent for campus planning was more closely tied to America.

That Bowden drew precedent from MIT and the United States in general is significant. In the architectural journals of the early 1950s most new university buildings were from the United States. The architects for the College must have been aware of expansion and master plans in US institutions and in spirit, if not in scale, it is William Wurster's campus plans for UC Berkeley (1951, 1955 and 1956) that can be compared to the College.[83] Wurster was Dean of the School of Architecture and Planning at MIT between 1944 and 1949, before assuming the equivalent post in California. He was 'singled out' by Lewis Mumford as one modern architect who had adopted a regionalist 'idiom'.[84] He corresponded regularly with Alvar Aalto and was responsible for Aalto's appointment as professor at MIT and subsequent commission for the Baker House dormitory block.[85]

In his final year as Dean of MIT, Wurster presented a talk about 'architecture as social art'. It is this central concept that can be seen to underpin the 'utopianist' ideas of the various international post-war higher education programmes.[86] For Bowden, the life of the students and their proximity to both study and amenity was crucial in his conception of a university. Like the

---

81 The comment in relation to patronage was made by Gordon Hodkinson in interview, 1 October 2012. Bowden and Gibbon also travelled together to visit Scandinavian universities. Minutes of the Planning and Development Committee, 29 March 1963, p. 643. UoMA: TGB/2/5/2.

82 This could be one reason for C&S's appointment at the College, but equally the well-connected H.T. Seward may have had his own professional relationship with Bowden.

83 The scale of the two campuses is not comparable; Berkeley had 10,000 students before 1939, and the College had fewer than 1000 full-time students by 1956. There were a further 5000 part-time students engaged in 'non-university' level study. Bowden, *Proposals for the Development of the Manchester College of Science and Technology*, p. 137.

84 See Moran, B.D. (2013) 'Toward a "Nation of Universities" Architecture and Planning Education at MIT circa the 1940s', in Dutta, A., *A Second Modernism. MIT, Architecture and the 'Techno-Social Movement'* (Cambridge, MA: MIT Press), pp. 686–715, p. 687. Moran quotes Mumford, L. (1947) 'The Sky Line: Status Quo', *The New Yorker*, Vol. 23, No. 34, 11 October 1947, pp. 106–109.

85 Marc Treib suggests Wurster's 'influence' on the campus planning at MIT. There was no overarching master plan, but his patronage of Aalto and others meant a break from tradition. Treib, M. (ed.) (1995) *An Everyday Modernism: The Houses of William Wurster* (Berkeley, CA: University of California Press), p. 96, n. 29.

86 Muthesius, *The Postwar University*.

College, Berkeley had to expand into adjacent urban fabric. Each institution protected its character from over-development, despite land premiums, by the preservation of open space – referred to as 'greenbelt' by both.[87] Wurster's plans were developed according to guidance from the Educational Facilities Laboratories and, it is suggested, informed by Gropius's imported form of Modernism at Harvard and MIT.[88] The expansion of Berkeley required 'demolishing many older buildings, and minimizing automobile circulation on the campus through perimeter parking' as well as the tower and open space programme – all strategies that emerged at the College as the campus plans developed in parallel with the new buildings.[89] These characteristics may not have been apparent in Worthington's early drawings, but it is fair to assume that Gibbon was familiar with Wurster's approach. The parallels don't simply extend to the organising devices of the plan, though; halls of residence in Berkeley and in Manchester were designed using bespoke prefabricated systems. Furthermore, the city of Berkeley aided the university expansion in a mutually beneficial deal that resonated with the assignation of land by Manchester Corporation to the College. It was, then, the physical *and* political fabric with which the institute engaged.

There is one image that seems to capture what the architects were trying to do at UMIST. It is a photographic print in an elongated landscape format of a painting by architectural perspective artist Peter Sainsbury [Figure 3.10]. The image is unusual in its format. Notable is the position from where the view was taken; it's from the south and shows the proposed campus with the city of Manchester behind it, as approached from London Road, one of the city's main arteries. It is cleverly composed in two-point perspective, the centre deliberately positioned at the south-east corner of the proposed maths tower. Two darker and domed Victorian towers (Refuge Assurance Building and London Road Fire Station) flank the bright white orthogonal volumes of the campus and the modern city is recognisable by the white slabs of Rodwell House (Douglas Stephen & Partners, 1965) and Piccadilly Station (R.L. Moorcroft, 1964) set in

---

87 Area 'C' Development sub-committee, 3 June 1960. Minutes of the Planning and Development Committee, pp. 579. UoMA: TGB/2/5/1; Wurster, quoted by Allen, from papers 'Campus Planning' and 'Keys to Campus Planning', Wurster, Bernardi & Emmons Collection (1922–74), Environmental Design Archives, College of Environmental Design, University of California, Berkeley. See Allen, P. (2011) 'The End of Modernism', *Journal of the Society of Architectural Historians*, Vol. 70, No. 3, pp. 354–374.
88 The Educational Facilities Laboratories was an organisation founded by the American Institute of Architects in the late 1950s and advocated modern planning and architecture. Muthesius introduces Wurster as having 'imbued' various European influences; Allen introduces the 'organic' nature of the master plan as well as the modernist tendencies in the promotion of towers. See Muthesius, *The Postwar University*, p. 47; Allen, 'The End of Modernism'.
89 Allen, 'The End of Modernism', pp. 359–360.

Figure 3.10 Perspective painting by Peter Sainsbury for Cruickshank & Seward of the new campus. The new white buildings contrast against the soot-blackened Victorian city in the background.

the background on the far right and above the shadowy viaduct that sinks into the campus mass.

Knowing now that Gibbon was charged with the control of the final pieces of the master plan, and that he quickly commissioned a model to specifically examine the massing and composition of the new elements, this accompanying illustration has new purpose. The officers of the City were prominent as they vocalised their ambitions in a new wave of central planning in the 1960s.[90] The Corporation was instrumental in forcing the University to appoint a consultant planner, unhappy with the quality of the buildings erected through the 1950s around Oxford Road. Unfortunately, the University buildings came mostly from the office of H.S. Fairhurst and within the master plan by Sir Hubert Worthington! This must have brought the College development into sharp focus and I believe Gibbon's appointment to oversee the latter stages of planning, and Sainsbury's painting under his direction, is evidence of such.

As the perspective indicates, the city and campus were combined at UMIST. Unlike the other HE institutions in the city, UMIST remains a permeable landscape through which staff, students and public have equal access. Its proximity to Piccadilly railway station means that the campus is regularly traversed. There is more than one route through the group of buildings and spaces, which gives an impression of free choice but the sequence is subtly controlled, by datum, by

---

90 The *1945 Plan* was not ratified until the approval of a Development Plan in 1961. With the approval came an instruction to revisit the central area and a new department was formed under the guidance of the first City Planner of Manchester, John Millar. See Brook, R., and Jarvis, M. (2013) *Trying to Close the Loop: Post-war Ring Roads in Manchester* (Birmingham City University, Centre for Environment and Society Research, Working Paper Series, no. 24).

mass, by edge and by path. The UMIST campus master plan, as built, allowed the interface of 'town and gown' in a way that the proceeding 'streets in the sky' of the University campus would not. The architects understood the importance of green space and in more than one instance low-rise buildings were designed to allow sunlight into the courts. Manchester is historically lacking in parks in the city core and on sunny days the campus doubled as a recreational space for all who chose to use it. Where the campus planning swept away the old grain, the city adjusted itself to the new form.

Formally, the group of high-rise and low-slung buildings combined the city, the square, the street and the park. This was not to preserve the landscape like Capon aimed to do at the University of Essex, but to assimilate ideological aims in the creation of a university society with a site that was a part of a bigger city system.[91] Bowden was certainly influenced by his time in the United States and MIT was one institution to which he repeatedly referred.[92] His cause was not a selfish one, designed to construct his own empire, but a genuine conviction of the power of science and technology to change society. This is clear in his prose and in the extensive research required to reinforce these values in his published works. Even as Imperial College, Manchester and Glasgow were expanding and after introduction of the CAT programme, Bowden still felt that provision for the sciences lagged behind advances in continental Europe and continued to champion them.[93] The fact that models of education and architectural inspiration drew on international precedent is testament to the pioneering spirit within which UMIST came to be. But it is also symptomatic of the lack of progressive design of curriculum and construction in British universities at the time, a situation observed by Robert Gardener-Medwin in 1956:

> One also looks to the universities to adopt a progressive attitude to architecture ... Unfortunately, however, most universities seem to be puzzled by modern architecture and are therefore tempted to play safe.[94]

As we will see in the following section of this chapter, the architecture sponsored by the College and Bowden challenged this view of British university architecture and definitely sprang from social and scientific advance.

---

91 See Lubbock, J. (2002) 'The Counter-Modernist Sublime: the Campus of the University of Essex', *Twentieth Century Architecture*, No. 6, *The Sixties: Life: Style: Architecture* (London: The Twentieth Century Society), pp. 106–118.
92 See Bowden, B.V. (1960) 'Too Few Academic Eggs', *Higher Education Quarterly*, Volume 14, Issue 1, November, pp. 7–23 and Bowden, *Proposals for the Development of the Manchester College of Science and Technology*.
93 Bowden, 'Too Few Academic Eggs', p. 12.
94 Gardner-Medwin, R. (1956) 'The Decline of Architecture', *Higher Education Quarterly*, Vol. 10, no. 2, pp. 132–142; p. 135.

Site, architecture, form and grain

The buildings at UMIST are often referred to as a group and it is in the decisive ordering of the site that its strengths as a piece of modernist cityscape are most evident. In terms of the overall appearance of the development, the Committee prepared a design-briefing document entitled 'Some canons of good design'.[95] In a manner befitting a technological institution, the functional demands of spaces were assumed as the primary organising factor in the design of buildings. However, aesthetics were also of concern and referred to under the banner of 'pleasing appearance'. This short treatise extended to the massing and proportion of new buildings, a tacit instruction as to the honesty of facades and to a simplicity informed by economy, lack of 'fuss' and the use of modern materials that would not deteriorate with age in the Manchester climate. One clause stipulated, '[t]he use of modern materials, constructions and techniques is desirable' but also that 'they must have a raison d'etre [sic] other than a mere exercise in technological ingenuity'.[96] As the master planning ran alongside the design of the buildings to populate it, form and appearance were decisions reached by consensus.

The first such agreement hinged upon the retention of Jackson's Mill in the centre of the campus. Delays to the Manchester Corporation Bill meant that funds from the UGC were reallocated to protect the College building programme for 1959.[97] In quick and decisive mode it was acknowledged that a small addition to the mill was the only construction project that could be achieved within the allotted period and for the designated sum.[98] Retaining the mill redefined the proportions of the open spaces envisaged in Worthington's early plans. The small extension was considered to 'form a more satisfactory southern boundary to the second court'.[99] It consolidated the implied squares and created stronger orthogonal boundaries [Figure 3.11]. Its development was viewed as an important element of the overall master plan and can be seen in Scheme 5 [Figure 3.12] adjoining the mill in the centre of the plan. The plan form of 'Staff House building with cloister and concourse' was intended to complete the two self-contained 'quads'.[100] Here is the traditional language of an

---

95 Note attached to Minutes of the Planning and Development Committee, 19 September 1957, p. 83. UoMA: TGB/2/5/1.
96 Ibid., para. 3.
97 The realignment of the culvert needed an Act of Parliament and if passed before CPOs had been completed would have artificially inflated prices on outstanding acquisitions.
98 Meeting of Staff House Exploratory Committee, 24 November 1958. Minutes of the Planning and Development Committee, p. 297. UoMA: TGB/2/5/1.
99 Sub-committee meeting to consider Revision of Layout Scheme 3, 28 April 1958. Minutes of the Planning and Development Committee, p. 212. UoMA: TGB/2/5/1.
100 Worthington raised the accommodation to create a colonnaded cloister for sheltered transition between the Lecture Room Block and the proposed Students' Union. Raising

Figure 3.11 Staff House (L) (Hubert Worthington, 1960), with the Renold Building (Cruickshank & Seward, 1962) in the background. The two buildings flanked the first inner quad of the campus.

Oxbridge College – cloister and quad – in combination with the development of contemporary modern architecture. It might be argued that the 'Some canons' treaty was a dilution of modernism for the production of acceptable mainstream architecture – Staff House was the first new building to be completed on the campus and could well fit this classification.

The following year, however, saw the completion of perhaps the most striking structure, the Renold Building, designed by Gibbon, assisted by Gordon Hodkinson.[101] It was intended that this building brought together disparate, department-related lecture rooms of the College to one central location, the first such building in the UK.[102]

---

the staff areas afforded a greater sense of privacy and had the dual function of masking 'a drab area of old and irregular brickwork' on the existing mill. The construction was steel framed with precast concrete floor slabs. The external walls were metal units infilled with glass or wall panels as required by the corresponding internal function. Its façade was described as an 'uncompromising frame of big squares', but it is its presence and formal configuration, rather than appearance, that is of note here. Minutes of the Planning and Development Committee, p. 403, 404. UoMA: TGB/2/5/1; Hartwell, *Manchester*, p. 125.

101 Interview with Gordon Hodkinson. Hale, 1 October 2012.
102 'Lecture Room Building', *The Builder*, 10 June 1960, p. 1092.

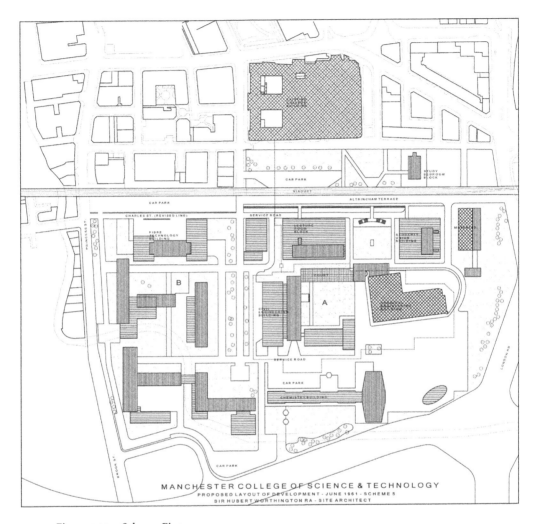

Figure 3.12   Scheme Five.

The lecture room block (Renold Building)

A scheme for the lecture room block, 'comprising eight storeys', was proposed in May 1957.[103] The overall master plan was still in flux and responsibility was handed to C&S to resolve the finer details of siting in consultation with Worthington. In agreeing the alignment and general form, the architects

---

103   Minutes of the Planning and Development Committee, 7 May 1957, Item 3, p. 43. UoMA: TGB/2/5/1.

consolidated the idea of 'quadrangles' as organising devices for a sequence of buildings.[104] The scheme eventually took the form of a podium and tower and is one of the earliest examples of this arrangement in the country.[105] The podium housed large lecture theatres and the tower contained smaller theatres and seminar rooms. The angled east façade of the tower was the result of an acoustic study and followed the profile of the rear of the vertically stacked smaller theatres. The tower was positioned as far away from the adjacent railway viaduct as possible and the podium was acoustically insulated by virtue of the significant topographical shift between the viaduct, the parallel street and the rest of the campus to the south.[106] The provision of two entrances, one at first floor level to the north side and one at ground level to the south, exploited this difference in datum. It also required the provision of a bridge link from Altrincham Street that traversed the site service road below.

Although the Renold Building was the second building to be completed it had a longer period of gestation than the rapidly delivered Staff House. As such, the treatment of its façades was a forebear to the rest of the campus architecture. The building was first discussed in terms of its appearance after H.T. Seward tabled artist's impressions [Figure 3.13]. Comments recorded in the minutes centred upon the style of the elevations, described as 'contemporary'.[107] Worthington emphasised the importance of the decisions attached to the lecture room block as 'it would tend to set the general style for the whole of our development'. The Committee was 'strongly in favour' of C&S's treatment 'rather than an adherence to more traditional lines'.[108] The assembled group also decided that it was not necessary to finish each new building in the same material; harmony could be achieved in other ways, through the formal association of elements and the 'treatment of paths, paving and retaining walls which would draw the campus together'.[109]

---

104 Minutes of the Planning and Development Committee, 10 April 1958, Items 8 and 11, pp. 186–187. UoMA: TGB/2/5/1.

105 Skidmore, Owings & Merrill's Lever Building (1952) is generally acknowledged as the first of this type. John Madin's Post and Mail building has also been cited as an early UK example, but was not completed until 1964. See Clawley, A. (2011) *John Madin* (London: RIBA, English Heritage).

106 Gibbon, W.A. (1963) 'Manchester College of Technology', *The Guardian*, 9 April 1963, p. 12.

107 Minutes of the Planning and Development Committee, 16 July 1957, Item 9, p. 60. UoMA: TGB/2/5/1.

108 In the first instance the preferred cladding for the first new building was Travertine marble. In the event that the UGC vetoed this choice then a cheaper alternative, Portland stone, was envisaged. Ibid.

109 Report of meeting held 29 July 1958. Transcript. Minutes of the Planning and Development Committee, p. 262. UoMA: TGB/2/5/1.

IN ADVANCE OF PROGRESS

Figure 3.13   Perspective painting of the design for the Renold Building.

Members of the Committee were invited to inspect other sites before making final decisions about the stylistic treatment.[110] A special meeting was held to discuss the material finishes for the lecture room block and one outcome from these inspections appears to have affected material selection: Sir Charles Renold stated 'that there appeared to be a general opinion in favour of Portland stone'.[111] Any exposed concrete was white, to match the stone, as were the adjustable louvres on the south façade, deliberately manufactured in white fibre-cement.[112] The louvres are long gone, but one anecdote concerning their manufacture is redolent of the threshold between craft and mass production so encountered during the

---

110   Visits to ICI facilities were seen as able to provide insight for new technical spaces. Serge Chermayeff's celebrated laboratories (1936) at Blackley in Manchester were examined by the Committee, as were the new buildings of ICI's Plastics Division at Welwyn (E.D. Jefferiss Mathews, 1955). Minutes of the Planning and Development Committee, 19 September 1957, Item 6, p. 78. UoMA: TGB/2/5/1.

111   Minutes of the Planning and Development Committee, 11 October 1957, Item 7(ii), p. 107. UoMA: TGB/2/5/1. Report of meeting held 29 July 1958. Transcript. Minutes of the Planning and Development Committee, p. 262. UoMA: TGB/2/5/1.

112   Report of meeting held 29 July 1958. Transcript. Minutes of the Planning and Development Committee, p. 263. UoMA: TGB/2/5/1.

Figure 3.14 *Metamorphosis*, Victor Pasmore. Painted by Pasmore and assistants in 1968 in response to charges of a lack of focus on culture and humanities in the institution.

mid-century. Project architect, Gordon Hodkinson, visited the cement factory charged with making the louvres and drew the S-curve of the profile on the factory floor with a piece of chalk, this was traced over and used as the template from which the louvres were formed! Modern did not always mean machined, or cold or monochromatic. Gibbon introduced a blue band of faience to the exterior of the ground floor, subtle colouration to the spandrel panels and proposed the use of colour internally, to be glimpsed from the outside. These materials and colours informed much of the proceeding development.

In the interior Gibbon wanted the vivacity of the student population to provide life and colour. The Committee embraced this approach and the large circulation areas on the ground and first floor were seen as a 'valuable aid to creating a communal life'.[113] These spaces were treated neutrally with contrasting polished wood and simple rough concrete and eventually provided the backdrop for a period, abstract mural, *Metamorphosis* by Victor Pasmore, in the lower of the two halls [Figure 3.14].[114] The visual separation of the tower was achieved by using elegant birds-mouth beams that facilitated the continuous

---

113 Concentration of Lecture Room Accommodation. Note attached to Minutes of the Planning and Development Committee, 17 January 1958, p. 157. UoMA: TGB/2/5/1.

114 The Edwin Abbey Memorial Trust were consulted on funds to provide a mural in the Civil Engineering building in 1961. Vincent Harris inspected the site on behalf of the trust and rejected the proposed space due to the poor quality of the space and its daylight conditions. The idea was not lost, though, and after Pasmore inspected the

Figure 3.15   Bird's-mouth beams and open staircase.

clerestory window at the junction of the two formal elements. These 'cantilever pre-stressed reinforced concrete beams' were sufficiently experimental for the College, the architect and the engineer to test the solution on a model in the Department of Structural Engineering and the results were published in a journal.[115] The subcommittee commented that '[a]n unusual feature of these beams is the slot which runs full length on both sides and into the cantilevered splayed ends. The slot is an architectural feature' [Figure 3.15].[116]

The most prominent device for display and circulation, however, was the stair tower, a perpendicular projection of perilously thin glazing bars. This element was part of the evolving modern language of the firm, had its predecessors in their buildings at Wythenshawe and its growing family in the College and University buildings to come. Here, it was purposefully employed to encourage

---

site himself and selected an area in which to work the funds were provided. Minutes of the Planning and Development Committee, 10 November 1961, p. 235. UoMA: TGB/2/5/2; Minutes of the Civil Engineering Building sub-committee, 7 June 1962. the Minutes of the Planning and Development Committee, p. 375. UoMA: TGB/2/5/2. Minutes of the Planning and Development Committee, 1965, p. 174. UoMA: TGB/2/5/3. Campus Development sub-committee, 12 November 1965. Minutes of the Planning and Development Committee, pp. 509–510.

115   Smith, R.B.L., and Merchant, W. (1956) 'Critical Loads of Tall Building Frames', *The Structural Engineer*, No. 34, pp. 284–292.

116   Meeting of the LRB sub-committee, 14 September 1960, p. 621. UoMA: TGB/2/5/1.

students to use the stairs, by affording great views, and in turn put the students on display.[117] Conscious that the lid of the podium would be exposed to those ascending, Gibbon applied a diamond check pattern in bonded gravel to the roof and positioned rooflights in a deliberate composition. In a final flourish for the exterior, and with a nod to Niemeyer and Nervi, Gibbon instructed Gordon Hodkinson, in full view of the design team, to define the curved profile of the rooftop plant enclosure. With a single freehand sweep Hodkinson made his mark and was then instructed to set out the curve![118] Strong volumetric elements that housed plant equipment on roofs were another hallmark of C&S schemes across Manchester and further afield.

The Civil Engineering building

Funding provided by the UGC affected the sequence of construction. This was exemplified by Fairhurst's proposals for the Civil Engineering building. The sub-committee controlling its development thought the design lent itself more readily to completion in one operation, but also felt the UGC might wish to see this extended over several years.[119] The result was composed of three distinct formal elements, a tower with two workshop blocks flanking it that could be built in one or more phases as required. The nine-storey tower was built on a north–south axis, perpendicular to that of the Renold Building and enclosed another quad. It was serviced from the west and the south, to enhance the traffic-free qualities of the site. The structure of the tower as envisaged by the Project Architect was to 'express its function externally', in line with design guidance.[120] The top two floors housed mechanical plant and a rooftop laboratory. These were expressed by means of material differentiation and clad in copper, much like other Fairhurst schemes along Brunswick Street for the University.[121] Bowden suggested the use of new buildings as a study aid for understanding the 'science of building construction'. A hut was provided for students on site and further studies were published by academics as the scheme went up.[122] This idea permeated the architecture of the completed scheme, the structure was 'exposed ... so that it can itself be used as a teaching aid' and the veneers varied on the doors of the Building Department 'to include all the commonly used timbers'.[123]

---

117 Interview with Gordon Hodkinson. Hale, 1 October 2012.
118 Ibid.
119 Minutes of the Civil Engineering Block Planning Sub-Committee, 11 October 1957, Item 3, p. 102. Minutes of the Planning and Development Committee. UoMA: TGB/2/5/1.
120 Ibid.
121 Ibid.
122 Minutes of the Planning and Development Committee, 21 January 1957, Item 3(h), p. 8. UoMA: TGB/2/5/1.
123 'Civil Engineering Building for Manchester College of Science and Technology', *Official Architecture and Planning*, May 1963, pp. 417, 420.

However, technological education moved as rapidly as the industries it served and Bowden often speculated on possible future subject areas.[124] Aware that the building might be used for alternative functions before the end of its life, the architects designed the standard floor plates to be as 'flexible as possible'.[125] Despite designing for flexibility, the rather crude separation of the building's formal elements in response to UGC funding streams inhibited the imagination of the architects. Whilst the Civil Engineering Building refers to earlier work by the firm, Fairhurst's, unlike C&S, seemed encumbered by their stylistic history.[126]

The dormitory block (Chandos Hall of Residence)

C&S were appointed as Project Architects for both the Students' Union and dormitory block in 1960. There was very little in the way of research into halls of residence in the UK, despite calls over a decade earlier for more investigation and experimentation.[127] Chandos Hall was one of the earliest halls in the country and the first to assume a tower form [Figure 3.16]. The lead here may also have been taken from Berkeley, where three nine-storey towers had been completed by 1960 following a competition-winning design of 1957 by Warnecke and Warnecke.[128] Gibbon travelled to Scandinavia with Bowden to examine similar schemes and visited Weeks Hall (Sheppard Robson, 1957) at Imperial College. They learned that the ancillary spaces of kitchen and laundry were more important to the students than the architects had anticipated. These spaces were carefully considered for Chandos and the social life of the kitchen was part of the ergonomic study [Figure 3.17]. Common rooms were viewed as under-utilised and the impression was that there was no need for

---

124 Bowden would appear to have been the driving force behind imagining the need for new types of spaces to accommodate new fields. At one point he specified 'Aeronautical Engineering, Nuclear Power, Communication Engineering and Radio, Electronic Measurements, Production Engineering, Polymers and Plastics' as evolving areas of research with which the College should be associated. Minutes of the Planning and Development Committee, 5 March 1957, Item 4, p. 20. UoMA: TGB/2/5/1.
125 Ibid., p. 417.
126 This building and those on Brunswick Street for the University are clearly of a family. The tone, materiality and detail of each are developments of earlier architectural language developed by H.S. Fairhurst in the pre-war period. Fairhurst were still very much a family firm at this point. See Whittam, W. (1986) *Fairhursts Architects: The History of a Manchester Practice* (Manchester: Department of History of Art and Design, Manchester Polytechnic).
127 'These circumstances would have told less if there had been any accepted theory or philosophy of Halls. There has hardly as yet been time for a philosophy to take shape: the experimentation is still recent and on a small scale', Murray, J (1949) 'Halls of Residence in Universities', *Higher Education Quarterly* Volume 3, Issue 2, February, pp. 563–570.
128 Allen, 'The End of Modernism', p. 361.

Figure 3.16 Chandos Hall viewed from the stairwell of the Renold Building.

Figure 3.17 Student-shared kitchen in Chandos Hall.

a television room as 'facilities were made available in the Union Building'.[129] Halls of residence were considered in light of the UGC's Niblett report, which emphasised the educational benefit for students who lived on campus, a view that was novel at the time, but aligned with Bowden's US experiences.[130]

Chandos Hall of residence appeared to stand alone, almost monolithic. This was a product of its situation and its construction. British Railways (BR) demanded an easement of six metres from the viaduct and space was maintained around all sides of the base at the behest of the fire authorities. Gibbon proposed a cross-wall construction using reinforced concrete and was keen to use 'prefabricated methods of construction, as far as possible'.[131] This was a reaction to earlier difficulties in keeping labourers, especially sub-contracted joiners, on site. There was a general shortage of skilled labour and construction was booming in Manchester. The use of prefabrication made for an honest, if repetitive, façade that was not universally popular. Its white gridded surface grew from the contrasting void of a yard that was retained on three sides. The site and construction method created a formal tension between the building, its hollow seat and the massive viaduct. The elegant stair, again articulated as its own filigree, glazed tower, was delicately engineered. Views across the city from the head of the stairwell were a full, and breathtaking, 270°. The completed building had thirteen residential floors with a mixture of single and twin rooms, served by communal kitchens. The top floor housed the warden's residence with access to a roof terrace and a larger common room. So new was the building type that full-scale mock-ups of study bedrooms were built inside a room in the Sackville Building. The scheme was criticised for the monotony of the elevation but praised as a successful prototype for living in a communal way.[132]

Students' Union (Barnes Wallis Building)

Much of the early construction, beyond the quickfire provision of teaching accommodation in Jackson's Mill, was about the idea of campus. The Renold Building housed lecture theatres that were shared between disciplines and Chandos Hall brought students together and close to their place of learning. The third of C&S's white concrete buildings was also associated with the community

---

[129] Despite this impression, the student cuncil soon lobbied for a television after the halls were occupied. Third meeting of the Students' Union building planning sub-committee. 5 May 1960. Minutes of the Planning and Development Committee, p. 542. UoMA: TGB/2/5/1.

[130] Niblett, W.R. University Grants Committee (1957) *Report of the Sub-Committee on Halls of Residence* (London: HMSO).

[131] Third meeting of the Students' Union building planning sub-committee. 5 May 1960. Minutes of the Planning and Development Committee, p. 647. UoMA: TGB/2/5/1.

[132] 'Hall of Residence, Manchester University; Architects: Cruickshank & Seward', *Architects' Journal*, 29 April 1964, pp. 979–990.

of the College. It was an additional hall of residence combined with a students union. Its position was largely determined by the completion of the enclosure of the quad and the perimeter service road and its form was part of the overall site composition.[133] The massing of the podium was 'related to that ... of the nearby Lecture Room Block' and the tower designed to be 'in balance' with those built and proposed.[134] The Union and residences shared a refectory. The Union connected directly to the halls, to Altrincham Street via a bridge and a link to the staff house was also formed. The scheme was about connecting the campus and its occupants and addressing the heart of the campus, the quad it completed: Gibbon referred to it as 'the Great Lawn'.[135]

As the overall scheme developed, demands to increase student numbers met with the UGC's objectives to reduce unit costs for construction. To try and explain the pressures of development specific to the College, UGC staff were invited to visit the site to see the constraints for themselves.[136] The changing relationship and tightening audits and budgets began to affect the perception of design in the eyes of the Committee. The deep projecting beams of the main hall [Figure 3.18] were designed to eliminate the need for columns and also to control glare from direct sunlight. Their illustration at design stage intrigued the Committee but also created concern that the UGC, without a good explanation of their purpose, might view the beams as architectural frivolity and not see the need for them.[137] Design gestures like this and the expressive use of volumetric forms were not only a motif of C&S's buildings, but more generally can be seen to typify mainstream modernism. Often limited by budget in commercial or provincial settings, the simple modularity of orthogonal, framed buildings risked monotony. Any opportunity to interrupt this with justifiable architectural intervention was seized upon. In the case of C&S stairwells, plant enclosures and lift heads all offered such opportunities [Figure 3.19].

It was, however, such formal flourishes and their composition that turned modest conjunctions into finely assembled volumes. Part of the west wall of the tower above the Students' Union building was angled to provide more space to the kitchen areas. This in turn allowed a vertically glazed slot to mirror that of the stairwell on either side of the solid wall of the lift shaft. The solid element, flanked by the two visual voids, terminated in an open flourishing gesture at the head of the lift motor room, described as 'a somewhat novel treatment'.[138]

---

133 Students' Union Building Planning Sub-committee, 27 February 1961. p. 58. Minutes of the Planning and Development Committee, UoMA: TGB/2/5/2.
134 Minutes of the Planning and Development Committee, 26 September 1961, p. 629. UoMA: TGB/2/5/2.
135 Ibid.
136 Ibid, 26 September 1961, pp. 221–222. UoMA: TGB/2/5/2.
137 Minutes of the Planning and Development Committee, p. 384. UoMA: TGB/2/5/2.
138 Minutes of the Student Union Building Plannig sub-committee, 25 March 1963. Minutes of the Planning and Development Committee, p. 606. UoMA: TGB/2/5/2.

IN ADVANCE OF PROGRESS

Figure 3.18   Interior of main hall with sculptural lighting units by Anthony Yeomans.

Figure 3.19   The stair and lift tower of Wright Robinson Hall.

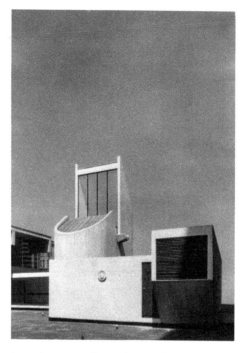

Figure 3.20 Expressive volumes on the roofscape of the Barnes Wallis Building.

These subtle formal alterations distinguished this tower from Chandos, despite the use of the same prefabricated façade modules – it was possibly a response to criticism of the monotony of the earlier scheme. There was more than a hint of Corbusier in the up-ended arrow-like extrusion. It was complemented by further expressive volumes on the roof of the Union building where, as originally intended, students would be able to use the space as a terrace. The chamfered extruded pill form of the secondary stair and the wedge and cylinder of the air intake and extract were simultaneously functionalist and formalist [Figure 3.20].

The southern edge

As the precise alignment of Link Road 17/7 was already determined, the Corporation had an interest in how the buildings on the southern edge of the campus would meet it. City Engineer and Surveyor, Rowland Nicholas was close to retirement by this stage, but was nonetheless prepared to assert the position of the local authority. The proposal for the Chemistry building shown in Scheme 5 [Figure 3.12] was subject to continual adjustment as Nicholas deemed its siting and appearance unsatisfactory. A lack of consultation by the Project Architect, Fairhurst, its lack of density and the manner by which it precluded the full development of Area A, all combined to delay the design phase. Nicholas viewed the form of the southern edge of the campus as integral to the aspect from the new road; he insisted on 'unification' in terms of appearance and 'maximum capacity' in terms of density. As a direct response to Nicholas's demands Gibbon tabled the first designs for a tower on the south-east corner of the site that would become the Maths and Social Sciences building.[139] The scheme presented by Gibbon followed instruction from the Committee; however, Gibbon sought advice from Nicholas before preparing his massing proposal, which extended to the eastern boundary of London Road and included a 'two or three storey building'.[140] None of these proposed buildings had assigned functions and at this stage Gibbon's intervention was a formal sculptural exercise. Gibbon was astute enough to have consulted Nicholas independently of the activities of the Building Committee and, with solution in hand, effectively imposed his personal authority on the continued development of the master plan. The Committee were of the opinion that Gibbon's speculative massing for a building would 'no doubt it will properly fit into the academic requirements of the College when they become specific'![141] This was not a conventional method by which to procure.

Specificity did not aid Fairhurst's in their extended attempts to reconcile the requirements of the Chemistry Department with a new building. They were appointed in February 1961.[142] The brief was loose from the beginning with only a schedule of areas to work from. Fairhurst's first proposal was the outline shown in Scheme 5 and his approach, on paper, was not dissimilar to Gibbon's. He was conscious of the relationship to the other buildings and that the proximity to Link Road 17/7 meant 'design and massing were ... more than ordinarily important'.[143] The minutes of the Committee show an extended and tortured development of the Chemistry Building, commissioned earlier than the Maths and Social Sciences department, but delivered concurrently. Part of the reason for this was that the scheme was actually too large for the remaining portion of Site A and Site B had not yet been released for development.[144] It was Gibbon's massing study that forced the recommencement of Fairhurst's design phase in 1963 and Fairhurst was instructed to consult with Gibbon over the prospective

---

139 Minutes of the Planning and Development Committee, 7 February 1963, p. 518. UoMA: TGB/2/5/2.
140 This was eventually realised as the Chemical Engineering Pilot Plant by H.S. Fairhurst and Sons. Ibid., p. 520.
141 Ibid., p. 521.
142 Chemistry Building Planning sub-committee, 10 Feb 1961, p. 61. Minutes of the Planning and Development Committee. UoMA: TGB/2/5/3.
143 Ibid., p. 63.
144 The release of Area B was wrapped up in the Manchester Corporation Bill 1958 and the route of the Medlock culvert.

Figure 3.21   The Faraday Building.

siting and mass of the unresolved scheme.[145] The Chemistry Building was named the Faraday Building upon its completion in 1967. It was unlike other Fairhurst projects of the time and its white concrete mimicked that of the C&S buildings. How much influence Gibbon exerted over the material specification of the Faraday Building is open to speculation. Perhaps indicative of a lack of confidence, Fairhurst invited artist Antony Hollaway to prepare designs for textured precast panels for the solid gable walls of the tower [Figure 3.21]. Hollaway went beyond his remit and provided instructions for the entire façade.[146] The Faraday building was constructed in two blocks, with a link bridge over one of the exit spurs from Mancunian Way. The campus planning and the aims of the city to create greater urban mobility came together in an unusual form that was emblematic of the complex relations of wholesale urban renewal.

---

145   Minutes of the Planning and Development Committee, 29 March 1963, p. 574. UoMA: TGB/2/5/2.
146   Chemistry Building Planning sub-committee, 1 April 1963. Minutes of the Planning and Development Committee, pp. 642–643. UoMA: TGB/2/5/2.

The Maths and Social Science Building and Electrical Engineering (Ferranti) Building

The last of C&S's building on the campus Area A was 'positioned to form a strong visual feature as one proceeds towards the city'.[147] The Maths and Social Science Building sub-committee was convened in June 1963.[148] The department was seen as a convenient fit to the tower already proposed by Gibbon. The Electrical Engineering department was housed adjacent and the two were commissioned together and included in the same contract, which was seen as expedient for construction and efficient in the eyes of the UGC.[149] The perspective [Figure 3.13] showed the considered balance of the composition, but, despite his newfound prominence amidst the Committee, Gibbon had to accommodate the recommendations of others.[150] Restrictions on the height of the Electrical Engineering Building imposed by the City meant that the lecture theatres attached to the department had to be situated elsewhere in the new construction.[151] The base of the tower was considered, but the diminishing UGC cost targets demanded ruthless standardisation and it was cheaper to build the lecture theatres in a standalone, adjoining block and keep the tower simple. The lower elements flanked the tower in its pivotal position at the south-east corner of the campus and the bright white assembly announced the advance of science and technology to those arriving to the city from the south [Figure 3.22].

Formally, the cluster was the least expressive and the most orthogonal of the group of white buildings by C&S. The structure of the tower was honest, but not explicit. The in-situ cast, structural elements, characterised by board marked concrete, were connected by precast sheer wall panels. It was possible to read both on the façade, but the elegant composition of the rectilinear volumes created an assemblage that was more than the sum of its parts. The solid mass of the lecture block at the foot of the tower formally exposed its internal function with projecting sloping faces to the east and west walls. The two-storey Ferranti Building was engineered to shut out noise from the traffic running parallel to its

---

147 'Institute of Science and Technology, University of Manchester; Architects: Cruickshank & Seward', *Architecture North West*, April 1968, p. 14.
148 Minutes of the Maths and Social Science Building sub-committee, 7 August 1963. Minutes of the Planning and Development Committee, p. 793. UoMA: TGB/2/5/2.
149 Minutes of the Maths and Social Science Building sub-committee, 26 September 1963. Minutes of the Planning and Development Committee, p. 796. UoMA: TGB/2/5/2.
150 Gibbon had to consult Hugh Wilson and John Millar. Minutes of the Planning and Development Committee, 3 December 1963, p. 812. UoMA: TGB/2/5/2.
151 The Committee were conscious of the demands of the authority and commissioned a study model to address the massing of the buildings in context alongside their primary concern of layout. Minutes of the Planning and Development Committee, 3 December 1963, p. 818. UoMA: TGB/2/5/2.

Figure 3.22   Maths and Social Sciences Building.

long axis and its height determined to permit maximum daylight to the lawns beyond. The long block terminated as it met the High Voltage Laboratory, for which Gibbon originally proposed a dome. It is possible that American precedent again informed this inclusion: Eero Saarinen's domed auditorium and cylindrical chapel at MIT (1950–55) had caused a stir in the architectural press.[152] Ultimately, the gesture was deemed inefficient in its provision of useful areas and expensive in its construction, a rectilinear, metal clad volume was realised in its place.

Chemical Engineering Pilot Plant

Just to the north of low lecture block Fairhurst realised their most adventurous project on the campus. The Chemical Engineering Pilot Plant (1966), and the adjoining sculptural wall by Antony Hollaway, formed the eastern boundary of the campus.[153] The bold coloured volumes of the roof-mounted cooling plant had a plastic quality. The floating fluid shapes above contrasted against the orthogonal form below. The building was effectively divided in two: this was expressed clearly by the use of curtain wall glazing to one end and blue engineering brick

---

152   'Saarinen Challenges the Rectangle', *Architectural Forum*, June 1953, pp. 126–133.
153   www.c20society.org.uk/botm/hollaway-wall-manchester/ [Accessed 19 March 2014].

Figure 3.23 Chemical Engineering Pilot Plant.

to the other [Figure 3.23]. The glazed section was open through all four floors, designed for undertaking large-scale experiments and handling big pieces of scientific equipment. It was intended to exhibit the students' experiments to those passing on London Road, perhaps with the earlier Daily Express Building (Sir Owen Williams, 1938) in mind, whose printing machines were on display to passers-by on Great Ancoats Street.[154] Specific colours defined the utility service runs, five years before Rogers and Piano designed the Pompidou Centre. Without explicit design intent, the filigree lattice of kit, transoms and mullions and the reflective nature of the glass provided a visual sense of science and its complexity. At each floor a narrow band within the curtain wall extended laterally across the brick façade to provide clerestory windows to the labs and offices. This lightened the whole building by defining the masonry as cladding rather than structure. The entire block was grounded by the use of a plinth wall at grade that extended to enclose the service yard. This was the most functionally defined of Fairhurst's schemes and yet the most progressively modern.

The first wave of campus development was completed by 1967. The architectural language established within the campus was evident in all the schemes that followed, despite tightening budgets. Gibbon also had a final contribution to make. The very first formal proposal for the campus described in this chapter

---

154 Chemical Engineering Extension Building Planning sub-committee, 3 September 1963. Minutes of the Planning and Development Committee, p. 803. UoMA: TGB/2/5/2.

Figure 3.24   The Renold Building viewed from beneath the Sir Hubert Worthington Stair.

was the stair from Altrincham Street to the first quad. The Site Architect, Worthington, was responsible for the design of this stair. As the master plan developed and the lower-level service road required bridging, Worthington and Gibbon were to collaborate over the design of the bridges to ensure harmonious style.[155] Following Worthington's death Gibbon assumed the role of designer for the stair, as well as the bridges to the Renold Building and Union [Figure 3.24]. He originally proposed the curved sweeping flights onto his 'great lawn' to be without a handrail – a beguiling Brazilian style gesture, clearly referential to Niemeyer.[156] The handrails were added and made from bronze. The rail at the head of the flight, from where one has a commanding view across the campus, was inscribed 'The Sir Hubert Worthington Stair'.

The joint scheme

A joint planning exercise with the University brought about some change to the continuing development of the College. Discussion concerning the provision of

---

155   Area 'C' Development sub-committee, 16 September 1960, p. 658. Minutes of the Planning and Development Committee, p. 780. UoMA: TGB/2/5/2.
156   Area 'C' Development sub-committee, 16 July 1963. Ibid., p. 780.

residential accommodation for the expanding student body of the University began in the late 1950s. The expansion of teaching spaces was aligned with growing numbers and as talks began in 1960, both the College and the University had their own development plans. By March 1961, the University had already completed as much as £2.5 million worth of construction work and had more programmed, up to 1965.[157] Both institutions wanted to expand, more or less towards one another. A shortage of housing meant that the sites earmarked by the joint committee, which contained mostly run-down residential property, were a political issue. The continuing lack of statutory approval for the 1951 Development Plan meant that their land use was not formally designated and negotiation with the council became necessary. Rowland Nicholas advised that a joint scheme for 'city development' would strengthen the case of each institution.[158] In response, Bowden's directive was that a well-resolved and boldly comprehensive architectural scheme would help to sway the City when making their decision.[159] He asked Worthington, Fairhurst and C&S, each to prepare designs for the portion of the site that the College needed for its 'Student Village', north of Mancunian Way. The C&S version was published in the proceedings of the Annual Meeting of the British Association for the Advancement of Science, held in Manchester in 1962.[160] A model of the same scheme was commissioned by the University to integrate with their revised plan by Worthington.[161] Surviving drawings and photographs of models [Figure 3.25] show C&S's third-wave mainstream modern approach that indiscriminately adopted as much Corbusier as it did Niemeyer – Bowden also funded Gibbon's travel to Stockholm to look at Swedish halls of residence.[162]

---

157 Vice-Chancellor's notes for Meeting with the Representatives if the City Council Concerning Residential Accommodation for the College of technology, 8 March 1961. Held at Manchester University Archives. Ref: VCA/7/386 Folder 1.

158 Charles Renold, *Joint Scheme for the Designation by the City of Additional Land for Development*. Minutes of the Planning and Development Committee, pp. 562–564. UoMA: TGB/2/5/1.

159 All three firms, C&S, Worthington and Fairhurst prepared plans for the area to the south of Link Road 17/7 in 1960. University of Manchester and the Manchester College of Science and Technology (1960) *Joint Submission to Manchester Corporation Respecting Future Developments*. JRUL Store: C149352.

160 The plan was included as an appendix to the handbook to accompany the 'meeting'. British Association for the Advancement of Science. Manchester Local Executive Committee (1962) *Manchester and its Region: A Survey Prepared for the Meeting [of the British Association for the Advancement of Science] held in Manchester, August 29 to September 5, 1962* (Manchester: Manchester University Press for the British Association).

161 In written correspondence with John Sheard, December 2008–October 2009.

162 Letter from B.V. Bowden Principal of the Manchester College of Science and Technology to W. Mansfield Cooper, 10 May 1960. Held at Manchester University Archives. Ref: VCA/7/386 Folder 1.

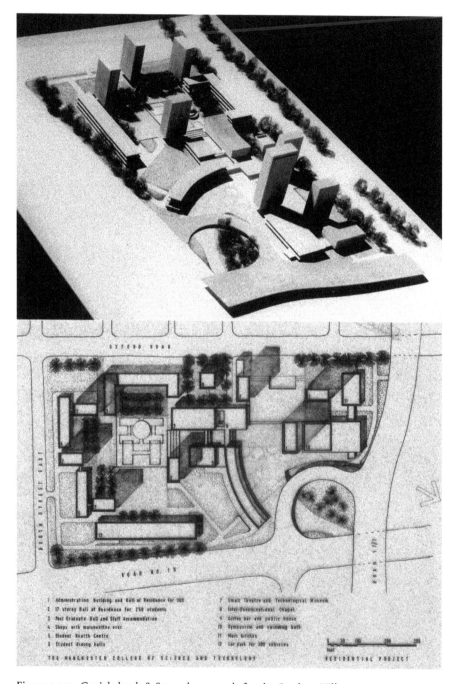

Figure 3.25 Cruickshank & Seward proposals for the Student Village.

The student village itself was intended to continue the spirit of campus, community and shared space already established on the main site. As well as halls, it was to provide a small theatre and technological museum, interdenominational chapel, coffee bar, pub, gym, swimming baths and health centre. The open space between the buildings was deliberately varied in scale and level. C&S also speculated on the form of the future BBC North HQ building, which was shown as a contemporary tower and podium form, with a substantial inner courtyard. By contrast, Worthington's revised scheme on behalf of the University was lowest common denominator planning of the most conventional type. It was governed by perimeter blocks, gestural axial organisation and an oddly imbalanced symmetry. It was really an extrapolation of the same principles that governed his work in 1945 and was as outdated as it was lazy. Despite the council's agreement to surrender the land at rates amendable to the UGC, which roundly signalled their support for expansion, they were less than enamoured with the quality of either the University's new buildings or its planning proposals.[163]

In September 1961 the Corporation's Town Planning Committee approved, in principle, the reallocation of zoning as proposed by the College and University. However, as the statutory approval from Whitehall remained outstanding, formal zoning amendments were in abeyance, effectively halting the development.[164] The College had funds from the UGC to proceed and, with pressing matters of funding and deadlines, Bowden thought that the institutions should strike out to develop their own detailed proposals.[165] By the end of 1961, however, it would seem as if a general mood of dissatisfaction had taken hold. In a letter to Rowland Nicholas, Mansfield Cooper acknowledged his recent representations over 'the appointment of a Town Planner to advise on the development of the new areas'.[166] It appeared that the combined study proposals raised concerns and Nicholas intervened and was keen to stress the need for a planner over that of an architect.

It was Nicholas who opened exchange as to who should be appointed too – Sir William Holford, Chamberlin Powell & Bonn, Robert Matthew Johnson Marshall & Partners (RMJM) and Sir Hugh Casson were all suggested.[167] Holford

---

163 Letter from Lady Simon of Wythenshawe to the Vice-Chancellor, 5 April 1961. Held at Manchester University Archives. Ref: VCA/7/386 Folder 1.

164 Letter from P.B. Dingle, Town Clerk, to W. Mansfield Cooper, 7 September 1961. Held at Manchester University Archives. Ref: VCA/7/386 Folder 2.

165 Letter from B.V. Bowden, Principal of the Manchester College of Science and Technology to W. Mansfield Cooper. 11 January 1962. Held at Manchester University Archives. Ref: VCA/7/386 Folder 2.

166 Letter from W. Mansfield Cooper to R. Nicholas, City Surveyor. 28 December 1962. Held at Manchester University Archives. Ref: VCA/7/386 Folder 2.

167 Letter from R. Nicholas, City Surveyor to Councillor Maurice Pariser, 2 January 1963. Held at Manchester University Archives. Ref: VCA/7/386 Folder 2.

had considerable experience in the planning of universities, Chamberlin Powell & Bonn were responsible for the development planning of Leeds University and recently appointed by the City of London for the Barbican master plan; Sir Hugh Casson had famously coordinated the Festival of Britain site; and RMJM had contracts with York and Edinburgh universities for similar commissions. Mansfield Cooper was largely in agreement with Nicholas about the need for a well-known and skilled planner. He was keen to promote 'civility' to parts of the city he considered 'sordid' and cited recent Scandinavian city planning as exemplar. His preferred lead consultants were Sven Markelius or Sir Leslie Martin, a Manchester graduate and lead designer (not architect) of the Royal Festival Hall, a building he admired.[168]

Discussions on the lead consultant gave way to ideas about who might join them on a consultant team. Other firms mentioned, in a protracted period of stagnation, included Richard Sheppard Robson & Partners, Yorke Rosenberg & Mardall, Ove Arup, Cubbitt Atkinson & Partners and Sir William Holford. Holford, whilst willing to comment on the structure of the assembled team, dismissed himself as a possible chair due to standing commitments at University College London.[169] Prompted by the question, 'What is this great mass of students to do during the hours they are not in lecture and not in the refectory?' the committee also considered social cohesion and the closer integration of 'town and gown'.[170] Months later, the Robbins Report (1963)[171] reinforced the notion that university campuses should be like communities. The need for specialisms in sociology, traffic, civil engineering and architecture was accepted, but nothing was acted upon before a planner with 'very wide over all experience' could be appointed.[172]

The 'Policy Committee' (later the Joint Planning Committee) was officially formed following a meeting in March 1963 and was comprised of three representatives each from the City, the College and the University.[173] In Gibbon's view, the formal joint venture for an 'Educational Precinct' effectively put

---

168 With reference to Belle Vue as a leisure centre and its comparison with the Tivoli in Copenhagen. Letter from W. Mansfield Cooper to R. Nicholas, City Surveyor, 3 January 1963. Held at Manchester University Archives. Ref: VCA/7/386 Folder 2.
169 Letter from R. Nicholas, City Surveyor to W. Mansfield Cooper, 26 February 1963. Held at Manchester University Archives. Ref: VCA/7/386 Folder 2.
170 Record of meeting of the Joint Planning Committee, 16 January 1963, CVR cites Mr G.H. Kenyon as using this statement to introduce the idea of the sociological aspects of the planning task ahead. Held at Manchester University Archives. Ref: VCA/7/386 Folder 2.
171 *The Report of the Robbins Committee on Higher Education* (1963).
172 Letter from W. Mansfield Cooper to R. Nicholas, City Surveyor, 27 February 1963. Held at Manchester University Archives. Ref: VCA/7/386 Folder 2.
173 Informal Meeting of the City-College-University Planning Group in the Vice-Chancellor's Room. Monday, 4 March 1963 at 3.30 p.m. Held at Manchester University Archives. Ref: VCA/7/386 Folder 2.

pay to the 'entirely viable' Student Village previously proposed by C&S. He reported it as 'improper' to burden the incoming planner with preconceived ideas.[174] Rowland Nicholas left office at around the same time, his 23-year tenure ended amidst restructuring. In correspondence Sir Charles Renold referred to Nicholas's 'resignation' altering the 'climate' surrounding the negotiations over the planning – elsewhere it was reported as retirement.[175] Less than a month prior Nicholas had written, 'I cannot help wondering whether we may be exaggerating the planning task which is involved. It seems to me that much of the research has already been done by, or could be done by, the College and University themselves.'[176] This contradicted his earlier advice that stipulated the need for a planner. One of the officers replacing Nicholas was John Millar who would head the new planning department. It could be argued that Nicholas was trying to play down the need for planners more generally due to the restructuring of what he saw as his domain and with which he disagreed. Regardless, his intervention was futile and only served to prolong the period of stagnation.

Eventually, Dame Evelyn Sharp, Permanent Secretary, intervened, on behalf of the MHLG. She wrote to Town Clerk Sir Philip Dingle, 'there are few more important projects coming forward than this educational precinct in Manchester' and, having been dissatisfied with Architects Co-Partnership and not having seriously entertained Chamberlin Powell and Bonn, 'Another possibility... is Mr. L.H. Wilson, who is the planning consultant for the new town of Skelmersdale.'[177] She went on to refer to Wilson's experience at Cumbernauld and in the reconstruction of Canterbury, advising that he 'would recruit a team for any job that he took on'.[178] Following informal interviews and discussions with Wilson, the Joint Committee approved his engagement as lead consultant in November 1963 and charged him with assembling a professional team, based in Manchester, to deliver a full report in eighteen months.[179] Shortly afterwards Wilson approached Lewis Womersley, City Architect of Sheffield to join him in partnership.[180] The commission for the Education Precinct drove the formation of the partnership and they would go on to shape large parts of Manchester, including its Arndale Centre and the infamous Hulme crescents.

---

174 Ibid.
175 Letter from Sir Charles Renold to W. Mansfield Cooper, 13 March 1963. Held at Manchester University Archives. Ref: VCA/7/386 Folder 2.
176 Letter from R. Nicholas, City Surveyor to W. Mansfield Cooper, 26 February 1963. Held at Manchester University Archives. Ref: VCA/7/386 Folder 2.
177 Letter from Dame Evelyn Sharp to P.B. Dingle, 4 October 1963. Held at Manchester University Archives. Ref: VCA/7/386 Folder 4.
178 Ibid.
179 Letter from R.A. Rainford, University Bursar to L.H. Wilson, 18 November 1963. Held at Manchester University Archives. Ref: VCA/7/386 Folder 4.
180 In conversation with Malcolm Cundick of Alphaplus Architects who worked for Wilson & Womersley on the Arndale and Regional Sports Centre proposals.

As the College expansion was almost entirely programmed and the University had significant works completed or under way, Wilson & Womersley (WW) had to act quickly. Their final report of 1967 was preceded by a rapidly composed interim plan in 1964, which created a flurry of press reports about its large scale and ambition.[181] It addressed the projected statistical demands for student numbers, the volume of bus and private vehicle journeys, and parking requirements. Colin Buchanan provided a preliminary report into some of these matters including the Corporation's highway planning, that was intrinsically bound with the study area.[182] Planning for roads around the Education Precinct was largely complete. The South-East Lancashire North-East Cheshire (SELNEC) study of 1962 effectively ratified the ring and radial road proposals of the *1945 Plan*. The inner and intermediate ring roads were to cut at right angles to the long axis of the Precinct and the main University campus area would be flanked by the realigned and re-engineered carriageways of Upper Brook Street and Cambridge Street.[183] This was intended to facilitate the closure of Oxford Road to all but local service traffic and enable more of a parkland setting to the campus, which included the soft landscaping of Brunswick Street. Thus, between 1945 and 1963 the University built all of its new estate within the framework of the *1945 Plan* and much of the 1967 proposal was also driven by concessions to the Corporation's transport strategy.

This fact did not escape Mansfield Cooper and towards the end of 1968 he wrote in uncharacteristically terse tones to the Town Clerk; 'It would be a great pity if the City were now to reverse matters which were considered agreed upon many years ago and thus make the University open to criticism for wasting money on schemes which will not now be properly completed and which would certainly raise the whole question of the value of forward planning.'[184] He suggested that had they been aware of this possibility in 1946 their plans would have been 'radically different' and directed with more certainty to the areas of land fully within their control. Just how radical, or different, is impossible to gauge, but WW forged ahead with their own plans that captured the planning zeitgeist.

Buchanan's *Traffic in Towns* was not long in print when he made his recommendations for the Education Precinct. He proposed a separate system of

---

181 Letters in and around November 1964. Held at Manchester University Archives. Ref: VCA/7/386 Folder 4.
182 Colin Buchanan and Partners, 'Appendix "B" Preliminary Report upon the Road and Traffic Aspects of the Proposed Redevelopment' in Wilson, H., and Womersley, L. (1964) *Manchester Education Precinct. The Interim Report of the Planning Consultants*, p. 41.
183 South-East Lancashire and North-East Cheshire Area Highway Engineering Committee (1962) *SELNEC A Highway Plan* (Manchester: SELNEC Committee).
184 Letter from W. Mansfield Cooper to P.B. Dingle, Town Clerk, 28 October 1968. Held at Manchester University Archives. Ref: VCA/7/386 Folder 5.

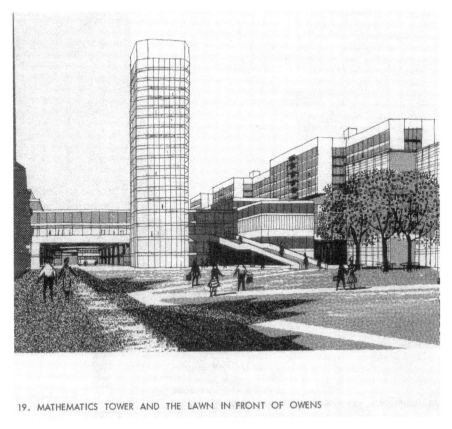

19. MATHEMATICS TOWER AND THE LAWN IN FRONT OF OWENS

Figure 3.26   Preliminary drawing for the Maths Tower showing the early idea of a ramped access up to an elevated pedestrian realm. Oxford Road is closed on this image and an overbridge connects the Maths Tower to other proposed buildings.

pedestrian walkways above ground level, but made no allusion as to how people would perambulate amidst the new parkland campus. The problems thrown up by such a proposal did not escape Professor Kantorowich of the School of Architecture and Planning:

> The idea of largely handing over the ground level to cars, and providing concrete deckways above for pedestrians will profoundly affect and limit architectural form in the Precinct, and will pose great practical and aesthetic problems, not least in the early and middle stages of development. It should be carefully studied from all angles before it is accepted.[185]

---

185   Extract from *Comments on the Interim Report on the Manchester Education Precinct* by Norman Hanson and Roy Kantorowich on behalf of the Buildings Committee, 30 October 1964. Held at Manchester University Archives. Ref: VCA/7/386 Folder 4.

Figure 3.27 Early proposals for the Maths Tower from Scherrer & Hicks. This powerful sketch shows the adoption of ideas set out by Wilson & Womersley, most notably the ramp.

Such a view had not previously prevented Kantorowich undertaking his own study into aerial travellators along Oxford Road, 'which would run approximately 40 ft above the ground and connect all key parts of the education sector'![186] The ultimate flexibility of the pedestrian deck (according to Womersley and accepted by Kantorowich) was sufficient to allow existing schemes, like the Mathematics Building, to progress with no adverse effect on the ultimate campus form.[187]

The Mathematics Building, referred to at the opening of this chapter, was the first major built component that configured with WW's plan. In the interim report they suggested a tower [Figure 3.26] to act as a landmark in the centre of the campus. The Buildings Committee thought that the site was too central and the location would be better for a library that could act as a hub. Also of concern, were the prospective CPOs, which could slow down the procurement

---

186 Minutes of the Buildings Committee. 15 May 1962.
187 Ibid.

IN ADVANCE OF PROGRESS

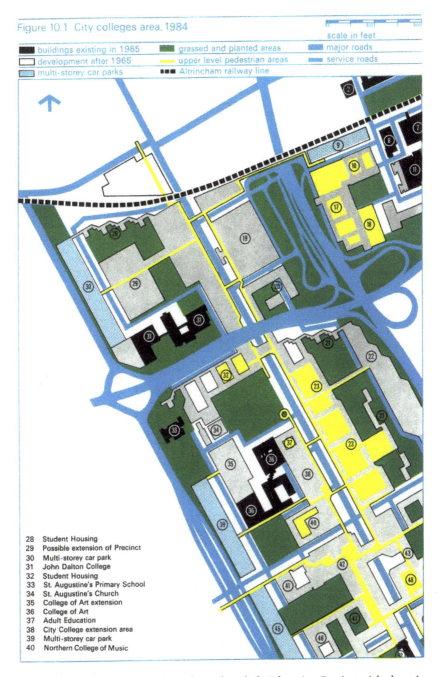

Figure 3.28 Aerial walkways throughout the whole Education Precinct picked out in yellow. This vision for 1984 shows the elevated connection as a total vision extending for approximately one mile.

Figure 3.29 Ramped approach to the entrance of the Maths Tower, with the sloping soffit of the lecture theatre providing cursory shelter.

phase and put UGC funding at risk. Womersley thought that the initial proposals [Figure 3.27] put forward by Scherrer & Hicks would offer much needed enclosure to the Owen's 'Quad' and neatly obviated the seemingly irresolvable highway matters of the growing campus. He also admired the design, stating that 'the imaginative sculptural quality of the building itself will herald new and higher standards of architecture'.[188] Jack Lynn, representing Wilson & Womersley, 'stated that the planning consultants did not wish to determine the exact form of the building, and although the interim report had shown the building as a tower it did not necessarily need to be so, although they would wish to see a tall building on the site'.[189] In October 1964, the Buildings Committee accepted Scherrer & Hicks's proposal for a tower, situated where WW proposed and not to interfere with Oxford Road, which, it appeared, would not be closed to through traffic.[190]

By virtue of its connection to wider transport planning, Oxford Road's closure or diversion could never be resolved in the context of WW's plans.

---

188 Letter from J.L. Womersley to G.H. Kenyon, 24 December 1964. Held at Manchester University Archives. Ref: VCA/7/386 Folder 4.
189 Ibid.
190 Minutes of the Buildings Committee. Mathematics Building. Report of the Third Meeting of the Planning Sub-Committee, 30 October 1964.

Yet, their report ultimately had to acknowledge the ambition of the city. This tension caused much concern in the intervening period between the interim and final reports.[191] The pedestrian decks afforded WW the opportunity to refer directly to Worthington's earlier plans and the termination of Oxford Road around the line of Booth Street. Their terminus, however, could exist with or without the closure of Oxford Road, as it was proposed as a high-level bridge link. The final proposals were criticised, as the radial roads, which admittedly were not of WW's design, were viewed as divisive and as potentially separating the local community from the academic enclave, thus amplifying differences between the two groups rather than bringing them together. The realisation of certain sections of the aerial walkway was similarly charged as exclusive and elitist, despite sections of it being publicly accessible.

Issues over the legal dedication, adoption and maintenance of the pedestrian walkways were only raised after their construction commenced.[192] The University was coming to realise some of the problems presented by the complexity of its ambitious undertaking, which were, in part, a result of the input from the planning consultants. This affords Nicholas's parting comments, about the need for a planner at all, some validity. Furthermore, some of the reasoning for the Corporation's insistence on a planner was quite superficial and can be found in archives: According to Councillor Hatton, Chairman of the Education Committee; 'What sparked off the Precinct idea was the concern of some members of the city council about the external appearance of the development' and that 'parts of the area [were] allocated to the City for developing their own colleges.'[193] A similar account can be found in a letter from Philip Dingle to the City Librarian, where he wrote that 'the Joint Planning Committee was originally set up because there was wide felt dissatisfaction with the architectural design and development of the University'.[194] The walkways and other built elements of the plan were the spatial and formal outcomes of many sequences of overlapping decisions, political interplay and hierarchies. The drawings and models produced by the planners to visualise their ideas were agents of the institutions who commissioned the plan.

---

191 Letter from W. Mansfield Cooper to P.B. Dingle, Town Clerk, 2 April 1965. Held at Manchester University Archives. Ref: VCA/7/386 Folder 5.

192 Letter from W. Mansfield Cooper to G.K. Daniels of Tatham, Worthington & Co. Solicitors asking for legal advice about the status of the pedestrian paths in the sky, 26 June 1969. Held at Manchester University Archives. Ref: VCA/7/386 Folder 6.

193 From the transcript of a conversation between Sir William Mansfield Cooper, Lord Bowden, Councillor Hatton and Sir Maurice Pariser, recorded by Boris Ford of the School of Educational Studies at the University of Sussex. December 1965. Held at Manchester University Archives. Ref: VCA/7/386 Folder 6.

194 Manchester Corporation Interdepartmental Memorandum, 12 July 1965, held at GMCRO, ref: M740/2/8/3/43.

Figure 3.30 The upper-level entrance to the Kilburn Building (Computing) via a bridge link from the head of the ramp to the Maths Tower.

Manchester Education Precinct: The Final Report of the Planning Consultants was published in May 1967.[195] It contained the unerring adhesion to the principles of pedestrian separation and proposed an extended deck over an area about a half of the length of the entire study area [Figure 3.29]. The closure of Oxford Road no longer featured, but a large proportion of the movement analysis remained dependent on the Corporation's unrealised highway planning. Despite its scale and the considerable effort expended in its production, it was a document of uncertainty and compromise, loaded with caveats and demands for further studies. The report and its plan could not capture a fixed moment – as reported in *The Guardian*, a significant number of architectural schemes were 'already in hand' when it was published.[196] Amongst these was the only architectural commission that befittingly fell to WW – the Precinct Centre.[197] It was to contain shops, a pub, a community library, a post office and a 'motorway style

---

195 Letter from W. Mansfield Cooper to Sir John Wolfenden of the UGC, 26 April 1967. Held at Manchester University Archives. Ref: VCA/7/386 Folder 6.
196 George Hawthorne, 'A Campus for 43,000', *The Guardian*, 12 May 1967, p. 10.
197 Correspondence between Keyser Ullman Limited and R.A. Rainford, University Bursar. 16 February 1968. Held at Manchester University Archives. Ref: VCA/7/386 Folder 5.

restaurant' in a bid to emulate a town centre and to be a public hub for the combined campuses and their nearby communities.[198]

As a microcosm for the entire proposal, the Precinct Centre mirrored the unifying ambition of the wider plan. As it struggled to find tenants, it also served as an unfortunate metaphor for a lack of cohesion and the inability of achieving shared institutional health centres, libraries and residences.[199] Despite early calls by the joint committee for 'one voice ... for four ministries', they were forced to seek permissions variously from the Ministries of Education, Health, Housing and Local Government and the Treasury. The egalitarian Lady Shena Simon (feminist and educationalist) bluntly asked of Mansfield Cooper, 'Has the idea of common facilities been given up entirely?'[200] to which Mansfield Cooper replied that Whitehall was 'more rigidly "departmental" than I would want them to be'.[201] As a result, rather than sharing resources, as desired, each institution had their own chaplaincy, library and halls. Seemingly, the only way in which the plan could unify was through the physical connection provided by its aerial walkways.

From the south, the sequence of ramps, bridges, courts and plazas began at the Maths Tower [Figure 3.31] where a ramp from Oxford Road took students to its main entrance at first-floor level. From here a bridge connected it to the Computer Building (BDP, 1969–72) [Figure 3.30], where the route continued through an elevated courtyard and on to the entrance point of the University Chaplaincy (Cruickshank & Seward, 1976). A small flight of stairs joined the chaplaincy to the deck of the Precinct Centre, where an internal plaza served the shops and post office [Figure 3.31]. Continuing northwards, a bridge over Booth Street West connected the Precinct Centre to the Royal Northern College of Music (RNCM) (Bickerdicke Allen Rich & Partners, 1968). The RNCM also had its main entrance at first-floor level and was designed to accommodate further extents of aerial deck [Figure 3.32], but this was as far as the streets-in-the-sky proceeded. One block removed, the City Architect's Department had designed a new adult education college (1973), itself primed to receive the onward walkway once the building between it and the RNCM was constructed. Had such a link been created, the walkway was scheduled to descend into All Saints Park via a spiral ramp. The gap was not closed until 1999 when the Geoffrey Manton Building (Sheppard Robson) was completed. Of course, by this time there was no surviving joint committee and the idea of a unifying plan was consigned to history.

---

198 'Work Starts on Education Precinct Plan', *The Guardian*, 27 September 1968, p. 6.
199 Dennis Johnson, 'Shops Go a-begging in University Precinct', *The Guardian*, 8 June 1972, p. 10.
200 Letter from Lady Simon of Wythenshawe to W. Mansfield Cooper, 11 May 1966. Held at Manchester University Archives. Ref: VCA/7/386 Folder 6.
201 Letter from W. Mansfield Cooper to Lady Simon of Wythenshawe, 13 May 1966. Held at Manchester University Archives. Ref: VCA/7/386 Folder 6.

Figure 3.31 Inside the upper level of the Precinct Centre.

Figure 3.32 Bridge connecting the Precinct Centre to the RNCM.

IN ADVANCE OF PROGRESS

Figure 3.33 Artist's illustration of the long facade of the Medical School (H.S. Fairhurst & Sons, 1972–74). The soft landscaped area in front was reserved for the path of the inner ring road that was never constructed.

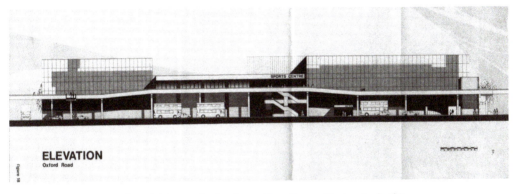

Figure 3.34 Wilson & Womersley's scheme for a Sports Centre (unbuilt) encompassing their ideas for an upper-level pedestrian realm.

The partial, and eventually rather forlorn, sequence of space did not 'inject on to the resulting complex an organic life of its own'.[202] Nor did it create 'a single community with a shared identity, a town within a city, dedicated to advance education'.[203] As with many urban master plans, the funding, sequencing, local authority controls and parliamentary decisions that might affect them were often slow and frequently unpredictable. The MEP plan was reviewed in 1974.

---

202 Dennis Johnson, 'City Campus – a World Pioneer or a Monster Beyond Control', *The Guardian*, 15 December 1969, p. 6.
203 Ibid.

It listed the major changes that impacted upon the aims of the original plan. The most significant were the 'designation of the Polytechnic in 1970 which incorporates some of the buildings previously described as the City Colleges' and 'the delay in the up-grading of the main highways until after 1984'.[204] Both of these wrought their own impact. Areas around All Saints Park that were scheduled for a sports arena, student housing and unspecified 'academic extension areas' became part of the parcel that Sheppard Robson were asked to interrogate as they formed their master plan for the newly constituted polytechnic that drew together the city colleges as a single institution from 1970.

Whilst Mancunian Way was completed and some upgrading of Upper Brook Street took place, the rest of the highways planning faltered and Oxford Road remained a major thoroughfare. The review also contained a list of 'Buildings which have been completed within the Precinct since 1967 or are now in course of design or construction' that highlighted the institutional patronage bestowed on a small number of firms.[205] It showed images of completed buildings, the Medical School (H.S. Fairhurst, 1972–74) [Figure 3.33] the Maths Tower and the RNCM as well as an impression of WW's proposed sports centre [Figure 3.34] (now the site of Manchester Aquatics Centre, built for the Commonwealth Games in 2002). The upper-level walkway was lauded as a success and a new multi-storey car park heralded as the first of many in the strategic vision. In fact, the car park, that served the College was already planned in 1963, prior to the consultants' appointment.[206] This type of claim signalled some of the futility of planning when so much was outside the control of the commissioning body. It was inevitably the transportation solutions upon which so much rested and these were partial and forlorn too.

The closure of Oxford Road was one of the most striking features of the *1945 Plan*, gifting a collegiate atmosphere to the proposed campus, free from cars and buses. This in turn rested on the wider delivery of the ring road proposals that were the perennial dream of the city's planners and engineers (see Chapter 6). Studies in the mid-1960s affirmed the ideas of the 1940s. Thus, WW were forced to produce a vision that would permit Oxford Road to remain open, but to function were it to close – the upper-level walkways were a convenient answer to this uncertainty and reflected thinking of the time and the experience of Wilson at Cumbernauld and Womersley at Park Hill in Sheffield.

A considerable number of University buildings were under construction as the MEP plan was commissioned and developed. Their progress was recorded

---

204 Wilson, H. and Womersley, L. (1974) *Manchester Education Precinct. A Review of the Plan* (Manchester: Joint Committee for the Comprehensive Planning of an Education Precinct), p. 8.
205 Ibid., p. 4.
206 Letter from B.V. Bowden, Principal of the Manchester College of Technology to Sir Keith Murray of the University Grants Committee, 30 August 1963. Held at Manchester University Archives. Ref: VCA/7/386 Folder 3.

Figure 3.35   University of Manchester Business School (Cruickshank & Seward, 1972).

in the minutes of the University Buildings Committee, which pay little heed to the work of the Joint Committee and present a matter-of-fact approach to procurement and construction aligned to existing processes and approvals procedures. The MEP Plan captured a particular moment and gave a framework to the sequence of development. It drew on earlier ideas and visions of the Corporation and brought the schemes for the College and the University Hospitals (Fry & Drew) into its hegemony. Its greatest gift was probably the assurances and the agency it gave to the local authority about the onward development of the education economy. Spatially and materially, the notion of reducing traffic and increasing pedestrian movement in a parkland setting is one that prevailed – Oxford Road is now largely limited to bus-only traffic and Brunswick Street was finally closed and landscaped in 2019.

Campus concluded

The conditions by which the College and the University's master plans came about were quite different; albeit they were co-opted and contained in local authority plans as a single entity. The College (UMIST) was a city and institution in both a literal and metaphorical sense. Its first new buildings were civic in their function, communal spaces to learn, relax and refresh. Its position, as

Figure 3.36 Loxford Tower (City Architect's Department, 1971–74), which became part of the Polytechnic campus.

of and in the city, was advantageous as the nation sought to address its future through education, research and development in the technology sector. The assembled architects were elder statesmen of an architectural establishment that remained very traditional in the face of a modernising society. This did not prevent H.T. Seward putting his faith in a young Arthur Gibbon and Gibbon's relationship with Bowden asserted his influence on the campus architecture. Expressive of his admiration, Bowden remarked:

> I have seen several of Aalto's buildings both in America and in Scandinavia, and I do not believe that any of them are any better, if as good, as the Renold Building which Mr. Gibbon designed for us. This of course is only the opinion of one amateur, but my own belief in the merit of this building has been supported by one of the city planners of Rotterdam, who told me it was the finest building he had seen in Europe.[207]

The development of the College did not, however, stem from one good idea and did not have a sole champion, although Bowden undoubtedly had

---

207 Letter from B.V. Bowden Principal of the Manchester College of Science and Technology to W. Mansfield Cooper, 17 January 1963. UoMA: VCA/7/386 Folder 2.

the vision actively sought by the Education Committee and the UGC when making the appointment. He was described as 'a visionary and expansionist, who would have been quite frustrated in the present era of efficiency gains and tight budgetary control'.[208] It is perhaps fortunate then, that the UGC was inexperienced in the stewardship of large-scale development and that cost targets for construction were less restrictive in the early years of building. Nor was the campus formed from a single source of precedent. It was an application of Continental and North American ideas in a collaborative atmosphere. In 1962, as the first wave of new buildings were about to be handed to the College for occupancy, the Planning and Development Committee proposed that the project architects be invited to comment upon *any* material proposals for new buildings, signage, furniture or landscape in the following two years.[209] This was symbolic of the spirit of shared endeavour and in this sense the campus and institution could be described as 'utopian'.[210]

At the University, the pattern for development through its committees, approvals and departmental structure was an established one. In some sense it was this status quo that stultified the planning and architecture of its 1950s development and led to its criticism in the press and by the local authority. In many senses, despite the questionable impact of Wilson & Womersley's planning, their appointment shook the University out of its stupor and dragged it into the twentieth century. The scale and scope of the project was, however, unprecedented and the ambition to engineer socially as well as structurally truly reflected the momentum of the expanded field of planning in the 1960s. In this way, the MEP, in its totality, may also be understood as utopian. By 1974, as the review was published, the existing structures of local governance were overturned in the creation of the new metropolitan county and the work to develop the Polytechnic campus was well under way. Nonetheless, the major buildings of the early 1970s, the Business School [Figure 3.35] (Cruickshank & Seward, 1972) and Loxford Tower [Figure 3.36] (City Architect's Department, 1971–74) took account of the defensive aspects proposed for perimeter residential blocks and turned their backs on the new highways. The continuing connection of the aerial walkways persisted in the minds of WW and a section of the 1974 review speculated on how these might be achieved in Sheppard Robson's Polytechnic buildings and elsewhere. A new establishment was formed by the processes of development, but it was an open and consultative forum that included the major partners in joint decision making.

In the development of both campuses and the wider MEP area the relationship between the networks of government and the governance of the

---

208 Wood, G.C. (1993), 'Conference Introductory Paper why Manchester?', *Corrosion Science*, Vol. 35, Issues 1–4, pp. 1–12.
209 Minutes of the Planning and Development Committee, 15 August 1962, p. 405. UoMA: TGB/2/5/2.
210 Muthesius, *The Postwar University*.

institutions affected the spatial and material outcomes. At the College, the central government demand for the expansion of technological education met with a strong local tradition and institutions with long histories. Whitehall and Manchester Corporation had to cooperate with one another to achieve their collective aims. The local committees were in almost constant communication with the UGC. In the early stages of development, the UGC was learning from the active construction and latterly began to exert more financial control, which in turn impacted upon the architecture. There was considerable discussion locally between the various bodies charged with delivery and the local authority. The inner-urban motorway and river culvert determined certain massing and form, as did the conditions imposed by BR. At the university it was the spectre of highways planning that pervasively influenced much of the thinking and ideas of connectedness and community that impacted on form. In both circumstances political interplay, policy, planning and infrastructural conditions were all filtered through an assembled group of architects and other committees working in very specific geographic location. The local actors were strong influencing factors in the formation of Manchester Education Precinct. In the following chapter we see how local interests were powerless in the face of global finance.

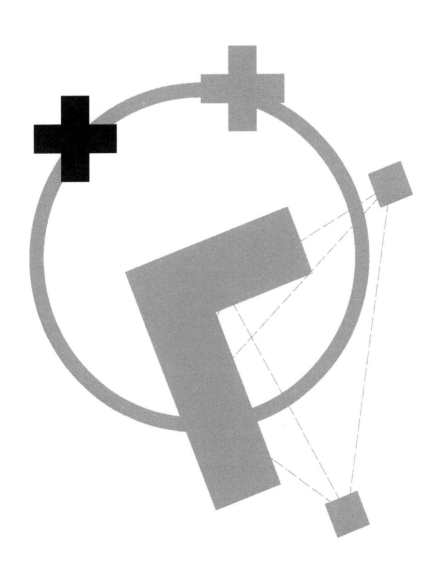

4

Intractable investment: the Crown Agents and Central Station

Introduction

Renewal cities were beholden to inward investment, particularly in the commercial sector. In the previous chapters we have read how central government spending on defence and education fed into construction; how networks connected various planning and architectural schemes, and how global events, like the Cold War, impacted on the local physical realities of Manchester. The story of Central Station brings us to another international context, that of decolonisation. Central Station was mooted for closure in 1965 and finally did so in 1968. The story of the proceeding decade and a series of unbuilt proposals for the station, demonstrates how local conditions were affected by post-colonial dealings, as well as by, the now familiar, political interplay between national and local government.

Mainstream modern architecture ran amok in the renewal cities. This form of modernism unashamedly adopted and adapted the international style to its own ends. Architects working at the commercial end of Britain's booming 1960s inner-city development were influenced by first and second generation modernists, the study of whom was prevalent in British schools of architecture by the middle of the 1950s. The architecture of much large-scale, comprehensive development drew on manifold formal tropes in discombobulated, intellectually diluted assemblages. Developers were afforded new freedoms as levies were reduced and building licences abolished. In a development boom based 'on institutional finance and individual talent', speculative entrepreneurs made fortunes and their bottom line was frequently cost over quality. Amidst the landscape of the 1960s 'boom cities' one of the major tools available to local authorities to control development was the Comprehensive Development Area (CDA).[1]

---

[1] Selina Todd took the phrase 'boom cities' from a campaign run in the *Daily Mirror* in 1967 that celebrated growth in urban Britain. Todd, S. (2015) 'Phoenix Rising:

Local planning authorities also had control of the design of new road patterns.[2] In Manchester, as elsewhere, the CDA allocation was bound with highway planning. The use of CDA powers was firmly consolidated in the Town and Country Planning Act 1962 and their application was seen as able to 'channel the buoyancy of private enterprise' and to 'stimulate economic as well as social change'.[3] These converging private sector interests and public sector powers facilitated the large-scale investment and redevelopment in the renewal cities from the early 1960s through to the middle of the 1970s.

Comprehensive development

Reflecting on the situation in 1971, planner Nathaniel Lichfield pointed to the war and subsequent Town and Country Planning Acts as having influenced ideas of comprehensive planning and development.[4] Under the Town and Country Planning Act 1944, local authorities were given the powers to designate land for comprehensive development, in the guise of the Declaratory Order. The designation and acquisition of sites did not always mean immediate demolition. Some land was purchased by councils to ensure that their long-term ambitions could be realised – many set in place in plans published between 1941 and 1952.[5] Some types of reconstruction were contested; idealists wanted to grasp the opportunity for optimistic wholesale replanning and rebuilding in a modern fashion and saw the statute as a means of directing such.[6] Others wanted certainty that bomb-damaged areas would take priority over blighted areas and be reconstructed much in the same image as before.

The 1944 Act sought to deal primarily with the comprehensive redevelopment of war damaged areas. Even though local authorities were given the power to use compulsory purchase for land assembly, decisions were still approved in Whitehall. Declaratory orders could be used to further expand sites, to enable comprehensive development – these too were subject to government

---

Working-Class Life and Urban Reconstruction, c.1945–1967', *Journal of British Studies*, Vol. 54, No. 3, pp. 679–702.
2 Cherry, *Town Planning in Britain Since 1900*.
3 Hart, T. (1968) *The Comprehensive Development Area. A Study of the legal and administrative problems of comprehensive land development with special reference to Glasgow*. University of Glasgow Social and Economic Studies Occasional Papers No. 9 (Edinburgh and London: Oliver & Boyd), p. 20.
4 Lichfield, N. (1972) 'Renewal of Central Areas' in Davidson, A.W., and Leonard, J.E. (eds) (1972) *Urban Renewal* (London: Centre For Advanced Land Use Studies), pp. 38–48.
5 This was the most intensive period of production of 'Reconstruction Plans', many of which were simply development plans. Larkham and Lilley, *Planning the 'City of Tomorrow'*.
6 Hart, *The Comprehensive Development Area*, pp. 14–15; Town and Country Planning Bill. HC Deb 29 January 1947 vol 432 cc.947–1075, http://hansard.millbanksystems.com/commons/1947/jan/29/town-and-country-planning-bill [Accessed 5 July 2013].

approval.[7] Such approval for war damaged sites led to the release of Exchequer grants towards reconstruction costs. Local authorities could also use CPOs for a wide variety of other purposes, including to combat 'bad layout and obsolete development'.[8] This, rather ambiguous phrase, encompassed ideas of reconstruction *and* renewal and effectively opened the use of powers to local interpretation as to what might constitute comprehensive redevelopment. In the context of 1960s planning, this inherent characteristic of the legislation is notable – national policy, even in the form of an Act of Parliament, can never be implemented without local interpretation. Even evidently statutory obligations are actually guidance. The combined devolution of powers and the evolution of new legislation created the conditions for the interplay of policy and proposals between local and central government departments.

Whilst the 1947 Act brought little in the way of alteration to the terms of designation, local planning authorities were granted full power to deliver their ambitions through the use of Development Plans. The Development Plan and CDA were designed to operate in a complementary fashion – Part I of the *Explanatory Memorandum* (1947) envisaged that Development Plans would allocate large swathes of towns as CDAs. Part II alluded to the utilisation of the CDA for slum clearance and 'for other purposes defined in the plan'.[9] The room for interpretation by local authorities presented many development options. Also instituted in 1947 was the role of the local planning authority as the body that would award permission for new development. The rules around the designation and assembly of CDAs were sufficiently relaxed for a local authority to achieve almost any purpose contained within an approved Development Plan. In principle this relaxation handed more powers to be administered locally, but it relied on a Development Plan that had been signed off by MHLG – something that Manchester did not have. The impact of this was twofold: first, very little planning work to develop a deliverable plan took place; second, only schemes that did not jeopardise the *1945 Plan* were allowed to proceed. As such, the CDA tool was not used by the planning authority in Manchester until the 1960s.

Conditions to truly test development powers for local authorities only emerged during the 1950s. In Coventry, one of the towns at the vanguard of reconstruction, it was not until the Development Plan of 1951 that the first CDAs were identified.[10] One reason for this delay in the use of powers by local authorities was due to the national political structures implemented

---

7 Hart, *The Comprehensive Development Area*, p. 11.
8 Town and Country Planning Act 1944. The phrase was used repeatedly throughout the text of the Act, but was headlined in Section 9.
9 MHLG (1947) *Town and Country Planning Act, 1947: Explanatory Memorandum* (London: HMSO).
10 Coventry City Council (1951) *Coventry: The Development Plan*, see www.coventrysociety.org.uk/coventry-neighbourhoods/hillfields.html [Accessed 1 June 2013].

to oversee development in the immediate post-war period. Post-war building licensing controlled development through regional committees until November 1954. The committees, under MoW chairmanship, were composed of representatives from the Ministries of Health, Labour and Supply, the Board of Trade and the MTCP.[11] They controlled the supply of labour and materials in the process of rebuilding. Resources were channelled towards schools, the health sector and new homes; redevelopment of central areas, whether residential or commercial property, was not a high priority. Ultimately, the cessation of strict licensing was one of the early catalysts for the upsurge in private sector development.[12]

City centres were fertile territory for young rapidly expanding property firms who injected fervour and commercially tinged professionalism into the act of developing. These companies, as well as being supported by state activities, were financed by the growing investment fund sector 'who realised that real estate, bricks and mortar' was a 'good thing to get into'.[13] A real term increase in wages created greater public spending power and retail environments were transformed to accommodate the consumer boom. The Conservative Government in particular put an emphasis on public–private partnerships in the renewal of town centres, but local Labour run councils contentedly adopted the model.[14] This heightened activity, on the part of the private sector and encouraged by central government, did not meet with equal resources within local authorities that 'faced with cumbersome procedures, financial limitations and inadequate staff, local planning authorities [were] unable to make much progress with comprehensive development'.[15] This was certainly the case in Manchester which, according to Chief Planner John Millar, before restructuring, 'had two architect planners available, one of whom was me, but there were no less than one hundred working for them [the private developers]. It was absurd.'[16]

The relationship between CDA powers, the role and status of the Development Plan, governmental interplay and local conditions is a complicated matrix of space, capital, will, expertise, material and policy. The story of the Central Station CDA in Manchester is one example of many similar developments. The networks of finance, policy, personnel and expertise involved in the unbuilt project were global, national and local and all influenced decision making around design.

---

11 See Ministry of Works: Regional Building Committees: Minutes, NA: WORK 49. Administrative / biographical background http://discovery.nationalarchives.gov.uk/SearchUI/details?Uri=C14650 [Accessed 28 May 2013].
12 Scott, *The Property Masters*, pp. 132–165.
13 Ibid., p. 41.
14 Hart, *The Comprehensive Development Area*, p. 21.
15 Ibid., p. 2.
16 Turner, *The North Country*, p. 70.

Comprehensive Development Areas, advisory schemes, models and Manchester

For a brief period in the 1940s it was assumed that cities would undertake a significant amount of their own rebuilding. It is argued that this is one reason for the grand visions in many of the early post-war plans.[17] From 1951 to 1974, in order to best serve the city and the citizen, the local authority architect-planner had to prepare a Development Plan with defined CDAs. The CDAs were supposed to simultaneously attract investment and protect the environment and amenity of public space. The skills of a Chief Planner and their team would affect the detail in the visual and spatial representation of their advice. In turn, the architectural schemes promoted by developers would respond to the proposed frameworks of the planning department (as well as the breadth of other influencing factors). Of course, all British architecture has had to respond to regulation of some form or another for most of the twentieth century.[18] In 1951 the Development Plan was instituted and, by 1974, the Structure Plan was its universal replacement. The CDA, within the context of the development plan system, was a very particular planning tool and its effectiveness was dependent on skilful interpretation.

Following John Millar's appointment in 1963 and the ensuing planning work, Manchester's six CDAs were published in 1967.[19] The development plan within which they were presented was approved by 1968. This was the first statutory document that could be used to control development in the central area of the city. The designation of the CDAs was the most far-reaching outcome in terms of the shape of the central city as much of its twenty-first century form was instituted in the words and images published in the 1960s. These were, however, explicitly 'advisory plans' and subject to discussion and amendment prior to development.[20] This type of outline guidance acknowledged the limits of the local authority and the lack of financial resources necessary to implement projects themselves. It was a reaction to the pressures exerted by the private sector and a need to provide some form of control that would protect the overall character of the city – developers would not wait to participate in a broad vision when there was money to be made in the now.

---

17 Ravetz, A. (2013) *The Government of Space: Town Planning in Modern Society* (London: Routledge), pp. 69–70.
18 The Housing, Town Planning, &c. Act 1909 (c. 44) was the first piece of British legislation to control development. Cherry, G.E. (1988) *Cities and Plans. The Shaping of Urban Britain in the Nineteenth and Twentieth Centuries* (London: Edward Arnold), pp. 71–72.
19 Millar, J.S. (1968) *City and County Borough of Manchester: City Centre Map, 1967* (Manchester: City Planning Department).
20 Telephone conversation with Robert Maund, former Assistant City Planning Officer, 5 July 2013; Interview with John Millar. Wilmslow, 19 August 2013.

Figure 4.01   Rodwell House (Douglas Stephen & Partners, 1965). The base of the building straddles the Rochdale Canal, which runs beneath it.

The pace of development in 1960s Manchester was accelerated and several CDA allocations simply reflected deals already made between the local authority and the private sector, such as the dedication of the Market Street Area, which eventually became the Arndale Centre.[21] A host of commercial developments including Piccadilly Plaza (Covell & Matthews, 1962–65), Portland Tower (Leach Rhodes Walker, 1963) and Rodwell House (Douglas Stephen & Partners, 1965) [Figure 4.01] had already begun to change the landscape of the city and it was the free market, rather than the local authority, that was shaping the streets. That isn't to say that these developments were ignorant of the greater aims and ambitions of the corporation. Many proposals took account of the route of the proposed city centre road – several buildings drew their line or aspect from the unrealised scheme and ultimately became slightly incongruous in their setting.[22]

Indicative of the pressures exerted by private developers, several of the advisory plans were reported in the architectural press before being formally

---

21   '£15m Redevelopment Plan for City Centre', *The Manchester Guardian*, 14 January 1965, p. 18.
22   See Chapter 6.

published by the Planning Department. These included the Cathedral Area and the Civic Area [Figure 4.02], which were provisionally endorsed and received very little in the way of analytical critique.[23] Prior to the approval of the development plan, these types of advisory schemes were mostly reactive in their production, a fast way to wrest some control over a landscape subject to change and without a statutory framework. The particular skills of Millar's department and their negotiation between national guidance and local concerns resulted in quite specific three-dimensional proposals for the central area and the CDAs especially. The department produced a series of advisory schemes and used drawings and models to illustrate their favoured approaches to particular sites. The advisory schemes were intended to act as outline frameworks for developers, but appeared quite authoritative, particularly when presented as a totality in a model of the entire city.

The architect-planners of the post-war era were equipped with design skills and produced diagrams, drawings and visualisations of their recommendations that could give the impression of definitive proposals. The skills of officers and the provision of outline planning advice also varied from city to city. Some cities, like Leicester under the direction of Konrad Smigielski, mirrored the level of production seen in Mancunian guidance, others stuck steadfastly to two--dimensional zoning and the basic package of statutory instruments.[24] Not all local authorities had personnel with the same skill set and guidance on the production of development plans left the level of formal definition in their hands. Not all cities had a planning department and some appointed consultants to prepare their plans.[25] In Manchester, Millar was a good communicator and he wrote and published on the work of his department. The Corporation also

---

23 'Manchester Reunited: Proposed Cathedral Area Development', *Interbuild*, February 1963, pp. 40–41; 'Planning Proposals for Manchester Civic Area', *Interbuild*, July 1962, pp. 12–15.

24 Smigielski, K.R. (1968) *Leicester Today and Tomorrow* (London: Pyramid Press). City planning officers came from a variety of backgrounds, many from the office of City Engineer. The City Engineer was an intrinsic part of local government as authorities had controlled their own water and sewage undertakings since the middle of the nineteenth century. Often, engineers responsible for planning would revert to disciplinary conventions of technical and empirical measure and layout. A good example is Stanley Gordon Wardley in Bradford. See Gunn, S. (2010) 'The Rise and Fall of British Urban Modernism: Planning Bradford, circa 1945–1970', *The Journal of British Studies*, Vol. 49, No. 4.

25 For example, Liverpool, who commissioned Graeme Shankland to prepare their 1960s plan. Shankland, G. (1965) *Liverpool City Centre Plan* (Liverpool: City and County Borough of Liverpool); Shankland, G. (1964) 'The Central Area of Liverpool', *Town Planning Review*, Vol. 35, No. 2, p. 105; Bor, W. and Shankland, G. (1965) 'Renaissance of a City. A study of the redevelopment of Liverpool', *The Journal of the Town Planning Institute*, January, Vol. 51, No. 1, pp. 20–32; Smith, O.S. (2014) 'Graeme Shankland: A Sixties Architect-planner and the Political Culture of the British Left', *Architectural History*, Vol. 57.

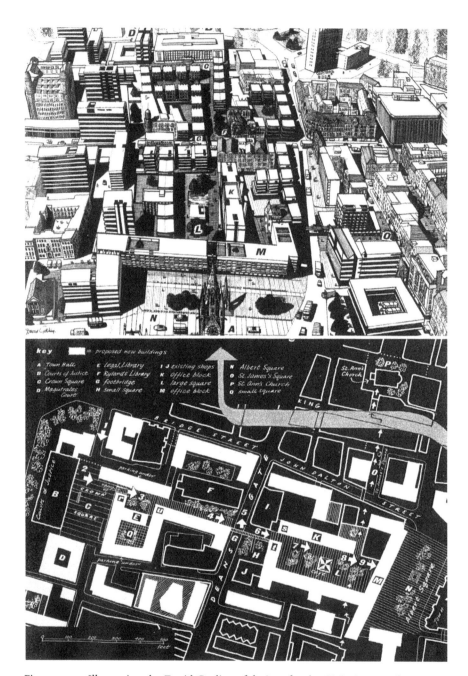

Figure 4.02 Illustrations by David Gosling of designs for the Civic Area. In the foreground of the upper image is the tower of the Town Hall. The building at the very top of the image is the Crown Court. A processional way would link the two civic buildings.

kept the public informed of evolving proposals and saw fit to put on display a model of the entire city centre, built by the planners, to enable citizens to view architectural proposals at an early stage.[26] The model was promoted as giving 'an exciting visual dimension to the spate of official planning reports' and seen as 'much more than a table toy town'.[27]

This, then, was the three-dimensional spatial representation of the planning department's development ideals and an act informed by national guidance but shaped creatively using local knowledge and experience. The production of the reports, drawings and models is a formalisation of the interplay between Whitehall policy and local application. It is also representative of the steady handing of powers to local authorities to enact their own planning policy and approvals and the uncertainty and tension inherent in such a transition. The quality of development plans, for example, varied widely.

Manchester's 1968 development plan was comprehensive. The Corporation published separate reports on car parking and the ring roads during the same period.[28] Read collectively these documents are more definitive than the proposals in the *1945 Plan*. Millar recalls the road programme as a measure designed to secure 'their' (the Planning Departments) aims of conserving the historic core of the city and to create a more pleasant pedestrian environment by banishing cars to the edge of the centre.[29] This recollection is important in relation to Central Station; as will be seen, the historic train hall did not feature in all of the architectural schemes for the site. Understandably, the published reports did not reveal Millar's personal love of Victorian railway heritage.[30] The apparent primacy of the road programme and all of the new development it both required and implied was at odds with Millar's personal view. The architect-planners were not just decision makers working with exclusively quantitative data, they were aesthetes, with subjectivity; another chief planner may have cared less for history. A rise in regulatory systems and an increase in their dissemination meant that interested parties were able to acquire knowledge of the planning system and to judge the competencies of their public officers. The formation of the Civic Trust in 1957 highlighted some general and lay concern in the acts and the results of town planning.

As the general appreciation of historic buildings grew and coalesced with Millar's personal ideal and his professional advice, the architecture of the schemes for Central Station would be directly affected. Alongside burgeoning public-sector planning activity, new social attitudes were being formed by

---

26 'Permanent Display of the Changing Manchester', *The Manchester Guardian*, 20 September 1965, p. 5.
27 Ibid.
28 Manchester Corporation, *Joint Report on Car Parking in Central Manchester*; Hayes, J., City Engineer, *Manchester City Centre Road*.
29 Interview with John Millar. Wilmslow, 19 August 2013.
30 Ibid.

Figure 4.03   Central Station looking rather forlorn in 1975 after its closure in 1968 and its use predominantly as a car park in the intervening years.

non-governmental organisations that published their own advice and guidance concerning comprehensive development.[31] Despite this broader public interest and the most determined efforts of the planners, it was inevitably national policy that shaped local decisions. The closure of the Central Station was in the hands of British Railways (BR) and the Minister of Transport.

Central Station: closure to CDA status

Manchester Central Station was designed by architect Sir John Fowler and constructed for the Cheshire Lines Committee between 1875 and 1880.[32] The Midland Railway used Central Station as the terminus for its services from London St Pancras. The trains would arrive in the magnificent train hall that is enclosed by a single span wrought iron truss structure, 64 m in width and 168 m in length [Figure 4.03]. Its height at the apex is 27 m. A significant portion of the arched roof was glazed and the building compared to the Continent's finest

---

31   See for example: Town Planning Institute, *Memorandum on Central Area Development*, 1960; Civic Trust, *Rebuilding City Centres – Report of the Conference*, 1960; Town Planning Institute, *Further Memorandum on Comprehensive Development*, 1961.
32   Parkinson-Bailey, *Manchester: An Architectural History*, p. 53.

stations of the same era. Its value was recognised in December 1963 when it was listed at Grade II*.[33]

To the Corporation the site was important. It covered a huge swathe of central land and directly served the traditional civic and financial sectors of the city. Close to the site were the Free Trade Hall (Edward Walters, 1853–56), The Midland Hotel (Charles Trubshaw, 1903), the Oxford Road entertainment district. The recently published Rapid Transit Study had proposed a new underground station for nearby St Peter's Square [Figure 4.04].[34] The site was also the effective terminus of traffic travelling along the M56–A56 corridor from affluent Cheshire and would become even more strategically prominent should all of the city's highway ambitions be realised. The station's demise, or more precisely its decay, would be there for all to see and would not the symbol or message that politicians wished to represent Manchester.[35]

Figure 4.04 Proposal for new underground station at St Peter's Square, part of the Picc–Vic project that was abandoned in the mid-1970s.

---

33 G Mex, Manchester. Listing Report. Listing NGR: SJ8373797786, https://historicengland.org.uk/listing/the-list/list-entry/1270514 [Accessed 17 April 2022].

34 De Leuw, Cather & Partners, Hennessey, Chadwick, O hEocha & Partners, Manchester City Transport (1967) Manchester Rapid Transit Study, Vols. 1–3. See Brook, R. and Dodge, M. (2012) Infra MANC (Manchester: Bauprint).

35 A view clearly communicated by John Millar. Interview with John Millar. Wilmslow, 19 August 2013.

As a functioning station, Manchester Central fell victim to the British Transport Commission's *Modernisation Plan*.[36] Only one passenger service to the station was to be cut on the advice of Dr Beeching.[37] John Millar, whilst asserting that there were 'no firm plans' for its reuse in 1965, acknowledged that 'it would be an extremely fine building for an exhibition hall'.[38] The Corporation saw the need for an exhibition hall in the city and the revenue and business it could bring.[39] Other sites were under consideration but Central Station was thought preferable because of the architectural calibre of the existing building and the expense that would be incurred to realise a new building of the same quality.[40] It was suggested that the exhibition hall could be planned alongside the existing proposals for the entertainment centre in the Mosley Street CDA.[41] Later the same year councillors added to the commentary, stating, 'the site has untold possibilities. It is close to hotels and it is right on the spot as far as road development is concerned.'[42]

While Millar publicly disputed the rigidity of any proposals, the report of 1964–65 from his department made clear reference to the possibilities of the site as an extension of the entertainment and leisure quarter proposed for the Mosley Street CDA that would connect the station site to the Piccadilly area of Manchester.[43] Suggestions as to the formal configuration of the scheme were even put forward; it was proposed that an upper-level pedestrian deck could connect the two CDAs. This type of proposed separation between vehicles and pedestrians had been around since the 1950s and was seen as a way to improve the amenity of the public realm.[44] Its wide adoption, at least in plans,

---

36 British Transport Commission (1954) *Modernisation and Re-Equipment of British Rail*. The Railways Archive (Originally published by the British Transport Commission), www.railwaysarchive.co.uk/docsummary.php?docID=23 [Accessed 23 September 2013]; 'Station as Exhibition Hall?', *The Manchester Guardian*, 11 February 1965; 'Central Station May go Next in Dr B's Axe', *Manchester Evening Chronicle*, 9 July 1963.
37 British Railways Board (1963) *The Reshaping of British Railways* (London: HMSO).
38 'Station as exhibition hall?'
39 It had been an ambition since 1946 and the subject of a clause in a parliamentary bill in 1957/58. *Report of the County Planning Officer to GMC Planning Committee*, 1 July 1974. Archives+: GB124.GMC/4/Box 28.
40 'D-Day for Hall Plans', *Manchester Evening News*, 5 June 1967.
41 The area between Mosley Street and Portland Street had been scheduled as a centre for entertainment and leisure since 1945 and had been the subject of various proposals by City Architects and commercial architectural firms. 'Big Development Plan for Manchester "A Focus of Civic Life"', *The Guardian*, 13 April 1961, p. 2; 'Station as Exhibition Hall?'
42 'Station Site to Become Show Hall?', *Manchester Evening News*, 23 August 1965.
43 Millar, *Manchester City Centre Map 1967*, Cl.43.
44 There were several notable schemes, both built and unbuilt, that influenced a generation of architect and planners, including Sergei Kadleigh's 1952 proposal for High Paddington and the design competitions for Golden Lane Estate (1952) and Sheffield University (1953). Particularly influential were Park Hill estate in Sheffield (1957–61)

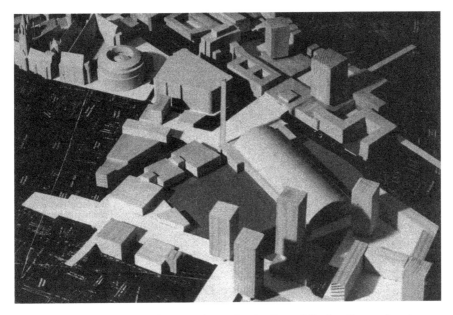

Figure 4.05 Model of the Advisory Scheme for the Central Station Comprehensive Development Area. The station hall is shown surrounded by pedestrian decks connecting to the rest of the city.

was in large part due to the recommendations of national guidance prepared by Colin Buchanan and published as *Traffic in Towns*.[45] By the time the 1966–67 report of the planning department was published an advisory scheme had been prepared for the site that outlined the approximate area allocation of various components for a mixed-use development. A model was built suggesting the massing and positioning of formal elements that might be acceptable to the authority [Figure 4.05].[46]

BR formally announced the closure of Central Station in September 1965.[47] However, the closure of the station was not a local decision, nor was it exclusively in the hands of BR or the train companies; it was subject to approval by the Minister of Transport, Barbara Castle, and a public inquiry.[48] Locally, the

---

and Cumbernauld town centre (1958–67). See Gold, J.R. (2006) 'The making of a megastructure: architectural modernism, town planning and Cumbernauld's Central Area, 1955–75', *Planning Perspectives*, Vol. 21, No. 2, pp. 109–131.

45 Buchanan, *Traffic in Towns*.
46 Millar, *Manchester City Centre Map 1967*, p. 22.
47 'Manchester Central may be Closed', *The Guardian*, 17 September 1965, p. 1; 'Economics of Central Station', *The Guardian*, 15 June 1966, p. 3.
48 '1880 Station may Become Show Site', *Daily Telegraph*, 17 September 1965.

Town Planning Committee agreed that there was a case for the Corporation to acquire the Central Station site with a view to its use as an exhibition hall or car park.[49] Objections to the closure were heard in Manchester over a six-week period.[50] At the inquiry it was suggested that 'the railways' had 'not taken into account the tremendous increase in road traffic that would come in the next five to ten years'.[51] Ironically, the lack of a central ring road (still on the drawing board, yet intrinsic to the central planning of the city) posed as pivotal to servicing the developed site, was not seen as problematic. The combined predicted increase in car use and the additional traffic generated by railway closures was considered as a local issue and did not seem to affect national strategic planning.

The Minister was not forthcoming with her decision and during the rest of 1966 local lobbying and speculation over the future of the site continued. It was reported in December that, 'any scheme for the station would have to fit with the comprehensive redevelopment of a district to which the corporation planning department attaches considerable importance'.[52] Eventually, in August 1967, Barbara Castle approved the closure.[53] The following day a representative of BR said that 'the railways would not necessarily put the site up for sale. They could lease it to a development group or develop it themselves.'[54] The site was not sold immediately and during the following few years several ideas and architectural schemes were prepared for the site.

The interest of private developers was sparked and, by October 1968, the Taylor Woodrow Group (TWG) published speculative proposals for the development of the site and its surroundings [Figure 4.06].[55] In the interim, figures released by the Corporation to the press suggested it would take approximately £11m to redevelop the entire site. The city's blueprint, in the form of the advisory scheme, provided for the transformation of the main building into an exhibition hall, the provision of associated car parking and up to 600 city centre homes.[56] The TWG proposals largely mirrored the planning department guidelines and were presented in a short report with accompanying

---

49 'Manchester Thinks of Houses in the Centre of the City', *The Guardian*, 21 September 1966, p. 22.
50 *Manchester Chronicle*, 4 May 1966.
51 'Railway Pledge is Attacked as Naïve', *Manchester Evening News*, 23 June 1966; 'Rail closure objection', *The Manchester Guardian*, 26 May 1966.
52 'Hall plan could "save station"', *Manchester Evening News*, 20 July 1966; Whiteley, G., 'Decision Soon on Exhibition Hall Site', *The Guardian*, 13 December 1966.
53 Services would be diverted to the city's other mainline railway stations. 'Central station to be axed next year', *Daily Telegraph*, 17 August 1967.
54 Whiteley, G. 'Manchester to Lose a Station, but no cut in Services', *The Manchester Guardian*, 18 August 1967.
55 '£1m Arena Plan for City Station', *Manchester Evening News*, 17 October 1968; 'Station may be Exhibition Centre', *The Guardian*, 18 October 1968, p. 6.
56 'Central Station: Action Soon?', *Manchester Evening News*, 5 May 1967.

Figure 4.06 Taylor Woodrow Group sponsored proposals for Central Station, designed by BDP. These largely mimic the massing proposed in the Planning Department's Advisory Scheme.

drawings.[57] The historic train hall was labelled as 'exhibition and sports building' – two of the clear uses that were part of the advisory scheme and suggested in earlier press reports. The rest of the site was shown as a mixture of office, residential, retail and public space. The most prominent feature of these early proposals was a cylindrical tower situated close to the drum form of the Central Reference Library (E. Vincent-Harris, 1930–34). Designed to house a hotel and conference centre, the drawing of the proposed section through

---

57 'Proposals for Central Station', *Manchester Evening News*, 9 December 1968; Taylor Woodrow Group (1968) *Manchester Central Station* (Report). Manchester Central Reference Library, Local Studies Unit, ref: Q725.31Ta1.

the site shows the label 'beacon' applied to the tower. The accompanying text (presumably that of the architect) stated that 'such a marker is valuable to draw attention to the site from the rest of the city cut off as it is by a rank of older buildings; to counterpoint the long barrow of the train hall; and to guide traffic from Princess Parkway into the parking terminal'.[58] Here was the idea of a sentinel to the city, designed to operate as a sign and a landmark, that would re-emerge in later proposals.

The Corporation, who required broad consensus to approve a plan as bold as this, still did not own the site. TWG's aim, with BDP as their architects, was to convince the Corporation to appoint them as preferred partner if the local authority could make the acquisition.[59] Another site, at Belle Vue, was owned by the Corporation and also proposed for a new exhibition hall. The Development Committee was asked in July 1967 to make a decision as to which one it should back.[60] Perhaps unfortunately for the city, they chose to support the Central Station site, over which the authority actually exerted little or no control – the decisions to close the station and the disposal of it as an asset were firmly held by national organisations. Local press coverage reflected the apparent powerlessness of the situation from the city's perspective.

Throughout 1967 stories appeared regularly enough in the local press to keep the issue in the minds of readers. An unusual joint Corporation-University working party investigated the possibility of the station's use as an industrial museum and a student of architecture had his thesis project for an exhibition hall published as a 'viable proposition'.[61] In the following year it was reported that Manchester's planning chiefs were discussing proposals with an unnamed London firm of architects and that BR were also poised to submit their own planning application for the redevelopment.[62] Finally, in February 1971, the City Council gave the go ahead to commence negotiation with BR and the Minister for the Environment over the purchase of the site.[63] The £2m offer made by Manchester Corporation was rejected and the station was sold to an unnamed buyer for an undisclosed sum in June 1972.[64] The planning machinery of the CDA process likely had its own impact on the sale. Nearly ten years earlier, Franklin Medhurst, speaking in his role as director of the Civic Trust for the North West, suggested that local authority schemes were being jeopardised

---

58 Taylor Woodrow Group, *Manchester Central Station* (Report), Section V, Para. 55.
59 Ibid., Section I, Para. 2.
60 'D-Day for Hall Plans', *Manchester Evening News*, 5 June 1967.
61 'Station May be Museum of the Steam Age', *Manchester Evening News*, 20 June 1969; 'Station is a Likely Site for Museum', *The Guardian*, 21 October 1969, p. 4; 'Station Could be City Show Centre', *Manchester Evening News*, 24 June 1970.
62 'Station Site Development Talks', *Manchester Evening News*, 14 July 1970.
63 'Council May Buy Former Station Site', *Daily Telegraph*, 4 February 1971.
64 'City Centre Station Sold', *Daily Telegraph*, 1 June 1972.

by their very publication. His argument centred on the fact that land values rose as speculators raced to secure sites in and around areas scheduled for comprehensive development.[65] This situation was certainly evident in the financial dealings around Central Station.

The CDA, however, was the best tool that Manchester planners had to control development. The setting out of central area of the city was not within the 1961 approval and, soon afterwards, Development Plans were being replaced as Wilson's incoming Labour Government instituted change. In 1965, through the PAG, *The Future of Development Plans* was under discussion and the 'Town Centre Map' and 'Action Area' were to be implemented to replace the Development Plan and CDA.[66] Millar worked hard to negotiate a medium ground with Whitehall that enabled the onward work of his fledgling department, supported development in Manchester and met with the changing requirements of the planning system.[67] Their advisory schemes prevailed as the only real device with which to direct architects and developers. This was the officers of the Corporation utilising a selective part of the planning machinery to serve the interests of the city. Three-dimensional frameworks of this type, generated by local authority departments, were products of local action and interpretation in response to national policy. The nuanced situations of individual cities relied on the aptitude of personnel to work between the complicated legislative landscape. Each renewal city had its own actions, reactions and interplay within similar parameters – those orbiting Manchester's Central Station were global, national and locally influenced.

The Crown Agents and English and Continental Property Company

The mystery surrounding the acquisition of Central Station in 1972 concealed a murky set of financial exchanges. The nature of these dealings ultimately led to the collapse of the development proposals but not before a lot of design work was done. In a complicated series of transactions involving businesses registered in the Channel Islands, conditional share capital acquisitions and holding companies, two developers, Ramon Greene and Jack Walker, saw the speculative opportunity in Central Station and how it could be manipulated to twice yield a profit – in its acquisition and in its development. The mystery buyer was later revealed as Arkle Holdings and it was funded by a post-colonial oddity of an

---

65 'Speculators "disrupting cities"', *The Guardian*, 2 October 1963, p. 6.
66 Planning Advisory Group, *The Future of Development Plans*, pp. 26–30. The Town Centre Map was a non-statutory tool to replace the Development Plan. See Planning Advisory Group (1962) *Planning Bulletin No. 1. Town Centres – Approach to Renewal* (London: HMSO).
67 Correspondence at NA/HLG 144/86.

organisation known as the Crown Agents (CA), formerly, and officially, the Crown Agents for the Colonies.[68]

The CA were effectively civil servants but, because their work was for colonial governments, their appointments were made by royal prerogative and not by parliamentary authority. Constitutional lawyers described them as 'an emanation of the Crown'.[69] Following the dissolution of most of the British Empire in the 1950s it was anticipated that the organisation would 'wither away and eventually vanish'.[70] This view discounted the resilience of a large professional staff in dignified London headquarters and their appetite for survival. Their numbers did diminish but certain activities in procurement continued. One of the services the CA provided in colonial days was in the financial sector, raising loans and managing investment funds.[71] It was this branch of the organisation and its expansion that ensured the continued existence of the CA. The indistinct hierarchical structure of the CA combined with their operating procedures, which was effectively a cooperative, eventually led to poor record keeping and a large-scale mismanagement of funds, though no personnel were ever charged with fraud. Their finance department was left to make decisions about tens of millions of pounds of investments with little or no consultation with the board.

Walker initially acted as a solicitor for the CA, but in one particular property venture he became projects director for Australia and soon developed other property interests with them.[72] Through a series of insider dealings the CA had its own subsidiaries, secondary banks and a number of interests. Amongst these was Keepsake Homes Ltd, formed in 1969 by Walker, Henry Kaye and the Greene brothers, Ramon and Lionel (whom Walker had met in 1968) and funded by the CA.[73] In December 1969 Keepsake Homes Ltd became English and Continental Property Company (E&C) and, in a few exchanges, by 1971 the majority shareholders became Walker and Greene.[74] The CA agreed to provide

---

68 *Report by the Committee of Inquiry appointed by the Minister of Overseas Development into the circumstances which led to the Crown Agents requesting financial assistance from the Government in 1974* (London: HMSO), 1977. Para. 8, p. 2.
69 Ibid.
70 Ibid. Para. 11, p. 3.
71 Ibid., Para. 9, p. 3. Cain and Hopkins suggest: (1) that the empire was always mainly about finance, and (2) after the Second World War, finance was reorganised, no longer needing an empire, but the financial sector sailed right along. See Cain, P.J., and Hopkins, A.G. (1993) *British Imperialism: Innovation and Expansion, 1688–1914*, Vol. 1 (Boston, MA: Addison-Wesley Longman).
72 Ibid., Para. 54, p. 22.
73 Ibid., Para. 77, p. 30.
74 Ibid., Para. 76, p. 29. Walker and Greene each held 24.5 per cent. The Crown Agents' interest was 51 per cent.

up to £3m loan capital and the company was 'vigorous from the start'.[75] 'Comfort letters', not legal agreements, as a form of guarantee, secured further loans. The status of the CA meant that they were not subject to much scrutiny or properly audited and it was mid-level personnel who distributed millions of pounds. E&C went on to raise further capital from the markets via their association with the CA, who were seen by speculators as a reliable guarantor of their investments. The exact amount loaned to E&C was unknown but was approximated to be at £38m at its peak in April 1973.[76] Financial relations between E&C and the CA were so interwoven that were the E&C to fail the CA could not jettison their subsidiary – they were actually obliged to underwrite their debt![77]

Earlier, in August 1971, questions were raised over the CA in the House of Lords.[78] This was the first time in any parliamentary context that the CA problem was posed and the Lords 'appeared to be somewhat perplexed at the nature and accountability of the Crown Agents'.[79] The sale of Central Station was also eventually subject to parliamentary questions that brought to the fore issues of the relationships of nationalised industries and commercial development.[80] This was not the first time that E&C had been under scrutiny, but earlier investigations had largely concluded that, although there was some financial irregularity, the dealings of the CA were not illegal.[81] Legalities aside, the funding of the purchase of Central Station by E&C and the fees for the professional services of the design team existed as a consequence of the shifting political scales of the Commonwealth. The distant impact of the financial dealings coalesced with the reshaping of the national railways and the local situation of Manchester's planning mechanisms to inform its architecture.

English & Continental, Cruickshank & Seward and Central Square

Despite the various inquires, E&C's activities remained buoyant and apparently unaffected by the questions raised at the highest levels. E&C officially acquired the Central Station site in January 1973 for a reported £3m.[82] E&C extended an

---

75 Ibid., Para. 76, p. 29.
76 Ibid., Para. 146, p. 61.
77 Ibid., Para. 214, p. 90.
78 Ibid., Para. 188, p. 79.
79 Ibid., Para. 188, p. 80.
80 'Station Site Enquiry Urged', *The Manchester Guardian*, 24 January 1973, p. 8.
81 See Crown Agents (Stevenson Report), HC Deb 24 July 1972 vol. 841 cc.1313–6. http://hansard.millbanksystems.com/commons/1972/jul/24/crown-agents-stevenson-report [Accessed 5 July 2013]; David Sunderland supports this view in his retrospective assessment. Sunderland, D. (2007) *Managing British Colonial and Post-Colonial Development: The Crown Agents, 1914–74* (Woodbridge: The Boydell Press), pp. 218–220.
82 'Central Station Changes Hands', *The Manchester Guardian*, 18 January 1973, p. 14; Joint Note of the City and County Planning Officers. Central Station Development. Para. 6.

invitation to the local planning authority to attend its meetings as the proposals were developed towards a planning application. C&S headed the consultant design team. The partner in charge at C&S was John Seward and this project, known as Central Square, was without doubt the largest scheme he or C&S were commissioned to design. Had the proposals gone ahead it would have propelled C&S to international standing and undoubtedly been the catalyst for reordering their company structure.

John Sheard and Eamonn O'Neill were also heavily involved in the development for C&S and among the consultants was John Whalley of Derek Lovejoy Associates who went on to become President of the Landscape Institute.[83] Whalley and Sheard first met in the office of Frederick Gibberd at Harlow New Town some time around 1949/50 and had a long working relationship that included C&S buildings for ICL and Sun Microsystems at West Gorton [Figure 4.07].[84] The work of the C&S architectural design team was explorative and one that considered a number of options and possibilities for the site. Seward directed the programming and design of the scheme and his clients were open to his ideas.[85] The local spatial planning framework here interacted with the matured mainstream modern architecture of C&S, who had developed their language over nearly twenty years with Seward and Gibbon at the helm.

Surviving in archives are photographs of models produced by C&S in the period leading up to the outline planning application. The earliest model [Figure 4.08] was produced by C&S in-house model maker and perspective artist David Fricker, most likely to represent the drawings of an unnamed Dublin-based practice who were commissioned by Arkle Holdings prior to the transfer of ownership to E&C.[86] It is not uncommon for jobs to pass from one practice to another when a scheme moves from feasibility study to planning application. In all probability this first model was the starting point for discussions about how to further develop the design intent. This proposal was seen by C&S as addressing the main elements of the advisory scheme set out by the City in 1966 and the production of the model was a quick method for ascertaining the general massing of the scheme at an early stage.[87] The slab block of the tower bore resemblance to Rodwell House in Manchester Piccadilly [Figure 4.01] – the expressed structural columns outside of the floor plate could have been

---

Enc. To letter from L. Boardman, 21 February 1975, Director and Deputy Town Clerk. Archives+: GB124.GMC/4/Box 28.

83 Interview with John Sheard, Torquay, 5 August 2011; Interview with Eamonn O'Neill, Heaton Mersey, 7 February 2013. Telephone conversation with John Whalley, 20 May 2013.
84 Telephone conversation with John Whalley, 20 May 2013.
85 Ibid.
86 Pers. comms with Eamonn O'Neill, 23 June 2013.
87 Ibid.

Figure 4.07 Landscaped courtyard at ICL, West Gorton. Designed by John Whalley for Derek Lovejoy and Partners.

conceived to straddle the junction canal that ran beneath the station, in the same manner as the tower at Piccadilly. The model shows the complete removal of the historic train hall and a number of flanking building arrangements outside the main site. This was not aligned with the view of the planning authorities, one of whose aims was to 'preserve Central Station'.[88] The proposed city centre road is clearly shown in the foreground of the image and presents a significant barrier to the connectivity of the scheme, overcome by some form of extended bridge link to Knott Mill (Deansgate) Station – shown bottom left.

Initial models of C&S's early proposals showed the partial retention of the train hall [Figures 4.09 and 4.10] albeit with the apparent removal of the flanking walls. Both schemes show significant plaza-type landscape arrangements. Here too was their first visualisation of cylindrical towers; one option showed them as dispersed and the other clustered, with the latter form reminiscent of the BMW Headquarters in Munich (Karl Schwanzer, 1972). Seward visited the Munich Olympics in 1972 and it is probable that this influenced the form and configuration of this element of the scheme.[89] Seward made reference to the idea of open space as stemming from the work of the City Planning Department. He argued, like BDP previously, that the curvilinear forms of their proposal responded to

---

88 Telephone conversation with Robert Maund, 5 July 2013.
89 Telephone conversation with John Sheard, 2 May 2013.

Figure 4.08 Model 01. Preliminary model by Cruickshank & Seward. Thought to have been built by Dave Fricker to record a feasibility study by unknown architect.

Figure 4.09 Model 02. A group of cylindrical towers proposed at the corner of Deansgate and Peter Street. The station hall is shown as retained, but with significant intervention in the form of stepped floorplates.

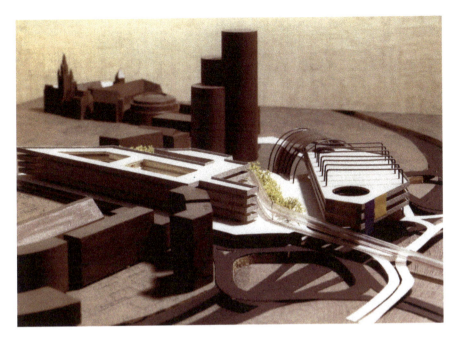

Figure 4.10 Model 03. The clustered cylindrical towers are shown to the south-east corner of the site. The train hall is only partially retained and a new building inserted into its frame. In the middle ground are clear tubes, indicative of a proposed bridge link above the new ring road to Knott Mill Station.

the arched structure of the train hall and that the cylindrical towers were in a formal dialogue with the drum of the Central Reference Library.[90] One of the sunken gardens appears similar in volume to the Library and could be described as its negative. The stepped profile of the clustered towers was intended to be visually dynamic and the exact truncation of the skyline would be determined at detailed design stage.[91] Their curvilinear form, as well as being responsive to context, was intended to 'set it apart from the anonymity of the lesser breed of slab sided modern office towers'.[92]

An alternative to the cylindrical option was imagined as a narrow slab block [Figure 4.12] positioned towards the south-west of the site. In this option the train hall was fully retained, whereas in the preceding schemes a form of

---

90 John Seward, *The Development Objectives of Central Station, Manchester*, p. 4. Archives+: GB124.GMC/5/Box 89.
91 Correspondence from John Seward to Brian Parnell, Chief Planning Officer, 26 November 1974. Archives+: GB124.GMC/5/Box 89.
92 John Seward, *The Development Objectives of Central Station, Manchester*, p. 4. Archives+: GB124.GMC/5/Box 89.

Figure 4.11   Perspective painting by Peter Sainsbury of proposal shown in Model 03 (Figure 4.10). This bold vision shows the partial retention of the structure of the historic train hall as a sort of fascinator for a new building colliding and cutting through it.

new architectural intervention seems to formally interact with a portion of the historic structure. The proposed linear block, shown in this option running parallel to Deansgate, was typical of other commercial architecture by C&S in its horizontal emphasis and setback upper level.

In a further option [Figure 4.13] other additions to the train hall were considered and rolls of masking tape were used to represent a conference centre! Both the slab and clustered cylinder options showed a high-level link to Knott Mill and each of the early proposals had landscaped areas. The most significant open space was represented in the slab option and includes a body of water. John Whalley referred to this as a 'reflective pool' and central to the landscape proposals [Figure 4.14], which were a 'serious component' of the scheme and not a 'cosmetic' gesture.[93] Also physically striking, and clearly visible in Figure 4.10, are the complex levels of the proposed city centre road and the various spurs imagined as necessary to provide vehicular access to the site. The preservation of the route of this ring road was still important to the City despite its having been

---

93   Telephone conversation with John Whalley, 20 May 2013.

INTRACTABLE INVESTMENT

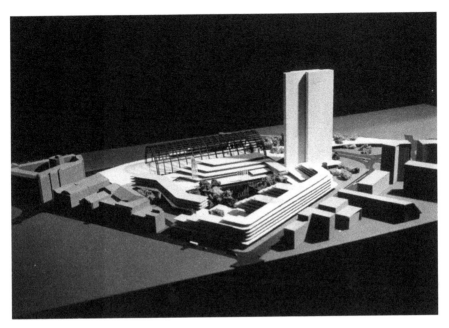

Figure 4.12　Model 04. Slab form tower to north-west of site. Long linear block to Deansgate.

on the drawing board, and without implementation, in one form or another since 1945.[94] This is demonstrable of the primacy of the motor vehicle in the mid-century and the perceived importance of this particular component of the city's renewal (see Chapter 6).

Model 06 [Figure 4.14] illustrated a consolidation of the scheme elements; the entirety of the train hall was retained without any additions that would compromise its form, the clustered cylinder tower was sited to the south-west and the public open space faced the city at the junction of Peter Street and Deansgate. The towers acted as a hinge between the strong geometries of the train hall and Deansgate itself. This succession of models testifies to the consideration of the overall formal composition. The influence of the train hall, the main thoroughfare, the proposed ring road and the civic core upon the organisation of the major elements is explicit throughout these three-dimensional studies. Deansgate is so inscribed in the grain of the city that it had to be addressed as an edge condition.[95]

94　Brook and Jarvis, *Trying to Close the Loop*.
95　Deansgate connects the Roman settlement of Mamchester (Castlefield) to the south and the medieval settlement to the north at the convergence of the Rivers Irk and Irwell. Until very recently its passage was essential to the mobility of the city. See Brook and Jarvis, *Trying to Close the Loop*.

THE RENEWAL OF POST-WAR MANCHESTER

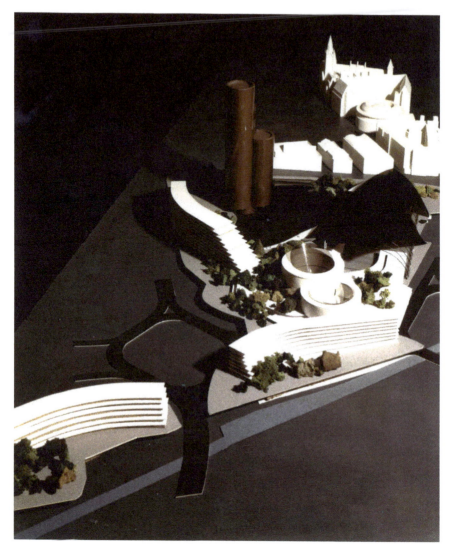

Figure 4.13 Model 05. A curvilinear response throughout this particular configuration.

The most malleable boundary was the existing approach from the northern end of the train hall towards the civic centre of the city. The concourse faced St Peter's Square, flanked by the Central Reference Library, the Town Hall extension and the Town Hall. Each option presented took advantage of the aspect and topography of the north-eastern corner of the site. The situation of the clustered towers was seen as a sentinel for the city at what was considered a 'gateway' site. It was thought to complement the other towers in similar settings

INTRACTABLE INVESTMENT

Figure 4.14　Model 06. A more public-spirited response, retaining the train hall and creating a public park with a large body of water at its centre which may have involved excavating to the level of the canal that ran beneath the site.

at other points in the city, namely the CIS Tower (G.S. Hay with John Burnet, Tait and Partners, 1961–62) to the north and the UMIST Maths Tower (C&S, 1968) to the south.[96] Visible in the next image [Figure 4.15] is a huge linear block stretching westwards towards St George's, an area of Hulme, and a group of shorter tower blocks on the edge of Castlefield (Byrom Street).[97] Quite what powers E&C exerted over these sites is unclear, but the combined extents of the

---

96　Pers. comms with Eamonn O'Neill, 23 June 2013.
97　A residential development was built at Byrom Street in 1979 by developer Wimpey at lower densities than imagined here.

Figure 4.15 Model 07. At the back of the model can be seen a linear block stretching out of the city centre towards St George's, part of Hulme.

proposals were colossal and perhaps represent the ambition and gall of Greene and Walker.

Jack Walker and Ramon Greene were larger than life characters and brought a cosmopolitan attitude to their dealings in Manchester. It was not unknown for them to arrive at the site by helicopter; Walker was a resident of Monaco and Greene resided in an apartment block called Shangri La in Monte Carlo![98] In 1973 they commissioned a promotional film that showed aspirational images from footage taken in Toronto and Chicago of similar conference and exhibition

---

98 John Brennan, 'Ramon Greene Has Debts of £15m', *The Financial Times*, 7 October 1977, p. 44.

centres. This type of pre-application lobbying was unheard of in Manchester and their perceptibly brash image may be one of the reasons why their initial personal approaches to the planning authorities in January 1974 were not particularly encouraging.[99] Nonetheless, the process continued and one model was taken to be critically reviewed by Sir Nicholas Pevsner.[100] A later model was presented to the Royal Fine Arts Commission at Carlton Gardens in November 1974.[101] Despite Walker and Greene's forthright approach, the design team appear to have worked tirelessly to satisfy all concerned parties and successfully negotiated the planning process.

C&S made an outline planning application on behalf of E&C in October 1974 for a comprehensive multi-use development. Reflecting on the process in 1979, John Millar noted that this application followed 'a long series of discussions with the architects ... and their clients Central Square (Manchester) Limited'.[102] According to Millar, a substantial amount of work by all parties, agreed through 'many meetings', went into the proposals.[103] Millar was seen as 'well informed' and a 'very effective city planner' as well as having a 'sharp mind'.[104] By the close of 1974, though, Millar was no longer Chief Planner for the city; he was now County Planner for the Greater Manchester Council (GMC) which was formally inaugurated on 1 April 1974 following the Local Government Act (1972). Nonetheless, his support of the proposals was important to their approval by the planning committee.

Millar and his successor to the city post, Brian Parnell, worked with each other and C&S as they developed their planning application. In order to reconcile any potential confusion over the respective aims of the newly formed county level governance and that of the city, the two authorities adopted the City Planning Department's Advisory Scheme of 1966 as their shared framework for development control.[105] In this situation, we can read the CDA allocation, and the advisory scheme for its development, as national planning guidance interpreted by local government officers. Its use as a tool by which to negotiate mass

---

99 Pers. comms with Eamonn O'Neill, 23 June 2013.
100 Ibid.
101 Ibid.; Correspondence from Royal Fine Arts Commission to Brian Parnell, Chief Planning Officer, 25 November 1974; Correspondence from John Seward to Brian Parnell, Chief Planning Officer, 26 November 1974. Archives+: GB124.GMC/5/Box 89.
102 Report by J.S. Millar, County Planning Officer to committee convened to discuss the future of Central Station, 21 March 1979. Archives+: GB124.GMC/4/Box 28.
103 Report of the County Planning Officer to GMC Planning Committee, 1 July 1974. Archives+: GB124.GMC/4/Box 28.
104 Telephone conversation with John Sheard, 2 May 2013; Telephone conversation with John Whalley, 20 May 2013; Telephone conversation with Robert Maund, 5 July 2013.
105 Joint Note of the City and County Planning Officers. Central Station Development. Enc. To letter from L. Boardman, 21 February 1975, Director and Deputy Town Clerk. Archives+: GB124.GMC/4/Box 28.

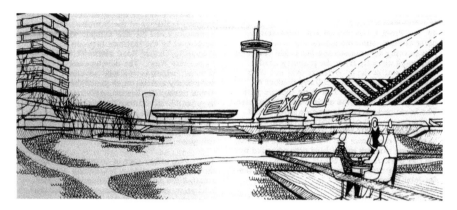

Figure 4.16 Illustrative sketch of the Advisory Scheme for Central Station.

and form with the architects was a development norm; however, the change of local and regional government structure added another tier to the political scale. The advisory scheme, in this context, turned from a piece of planning guidance to a type of contract between two arms of the state – a tool for development control became a mechanism for political consensus in spatial determination.

Two applications were made, one for the development itself and another for Listed Building Consent, related to conversion works that would impact on the Grade II* listed former train hall.[106] E&C also owned a significant portion of adjoining land that did not form part of the application. The proposals conformed generally to the planning department objectives of the *City Centre Map* and the advisory scheme [Figure 4.16].[107] About five of the twenty-three acres was still designated for the route of the inner relief (ring) road. The rest was proposed as a mixture of commercial, leisure and residential uses. The E&C-sponsored scheme by C&S was scheduled to contain a trade centre, exhibition hall, offices, hotel, housing, shopping and leisure facilities, open landscaped space and mandatory car parking. The application was the subject of a joint meeting of the City and County Planning Committees in February 1975, at which support for the scheme was expressed.[108] The Planning Application was

---

106 The outline application detailed many aspects of the development including the situation of the taller buildings, the access and egress by cars, service vehicles and pedestrians, the provision of public open space, parking and the formal relationships of the scheme to a number of centrally located conservation areas. Each of these were considered and discussed in correspondence prepared by the City and County Planning Officers. Joint Note of the City and County Planning Officers, 21 February 1975. Archives+: GB124. GMC/4/Box 28. Planning Ref. F01548/LB, Ref. F01547.
107 Report by J.S. Millar, County Planning Officer to committee convened to discuss the future of Central Station, 21 March 1979. Archives+: GB124.GMC/4/Box 28.
108 Ibid.

approved on 30 April 1975.[109] Only twenty-two conditions were placed on the approved scheme, none of which were particularly onerous or unanticipated. Some suggested conditions from the consultation process were not adopted, including the demand for a bridge link across Deansgate at an alignment to be determined by the local authority.[110] This implied a favourable view towards the developers on the part of the authority, a view underpinned by the preceding reports and minutes prepared at city and county level.

Manchester, in the mid-1970s, was in the depths of deindustrialisation; its docks were in decline and the city centre subject to depopulation.[111] In many respects the authorities were bound to accept the views of E&C as, without them, the site, which was already deteriorating and viewed as something of an eyesore, would simply not be developed. A county sub-committee provided support from a regional perspective and John Millar in his role as County Planning Officer was well aware of the site's capacity and possibilities. It was under his stewardship that the City Planning Department first prepared the advisory scheme for Central Station and mooted the idea of a 'Tivoli Gardens' type environment.[112] Ian Nairn writing in 1968 about the original advisory scheme recorded, in typically double-edged prose, that 'Central Station is suggested as an exhibition hall surrounded by a kind of Tivoli – not as unrealistic as it sounds, for Manchester is desperately short of both open space and fun-places.'[113]

John Seward penned his own statement to accompany the outline planning application that was eventually approved [Figure 4.17] and his words were measured and diplomatic. Speaking of developers in general, but perhaps making specific allusion to his client he referred to their 'tarnished image' and that this can only be countered if the 'quality of thought takes account of all of the essentials that ... will make a material contribution to the way of life of the City both in and around its immediate location'.[114] He is referring to the role of the architect as polymath, in this case as social engineer, and the mediation

---

109 Outline Planning Application notice, F01547. Archives+: Ref. GB124.GMC/4/Box 28.
110 Report of the County Planning Officer to the GMC Planning Committee and submitted to the City Planning Committee at its meeting on the 8 April 1975. J.S. Millar, County Planning Officer, 21 March 1975. Archives+: GB124.GMC/4/Box 28.
111 'Manchester Thinks of Houses in the Centre of the City', *The Manchester Guardian*, 21 September 1966, p. 22; Joint Note of the City and County Planning Officers, 21 February 1975. Archives+: GB124.GMC/4/Box 28.
112 In parallel to the planning process a sub-committee also existed at county level. They were supportive of the use of the site because of its 'central location, its accessibility, the suitability of the train hall and the preference shown by local operators'. Letter from R. Calderwood, Town Clerk to the office of the Chief Executive of the GMC, Mr G.A. Harrison, 10 July 1979. Archives+: GB124.GMC/4/Box 28.
113 Nairn, I, (1968) 'Manchester's Heart Operation', *The Observer*, 4 February 1968, p. 30.
114 John Seward, *The Development Objectives of Central Station, Manchester*, p. 1. Archives+: GB124.GMC/5/Box 89.

THE RENEWAL OF POST-WAR MANCHESTER

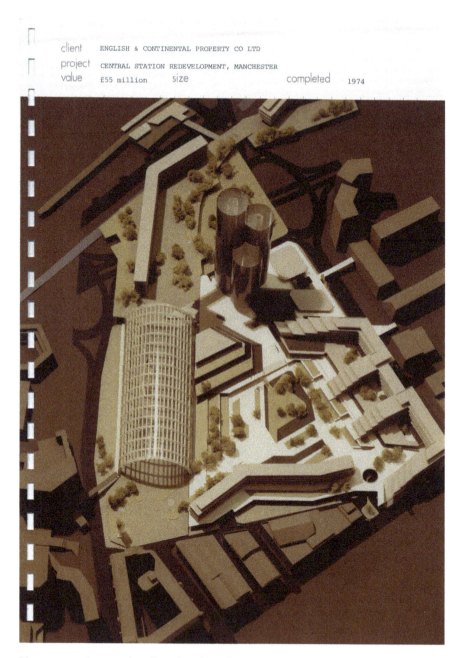

Figure 4.17 Approved outline planning scheme.

of place, policy and personnel in service of a design solution. Seward acknowledged the planning department on the first page of his design statement:

> The end product, as illustrated by the outline scheme now submitted for planning approval, can claim to have taken the City Planning Officer's original of a major open space within the main body of the site as a starting point, and extended this concept so as to provide what is in effect a linear park that could well influence the future development in a characterful way of such adjacent areas as the Castlefield Basin, and which could, as a total concept, provide a wide variety of much needed amenity for relaxation, recreation, exhibition and entertainment.[115]

To propose what amounts to an open-space landscape design framework for the renewal of further areas of the centre, C&S were in very close dialogue with the planning department. As we have seen, Millar and his team were proficient urban designers and their influence on the proposals, whilst not explicit in the acknowledgement or accredited authorship, was implicit in statements like that above and has a formal genealogy. The earliest sketches and models always retained the train hall; they also contained strong vertical counterpoints to the horizontal barrel form. The vertical organisation and creation of a new city datum for an urban park, as presented by C&S, was a primary aim of the city. The personal influence of Millar in the language used by Seward in relation to heritage and the celebration of the industrial past is not certain, but may be assumed.

By 1975 conservation architecture was well established and the juxtaposition of old and new artefacts and materials became a common approach to architectural continuity. The sense of architectural and cultural heritage in the scheme was not overt in the models, but was expressed clearly in Seward's text in relation to overarching character, spatial elements and material finishes. The use of existing materials and characterful spaces were described as 'incidents and moments ... that can be built into new forms and which will give a sense of continuity, character and consistency'.[116] Specifically mentioned was the exposition of a 'three level interchange hoist between canal, road and rail'. He cleverly couched the programme itself as derivative of the very nature of historic activities of trade in the city and tapped into the prevailing zeitgeist of post-industrial Manchester as a place for business to be conducted. Finally, he rounded off his informed disquisition with the following: 'the real truth is that a quality of thinking and imagination will yield a profit for the whole community – this can only come from an understanding of the real needs of all concerned. It can only be said that a great effort has been made by many people to achieve that objective before all else.'[117] In this prose, the regional experience

---

115   Ibid.
116   Ibid.
117   Ibid.

of the architect and their sensitivity to local concerns came to the fore. The formal language of the architecture proposed was undoubtedly international in its style, but John Seward managed to place this firmly and convincingly within a regional dialogue. The global nature of the financing and procurement of the site was ultimately anchored to a local setting by not only the words, but also by the actions, of the design team. The mainstream modern architecture proposed was sufficiently flexible (or could be described as such) in its form and material to satisfy an array of parties with different interests in the site – its principal arrangement was influenced by the existing listed buildings and the approach first outlined by the planning department; the major formal elements were said to respond to the wider city context and tie in to the proposed highway arrangement; and the amount of lettable floor space made the scheme financially viable to the developer. The metaphorical space between tiers of policy informed governance and detailed architectural proposal required knowledge, experience and skill to negotiate a universally agreeable outcome.

Unfortunately, the prevailing economic climate was not favourable to development and the shortcomings of the Crown Agents were beginning to catch up with E&C. Despite the outline approval, C&S never received instruction to proceed with detailed design, though the process of marketing portions of the site for acquisition by third parties had begun.[118] Walker and Greene effectively 'vanished' from any communication with the design team and other representatives of E&C continued to loosely manage the situation from a distance.[119]

City and county take control

Despite continuing parliamentary interests in the financial dealings of E&C, they remained owners of the site and continued to express a desire to develop some or all of it. Early in 1977 John Seward of C&S and a representative of E&C held talks with the City in light of the demise of the existing exhibition centre at Belle Vue in 1976. Their discussions centred on a reduced scheme that would see the creation of a new exhibition facility.[120] E&C were not prepared to relinquish any of their interests at this point due to the initial capital outlay and the 'high redevelopment value if it could be realised'.[121] Contrary to the messages relayed to the authorities, E&C's interest was not in developing the site, but in

---

118 As evidenced by sales pamphlet. Archives+: GB124.GMC/5/Box 89.
119 Telephone conversation with John Sheard, 2 May 2013.
120 Correspondence from the County Secretary to the Chief Executive of GMC, 6 July 1977. Orange folder marked Central Station Site, exhibition sub-committee. Archives+: GB124.GMC/4/Box 28.
121 Correspondence from the County Secretary to the Chief Executive of GMC, 6 July 1977. Archives+: GB124.GMC/4/Box 28.

disposing of it. They sold it in October 1977 to George Robinson (Manchester) Limited, a company specialising in demolition work.[122]

After a sustained period of inactivity, the whole area around the station became of concern to the GMC and in 1977, together with the City, they began to reinvestigate the site and those adjacent to it. The commercial demands in the city were vastly altered from those of the late 1960s and the GMC urged 'a more flexible approach ... that [was] not completely dependent upon a single comprehensive scheme.'[123] The City convened a Special Committee to consider the purchase of the site. On the recommendations of said committee the City Council decided to promote a Compulsory Purchase Order (CPO) under powers granted by the Community Land Act (1975).[124] This was just the lever required to facilitate discussions with George Robinson concerning the acquisition of the site by agreement rather than by use of a legal instrument.

GMC acquired the site in the summer of 1978 and quickly appointed Shankland Cox as planning consultants to make a formal reappraisal of the site and its possibilities. The assessment led to the creation of a Joint Venture Study Group and proposals to develop the train hall as a convention centre designed by favoured architects of the GMC, Essex Goodman Suggitt (EGS) rapidly evolved.[125] EGS's scheme also addressed the site of the Great Northern Warehouse [Figure 4.19], but ultimately funding was only available to construct the exhibition centre, which was named G-Mex, between 1982 and 1986. Following the IRA bomb of 1996 in Manchester, the city underwent a massive process of rebuilding and the remainder of the site that fell within the original CDA boundary was developed to include the Great Northern Warehouse, the Beetham Tower, a conference centre, residential accommodation and the Peter Street frontage to include a new public square, all at a disposition, scale and mass reminiscent of the Advisory Scheme of 1967 and the approved outline planning application of 1975. It is therefore possible to view the legacy of the CDA allocation in the shape and form of the city more than fifty years from its designation.

---

122 In fact, the purchase was largely underwritten by National Car Parks Limited (NCP) who secured a 99-year operational lease on the site. *City of Manchester, Central Station Site Manchester, Report of the Special Committee*, Report No. 761. Archives+: GB124.RB/Box 2.

123 *Central Station Site Manchester, Planning Appraisal*. County and City Planning Officers, January 1979. Archives+: GB124.GMC/4/Box 28.

124 Correspondence from R. Calderwood, Town Clerk and Chief Executive to The Chairman and Members of the Land and Development Committee, 7 April 1978. Archives+: GB124.RB/Box 2.

125 Central Manchester Joint Venture Study (1981) *Central Station: Proposals for Regeneration* (Manchester: GMC).

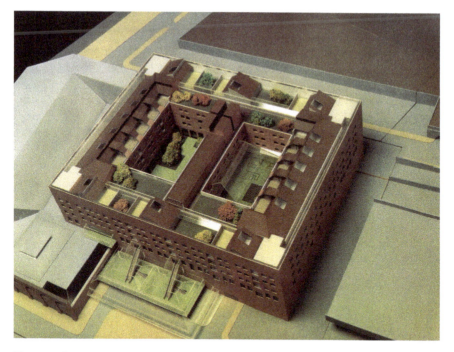

Figure 4.18   Essex Goodman Suggitt proposals for the Great Northern Warehouse.

International endings

Although C&S's huge scheme was never realised, the case of Manchester's Central Station shows very clearly how an international context, like that of decolonisation, can impact on regional and local concerns. It is interesting to note the tiers of discourse surrounding the development of the station. At one level there was a predominantly local or regional thread, which involved councillors, MPs and public bodies, whose voices, whilst looming loud in the local press, were largely without power or influence in the real negotiations. The second tier was internationally tinged; the CA were a former colonial body and provided funding, E&C had property interests across the globe including Australia and Singapore, Jack Walker was a resident of Monaco, John Whalley, the landscape architect, had studied at postgraduate level in Pennsylvania and the major new element of C&S's proposals was informed by European precedent.[126] Yet, it was the magnitude of the site and its situation in Manchester around which all of these forces coalesced to arrive at a formal architectural

---

126   Pers. comms with Eamonn O'Neill, 23 June 2013; Telephone conversation with John Whalley, 20 May 2013.

conclusion and the local knowledge of the design team, headed by C&S, that drove the scheme to its fruition, at least on the drawing board, and, ultimately, with approval success at the outline planning stage.

The narration of its turbulent procurement, yet inactive development, has highlighted the statutory frameworks of the Town and Country Planning Act and the planning machinery applied to enable development. In this example, as with many in other renewal cities, the statutory powers of government were interwoven with private sector finance. In terms of actual rebuilding, the delays to the post-war reconstruction of central Manchester were down to limited resources, a focus on housing, health and education buildings and the control exerted by central government on the construction of these building types and rationing of materials. Therefore, even though CDAs were part of the planning machinery from 1947, their application in development control was relatively slow – CDA powers were not really required in the central areas of renewal cities until the late 1950s and, more predominantly, into the 1960s.

Where CDAs were used as a planning tool in Manchester it was for two major purposes: CDAs were primarily used to assist the public sector in negotiations with private developers in the parcelling of sites with fragmented ownership. Robert Maund (Assistant City Planning Officer, 1963–74) referred to the advisory schemes as being used to 'fire the imagination' of developers and that the planners were 'happy to look at other options'.[127] It was a process of 'negotiation' and if negotiations were favourable then the authority would be willing to exercise their powers in support of the aims of the private sector. This corroborates arguments in relation to the entrepreneurial status of Labour authorities in the mid-century and the consensus of successive central administrations towards renewal.[128] CDAs were, in addition, used as a mechanism to protect the long-term interests of local authorities – as in the case of Central Station and the Education Precinct in Manchester.[129] The architects' role in this scenario was often as mediator first and as designer second. The architects acted as conduits to the approvals of local authorities and other concerned parties. Architects' local experience, particularly during the period under examination, was clearly important prior to the widespread international exchange of professional services. The CDA allocation in Manchester did not jeopardise reconstruction on smaller island sites and the comprehensive planning of the CDAs and the ring road effectively released certain locations for development.

---

127 Telephone conversation with Robert Maund, 5 July 2013.
128 See Shapely, P. (2011) 'The Entrepreneurial City: The Role of Local Government and City-Centre Redevelopment in Post-War Industrial English Cities', *Twentieth Century British History*, Vol. 22, No. 4, pp. 498–520; Smith, O.S. (2015) 'Central Government and Town-Centre Redevelopment in Britain, 1959–1966', *The Historical Journal*, Vol. 58, No. 1, pp. 217–244.
129 See Brook, R. (2010) 'Manchester Modern: The Shape of the City' (thesis) ch. 4. Copy held at RIBA Library, ref. ReAw/Brook.

The story of Central Station shows the agency of political tiers and at different scales; it shows the impact of political networks in the production of urban design, architecture and detailed specification. Larger factors came into play to prevent C&S realising their ambitious designs and it is ironic that the site was eventually developed by the newly formed GMC after fourteen years and the original unsuccessful bids of the City in 1968. Perhaps also tinged with irony is the fact that the GMC itself was dissolved in 1986, within months of completion of the G-Mex Centre, its most significant physical development. In this chapter we have seen the effects, impacts and ramifications of the networks of actors on an unbuilt central area scheme. In the next chapter I explore the development of another CDA in central Manchester, which was built – Market Place.

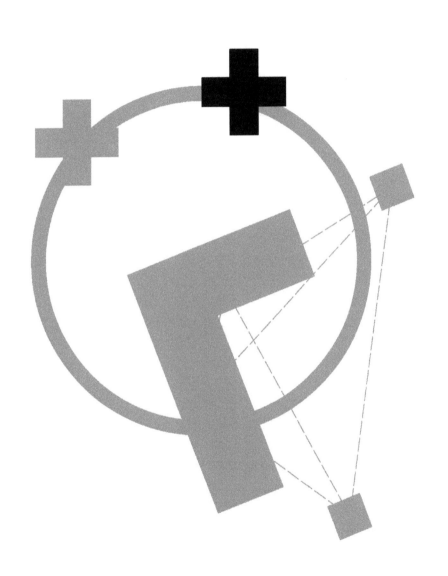

5

Bookended by bombs and drawn out development: Market Place

Introduction

On a Saturday morning in June 1996, Manchester city centre was ripped apart by the detonation of a bomb, planted in a van on Cross Street by the Provisional IRA. One of the enduring images of the post-explosion devastation was the survival of a Victorian pillar box, almost at the epicentre of the blast. Above the iconic red receptacle was another resilient form, the wavy concrete canopy of Michael House, home to Marks & Spencer, from where the rapid evacuation of the city centre commenced [Figure 5.01].[1] Architects, Cruickshank & Seward (C&S), designed Michael House as a shop and offices for Unicos Property Corporation in the late 1950s. It opened as part of the first wave of post-war central area development in Manchester in 1961 on a site known as Market Place. Market Place was one of several renewal schemes that were realised in central Manchester and similar to many others in Britain and Europe. As its names suggests, this was in the historic centre of commerce and exchange of the city, close to the Cathedral. The area was extensively damaged in the Manchester Blitz of Christmas 1940 and the first new building, Longridge House, was completed to designs by H.S. Fairhurst & Sons in 1959. The remainder of the site took a further fifteen years to construct, aand was completed in 1974.

Bookended by the Blitz and a bombing, the extended post-war narrative of this site, its planning and its architecture, shows how policy affected form and how local government and the private sector negotiated, using drawings and models to interpret legislation. One of the central threads of this book, through each of the chapters, is the shifting balance of regional and national interests.

---

[1] Williams, G., Batho, S., and Russell, L. (2000) 'Responding to Urban Crisis: The Emergency Planning Response to the Bombing of Manchester City Centre', *Cities*, Vol. 17, No. 4, pp. 293–304.

Figure 5.01 Cross Street Manchester, 15 June 1996. The wavy canopy of Marks & Spencer was partially destroyed at the epicenter of the blast. Also visible is the Portland stone cladding.

Earlier chapters have looked at schemes where central government played a strong part in the determination of site, mass, form and material. This chapter focuses on the activities of local government and the impact of its successive officers in affecting the architectural outcome of Market Place. It is Manchester's Arndale Centre that has received more attention from historians, mostly due to its monolithic beige tiled mass standing as a symbol of consumerism.[2] Market Place, as an earlier development, was built in parts, over a longer period of time and, as such, elaborates more nuanced discourse. Its circumstance reveals some of the debates central to post-war planning – those of conservation, mainstream modernism and urban renewal.

The IRA bombing was the catalyst for the second wave of twentieth-century renewal in the city centre of Manchester and instituted a number of public–private partnerships that were subsequently categorised as models for the 'Entrepreneurial

---

2 Historian Alistair Kefford has used Manchester's Arndale Centre to examine how urban managerialism fed the pre-neoliberal appetite for development and in turn fostered both consumerism and provided the economic foundations for later types of property-led urban regeneration. See, Kefford, A. (2020) 'Actually Existing Managerialism: Planning, Politics and Property Development in Post-1945 Britain', *Urban Studies* (September).

City'.[3] However, these collaborative arrangements were not unique to the burgeoning economy of the 1990s; similar relations were at play in the post-war renewal of many provincial cities from the late 1950s. In the 'renewal cities' of the Midlands, the North and Scotland, the political, cultural and economic conditions were very different to those of the earlier developed 'recovery cities'. As we have read, in 1960s Manchester, the entire city centre was considered by planners as a three-dimensional totality. The story of Central Station in Chapter 4 explained, in part, the role of local authority planners, their powers in relation to official advice and impacts upon architectural form. Here, we look at the how the physical frameworks proposed by successive officers of Manchester Corporation affected the design of Market Place. To do this will require a step backwards in time to the Manchester Blitz of 1940–41, and the subsequent planning and design eventually published as the *City of Manchester Plan* in 1945. The period between 1945 and the completion of the Market Place development in 1974 is crucial here, particularly with reference to changing cultures in British architecture and urbanism, that witnessed the full-scale adoption and adaptation of modernist ideas in architecture and city planning for the first time in the UK.

The act of construction forms only a short part of the development process and, as shown in earlier chapters, there are innumerable external forces acting upon the production of architecture. These forces are amplified in complex city centre sites where landowners and stakeholders are multiple and the wider economic and socio-cultural impacts are felt by large numbers of citizens. Such complexity can result in extended periods of consultation and approval that, in turn, have their own impact, as statute and conceptions of what constitutes good urban form shift according to new precedents, experience and theories. In the context of Market Place, there are a number of thresholds or transitions in ideas, policies, governance and personnel that influenced its formal outcomes. Most acute are the relationships between the two major urban plans for Manchester of 1945 and 1967, the influences of one upon the other and the prevailing urban design ideals manifest in each [Figure 5.02]. Ultimately, this chapter addresses the manner in which these plans and their negotiation impacted upon the design of Market Place by C&S.

Locally, the transition of office from City Engineer and Surveyor Rowland Nicholas, to City Planner John Millar was representative of the changing shape of local government and the roles and responsibilities of its officers. Planners became more important than architects in the interpretation of national guidance as the traditional act of civic design gave way to urban planning and urban renewal. Nationally, ideas published in *The Concise Townscape* (1961) and *Traffic in Towns* (1963) and the rise of the architectural preservation movement,

---

3 Williams, G. (2000) 'Rebuilding the Entrepreneurial City: The Master Planning Response to the Bombing of Manchester City Centre', *Environment and Planning B: Planning and Design*, No. 27 (August), pp. 485–505.

Figure 5.02 Extracts from Rowland Nicholas's plan of 1945 and John Millar's plan of 1967. The red rectangle picks out the area of the Market Place development. The solid black areas in Millar's plan indicate the intended areas of pedestrianisation.

also influenced discourse around the development of Market Place. Gordon Cullen's book, *The Concise Townscape*, captured the transnational rejection of commercial development in the UK, as Kevin Lynch and Jane Jacobs's works did in the United States.[4] Cullen's was an experiential approach based on his own first-hand observations of the 'serial vision' of various historic centres. Colin Buchanan's *Traffic in Towns* was similarly a warning against the destruction of the social life of cities, but aimed to address rising car ownership through planning, and synthesised many ideas about urban design that were prevalent at the time.[5] Multi-layered, mixed-use, retail, commercial and leisure centres with basement or multi-storey car parks, served by newly engineered ring roads, typified the development of the renewal cities. The model drew on US precedent, but also on earlier European modernist ideas of zoning. For planners this was a chance to test their training in forging city space by drawing together its functions in a designed assemblage. It also meant negotiating the demands of the private sector investors. For the public this meant new commercial and retail encounters.

---

4 Cullen, G. (1961) *The Concise Townscape* (London: Architectural Press), p. 9; Lynch, K. (1960) *The Image of the City* (Cambridge, MA: MIT Press); Jacobs, J. (1961) *The Death and Life of Great American Cities*. (New York: Random House).
5 Buchanan, *Traffic in Towns*.

Retail architecture in Manchester

Architecture for retailing in Manchester grew from its markets. The open aprons of Smithfield, to the north of the city centre, were covered with iron framed, glass lined structures in the middle of the nineteenth century. They were designed by a number of different architectural practices between 1846 and 1873.[6] The market halls of Upper and Lower Campfield (Mangall & Littlewood) were constructed along Liverpool Road in the 1880s. Affluence and economic buoyancy in the Victorian era led Manchester property owner John Hope Barton to adopt the Milanese model and to institute the first of a cluster of glazed *galleria*, the Barton Arcade, at a site on Deansgate (Corbett, Raby & Sawyer, 1871). This grouping of enclosed shopping spaces created a 'civic complex ... replicated in many other British towns';[7] the Corporation promoted its expansion across the city centre, but no new arcades were built.

The most significant new shopping experience of the twentieth century arrived following the completion of Kendal Milne's department store (J.S. Beaumont & Sons) in 1939. The outbreak of war the same year meant that the store was not occupied until after the cessation of conflict.[8] Thus, the first new retail experience in post-war Manchester was not in a sleek modern shopping centre, but was contained in Kendal Milne, the established well-mannered, late-deco styled institution that had traded in the city since 1836 [Figure 5.03].

Cruickshank & Seward's scheme for the new Marks & Spencer store in the early 1960s mimicked the Portland stone of Kendal Milne in its white concrete. However, the exuberant cantilevered canopy symbolised a city on the cusp of expansion and the store and office on the corner of Cross Street and St Mary's Gate, only yards from the Victorian arcades, embodied a new era of mainstream modernism in post-war Britain and encompassed formal ideas invested in the ideological and aesthetic shifts in architecture and urbanism after 1945.

Blitzed

In 1945, the publication of Nicholas's *Plan* heralded change in the city and signalled the professions' transition to modern zoning and modern architecture. Manchester had experienced several bombing raids on the city in 1940–41, the most sustained of which was the Christmas Blitz between 22 and 24 December 1940. This was the catalyst, though not the cause, behind the preparation of a plan to rebuild Manchester. The area around Market Place was significantly damaged [Figure 5.04]. Buildings were pulled down and sites cleared in the

---

6 Hartwell, *Manchester*, pp. 228–230.
7 Dobraszczyk, P. (2014) *Iron, Ornament and Architecture in Victorian Britain: Myth and Modernity* (Farnham: Ashgate), p. 191.
8 Parkinson-Bailey, *Manchester: An Architectural History*, p. 152.

Figure 5.03 Exterior of Kendal, Milne & Co.'s department store in Manchester, c.1950.

Figure 5.04 Extract from bomb damage maps to show area around Market Place. The buildings shaded in solid red were completely destroyed.

wake of the Blitz. Remaining standing amidst the levelled rubble was the Old Wellington Inn, a public house of medieval, half-timbered construction.

In Nicholas's 1945 vision for the city centre there was no place for the piecemeal retention of historic buildings. The Old Wellington was one of many surviving structures eclipsed by the ambitious replanning of the central area. Within the *Plan* only eight buildings were identified as 'historic', including the Cathedral, St Anne's Church, Rylands Library and the Art Gallery. Other buildings completed in the 1930s would also be retained; the Town Hall Extension, the Central Library, Kendal Milne and the Police Station all appeared in the illustrative plates drawn to accompany the *Plan*. The *Plan* did not, however, account for the retention of Alfred Waterhouse's neo-Gothic Town Hall of 1877! This was destined to be replaced by a modernist building in the manner of Hornsey Town Hall (Reginald Uren, 1933–35), which itself drew on Dudok's masterpiece at Hilversum (1931) and Östberg's City Hall in Stockholm (1923).

Nicholas's plan was a mixture of traditional civic design and modernist zoning, and the new buildings illustrated therein were also mixed in character [Figure 5.05]. Whilst the proposed Town Hall and bus and railway stations were imagined as contemporary, much of the commercial core and other civic buildings illustrated were rendered in a neo-classical style. The dirt and grime of the industrial age was to be cleansed and remnants such as the Old Wellington

Figure 5.05   Drawing by J.D.M. Harvey showing the new Town Hall (centre) and the proposed boulevard to connect Albert Square to the Law Courts beyond (see Figure 7.03). In the foreground on the left is the John Rylands Library.

were viewed as thorns in the side of progress. This particular thorn, however, was deeply embedded in the socio-cultural history of the city, and the preservation of the inn and its neighbour, Sinclair's Oyster Bar, would ultimately impact upon the form of the development to come.

Conservation was only one of the forces acting upon development. The Blitz and subsequent planning presented opportunities for the rationalisation of transportation systems; primary among these was provision for the motor vehicle. The design of highways 'to ease the flow of traffic' was first among four 'clear-cut' phases of planning that would enable 'future development'.[9] Despite the modernist zoning principles attached to the reimagined central area of Manchester, the new city was unable to fully obscure the patterns of the past. As in many other replanned centres, a series of ring roads were proposed that would link the radial routes that had traditionally converged on the core. These rings would 'relieve the city centre of all through traffic', 'clarify its road pattern' and take 'the fullest advantage of the scattered damage done by the 1940 air raids'.[10] Highway planning was designed to facilitate the proposed zoning within which landmarks would be established to create 'focal points' to afford 'coherence and architectural balance to the city centre'. Finally, the question of passenger transport would be addressed by improving rail connections.

This fourfold process, of highways design, zoning, focal points and rationalised passenger transportation, was spelled out in an assured manner by Nicholas but was nonetheless recognised as 'pointing the way to further inquiries'. Although the plan stipulated that 'none of the proposals [could] be regarded as final', the proposal for a city centre ring road would nevertheless overshadow and inform a significant amount of development for the following thirty years, including that of Market Place and the Cathedral Area.[11]

The published plan for the central area of Manchester in 1945, whilst overlooking large portions of the Victorian city now regarded as heritage assets, contained an ambition to create a precinct around the Cathedral [Figure 5.06]. The proposed traffic alignments were designed to remove vehicles from the front of the Cathedral and allow new gardens to be created over a culverted River Irwell. Amongst the highway works was a large roundabout whose situation would take 'full advantage of the blitz clearance'. As a further indication of the lingering and long-lived ambition of the *1945 Plan*, the Cathedral Precinct was envisaged for a second time in 1962 by Rowland Nicholas, in 1964 by John Millar, in 1988 by Fairhurst and again in 1996 by a consortium led by EDAW following the IRA bombing. It is the successive master plans, of 1945, 1962 and 1964 by the local authority that are most relevant here.[12]

---

9 Nicholas, *City of Manchester Plan 1945*, pp. 186–187.
10 Ibid., p. 187.
11 Brook and Jarvis, *Trying to Close the Loop*.
12 John Millar's plan of 1964 was part of the Development Map 1967, which formed the basis of the Whitehall approved plan in 1968.

Figure 5.06   Extract from central area plan (1945) to show precinct around Cathedral and the Market Place area immediately to the south.

Planning, preservation and public–private partnerships

The illustration of Nicholas's first plan of 1945 showed a group of three large commercial blocks of between 5 and 8 storeys tall, each with a central atrium. They were imagined in an orthodox orthogonal form and drawn in a manner that did not imply any particular architectural style [Figure 5.07]. Within the central area, the local authority had to work with existing legislation to determine the works that could be sanctioned and attract central funding from sources such as the War Damage Commission. A small Ministry of Town and Country Planning (MTCP) was hived off from the MoW in 1943 and the Town and Country Planning Act (1944) allowed for the development of areas of bomb damage or serious obsolescence. Market Place was one of nine official bomb-damaged areas that Manchester sought to repair and was scheduled as the first area in the city to be redeveloped under the guidance of the *1945 Plan*.[13] Lord Reith famously encouraged towns and cities to 'plan boldly and comprehensively' in 1941, but the powers to do so were not vested until revisions in the Town and Country

---

13   'Redevelopment in Manchester', *The Manchester Guardian*, 22 July 1948, p. 6.

Figure 5.07 Drawing by P.D. Hepworth of the Cathedral Precinct. Above the Cathedral are shown the first illustrations of the new Market Place, a rectangular road junction and a series of orthogonal commercial blocks.

Planning Act (1947).[14] Nonetheless, well-intentioned local authorities were still answerable to their electorate and in 1948 Nicholas's plans were presented at a public inquiry.

Prior to the preparation of reconstruction plans, the Old Wellington had not been protected. It was during the public inquiry that the first notion of its designation as a Scheduled Ancient Monument was mooted.[15] Such appeals were not limited to the inquiry. In his 1948 Presidential Address to the Royal Manchester Institution titled 'History and the City Plan', Liberal Party politician Philip M. Oliver called for the preservation of certain warehouses, merchants' palaces and 'little inns', including the Old Wellington.[16] Manchester City Council's application for the right to apply a compulsory purchase order to the 7.32-acre site was approved in January 1949. The approval came with the caveat that the

---

14 The then minister Lord Reith gave this oft-cited advice to delegates from Coventry in 1941 and recorded himself in 1949. Reith, J.C.W. (1949) *Into the Wind* (London: Hodder & Stoughton), p. 424.
15 'Redevelopment in Manchester', *The Manchester Guardian*, 22 July 1948, p. 6.
16 'Manchester's Past. Appeal to "Preserve the Heritages"', *The Manchester Guardian*, 13 October 1948; 'Royal Manchester Institution. History and the City Plan, by Philip M. Oliver' (President Address, 30 Jan. 1948). Archives+: GB127.M6/1/79/12.

Old Wellington should be protected and that any plans for redevelopment that would affect it should be referred to the MoW.[17]

With the exception of the Old Wellington Inn, the remaining property in the Market Place area was described as 'little better than commercial slums'.[18] The practice of building conservation before 1939 was largely focused on the preservation of ancient monuments and the upkeep of property owned by the National Trust.[19] It was not until the 1940s when articles about restoration of historic buildings in urban settings were published in the architectural press – a natural response to the destruction wrought upon towns and cities across Europe. Planning literature on conservation in the English language did not emerge until the 1970s.[20] There were two distinct choices for cities when conflict ceased: to reconstruct their historic centres or to design and build completely new districts; most places did a little of both. These approaches captured two popular desires, one for a return to the past and another imbued with progressive optimism following years of war.

In Manchester, despite a lack of regard for the neo-Gothic Town Hall, the modest and ramshackle public house reflected the public's appreciation of urban heritage and the increased professional focus on building conservation. Nicholas's initial plans did not account for the inn's retention, but in July 1950, by a huge majority, the City Council referred the scheme back to the Town Planning Committee. Not a single council member spoke in favour of the plans as proposed and several aldermen questioned the demolition of the 'irreplaceable' Wellington Inn and the adjoining oyster bar.[21] The protection and preservation of these buildings had significant impact on forthcoming proposals and the built scheme.

In January 1953 Nicholas's department presented revised proposals for the 'old Market Place'. His team prepared a 'rough model with moveable blocks' that was described as 'diagrammatic, and ... subject to alteration to suit the requirements of private developers'.[22] It was, however, intended to suggest potential phasing, the broad relationship between site and floor area, building heights and distance apart, much like the later advisory schemes for the CDAs of the city

---

17 'An Ancient Monument in War-damaged Area', *The Manchester Guardian*, 15 January 1949, p. 6.
18 'Redevelopment in Manchester', *The Manchester Guardian*, 22 July 1948, p. 6.
19 The first use of the term 'conservation' in the British architectural press was '"Our war-scarred heritage": Articles on the Conservation of Damaged Buildings', *The Builder*, 17 July 1942, p. 45.
20 Sutcliffe, A. (1981) *The History of Urban and Regional Planning. An Annotated bibliography* (London: Mansell Publishing), pp. 204–207.
21 'Wellington Inn Demolition. Plans Referred Back', *The Manchester Guardian*, 6 July 1950, p. 8.
22 'City's Plans for the Area Around the Old Market Place. Half-timbered Inn to be Preserved', *The Manchester Guardian*, 8 January 1953, p. 2.

centre. The Corporation lacked the funds to develop Market Place themselves, but were determined to use their powers to improve its feasibility for construction. Several interests on the site had to be addressed and through the assembly process they slowly acquired the necessary land to realise comprehensive development.[23]

In legislative terms, there were two major changes to the Town and Country Planning Act that altered the landscape for private developers and accelerated development outside London. The amendments of the 1953 Act lifted the development charge and, in the Act of 1954, building licensing was removed.[24] The Conservative administration of the early 1950s was increasingly reluctant to allow 'completely municipal central area developments'. They viewed the 'developer friendly system' created in 1954 as encouraging a speculative, commercial approach, which in turn satisfied a demand for the consumption of previously rationed goods and services.[25] The building boom in cities outside London was heralded by the first major development by Arndale at Jarrow in the north-east (1961). Arndale was formed in Bradford in 1950 by Arnold Hagenbach and Sam Chippindale and began by developing small parades of shops in Yorkshire.[26] Jarrow was a comprehensive development in cooperation with the local authority, a deal based on the model used in the blitzed recovery cities, where local authorities effectively leased the land to developers to configure with their existing statutorily approved master plans. This approach was relatively efficient in a town or city where wide areas were destroyed but subject to speculative acquisitions in places with less damage and multiple ownerships.[27] Manchester fell into the second category and Market Place was assembled through a series of such purchases.

Favourable conditions for development created by changes in legislation and the general economic recovery put local authority planning departments under pressure. They were supposed to direct, negotiate and approve plans that were progressing at an unprecedented rate. Comprehensive developments were managed using the CDA mechanism, which, by the 1950s, 'had largely superseded the 1944 Act's redevelopment areas'.[28] Using the drawings, models

---

23 NCP made a business buying bomb-damaged sites to use as car parking with little capital investment. Their lease was not renewed and the council took control of the parking until such time as the development would proceed. Other businesses had their applications for reconstruction denied as they were obstructive to comprehensive development. Town Planning and Buildings Committee minutes, 1953. GB127.Council Minutes/Town Planning and Buildings Committee/2/39, pp. 112, 348, 362, 489.
24 Ward, S.V. (1994) *Planning and Urban Change* (London: Paul Chapman Publishing), p. 114.
25 Ward, *Planning and Urban Change*, pp. 143–144.
26 Marriott, *The Property Boom*, p. 147.
27 Ibid., pp. 145–157.
28 Ward, *Planning and Urban Change*, p. 143; Hasegawa, J. (1992) *Replanning the Blitzed City Centre: A Comparative Study of Bristol, Coventry and Southampton 1941–50* (Berkshire: Open University Press).

and specifications of the advisory schemes was one way for local authority planners to influence the form and content of a CDA. The other important governing factor in the physical arrangement of proposals was the rationalisation of existing road systems, which often followed medieval patterns. The modernist organisation of space was not enough to undo the radial forces of the medieval market town. The geographic, economic and political orders that had established the morphologies of large British towns and cities were too ingrained to simply dissolve under the applied rules of modernism in planning. Despite the loosening of physical contextual strictures upon the act of design (the loss of the tradition of 'civic design')[29] the new city was unable to fully obscure the patterns of the past. Ring and radial roads that adopted and adapted existing routes were utilised widely as the proposed solution to the knotted congestion of the market town. Many contemporary accounts by local authority planners referred to the primacy of highways planning and its influence on the design and situation of new development.[30] Planning departments were thus trying to negotiate the complex long-term ambitions of highway engineering and a raft of applications for new development.

Shifting styles

As new development accelerated across the renewal cities, highway construction tried to keep pace. Ultimately, many cities only partially realised the extents of their ambitious post-war inner-urban motorway planning: Manchester's case is explored in the concluding chapter. Their construction was subject to delay due to complex land ownership patterns and funding that depended on public–private partnerships, which also took time to negotiate. Even though a road was as speculative a prospect as a development, the drawings of the proposed position of the city centre road and inner ring road in Manchester were much more precise than the information presented in the planning advisory schemes. The prevalent attitude was that roads had to be engineered first and buildings would follow. In the case of Market Place this meant that several highway designs informed its development and each left an incisive mark.

---

29 See Crinson, M., and Lubbock, J. (1994) *Architecture – Art or Profession?: Three Hundred Years of Architectural Education in Britain* (Manchester: Manchester University Press), pp. 123–125.

30 Among them are those in Burns, W. (1967) *Newcastle-upon-Tyne: A Study in Replanning at Newcastle-upon-Tyne* (London: Leonard Hill); the accounts of Birmingham, Leicester, Liverpool and Newcastle upon Tyne in Holliday, J.C. (ed.) (1974) *City Centre Redevelopment: A Study of British City Centre Planning and Case Studies of Five English City Centres* (London: Charles Knight); Milligan, J. (1986) 'Local Government and the City Centre: A view from 1960 – I', in Milligan, J. (ed.) (1986) *Strathclyde Papers on Planning. City Planners and the Glasgow City Centre* (Glasgow: University of Strathclyde, Department of Urban and Regional Planning).

Figure 5.08 Longridge House, H.S. Fairhurst & Son, 1959. Demolished 1996. View from Corporation Street.

The first new building on the Market Place site was Longridge House (H.S. Fairhurst & Sons, 1959) [Figure 5.08]. Its form and material related to ideas of the immediate post-war period and it appeared out of date when new. It is a useful example with which to consider stylistic architectural shifts (in the UK and in Manchester specifically) and the impact of policy guidance upon form. The eight-storey building was home to the British Engine Insurance Company and was designed in the Festival Style. Westmorland slate was used as a facing material and Portland stone dressed the openings. This was typical of Fairhurst's post-war approach to design and in contrast to the 'white' buildings by Arthur Gibbon for C&S that followed. Gibbon's buildings were designed for the new city, for the reimagined city of John Millar's team.

Longridge House belonged to Rowland Nicholas's city – it was designed and built with the future comprehensive development in mind, but according to road alignments established in the 1945 *Plan*.[31] The junctions defined in Manchester in 1945 were like those specified and illustrated in official documents where roads intersected in plan with diagonal lines, not curves – creating

---

31 'Longridge House', *The Guardian*, 11 November 1959, p. 12.

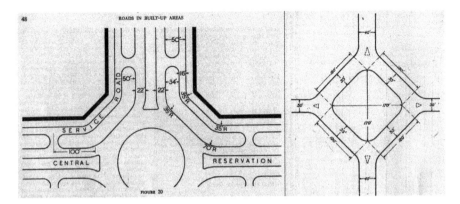

Figure 5.09 Extracts from government publications on highways and junction design from the 1940s.

'square-abouts' rather than roundabouts [Figure 5.09].[32] The footprint of Longridge House's plan followed the angles of the proposed junction, which mirrored published diagrams. The rest of Market Place was later developed within a revised plan for the city centre road that introduced plazas and high-level walkways to separate pedestrians from traffic. In this way Longridge House offers a view of the palimpsestic ghosts left by unrealised plans and of the awkward nature of urban and architectural design when dealing with decades of development. Its plan was of another age and its material expression similarly dated; the rear of the building failed to integrate with the new levels behind it. Longridge House was anomalous to the rest of Market Place; its completion date at the very end of 1959 offers a neat, if convenient, threshold into Manchester of the 1960s.

Mainstream modern

The architecture of large-scale development in renewal cities was invariably a form of mainstream modernism. As such its place in architectural history is not assured. Its ubiquitous presence in renewal cities, however, is important in understanding the forces shaping urban landscapes in the 1960s and 1970s. The development of central Manchester and Market Place were typical of the experiences of many British cities after 1959. As Oliver Marriot observed, '[f]rom about 1960 there was suddenly a switch of emphasis towards shops and the centres of

---

32 Advice on road layouts was published in Alker Tripp's *Town Planning and Road Traffic* (1942), the Ministry for War Transport's *Design and Layout of Roads in Built-Up Areas* (1946) and, later, Sir Colin Buchanan's *Traffic in Towns* (1963). Each of these documents captured the new 'science' of highway engineering and each had its impact on urban form.

provincial towns'.[33] There was also a political consensus towards renewal and continuity in central government support for such development.[34] Furthermore, regional policy for the dispersal of government offices led to a boom in the commercial sector through the 1960s.[35] These forces, combined with the earlier relaxation of building controls, made for an unparalleled expansion and renewal programme in provincial cities, especially the metropolitan centres.

Unlike other cities, where established businesses owned pivotal sites and '[t]he supply of land in existing shopping pitches was slowed down by the policy of some of the biggest retailers, notably Marks and Spencer' – Manchester accommodated Marks & Spencer in the first new speculative retail development of the post-war.[36] Unicos Property Corporation developed the site next to Longridge House in partnership with Manchester Corporation. The Corporation provided two levels of basement car parking and Unicos constructed the shops and offices [Figure 5.10]. Work was under way in 1958.[37] Discussions between the developer, C&S and the Corporation took place from 1956. Initial, rather sketchy, drawings of the proposed building, showing its podium and tower configuration, were lodged with the office of the City Engineer [Figure 5.11].[38] From the plan it can be observed that the original intention was to provide a number of smaller, subdivided retail units and the early iterations of the elevation did not include the distinctive wavy canopy. Nonetheless, the scheme was clearly of the modern idiom and typified the architectural approach applied to the centres of other renewal cities.

When Marks & Spencer opened their new store, it was touted as 'the big story of 1961' in their internal newsletter, *St Michael News*.[39] It was certainly the first modern retail building in Manchester [Figure 5.12] and one of the earliest schemes in the UK to assume a podium and tower configuration. In order to articulate the two formal elements of the building the plant equipment was housed in an intermediate floor with a narrowed footprint that visually separated the offices above from the shop beneath. The offices were let to other commercial tenants and accessed from the north in a situation that would eventually be subsumed by the wider development of Market Place.

---

33 Marriott, *The Property Boom*, p. 145.
34 Smith, O.S. (2015) 'Central Government and Town-Centre Redevelopment in Britain, 1959–1966', *The Historical Journal*, Vol. 58, No. 1.
35 Ward, S.V. (1994) *Planning and Urban Change* (London: Paul Chapman Publishing), p. 151.
36 Marriott, *The Property Boom*, p. 145.
37 'Manchester Landmark', *The Manchester Guardian*, 28 June 1958, p. 10.
38 The microcard library of the city engineer remains uncatalogued. Archives+: 5281 Unicos Market Street.
39 'Michael House, Manchester – that'll be the big story of 1961', *St. Michael News*, January 1961, p. 1. M&S Company Archive, Michael Marks Building, University of Leeds. Bound volume, open access, no ref.

Figure 5.10 Entrance to the Corporation's underground car park. In the right foreground are the Old Wellington and Sinclair's. In the background on the left is Longridge House and on the right Michael House is under construction.

Structurally, the in-situ concrete frame was on a regular grid and was a conventional solution for the time. The 'lively feature' of an 'undulating concrete shell canopy' was considered both expressive and exciting – it was only 100 mm thick and cantilevered over 2.5 m from the face of the building.[40] The shell was actually stronger than the equivalent slab canopy and, as it was thinner, was also comparable in terms of cost. The cost of commercial buildings was a severely limiting factor everywhere for architectural design, but was more marked in development outside London where much lower rental returns meant lower budgets for design and construction. In this sense, Gibbon's concrete specification may be viewed as a response to a constrained budget. Areas of the long street-level facades were clad in white Portland stone. Gibbon chose to match this with a white concrete product known as Snowcrete, a cement product also quarried from Portland, Dorset. White concrete was one of Gibbon's signatures

---

40 'Store and Office Block, Manchester; Architects: Cruickshank & Seward', *The Builder*, 15 February 1963, pp. 335–337.

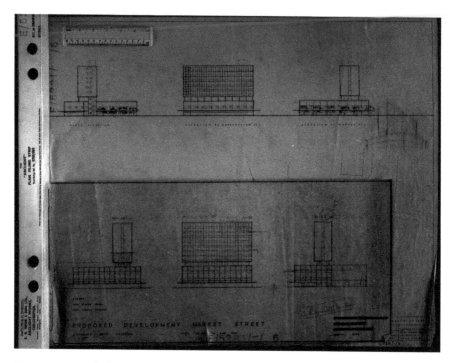

Figure 5.11   Early drawings of development for Unicos Property Corporation by Cruickshank & Seward, 1958.

in his later buildings and was especially well applied in the series of buildings at UMIST.[41] The tower element of the scheme had a lighter appearance than other C&S buildings of a similar scale. This was due to the primary structural columns being set inside the external wall line which permitted the use of narrow external columns, slender window frames and mosaic-faced spandrel panels, which all contributed to an airy appearance. This lightness was further emphasised in its contrast with the monolithic appearance of the stairwell. Much of the design could be considered as contemporary, but little could be described as unique. This was typical of the type of mainstream modern architecture realised in renewal cities and typical of Gibbon's approach – he was adept at identifying trends and applying them in new configurations to C&S projects.[42]

Another typical condition of mainstream development was the growth of the property companies and the rise of private sector investment. Between 1958 and 1962 the value of shares in property companies rose from £103m to over £800m. Companies expanded, more new companies came to the market,

---

41   See Chapter 3.
42   Interview with Gordon Hodkinson. Hale, 20 June 2012.

Figure 5.12 Michael House and Marks & Spencer. To the rear the cranes for the further development of Market Place can be seen. In the foreground are the hoardings around the site of the Arndale Shopping Centre.

more deals in shares took place and huge personal dividends were drawn down as the 'property boom' took hold.[43] In Market Place this played out over several years as Central and District Properties Ltd (C&D) gained interests in the site by piecemeal acquisitions.[44] They took over Unicos in 1959 and began to purchase other sites in an attempt at land assembly for comprehensive development. C&S put forward the first proposal for the rest of the site in November 1961.[45]

Amidst this landscape of expansion and mergers there remains little indication of precisely how Marks & Spencer came to be tenants, nor when C&S

---

43 Marriott, *The Property Boom*, pp. 18–19.
44 Central and District was owned by Johnny Rubens and Barney Shine. They used their main arm and a subsidiary company, Marine Properties, to make acquisitions. Marriott, *The Property Boom*, p. 226; 'Two More Skyscrapers Block Planned. Offices in Place of Theatre?', *The Guardian*, 25 March 1961, p. 12.
45 Custos, 'Investment Notes', *The Spectator*, 7 August 1959, p. 22; 'New Plans for Shopping Area. Another Tower of Shops and Offices?', *The Guardian*, 22 November 1961, p. 18.

became consultant architects for C&D, but the design for the rear of Michael House took account of the development to follow in a way that Longridge House had not: 'It was envisaged that this building [Michael House] would form the first phase of a larger Scheme [sic] and the western wall was in fact designed to permit a later extension.'[46] The inflated property companies, in a confluence with planning policy, were in a position to realise these large-scale projects that subsumed existing street patterns and defined new urban topographies.

New topographies

Elevated pedestrian environments, sunken vehicular carriageways, hovering monorails and aerial motorways were the motifs of a generation of architects and planners who sought to redefine our cities. Their popular production in the mainstream press heralded a new age for British inner-urban environments. As, Rowland Nicholas approached retirement age, in November 1961 he provided a report to the Town Planning and Buildings Committee that illustrated his understanding of how far urban design and commercial realities had shifted since his remarkable plan of 1945. He described the integrated nature of traffic, comprehensive development and environment as 'complex and completely interrelated'.[47] A number of specific statements reflected the changing planning ideals of the time. Nicholas accepted that his plan, as envisaged in 1945, was no longer an appropriate framework for development and underlined the need for the new style of urban planning that would eventually be delivered under John Millar's direction. The prospect of comprehensive development and its use in this interrelated landscape was 'coming to be accepted by developers' who understood 'that piecemeal building no longer provide[d] a satisfactory solution'.[48] The segregation of traffic and pedestrians would be achieved in several ways including the 'provision of overhead pavements'.

Nicholas also advocated that 'a plan in three-dimensions' should be prepared that would aid the selection of sites for comprehensive development and 'invoke designation procedure in order to bring about satisfactory redevelopment'.[49] Amongst the proposals as Nicholas made his report were 'several tentative schemes' around the Cathedral that were assessed to ensure that they conformed to 'an ultimate scheme for the area'.[50] The interrelation of sites allocated for comprehensive development was brought about by policy and popular imagination. Planning policy created the situation for great swathes of

---

46 Report by John Millar on the outline planning application for Market Place, 11 January 1967. Archives+, GB127.Council Minutes/Town Planning and Buildings Committee/2/67, p. 148.
47 GB127.Council Minutes/Town Planning and Buildings Committee/2/56, p. 902.
48 Ibid., p. 903.
49 Ibid., p. 902.
50 Ibid., p. 907.

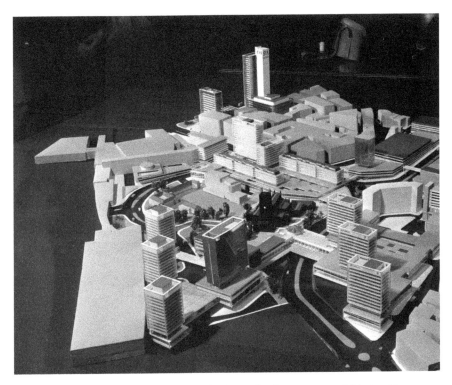

Figure 5.13 Rowland Nicholas's second scheme for the area around Market Place as published in 1962/63. The ring road can be seen in the foreground and W.S. Hattrell's scheme for the Corn Exchange sits behind the Cathedral.

cities to be conceived in their totality. The vertical programming of the city was imagined, theorised and illustrated in the early part of the twentieth century but became a voguish reality in Britain in the late 1950s and early 1960s. Of course, this context was also exploited by a burgeoning property sector that was effectively underwritten by state sponsorship.

Nicholas's revised advisory scheme for the area around the Cathedral [Figures 5.13 and 5.14], including Market Place was published in 1963.[51] The scheme clearly acknowledged the dramatic shift in the aesthetics of urban design, yet held steadfastly on to the highway plans of 1945. The city centre road still assumed the same route, above the River Irwell (see Chapter 6), but was no longer illustrated as a tree-lined boulevard and any sense of neo-classicism evident in the earlier civic design was erased. Instead, a complex, integrated, multi-level city was imagined where Market Place was linked by wide, habitable, bridges to the Cathedral Area and via a footbridge to the proposed Corn

---

51 'Cathedral Frame', *Interbuild*, February 1963, pp. 40–41.

THE RENEWAL OF POST-WAR MANCHESTER

Figure 5.14 Accompanying sketches, by David Gosling, to Nicholas's 1962/63 Scheme. Longridge House and Michael House can be seen centre left and beneath are three proposed towers on the Market Place site. A new pedestrian plaza and a series of linked pedestrian spaces are clearly visible. This style of drawing references Cullen's *Townscape* showing a sequence of enclosed squares, connecting passageways and landmarks as a means of orientation. Simultaneously, the drawing of the ring road illustrates the trend that was endorsed by Buchanan for the separation of pedestrians and traffic.

Exchange development, designed by W.S. Hattrell & Partners [Figure 5.15], which itself was intended to connect back to proposals for the Market Street Area (later Arndale).[52] Not only were the individual developments conceived comprehensively, here was the integrated planning for huge parts of the centre where public and private sector collaborated in its design. In the accompanying illustrations cars were shown cruising, unimpeded by other traffic, past the landscaped cathedral gardens whilst pedestrians relaxed in cafes and perambulated amongst linked plazas, free from noise and pollution. In this revision, the city

---

52 'Manchester Corn Exchange Project', *Architects' Journal*, 24 October 1962, pp. 946–947; 'Manchester Corn Exchange Redevelopment', *Architecture North West*, no. 11, pp. 14–15; 'Manchester Corn Exchange Redevelopment', *The Builder*, 19 October 1962, pp. 773–775.

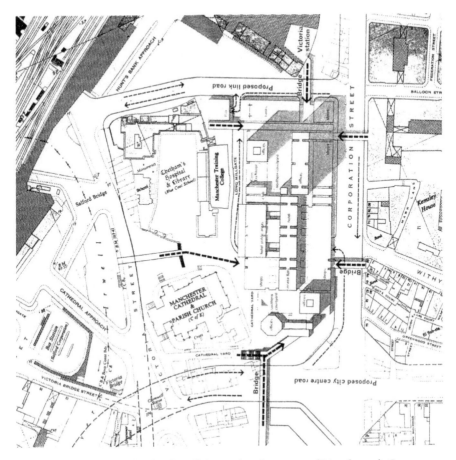

Figure 5.15 Proposals for the demolition and replacement of Manchester's Corn Exchange, W.S. Hattrell & Partners, 1962. This scheme was never built.

centre road became exclusively for motor vehicles and the pedestrian city found a new datum, a *tabula rasa*, from which to emerge.

At Market Place, this new datum was defined by negotiation and its definition was tied into the anticipated development of a much wider area. As with all of the CDAs in Manchester, the definition and development of Market Place was produced by the public and private sector in tandem. In this sense, it is worth considering the various advisory schemes as tools with which to influence discussions between agents of each. Nicholas's 1963 scheme may have been a response to that tabled by developers in 1961. Each of the successive schemes by the local authority had their influence on the eventual shape of the development and one defining feature of Nicholas's 1963 plans was the pedestrian plaza in the middle of the Market Place area, known as Shambles Square. This square was one new datum from where pedestrian connections would spring to the rest of the city – a bridge across Deansgate and another proposed above the path of the ring road aligned with Cannon Street, as well as the connection to the first floor of the existing Marks & Spencer store. The lateral and vertical position of the square became increasingly fixed during the proceeding revisions and refinements of the planning for the area. Beneath the level of the newly defined pedestrian environment new roads were designed to service the core of the city, much as outlined in *Traffic in Towns*. Above the precincts a series of towers were proposed, their projected height curtailed so as not to compete with the modest scale of the Cathedral.[53] This feature, of vertical containment, persisted through later revisions, though the alignment and form of the towers was also subject to discussion. Other mediations determined form too; the most contentious, and ultimately dramatic, negotiation was over the protection of the Old Wellington Inn.

Preservation

The means used to ensure the survival of the Old Wellington Inn and the adjoining Sinclair's Oyster Bar were as spectacular as any of the sweeping modernist visions superimposed on the city. Publicly valued, but viewed by the developers as an obstruction to progress, their preservation was tied to the desire for comprehensive multi-level development. They were famously 'lifted' to meet the new datum of Shambles Square, but not before the idea of moving them was explored, or the possibility of leaving them in a trench had been examined![54] Eventually it was considered feasible to raise the buildings on concrete stilts so that they would sit at the height of the new Shambles Square [Figure 5.16].

The Old Wellington was afforded statutory protection in the late 1940s, almost as a reaction to the first post-war proposals for the site. The act of securing the protection highlighted some of the perversities of regional government and a lack of coordination between ministries. In February 1947, as Manchester prepared the first of its Declaratory Orders for reconstruction, the Regional Director of the MoW was asked for his opinion on the proposals. The MoW requested additional copies of the documentation from the local authority and subsequently returned no comment on the proposals. In the background, and without further consultation, the MoW pursued the statutory protection of the inn as a Scheduled Ancient Monument.[55] The actions of the MoW only came to the attention of the Regional Controller of the MTCP via Manchester's Town Clerk. He was informed in May 1948 that the solicitors acting on behalf of the owners of the inn had received notice from the MoW of their intent to include

---

53 'Cathedral Frame', *Interbuild*, February 1963, pp. 40–41.
54 'Inns in Shambles May be Jacked Up', *The Guardian*, 18 January 1967, p. 16.
55 Memo from Regional Controller of the Ministry of Town and Country Planning to C.1. Division HQ. NA: HLG/79/407.

Figure 5.16   The Shambles being lifted up. The Old Wellington Inn (left) and Sinclair's Oyster Bar (right) elevated on concrete stilts during the construction process to meet the new datum established as part of the city centre stratification and separation of cars and pedestrians.

the building on a revised schedule.[56] The regional offices of the ministries were acting independently from one another and without local communications, and the matter was escalated, with some embarrassment, to central government to resolve. The view from Whitehall was that the protection of the Old Wellington Inn did not prejudice the status of the Declaratory Order as the plans for redevelopment were speculative and did not 'commit either the Planning Authority or the Minister to the particular layout'.[57] Despite this assertion, the protection of the buildings inevitably led to their preservation and certainly impacted upon the eventual form of Market Place.

Subsequent to the designation of the Old Wellington Inn as a Scheduled Ancient Monument, the development of Market Place stalled for a long time. Without private developers the local authority could do little as most of their resources were tied up in building new homes and schools in suburban areas. Even when C&S presented their first proposals in 1961, it was a further nine

---

56   Letter from Phillip Dingle to Regional Controller of the Ministry of Town and Country Planning. NA: HLG/79/407.
57   Letter from Regional Controller of the Ministry of Town and Country Planning to Phillip Dingle, Town Clerk, 19 July 1948. NA: HLG/79/407.

years until construction commenced.[58] During this time there were more versions of a master plan for Market Place, drawn and modelled as 'Advisory Schemes' within the CDA mechanisms and finally ratified in the *Development Map* (1967) and its approval in 1968. Within this series of plans, another set of formal characteristics emerged and were eventually built into the development. Meetings between the local authority and C&S, acting on behalf of the developer, were ongoing and undoubtedly the work of the planning department was influenced by these discussions. Nonetheless, during the protracted planning and legal phase, the local authority had their own objectives – the negotiations were not one-sided and did not necessarily kowtow to the demands of the private sector.

Negotiated design

The design of Market Place was subject to negotiation between the developer and the local authority through their respective agents. In the mid-century the legislative conditions for these negotiations gave the local authority planner considerable influence in the determination of form. The timeline of decision making over the form of the Market Place development and how decisions were communicated in published and archived drawings and models follows an imprecise path. The manner in which successive planning schemes were illustrated varied according to the audience and the purpose of the information. That which is legible from surviving records demonstrates the relationship between architect and planner in their negotiation of policy, finance and space. A series of reports from the mid-1960s captured the work of the planning department, which was engaged with planning huge swathes of the inner city as well as the central area [Figure 5.17].[59]

Among the reports are photographs of a series of models that were used to illustrate and communicate three-dimensional proposals prepared by the architect-planners under the direction of John Millar. Different models were used for different purposes, study models were used to develop ideas within the department [Figure 5.20], but one huge model of the city centre was on permanent display in the foyer of the planning department in the Town Hall [Figure 1.02]. This model was used as a tool for public discussion and information and was revised to become a formal exhibit on the occasion of the publication of the *City Centre Map 1967*.[60] 'The city centre map concept sprang from the work of the Planning Advisory Group (PAG) set up by the government to look at the future of development planning and reporting in

---

58 'Start on New City Centre', *The Guardian*, 16 October 1970, p. 6.
59 Millar, *Manchester Corporation. City Planning Department 1964–65*; Millar, *Manchester City Centre Map 1967*; Hayes (1968); Manchester Corporation (1967).
60 Maund, *Aspects of Planning in Manchester and Greater Manchester 1960–1975*. Personal private memoir received in correspondence, 29 January 2014.

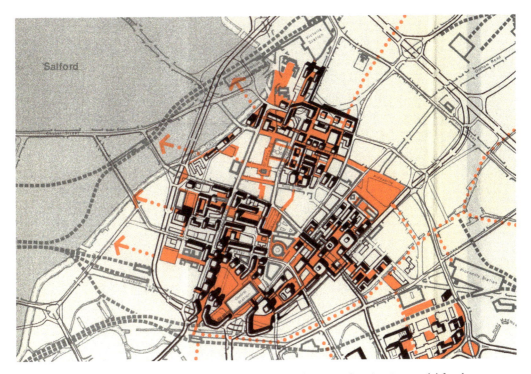

Figure 5.17 Extract from Map 9 showing 'Comprehensive Planning Proposals' for the central area. The red shows zones intended as pedestrianised and the buildings drawn with shadows are those proposed as new within the defined CDA boundaries.

1965.'[61] The major effect it had on the work of the planning department in Manchester was the combining of approaches to planning advocated in the existing statute and the new advice. The PAG recommended 'a lively and vivid style of presentation' which 'could include sketches and photographs, including photographs of design models' that 'should be in a form suitable for publication'.[62] As referred to in the preceding chapters, Millar's department combined these recommendations with the existing machinery of the CDA and produced a number of three-dimensional advisory schemes that described the approach for almost the entire city centre. The drawings and models produced in the period between 1962 and 1967 are used here to show their interrelation, their use as a planning tool, and to illustrate their influence on the eventual form of Market Place.

---

61 Ibid. Maund refers to the advice issued in the report: Planning Advisory Group, *The Future of Development Plans*. See also Delafons (1998).
62 Planning Advisory Group, *The Future of Development Plans*, p. 35.

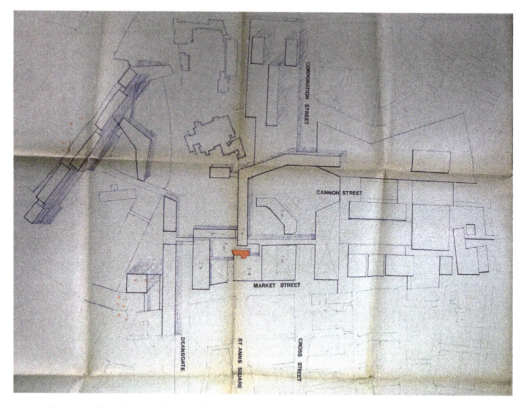

Figure 5.18   Advisory Scheme drawing. The Old Wellington Inn and Sinclair's are shown in red. Whilst rudimentary, this drawing from the Planning Department shows the interconnected nature of the vision for the central area. Buildings and bridges physically link developments flanking Market Place.

The advisory schemes for the comprehensive development areas were not routinely archived and surviving original documents are rare. None have survived in Manchester, but copies of the Market Place plans are held in Ministry files at the National Archives. One of the most striking features of the drawings [Figures 5.18 and 5.19] is the large numeric notation that indicated the desired levels (feet above sea level) for each part of the development. This suggests that the interconnected and new elevated layer of the city was important to the planners and that the connection of these levels across the city centre was as a matter for local authority guidance. In describing the context for his plan John Millar made direct reference to Manchester's comprehensive development and the advice contained in the Buchanan Report:

> Advisory schemes have been formulated for large parts of the central area which relate to each other as part of an overall framework plan, and following the

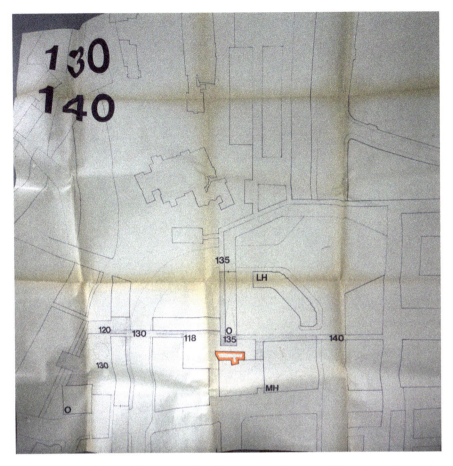

Figure 5.19 Advisory Scheme drawing. The connected nature of the sites to the north, east and west is shown here as high-level bridges at 135m, 140m and 130m above sea level. The apparent title of the drawing is '130 140' and indicates the concerns of the planner and the vertical separation of the city.

publication of the Buchanan Report which brought the greater official recognition of the essential inter-relationship between land-use and transportation planning.[63]

The desires to solve traffic congestion and to renew a huge portion of the central area were inextricably linked. Highways planning defined routes through the historic grain of the city and potential alignments created as many

---

63 Town Planning and Buildings Committee Minutes, July–Dec. 1967, pp. 1013–1014. Archives+: GB127.Council Minutes/Town Planning and Buildings Committee/2/68.

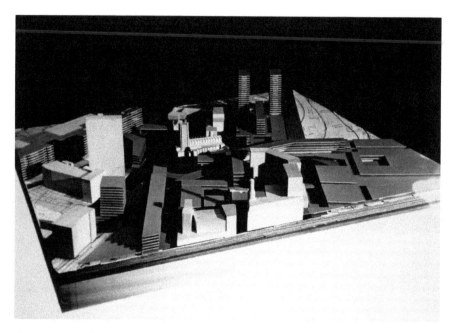

Figure 5.20 Advisory Scheme model. The Old Wellington Inn can be seen in red, with a public space carved in the centre of the scheme. Above the Inn is the proposed staggered form of the commercial block, rising towards the Cathedral. In the background is shown the anticipated development of the Corn Exchange site and a cranked, linear block connecting to the proposed Arndale Centre.

urban design problems as they solved. Whilst roads could flank and define edges for development, they could also sever sites and leave difficult plots for construction. The legislative control afforded to local authorities in pursuit of massive renewal programmes meant that cities could be conceived of as a whole so this paradox was not problematic in itself. The nationally instituted Acts gave local authorities the power and autonomy to design comprehensively in this way. The rebuilding of entire centres, combined with a plan for a ring road was the de facto solution to renewal in many British cities and mimicked, if not mirrored, advice outlined in exemplar maps that accompanied official planning documents [Figure 5.21].[64]

---

64 The 'Development Map' was the overarching structure for a town's future building programme and was instated via the powers invested to local authorities by the Town and Country Planning Act (1947). Visual material suggesting both form and notation for these plans was first published in 1951 and added to and amended with new publications and revisions until 1966. See *Reproduction of Survey and Development Plan Maps, Town and Country Planning Act 1947 Circular No. 92* (London: 1951); Ministry of Housing and Local Government (1962) *Planning Bulletin no. 1, Town Centres: Approach to*

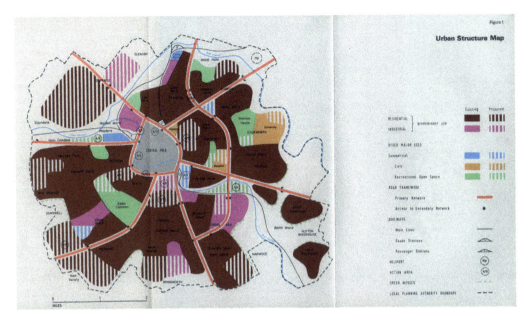

Figure 5.21 Urban Structure Map. This is the standard example provided by the Planning Advisory Group in their publication *The Future of Development Plans*. In this drawing the ideas of zoning and ring and radial road structure are clearly evident.

It is difficult to judge from archival sources precisely who were the biggest sponsors of the comprehensive redevelopment of Manchester's central area – the planners or the politicians. The planners acted with professionalism and proficiency. They believed in the virtue of their publicly held office and felt they had a responsibility to improve the built environment.[65] Local politicians supported development and ensured that the local authority were active partners in major schemes. During the development of the Arndale shopping centre, the City Treasurer proposed a short-term loan to the developer to sustain the programme when their major financial supporter, Prudential, was cautious about the risk.[66] This was an innovative approach that demonstrated two aspects of development: first was the faith invested in public–private partnerships – the assured powers of

---

Renewal (London: HMSO). The Planning Advisory Group examined the *Future of Development Plans* in 1965 and proposed that 'Development Maps' were replaced with 'Town Centre Maps'.

65 Conversations and testament from a number of planners who were employed by John Millar recall a genuine sense of the worthwhile improvements that could be brought to the city and its citizens (unpublished).

66 Maund, *Aspects of Planning in Manchester and Greater Manchester 1960–1975*. Personal private memoir received in correspondence. 29 January 2014.

Figure 5.22 Artist's impression of Market Place development. To the right are the earlier Longridge House and Michael House. In the centre, the staggered block that mimics the form proposed in the Advisory Scheme can be seen as well as the adjacent public space. To the left of the image is the hotel block that was Phase II of the development.

the CDA and CPO legislation gave the local authority a confidence that impacted positively upon procurement. Second was the need to underwrite private finance to ensure that development occurred. Negotiations for the development of Market Place were protracted, as the officers of the city council sought solutions for a larger swathe of city than that which C&D owned.[67] This was not just due the difficulties of land assembly; it was also down to the local authority wishing to fulfil their ambitions of comprehensive renewal. One site in particular, a narrow strip between Deansgate and the River Irwell effectively isolated by the proposed highway alignment, was not commercially attractive, but would likely remain undeveloped if it were not absorbed into the contract for Market Place – it became Phase II of the construction programme, a hotel. Other property firms owned ransom sites within the CDA boundary. These companies ultimately sold their interests to C&D, which was the catalyst for a viable partnership deal with the Corporation, and the site between Cross Street and the River Irwell was designed in totality [Figure 5.22] and delivered in two phases.[68]

---

67 Report of the City Estates and Valuation Officer on the planning proposals for the Market Place Redevelopment, 12 June 1967. Appendix 30 of Planning Committee minutes Jan.–June 1967, pp. 1078–1080. Archives+: GB127.Council Minutes/Town Planning and Buildings Committee/2/67.
68 Ibid.

The architectural form and mass of Market Place was significantly affected by negotiation – negotiation between the local authority and the developer, negotiation between the highways planning and the need for reconstruction, negotiation between heritage campaigners and central government, all of which was mediated using drawings and models as tools with which to inform decisions. The preservation of the Old Wellington Inn and its effect on determining levels for pavements and squares was one such negotiation, referred to by the Inspector of Ancient Buildings as 'virtually obligatory', something of a fait accompli.[69] This suggests ratification elsewhere within the protracted discussions of the planners, planning committee, councillors and developers that were ably visualised by the architects. The organisation and massing of the commercial blocks and open space was also largely determined by the successive schemes prepared by the local authority as they aimed to reconcile 'existing legislation and [the] new style thinking' of the PAG.[70] The determination of the local authority to ensure that the entire area they wished to be developed was included in the contract was demonstrable of the power invested locally to broker such deals.

It may appear here that the role of the architect in the design of the scheme is deliberately diminished – it is not the intent. The following section addresses the work of Cruickshank & Seward and their contribution. However, in the commercial sector, budget is invariably the master and is informed by investment costs and rental returns over a specified period of time. Thus, the physical conditions defined by political and planning negotiations were powerful and valuable parameters within which the architect operated – a formal mediation, or a discourse mediated by form. The architect had to mediate between the area required by the developer to realise a return on their investment and the area defined by planners in the advisory plans for the CDA. It is the role of the architect in this mediation, a role that no other professional can assume, that is skilful and cannot be underplayed when considered in scenarios like these.

The capacity to synthesise written information, imposed master plans, the demands of a client and the input of consultation into a design and then the realisation of a built scheme is a very particular skill. Cruickshank & Seward spent twelve years involved in negotiations about the form and mass of Market Place. Their drawings and models were informed, and were in conversation with those of the local authority. This act of negotiation is itself one part of the design of Market Place. This is not architecture as art, but design in practice. This manifold situation where the politics, economics, culture and heritage of

---

69 Report of the Inspector of Ancient Buildings of the Ministry of Public Building and Works on the planning proposals for the Market Place Redevelopment, 12 June 1967. Appendix 7A of Planning Committee minutes Jan.–June 1967, p. 159. Archives+: GB127.Council Minutes/Town Planning and Buildings Committee/2/67.

70 File note to Minister on occasion of his visit to Manchester, February 1967, from John D. Higham. NA: HLG 144/86.

The architecture of renewal

Cruickshank & Seward (C&S) began designing the area around Market Place in 1958. Construction commenced on the main phase of development in autumn 1970.[71] In the intervening twelve years C&S were retained as consultant architects and often acted as mediators between policy and form in the production of schemes that satisfied both their developer clients and the demands of the local authority. The western side of their first building, Michael House (M&S), was designed deliberately to be able to meet the wider development of Market Place that would abut its facade. This suggests a desire on the part of the architect to formally define this component of city as a multi-layered and mode separated landscape before the planning officers promoted such ideas. At Michael House all of the servicing and parking provision was subterranean, which established the pattern for the rest of the development.

Who proposed this is unknown, but there was either consensus or foresight on the part of the architect at this stage and the remaining scheme was informed by this initial striation [Figure 5.23]. Whereas certain formal conditions, like the retention of the pubs and the elevated connections, were apparently overdetermined by external control, the material, colour and more detailed treatment of the scheme is not recorded as of concern in surviving archival records. The extended urban piece eventually realised to the designs of Arthur Gibbon's team was predominantly white, predominantly concrete and particular in the strong horizontal projection of its fenestration and floor plates. The architecture may not have been at the cutting edge of design or technology, but the architectural language was cohesive and markedly of the office of C&S. It was also decisively mainstream modernism. It is this characteristic that may have led to the apparent lack of interest by the local authority in its overall appearance – it was modern, new and emblematic of a future that would be an alternative to the grime of Victorian Manchester [Figure 5.24]. It is its position in the mainstream that means that this and schemes like it are rarely considered in architectural history, but do feature in urban histories. The mainstream modern architectural development in this instance is inseparable from the development of the conservation movement, the period of urban renewal and the influence of planners and developers. As such, it helps to narrate the relationships between urban, planning and architectural histories.

Many things influenced architects' attitudes to developers, but the profession generally had low regard for the new breed of capitalists who made significant sums, often without developing at all. Lord Esher's inaugural address

---

71 'Start on New City Centre', *The Guardian*, 16 October 1970, p. 6.

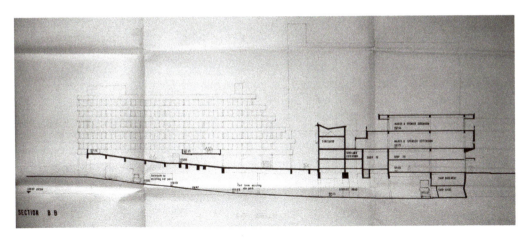

Figure 5.23 Section BB, extract from C&S drawing no. 1655/133 rev. A. This section cuts north–south from Cateaton Street to St Mary's Gate and shows the extensive subterranean area, the raised pubs (centre) and the retail block. In the background, in elevation, are the outline of Michael House and the staggered floorplates of the easternmost commercial block.

Figure 5.24 View eastwards along St Mary's Gate from Deansgate, 1980. The strong horizontal banding and the set back upper floor and extended canopy were typical motifs in Cruickshank & Seward's commercial work. In the background are Michael House and the buff-coloured tiles of the Arndale Centre and tower.

as President of the RIBA supposed that 'the only technical men they [the developers] employed at the evaluation stage were real-estate surveyors; the architect was not hired until the decision had been taken to go ahead, and of course it happened that by then the whole project was an architectural nonsense or a piece of vandalism'.[72] As with all generalisations, specific instances often counter popularly held views. C&S were involved with C&D from the earliest days of their interests in Market Place. The Royal Fine Arts Commission reviewed the scheme and the consultant architects to the Cathedral, Wilson & Womersley, also had their say.[73] Neither objected to C&S's proposals. This form of consultation did not guarantee design quality, but demonstrated the widely held consensus, or acceptance, about the physical form of renewal.

In the post-war commercial work by C&S the distinction between the projects directed by different partners became blurred. The commercial sector, whilst apparently booming in renewal cities in the mid-1960s, was subject to much tighter budgetary limits and left less room for architectural expression. Thus, architectural devices developed in other projects were deployed in this and other less well financed schemes and effectively became motifs common to many C&S projects – strong horizontal emphasis, volumetric expression of roof-mounted plant, expressive stair cores, recessed uppermost floors and oversailing roofs – there was definitely a language to the firm's work. In the renewal cities, large-scale development funded by inward investment was actually an opportunity for architects in the private sector, not a necessarily the threat as supposed by Esher.

The white buildings of C&S were not all designed by Arthur Gibbon, but it was Gibbon who introduced and propagated the bright, new additions to the city in the post-war period. The most significant civic and commercial schemes built in 1930s Manchester often used white Portland stone. In 1946 Manchester became the first place in Britain to institute a 'clean air' policy that was enforced in the central area from 1952.[74] The city was at its 'maximum blackness' around 1945–60 as crystallised, soot-laden facades met the pitch black of tarmacadam.[75]

---

72 'Inaugural address of the President, the Viscount Esher, given at the RIBA on 19 October 1965', *RIBA Journal*, November 1965, pp. 529–533.

73 Report by John Millar on the outline planning application for Market Place, 11 January 1967. Archives+: GB127.Council Minutes/Town Planning and Buildings Committee/2/67, p. 148.

74 The Manchester Corporation Act (1946) led directly to the first controlled zones in 1952, followed by 105 acres of central Manchester in 1956. Mosley, S. (2001) *The Chimney of the World: A History of Smoke Pollution in Victorian and Edwardian Manchester* (Cambridge: White Horse Press); Manchester Area Council for Clean Air and Noise Control (1984) *Twenty Five Year Review: A Review of Some Aspects of Air Pollution and Noise Control in the Area of the Council 25 Years after the Clean Air Act, 1956*.

75 Crompton, A. (2012) 'Manchester Black and Blue', *Bulletin of the John Rylands Library*, Vol. 89, No. 1, pp. 277–291.

Figure 5.25 Elizabeth House, St Peter's Square. Cruickshank & Seward, 1971.

Where Owen Williams produced the vitreous black glazed facade of the *Daily Express* Building (1939) as both response and resistance to the environmental conditions, the white buildings by C&S of the post-war period were similar. Elizabeth House (1971) [Figure 5.25] on the edge of St Peter's Square was supposed to be clad in Portland stone to address the Central Library opposite, but was eventually finished in white concrete owing to budgetary limitations.[76] The white buildings at UMIST and the National Computing Centre, discussed in earlier chapters, were deliberately designed to capture the 'White Heat' of technology.

There was something of the marketing man in Gibbon and, as well as being a capable designer, he was acutely aware of the need for identity, and the patronage that would follow. Gibbon commissioned high contrast black and white images of C&S buildings, produced by established architectural photographer Sam Lambert and oversaw the production of the practice's marketing material. In interviews with former principals, I have speculated that Gibbon's use of white was intended simply to stand out, both from his rivals and from

---

76 In conversation with Gordon Hodkinson. Hale, 3 October 2016.

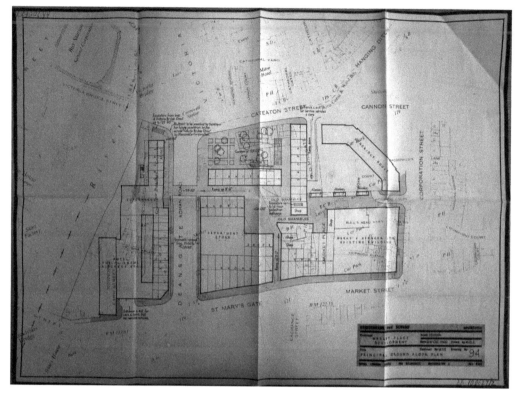

Figure 5.26 Master plan, October 1966. Drawn by Mark Edge. Whilst certain areas of hard landscaped areas remain unspecified on this drawing, the final form of the completed scheme assumed a plan very similar to that laid out above. Longridge House appears as a remnant of Nicholas-era planning and not integrated into the later scheme.

the blackened mid-century city. Those who knew him did not challenge my assumption.[77]

Gibbon established the white palette in the Portland stone and concrete of Michael House and continued it through Market Place itself and onwards to the new hotel on Deansgate [Figure 5.26]. The extended sequence of raised precincts was a safe environment and well patronised. It was also a new type of urban space. Spaces of this type existed across the UK and Europe and were products of capitalism and socialism. Here the capitalist mode of production met with the social ideals of modern architecture and planning taught in UK schools. The forms of the heroic egalitarian imagined cities of the early

---

77 In conversation with Gordon Hodkinson. Hale, 3 October 2016 and John Sheard 2 May 2013.

modernists were combined with the driving forces of mobility and consumption and made places and spaces that were particular to urban renewal in the 1960s. This was 'Buchananism'. I do not deploy this metonym lightly and I am not the first to do so – a commentator for *The Guardian* professed that, 'what is new about Buchanan (the name is sure to establish itself as a shorthand symbol for a whole philosophy) is that it gives shape and a cutting-edge to ideas that are already, albeit vaguely, in the air'[78] This 'shape' was the existing consensus between thinkers, planners, architects, engineers, policy makers and developers concerning ring roads, vertical separation and comprehensive renewal and it determined a very particular type of space in certain British cities. It is tempting to attempt to define this as some form of renewal style, a type of municipal modernism, but the incidents of such are varied in the UK and I have gone to great lengths to explain why style is a less useful way of considering the production of mainstream modern architecture. Yet, to use mainstream modernism as a lens can help to disclose a typo-morphology of the renewal city, its commonalities and its temporal frame.

Market Place exhibited characteristics that were common to other similar schemes: vertical separation was one. Others were sequences of passageways and pedestrian squares (which were often poorly engineered versions of Cullen's 'serial vision');[79] bridges that crossed roads in which the pedestrian had been engineered out, often dual carriageways with no pavement; escalators, travelators and ramps to seamlessly connect the new levels of the city; subterranean areas; and point and slab blocks rising from podiums. The bridge across Deansgate, with a ramp with a parade of shops on one side and escalators on the other, was how the future had been drawn [Figure 5.27]. Michael House was successfully integrated into the wider development and eventually linked via a further bridge over Corporation Street to the Arndale Centre [Figure 5.28]. However, the certainty with which the planners viewed the total renewal of the centre when they specified certain routes 'to be used only until the alternative pedestrian system at upper level is constructed' was fading.[80] Without a fluid connection to the north and with exclusively vehicular environments at grade, the development felt as if it had turned its back on the Cathedral and the new Shambles Square, instead of being integrated, was isolated.

Retrospectively we can view these as the forlorn spaces that many became during their decline [Figure 5.29]. However, these engineered environments were products of mensurable design inputs aimed to meet the ambitions of policy and the public. John Millar's words echo just this:

---

78 'To Live with the Motorcar', *The Guardian*, 28 November 1963, p. 10.
79 Cullen, *The Concise Townscape*, p. 9.
80 Cl. 4 of the conditions of the outline planning approval for Market Place. 24 February 1967. NA: WORK 14/2048.

THE RENEWAL OF POST-WAR MANCHESTER

Figure 5.27 Artist's impression by Peter Sainsbury of Phase II of Market Place development. The strong horizontal bands of windows are set against the diagonal of the ramp as it rises to meet the pedestrian footbridge over Deansgate.

Figure 5.28 Footbridge connecting St Michael House to the Arndale Centre. It was destroyed in the 1996 IRA bombing and replaced by a new bridge designed by Stephen Hodder.

Figure 5.29   Shambles Square in 1983. The half-timbered facades of the Old Wellington Inn and Sinclair's Oyster Bar sit rather incongruously against the stained white concrete of Market Place.

> The proposed development is in accordance with the principal of achieving wherever possible comprehensive development in which pedestrians and vehicles are separated ... it is hoped that it would recreate in modern terms something of the intimate scale that characterised the Old Shambles area.[81]

Regardless of the eventual state of Market Place and its disappearance following the IRA action of 1996, this narrative has shown the strong hand of local authority planners in their negotiation with architects in the service of developers. My aim is not to vindicate or to vilify any party, but to show the range of varying contexts for development – here, Whitehall had little interest in urban form, but policy still determined aspects of it. The drawn-out and piecemeal approach to what was eventually labelled as 'comprehensive development' has shown the impact of successive master plan proposals on the shape and form of this part of one city.

Similar places and spaces across Britain were created in these encounters between the policies, plans and production of renewal and, like Market Place, were often encumbered by the realities of total visions only partially realised.

---

81   Report by John Millar on the outline planning application for Market Place, 11 January 1967. Archives+: GB127.Council Minutes/Town Planning and Buildings Committee/2/67, p. 148.

Figure 5.30   The Arndale Centre, Wilson & Womersley, 1977.

In this sense, Market Place has offered a more typical view of the complexities of urban renewal in a period of unbridled expansion where statute struggled to keep pace with the influx of capital to provincial cities. The retail development that followed in Manchester, namely the Arndale Centre, was decisively more monolithic, literally and metaphorically, as it was realised in its totality and was much less compromising as a piece of urban design [Figure 5.30]. Despite its assertive presence, though, the Arndale still had to acquiesce to the demands of highway engineers and the plans for the ring road made an incisive cut through its beige mass. In the final chapter, the role of highway planning in influencing the shape of the city draws a ring around the central area development and ties this exploration back to the wider ideas of regional development with which we began.

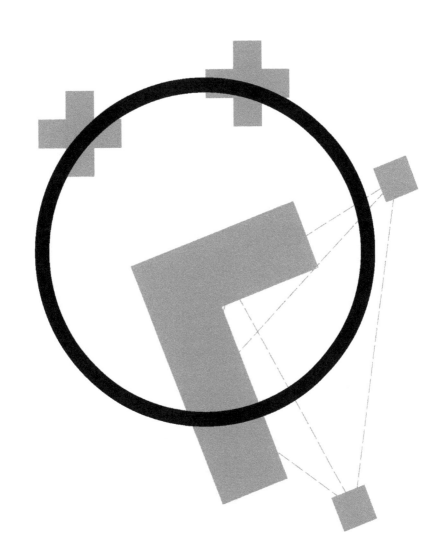

6

The redoubtable resilience of the ring road

Introduction

In Manchester's post-war planning, nothing was more determined than the route of inner ring road. As mentioned, there was a belief in the primacy of the motor vehicle and that, in making detailed engineered plans for vehicular circulation, the rest of the city would form around such routes. The focus towards serving the needs of the public as car ownership increased and the post-war economy recovered is widely recognised and the impact of inner urban motorways on central areas often discussed.[1] Conceptually, this chapter forms a lasso around the central area and ties the city's planning back to its regional context. In physical terms, the ring road was an integral part of the comprehensive plans of the 1960s and connected the majority of the designated development areas.

The first drawn plans for a series of concentric ring roads were presented in the *1945 Plan*. Versions of these were redesigned through the 1960s and certain sections were constructed before the policy was officially dropped in 1977. Plans were revived in the 1980s and a full loop around the city centre was finally completed in 2004. In looking at the 'city centre road', which was renamed as 'the inner relief route', we will explore its role in influencing the shape of the city, much in the manner that the rivers, canals and railways did before. We will also see the physical traces of the idea of the ring road and formal adaptations and concessions made in the city's architecture for sections of road that never arrived. It is the final part of a narrative that shows the connectedness of

---

1 See Kerensky, C.A. (1968) *Urban Motorways and their environment* (London: TPI); Hauck, T., Keller, R. and Kleinekort, V. (2011) *Infrastructural Urbanism. Addressing the In-between* (Berlin: DOM Publishers); Brainard, J.S., Jones, A.P., Bateman, I.J. and Lovett, A.A. 'Exposure to environmental urban noise pollution in Birmingham, UK', *Urban Studies* Vol. 41, No. 13 (2004), pp. 2581–2600.

infrastructure, planning and morphology and the influence of policy on form, using Manchester as its case.

The history of Manchester's ring roads

Ideas about a ring road for central Manchester first arose in the 1930s in response to the congested central streets of the regional hub served by radial routes from satellite towns.[2] Earlier proposals, in the 1920s, had considered the use of two pieces of infrastructure that would combine trams and cars on an inner circumference and trains and cars on an outer ring [Figure 6.01].[3] In the 1930s the Town Planning Committee, as well as supporting the idea of ring roads, recognised the need for a 'comprehensive [planning] scheme ... providing for proper zoning and layout'.[4] The first proposed route for the city centre ring would, as many proposals to follow, take the routes of existing streets that would be widened to prioritise traffic flow.[5] The scheme made the pages of the press at either end of the decade, 1932 and 1938 – its inception point and the eventual point at which the city council were due to make a decision on its progress.[6] Were it not for the outbreak of war the ring road may have proceeded as a single, standalone project and not bound to a comprehensive vision, as emerged in post-war planning. To date, this research has not uncovered any engineer's drawings for the schemes from the 1930s, the only visual representation of the routes has been sourced from the pages of the *Manchester Guardian* [Figure 6.02][7].

Rowland Nicholas's *1945 Plan* and the accompanying documents addressed the region. It is evident from his contribution to the cluster of reports and from his own words that Nicholas was a regional thinker. In 1942 as he began the task of replanning he penned a rare article in which he wrote of the 'practical regional planning of 'self purposing' areas, capable of providing their own requirements'.[8] Read together the combined post-war documentation presented

---

2 'Traffic Congestion in Manchester', *The Manchester Guardian*, 23 February 1937, p. 13.
3 'Manchester as it Might Be', *The Manchester Guardian*, 11 July 1929, p. 13.
4 'Easing Manchester's Traffic Congestion Problem', *The Manchester Guardian*, 26 October 1932, p. 11.
5 It was scheduled to be 'constructed at a width of 74 ft ... to provide a carriageway of 44 ft ... and two footways each 15 ft in width' and to cost just short of £700,000. 'Manchester's "inner ring" Road', *The Manchester Guardian*, 4 July 1938, p. 13.
6 The proposal would have then been subject to approval by the Minister of Transport for grant purposes.
7 *The Guardian* and *Observer* online archive has been invaluable in researching this period, particularly in relation to Manchester. *The Guardian* was known as *The Manchester Guardian* until 1959 and was produced in the city until 1964. After 1964 it still maintained strong regional news coverage, but the reporting bias slowly moved towards its now familiar national and international reporting.
8 Nicholas, R. 'Post War Planning', *The Manchester Guardian*, 15 May 1942, p. 4.

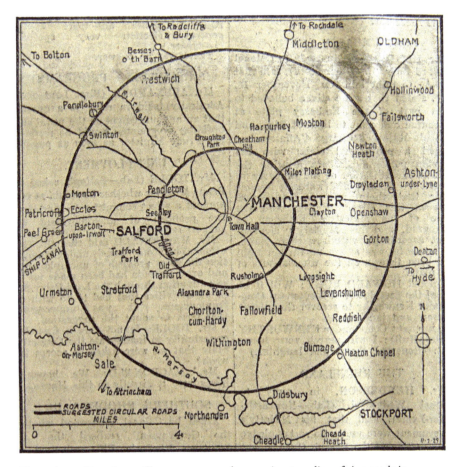

Figure 6.01 Drawing to illustrate proposed approximate radius of ring roads in relation to the city centre, 1929.

a regional system of comprehensive road planning that included four ring roads: the city centre road and inner, intermediate and outer ring roads [Figure 6.03]. The outer ring road would eventually become the M60 orbital motorway, though with a much closer southern radius to the city. The other three were all only partially realised but still had their own influence on the alignment, situation and form of buildings as the local authority sought to promote the plan by releasing some land and protecting other sites.

Policy context: national and local

As we have read, the statutory provision for planning in Manchester after 1945 was without a formal approval until 1961. Manchester's proposals were

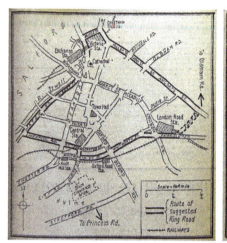 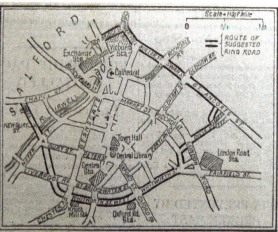

Figure 6.02(a/b)   Drawings to illustrate two possible routes for a city centre ring road. The conundrum of whether to cross the River Irwell into Salford and involve another borough in the planning and construction was evidenced in these early proposals.

essentially faithful to the *1945 Plan* and submitted to the Secretary of State in 1951. One indication of the primacy of highway planning was evidenced in that eleven of the forty pages of the Written Statement showed a table scheduling new road construction up to 1971.[9] The lack of detail in the 1951 Plan would come to define the production of architecture in the following decade. The lack of an overarching central master plan permitted short-term speculative development on sites which were known not to interfere with the broader aims of the planners, predominantly this amounted to protecting the proposed route of the ring road. John Millar's promotion to City Planning Officer in 1963 coincided with Rowland Nicholas's retirement and the arrival of a raft of new personnel, including a new City Architect and City Engineer. Despite this shaking up of officialdom the idea of a ring road persisted in the shaping of central planning policy.

In 1962, the SELNEC Highway Engineering Committee published a comprehensive report that used technical analysis and new methods of computation to examine the road network of Manchester.[10] Titled *A Highway Plan*, the report suggested that transport schemes proposed by the various local authorities within the wider conurbation were inadequate, as they wildly underestimated

---

9   Nicholas and Dingle, *Manchester Development Plan*.
10 The SELNEC Committee was formed in 1958 following a meeting of the Clerks and Surveyors to the County and County Borough Highway Authorities in South-East Lancashire and North-East Cheshire.

Figure 6.03 Extract from *Manchester Regional Plan 1945*, showing the full extents of the proposed outer ring road (D). A much larger area is encompassed compared to the final route of the M60. This drawing does not show the innermost 'city centre road'.

projected traffic levels.[11] An 'Overloading Diagram' [Figure 6.04] proved to be one of the most influential pieces of empirical data as it showed predicted traffic levels for 1965, which was not very far in the future. Alarmingly, the diagram suggested that 77 per cent of the roads in the SELNEC study area would have been overloaded [by 1965], with almost all major routes in Manchester city centre being overloaded by more than 150 per cent of their capacity.[12] The report also analysed the design and layout of the City Centre Ring Road from the 1945 Plan, commenting that the proposed junctions would create, 'a number of engineering problems ... [that would] have a serious effect on the

---

11 South-East Lancashire and North-East Cheshire Area Highway Engineering Committee (1962) *SELNEC: A Highway Plan* (Manchester: SELNEC Committee).

12 Brook, R. and Dodge, M. (2012) *Infra_MANC: Post-war Infrastructures of Manchester* (Manchester: Bauprint), p. 78.

THE RENEWAL OF POST-WAR MANCHESTER

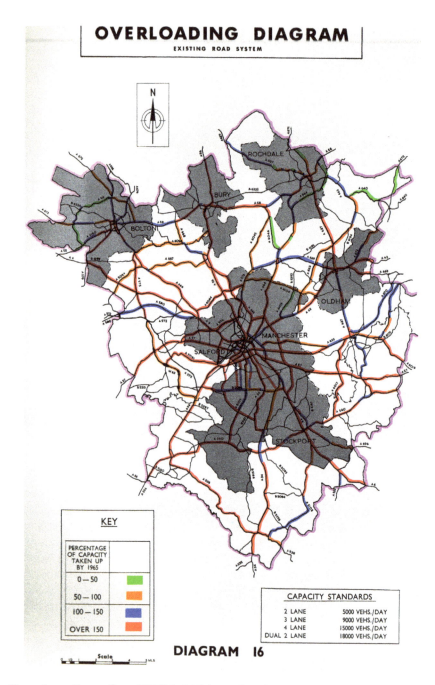

Figure 6.04 Extract from *SELNEC, A Highway Plan*, showing the anticipated overloading of the existing road network in and around Manchester. The red lines indicate overloading by more than 150%.

urban environment'.[13] The potential traffic flows around the ring roads were explored and the assessment emphasised the importance for the realisation of the route to 'discourage through-traffic', which would be 'essential to the future of the centre' in order for the main shopping areas and the Civic Area to become pedestrianised.[14] Millar's *1967 City Centre Map*, recommended the retention of the proposed ring roads and other road improvements from earlier plans and cited the SELNEC report as providing the techno-scientific proof of the urgent need for comprehensive road building.

In parallel to local planning discussions the problem of the incompatibility of pedestrian and vehicular flows and the impact of the motor car on townscape was investigated by groups commissioned by central government. Professor Colin Buchanan's influential 1963 report, *Traffic in Towns* seemingly proffered solutions to accommodate growing volumes of traffic.[15] Buchanan proposed a 'distributor hierarchy',where motorways would be situated below ground level, reducing noise and visual intrusion; local distributor roads would be at the existing ground level, offering good access and pedestrians would be elevated to first floor level [Figure 6.05].[16] This segregation of pedestrians and vehicles promised an improvement in safety and a reduction in accidents, where elevated walkways would become the 'new ground level for city life, a platform from which the buildings would rise'.[17] It was this vertical hierarchy that prevailed in the minds of planners in the 1960s as they implemented the advice.

The more subtle and sensitive suggestions embedded in the report, concerning the negative impact of the motor car and measures to mitigate against visual, acoustic and environmental pollutants, were widely overlooked.[18] Buchanan's work was often mistakenly appropriated as a blueprint for reconstruction when in fact 'it set fixed environmental standards and then offered a trade-off between the two variables – traffic and cost'.[19] In Manchester, the City Engineer acknowledged the idea of weighting and balancing 'accessibility, environment and cost' but concluded that 'the most important distributary routes in major towns would require grade separated intersections'.[20]

---

13 South-East Lancashire and North-East Cheshire Area Highway Engineering Committee (1962) *SELNEC: A Highway Plan*, p. 45.
14 Ibid., p. 45.
15 See Plowden, W. (1973) *The Motor Car and Politics in Britain* (Harmondsworth: Penguin).
16 Buchanan, *Traffic in Towns*, p. 135.
17 Ibid., p. 136.
18 For a good assessment of Buchanan's personal attitude to the motor car and his views of US policy see Ward, S.V. (2007) 'Cross-national Learning in the Formulation of British Planning Policies 1940–99. A Comparison of the Barlow, Buchanan and Rogers Reports', *The Town Planning Review*, Vol. 78, No. 3, pp. 369–400.
19 'The Buchanan Report: Twenty Years On' (Editorial), *Built Environment*, Vol. 9, No. 2 (1983), p. 91.
20 Hayes, *Manchester City Centre Road*, p. 4.

Figure 6.05   Illustration by Kenneth Browne from *Traffic in Towns* (Buchanan Report) to show vertical segregation of pedestrians and traffic.

The work of the planning department, from 1963 through to the publication of the *City Centre Map* in 1967, built upon the pioneering proposals of 1945 and combined these with emergent national policy guidance. The organising framework of the ring road concept remained and was augmented by the introduction of zoning and grade separation, as suggested by Buchanan. In *Traffic in Towns*, Buchanan supposed that small-scale road improvements were unlikely to be of lasting benefit, as congestion could only be solved by large-scale engineered interventions. The report proposed that the future of cities should be 'conceived as a patchwork of environmental areas', each with a dominant programmatic function.[21] These areas in turn would be separated and connected by distributor roads, with a street network designed to suit the capacity of each zone. The problems associated with through traffic would also be reduced, as each area would act as a 'terminus for traffic', with vehicles only entering if they had business there.[22]

This approach was mirrored in the proposals for central Manchester and the planning reports and development plans from Millar's department were

---

21   Buchanan, *Traffic in Towns*, p. vi.
22   Ibid., p. vi.

complemented by two documents produced by the City Engineer, John Hayes, concerning the city centre road and car parks.[23] Read together, it is easy to see the shared ambitions of the planners and engineers in service of the retail and commercial core. The innermost of the ring roads was presented as a terminus point for almost all personal traffic approaching the city and as a gyratory to move vehicles around, rather than across the centre. Car parks were proposed at the intersection of several radial routes and the city centre road as proposed would be something of a twentieth-century city wall [Figure 6.06]. This, it was thought, would release the central area from the pressures of cross-town traffic, permitting only service access for most functions other than public transport. The idea that the ring road might eventually inhibit growth was not foreseen as the scope for central area redevelopment at the time was vast and the adjustments to the road's alignment made in the late 1960s were actually promoted as providing an 'extended core'.[24]

Much of this core included the comprehensive development areas referred to throughout this book. Centrally located CDAs were essential to meeting the demand of the new car-borne consumer. The private sector, whilst willing to redevelop along the lines of the Buchanan Report, could not achieve radical alterations in highway configuration. The combined powers of CDA allocation and new road patterns, by virtue of the various Acts that had been passed from 1944, now lay with the local planning authorities. Each of the centrally located CDAs in Manchester took account of the route of the ring road [Figure 6.07] and, as they came to construction, physically adopted and delivered critical sections (some of which would never be formally connected to the ring road as it was eventually realised). As well as the CDA schemes, which effectively provided sections of the ring by proxy, there were also a number of significant architectural schemes that made provisions for the proposed alignments. Certain sites that were bomb damaged, but did not interfere with ring road planning, were released for development as well [Figure 6.08].

The formal ramifications of highways planning

Each successive permutation of the plan for the ring roads in Manchester had its own impact on the situation of new buildings. Despite the very definite alignments envisaged in the *1945 Plan*, its non-statutory nature, the complicated land ownerships and the lack of available finance made it impossible to realise with any immediacy. In truth Manchester's physical recovery, especially in the central area, was slow and typical of other provincial cities. Ultimately,

---

23 Hayes, *Manchester City Centre Road*; Manchester Corporation (1967) *Joint Report on Car Parking in Central Manchester* (Manchester: City of Manchester).
24 As evidenced by an overlay to drawing accompanying Hayes's 1968 report, which carries the term inside a dashed boundary that follows the route of the newly aligned road.

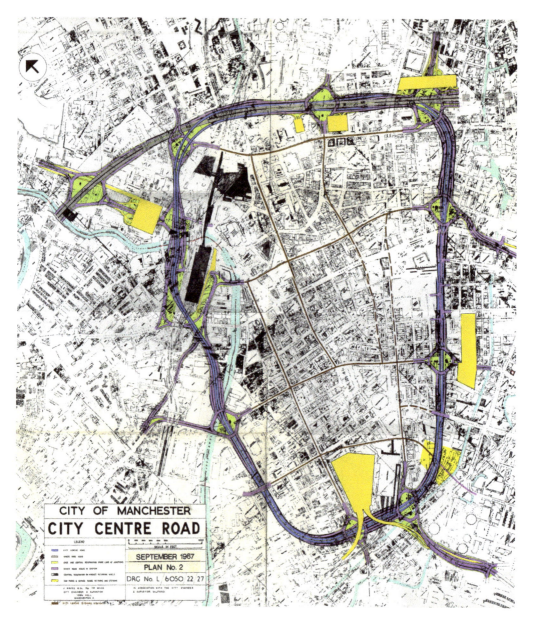

Figure 6.06 Map to accompany *Manchester City Centre Road*, 1968. The yellow blocks indicate the proposed sites for large car parking provision at the edge of the city centre.

Figure 6.07 Extract from 1965–67 Report of the Planning Department that shows the relationship between proposed comprehensive development areas and the Inner Relief Route.

the cessation of strict building licensing was one of the early catalysts for the upsurge in private sector development and the meeting of dream and demand would create a particular pattern in and around the city.[25] As the pressure on

---

25 See: http://hansard.millbanksystems.com/commons/1954/nov/02/building-licensing-termination [Accessed 31 July 2013].

Figure 6.08 Central Area Replanning, Sites Available for Development. Island sites such as these were subject to bomb damage, but their release did not interfere with the proposed route of any of the ring roads. Seen here is the area around Market Place, which was eventually subject to wholesale renewal as discussed in Chapter 5.

local authorities from private sector developers increased, the overarching plan for the ring roads as the central organising device for the economic success of the city became more focused and physically visible. A number of buildings of the late 1950s and early 1960s made provision for the route of the yet to be realised ring roads. Among the most prominent of these, visually and culturally, was the new headquarters for Granada Television to the west of the city centre and peculiarly situated perpendicular to the main radial route of Quay Street [Figure 6.09].

Following the Television Act (1954), Sidney Bernstein, founder of Granada Theatres Ltd, won a contract to become the sole broadcaster for the North of England. At the time of signing, Granada TV consisted of little more than a general idea of what the new television service should seek to attain, but there

Figure 6.09   Granada TV photographed in 1980. The road that runs perpendicular to the main facade is Quay Street. The cleared site was the proposed alignment of the ring road. This has now been developed as commercial office space.

were no tools or buildings with which to carry out the idea.[26] Bernstein acted quickly and formulated a simple vision for a television centre, 'to be the most advanced technically in the country'.[27] For the main studios, Bernstein identified a 4.5-acre site between Quay Street and Water Street that was already in the hands of Manchester Corporation, who had plans to use the land for a new exhibition hall. The Manchester Corporation Development Committee initially rejected Bernstein's offer, but after numerous meetings a sale was agreed. Ralph Tubbs, who had designed the Dome of Discovery at the Festival of Britain, was the appointed architect.

To ensure Granada was ready to broadcast by May 1956, the scheme was divided into five stages, with phase one being the first to be built in April 1955. It consisted of a 'small studio with ancillary rooms and a small office block'.[28] Phase two provided a second studio, completed in October 1957. Phase three, finished in March 1959, included a dressing-room block, technical department and a videotape recording room. The most significant building on the site and

---

26   Tubbs, R. (1958) *Year One* (Manchester: Granada), p. 11.
27   'Commercial TV in the North: Granada's Plans', *The Manchester Guardian*, 6 October 1955, p. 8.
28   'Granada Television Centre, Manchester', *The Builder*, 24 June 1960, p. 1178.

Figure 6.10   Courts of Justice, Crown Square (Leonard Cecil Howitt, City Architect, 1962). This view is from the end of Cumberland Street, c.1965, and in advance of the development of the Crown Square office complex (Leach Rhodes Walker, 1970).

that which has become synonymous with the organisation was the fourth phase. The construction of the ten-storey office block, the headquarters of Granada TV Network, began in August 1959, 'conceived as two vertical curtains of glass closed at each end by solid walls of brickwork'.[29] Tubbs didn't want the reinforced concrete structure to 'dominate internally or externally', so the concrete columns were set back from the face of the building, forming an unbroken surface of glass curtain walling from first floor to roof level; the first in the city.[30] Construction was completed in 1962. The new headquarters stood in contrast to the other recent completions that adopted the Festival Style or adapted classical techniques, styles and materials, such as the Portland stone clad Courts of Justice (L.C. Howitt, City Architect, 1962) [Figure 6.10]. The main elevation of Granada was supposed to flank the ring road and the sleek curtain-walled facade would reflect the gleaming metal of streamlined motor cars gliding past, at hitherto unknown speeds. As the ring road never adopted this alignment the incongruous setting of the gable wall facing the main road was established and never successfully resolved.

---

29   Truscon Ltd (1961) 'Granada TV Centre, Manchester'. *Truscon Review* (July), p. 31.
30   Ibid., p. 31.

Figure 6.11   The covered River Irwell as proposed in 1924 by E.L. Leeming, Borough Surveyor of Barton Upon Irwell. Drawn by Alfred Potter.

Close to Deansgate, the 1945 route of the city centre road was scheduled to cover the River Irwell, the boundary between Manchester and Salford. The reason for this was rumoured to be that Manchester could realise the plans under their own powers rather than have to negotiate with their neighbouring authority. It is more likely that the idea, which had been mooted years earlier [Figure 6.11] hinged upon the lack of value ascribed to the river and its role in the city. Long gone were the days of reliance upon the Irwell–Mersey Navigation for the import of goods and the discharging of all manner of effluent into the waterway was evident. One major objective of covering the river was to connect the city centre to a proposed new railway station, Trinity, which was intended to serve both Manchester and Salford [Figure 6.12]. Thus, the proposed new topography was to act in service of the city by facilitating both the gyratory and new public transport, both measures designed to improve the environment of the central area.

Highland House (Leach Rhodes Walker, 1966) was originally conceived and drawn in its relationship to the covered river [Figure 6.13]. By 1967 the idea to culvert the River Irwell was abandoned due to the excessive costs involved in engineering and the interference from Cold War era communication cables that ran beneath the riverbed.[31] Instead, the route of the city centre road was taken across the River Irwell and into Salford, scheduled to connect with the inner

---

31   See Brook, R. and Dodge, M. (2014) 'The Guardian Underground Telephone Exchange', *Lancashire & Cheshire Antiquarian Society Transactions*, 108, pp. 20–55.

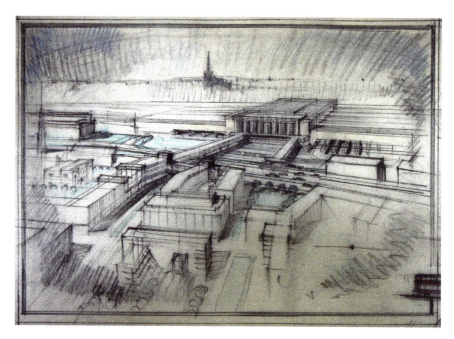

Figure 6.12 Extract from drawing showing proposed Trinity Railway Station, c.1947.

Figure 6.13 Sketch of Highland House (Leach Rhodes Walker, 1966). At the foot of the tower are vehicles shown driving on the covered section of the River Irwell as proposed again in the 1960s.

Figure 6.14 Cannon Street and the Arndale Centre, 2001. The ramp in the foreground was once the access to a multi-storey car park. The dual carriageway of Cannon Street passes either side. In the centre background is Highland House (Leach Rhodes Walker, 1966). Top right are the residential properties that were accessed from Shudehill.

ring road at a point north of Victoria Station. A viaduct was proposed to take the road over the railway lines at Exchange Station, with the amended route avoiding the need to demolish some valuable property.[32]

Following the line of the city centre road clockwise in an eastward trajectory from the Cathedral, two post-war building projects were designed to take specific account of the need for the route and its junctions. The first was Longridge House, the position and form of which was discussed in Chapter 5, the second was the Arndale Centre. The Arndale, which had been under discussion from 1962, completely filled the area dedicated as the Market Street CDA. In its original configuration the megastructure was effectively divided by a dual carriageway, Cannon Street [Figure 6.14], which, bereft of its adjoining sections of ring road, was an oddly over-engineered piece of infrastructure mostly serving bus passengers at the Arndale bus station. This was rumoured to have been one of

---

32 'New Route for City Centre Ring Road', *The Guardian*, 20 March 1968, p. 4.

Figure 6.15   CWS and CIS Towers.

the most polluted spaces in Europe! This section of road also disappeared in the wake of the 1996 bombing as the Arndale Centre was extended and modified to a new city master plan.

Indicative of the interwoven nature of decision making and the city centre, in the early 1960s, the Co-operative Insurance Society were engaged in discussions with the Corporation over two possible sites for their new headquarters. One was in Piccadilly, a site that was politically charged in so far as it was extremely central to the city and therefore highly visible to the public. Furthermore, its development would not interfere with the route of any major road plans. The second site was Miller Street. One condition of the Piccadilly site was that any scheme had to include shops and a hotel. Not wishing to compromise their autonomy, the CIS board chose the Miller Street site.[33] Designed by G.S. Hay in association with the CIS in-house architects the Co-operative Insurance Society (CIS) and Co-operative Wholesale Society (CWS) towers flanked the proposed route of the ring road and their footprints were deliberately set back from the proposed carriageway alignment on Miller Street [Figure 6.15].

---

33 'CIS Building, Manchester', *The Builder*, 8 March 1963, pp. 489–493.

The city centre road was paramount to the success of the reconfigured city, which meant the Corporation placed restrictions on the land that surrounded the route to ensure developments 'conformed with its [The Corporation's] requirements in respect of access, car-parking provisions, building lines, daylighting, density and the like'.[34] In March 1960, Ind Coope Ltd, a brewer based in Burton-on-Trent, announced the purchase of Queen's Hotel, situated on the junction of Portland Street and Piccadilly. In 1961 two schemes were submitted for planning approval for the redevelopment of the site. One scheme, which proposed an office block on the site, was approved, but the Town Planning Committee rejected the other scheme, which proposed a combination of offices and retail on the site. Under the City's redevelopment plans the building of shops on the outer fringe of the planned ring road was not permitted. The Town Planning Committee stipulated that all shops should be kept within the ring road and the road itself maintained for the free movement of traffic.[35] This was not the first scheme along Portland Street to be rejected, six months previously, a 25-storey block of shops and offices, and another 20-storey office block with retail on the two lower floors had their planning applications turned down for the same reasons.

Portland Street featured in both the 1945 and 1960s plans for the ring road and had suffered a concentration of bomb damage in 1940. Buildings on both sides of the road were designed to permit a proposed elevated dual carriageway and the splays and easements required for such a massive piece of engineering [Figure 6.16]. St Andrew's House (now known as Manchester One) was located on one site that was heavily bombed. The central situation of sites along Portland Street meant a good return for speculative commercial developers – the right to develop there was competitive. In 1959, four committees from the Corporation considered three schemes. The Corporation insisted on the inclusion of a large car park for the development of the site. One proposal was for an eleven-storey car park with vehicular elevators, another scheme a small office building that included parking areas with ramps between levels. A mixed-use development designed by Leach Rhodes & Walker was ultimately selected [Figure 6.17] and approved by the City Planning Department. It was composed of a 22-storey office block connected to a four-storey car park, itself sat above a new bus station.

This was an early commercial building by the firm, completed in 1963, and in their desire to optimise returns the architectural expression was somewhat compromised. The tower received a mixed reaction, with one critic describing it as an 'upturned matchbox' that was 'scarcely ... an adventure in architecture'.[36] The footprint of the tower was set back from Portland Street in anticipation of

---

34 'New Heart for Manchester', *The Guardian*, 15 June 1960, p. 18.
35 'Shop Schemes Rejected by Council', *The Guardian*, 19 July 1961, p. 14.
36 Dodd, K., 'St Andrew's House', *The Guardian*, 12 July 1963, p. 13.

Figure 6.16 Model showing proposed canyon and multi-level traffic engineering along Portland Street.

its widening and, acknowledging the trend for grade separation and the pending aerial highway, a first-floor access point was provided by a bridge link from the adjacent car park.

Next to St Andrew's House was Telephone House (Norman Bailey & Partners, 1961), a podium and tower configuration clad entirely in curtain wall glazing [Figure 6.17]. Like its neighbour, its footprint was set back from the existing street line in anticipation of the city centre road. On the opposite side of Portland Street the site at Piccadilly rejected by the CIS was subject to competition between developers and up to nine proposals were considered by the Corporation.[37] One of these was by the renowned modernist partnership of Fry & Drew, though the eventual selection fell to Covell Matthews and Partners on behalf of The Sunley Group.[38] The scheme became known as Piccadilly Plaza [Figure 6.18] and was one of the most substantial and prominent of Manchester's post-war buildings. In line with local authority ambition for a new elevated public realm the hotel and office towers of the Plaza were designed with entrance lobbies and parking at high level served by a spiral vehicular ramp, up which The Commodores once pushed Louis Kahn's broken down car![39]

---

37 'Piccadilly Site's Future. Nine Schemes Under Review', *The Manchester Guardian*, 12 May 1959, p. 15.
38 As evidenced by photographs held in the RIBA Library. Record Control No. P010785 Ref No. 285–5285/10, ON2642-ON2654.
39 A tale recounted by former Manchester School of Architecture lecturer John Proctor-Bishop who invited Louis Kahn to give a lecture in the 1970s.

Figure 6.17 Portland Street. In the centre, Portland Tower and behind Telephone House. Both buildings were set back from the original street line which is marked by the stone building to the left of the image, Britannia Hotel, former Watts Warehouse.

Figure 6.18 Piccadilly Plaza under construction. The smog-laden haze and soot-blackened Victorian buildings testify to the city's industrial roots.

Figure 6.19   The roof garden of Williams Deacon Bank.

The proposed elevated dual-carriageway section of ring road put the onus on this new city level; however, there were also other influencing factors. The earliest proposal for new elevated public realm in Manchester was promoted by developers in 1961 and designed by BDP. The site south of Oxford Street was intended for new residential flats, a new bus station, an air terminal, a hotel, offices, restaurants and entertainment centres, with 'attractive paving and gardens'.[40] It was eventually subsumed into the designation for the Mosley Street CDA, which was to be an arts and entertainment quarter founded on the existing City Art Gallery and its proximity to the cinemas of Oxford Street. Such a designation informed other buildings both within the proposed boundaries and on adjacent streets.

Within the curtilage of the Mosley Street CDA, Williams Deacon Bank building (H.S. Fairhurst & Son, 1965) on the corner of York Street and Mosley Street had a substantial roof garden that would have become part of the wider proposed public realm [Figure 6.19]. Further along Mosley Street, the Eagle Star House (Cruickshank & Seward, 1973) was designed to accommodate

---

40   'Big Development Plan for Manchester', *The Guardian*, 13 April 1961, p. 22.

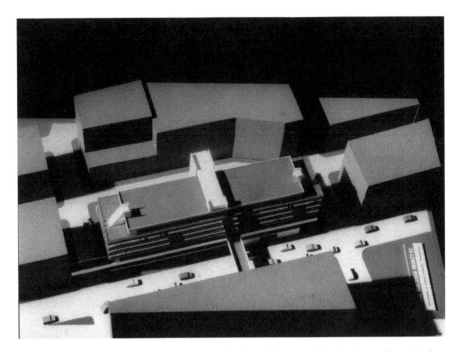

Figure 6.20 Model showing the proposed bridge link across Mosley Street from Eagle Star House.

a bridge link across to the new space [Figure 6.20]. Behind Piccadilly Plaza and facing Portland Tower, the Bank of England (Fitzroy Robinson, 1971) went even further in its response to the proposed highway planning. By the time it was commissioned, proposals for a 'depressed' section of primary carriageway along Portland Street and 'a secondary ground level system' were published.[41] The entire zone, including an Arts Centre, would be an inward focussed environment [Figure 6.21].[42] As such, the Portland Street elevation of the new building was without any fenestration and the architects did not attempt to form any relationship with the street on this side. The opposite side had an entrance at ground floor level as well as provision for an entrance at a high level and connection to the wider development that, along with the aerial roads, never came to be. That these buildings all made concessions to both the highway planning and the desire for comprehensive development made for an incoherent streetscape on Portland Street that festered for years. Bizarrely blank facades and glass walled towers that did not follow the established building line were interspersed with Victorian warehouses in various

---

41 Hayes, *Manchester City Centre Road*, cl. 42, p. 16.
42 Morris, M. 'Arts Centre to be Built on Platform', *The Guardian*, 29 January 1966, p. 3.

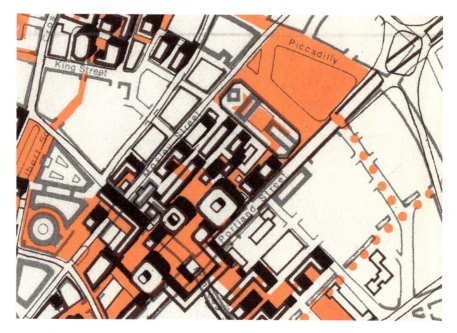

Figure 6.21   Extract from *City Centre Map*, 1967. The red areas between Portland Street and Mosley Street were scheduled as pedestrian plazas at first floor level.

states of decay.[43] This period of urban limbo was, in part, due to the collapse of the ring road proposals in 1973.

The very particular pattern of development brought about by the almost belligerent adhesion to the highways ambitions of the city was addressed in a newspaper article by lecturer, architect and town planner, Franklin Medhurst, in 1963.[44] His insightful observations concerned the relationship between the locations of the 'shining machined surfaces' of the office towers and the planned city centre road. To Medhurst, the corelation of the two was explicit and was clearly represented in a diagram that accompanied the article [Figure 6.22]. The cross-section through the city was becoming that of a crater, where the centre was formed of remaining Victorian warehouses of not more than six storeys and the edge of the city was ringed by a citadel of new towers. This contrasted against the growth cities of the early twentieth century in North America that had developed their commercial core at the centre of their cities and thus height and land value tapered with distance from the centre. The influence of planning on land values and development was clear and the disturbance of

---

43 See Canniffe, E., and Jefferies, T. (1998) *Manchester Architecture Guide* (Manchester: Manchester Metropolitan University Press), p. 90.

44 Medhurst, F. 'Out of Centre', *The Guardian*, 12 July 1963, p. 12.

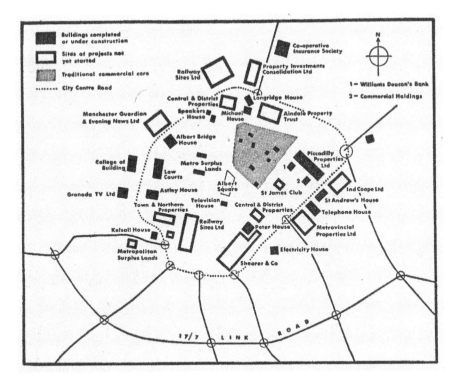

Figure 6.22   New construction in and around the city of Manchester in 1963. The dotted line is the proposed route of the ring road. It is clear to see the relationships between planning and development.

the ring road proposals had resulted in unexpected variance in prices for sites across the city.

A host of other buildings across the centre of Manchester were designed to take account of the highways planning that never came to fruition. Some made provision for first-floor walkways and others mostly adopted new alignments respective of proposed carriageway widening [Figure 6.23]. Whilst commercial pressures, market demands and cultural factors all influenced the situation and development of buildings amidst the lack of statutory planning guidance, it was the ring roads that were the most concrete organising principles as the city's new shape was formed. The eventual demise of the ambitious plans would coincide with an economic downturn in much the same manner as their evolution had aligned with the boom of the 1960s.

The end of the road

It was at a public inquiry into a 27-storey office block, designed by Leach Rhodes & Walker, proposed for 103 Princess Street [Figure 6.24] that one

Figure 6.23   John Dalton Street.

decisive nail was hammered into the coffin of Manchester's city centre ring road ambitions.[45] The highway scheme would have required the demolition of several sizeable and architecturally significant Victorian warehouses along Princess Street and Portland Street. Without the aid of a barrister, a team of local experts and architectural enthusiasts took on and defeated Castle Irwell Properties and its assembled professional consultants over the course of a three-day hearing in defence of the buildings. The Chair of the public inquiry praised the quality of the historic research prepared by the local team.[46] The proposal for new tower did not sit directly on the site of threatened buildings, York House and the Mechanics' Institute, but its construction along with that of the highway would have required the demolition of both.

---

45 Furthermore, GPO cable routing had forced the abandonment of the route for the ring road above the River Irwell in 1966, which immediately presented considerable issues with regard an alternative alignment and either a series of complicated land acquisitions or entry into the land controlled by Salford. See Whiteley, G. 'Proposed Route for Ring Road in City Abandoned', *The Guardian*, 12 February 1966, p. 14.

46 'City on Trial', *The Guardian*, 2 June 1973, p. 11. Among the local team were architectural historian and lecturer John Archer, conservation architect Donald Buttress, and a young architect, Ken Moth, who became a director at Building Design Partnership specialising in historic buildings.

Figure 6.24 The unbuilt Portland Tower. The gable wall on the left of the image is that of St Andrew's House (Manchester One).

It was really the first public debate of its kind concerning the wider value of Victorian and Edwardian buildings in Manchester. It set a new precedent and changed the landscape, metaphorically and physically, in terms of the appreciation of historic buildings *and* the realisation of the massive city centre ring road. In the immediate aftermath, in a churlish act, the City Council opted to demolish York House [Figure 6.25], despite the site no longer being required.[47] Its apparently wanton demolition in the 1970s was opposed by a significant

---

47 From a series of conversations with Ken Moth and John Archer of the Victorian Society between 2006 and 2009.

Figure 6.25   York House.

number of high-profile architects and designers, including James Stirling and Walter Gropius.[48]

A number of other convergent factors affected the plans for the ring roads. It is also important to remember that the likelihood of the city ever securing the funding outright to realise the plans was slight at best. The historically laissez-faire city, built on mercantile enterprise, never owned significant portions of the land within its boundaries. As such, land assembly, even with powers of compulsory purchase, was a convoluted affair at the best of times. The oil crisis and subsequent economic collapse of the early 1970s vastly changed the financial landscape of Britain and the post-industrial cities of the north felt the withdrawal of monies harder than the affluent south-east. Furthermore, local and regional political structures were subject to the most far-reaching changes

---

48   Parkinson-Bailey, *Manchester: An Architectural History*, p. 205, suggests that Gropius wrote a personal appeal. It is commonly held that Gropius had been to Manchester and shown the vast glazed facade of York House as an early example of modernist curtain walling. It was in fact governed by rights of light issues, but nonetheless pioneering. Gropius was referred to as 'Mr. Gropius, from the other Cambridge', by the Chair.

since the city of Manchester was incorporated under the Corporations Act (1838). The Local Government Act (1972) set in place the motion towards the creation of the metropolitan county of Greater Manchester and the creation of the Greater Manchester Council (GMC). The new organisation was designed to create systems of government with sufficient powers to administer metropolitan areas with a dominant economic core. Many local officers and politicians would embark on new careers under the new structures and the drawn-out aspirations to close the loop on the city centre ring road were without a single champion.

In 1976 the GMC abandoned the proposals entirely.[49] This was not before the press had criticised the policies that had created multiple vacant sites, preserved in anticipation of development, yet, in reality, were just a visible blight. The plans were considered as overly ambitious and referred to as an 'optimist's delight' and a 'library of schemes to be tackled when finances allow'.[50] One critic's assessment of the whole post-war landscape of recovery and development singled out the disparity between the plans and their implementation: 'Manchester suffered from a surfeit of ambition allied to a dearth of cash. The most dramatic gap between dream and reality lay in the county's transportation and road building programmes.'[51]

Regardless of political motion and motivation, the need for some form of circulatory route that could adequately bypass the city centre did not altogether vanish. The new county needed a new plan and, in 1979, the GMC published their first statutory document, the *Greater Manchester County Structure Plan*, which superseded Millar's 1967 Development Plan. The new plan offered an official explanation for the abandoned ring road schemes. It was explained that, in 1974, the GMC had 'inherited plans to construct or improve 460 miles of road' at a cost of over £800m.[52] Owing to a significant lack of funds, the council reviewed all road proposals. They decided only small-scale schemes were to be retained, as they were 'not dependent upon the completion of further works'.[53] Ironically, despite their scale and reach, the GMC thought that planning for bigger schemes was 'no longer possible nor desirable' and blamed overly ambitious schemes of the past for creating problems for contemporary planning.[54] However, the GMC did approve the completion of Manchester's Outer Ring

---

49 Parkinson-Bailey, *Manchester: An Architectural History*, p. 188.
50 Waterhouse, 'Eternity Ring', p. 16.
51 Ibid., p. 16.
52 Greater Manchester Council (1979) *Greater Manchester County Structure Plan, Written Statement* (Manchester: Greater Manchester Council), p. 70.
53 Greater Manchester Council, *Greater Manchester County Structure Plan, Written Statement*, p. 82. Examples of small-scale schemes included traffic management on existing roads, improved road junctions and refurbished roads.
54 Greater Manchester Council, *Greater Manchester County Structure Plan, Written Statement*, p. 69. In 1974 the introduction of the Transport Policies Programme (TPP) system meant that rather than procuring specific grants for individual schemes, the highway

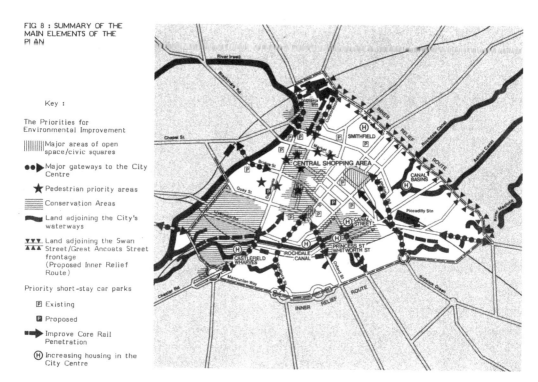

Figure 6.26 The proposed network from the 1980 report.

Road (eventually the M60), as they argued the county lacked a 'suitable north-south route through the urban areas on its eastern side'.[55]

While the GMC dealt with their restricted budget and curtailed road building programme, the City Council were still faced with the problem of central area congestion that had persisted since the Victorian era. In 1980 Brian Parnell, the City Planning Officer, published a report that highlighted the problems faced by the city centre and proposed guidelines on how to resolve them. It also identified Manchester's increasing decentralisation and the risks this presented

---

and trans portation authority was in receipt of a block grant from central government for all transport expenditure. This policy was introduced in conditions of severe financial stringency; new policy and planning was very difficult to achieve with the constrained budgets. See Gwilliam K.M. (1979) 'Institutions and Objectives in Transport Policy', *Journal of Transport Economics and Policy*, Vol. XIII, No. 1 (January), pp. 11–27.

55 Greater Manchester Council, *Greater Manchester County Structure Plan, Written Statement*, p. 69. The M60 Outer Ring Road was eventually opened in October 2000. http://news.bbc.co.uk/1/hi/uk/998291.stm [Accessed 7 August 2013].

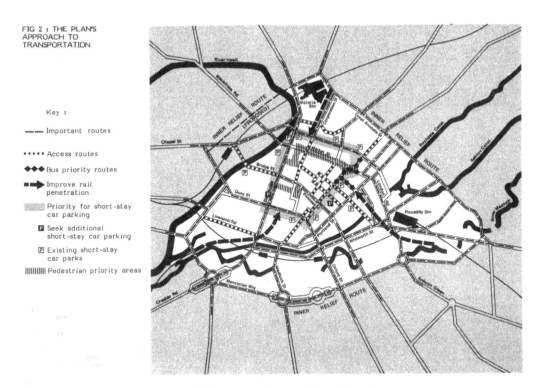

Figure 6.27　The diagram of the proposed network from the 1984 report.

to the inner city.[56] Parnell's solution was to make the city more accessible and he proposed a new road programme [Figure 6.26]. Predominantly formed of inexpensive, small-scale schemes, Parnell suggested two large-scale measures. The first was an Inner Relief Route, which provided a by-pass for through traffic, and the second was an Inner Circulatory Route, which would enable 'distribution round the centre itself.'[57]

In 1984, the City Council published the *City Centre Local Plan*. Together with the GMC's *1979 County Structure Plan*, it formed the new Development Plan for the city centre.[58] Unlike city plans of the past, the transportation

---

56　Manchester City Council (1980) *Manchester City Centre Local Plan: Report of Survey/Issues and Choices*. (Manchester: Manchester City Council), p. 9. The decentralisation of Manchester brought many benefits, including a lower density of housing and reduced pressure for development. However, decentralisation also meant that fewer people lived in the immediate vicinity of the city, and its centre was no longer the primary venue for the needs-based consumption of goods.

57　Ibid., p. 46.

58　In March 1981, the *1979 Greater Manchester County Structure Plan* was approved by the Secretary of State for the Environment.

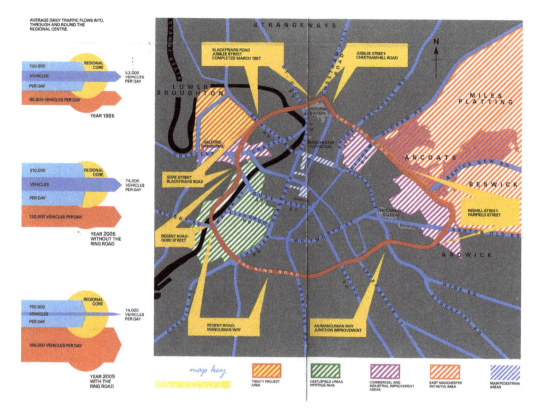

Figure 6.28 The Ring. Stylised graphical representation of the route of the Inner Relief Road.

proposals [Figure 6.27] were heavily weighted towards public transport and the environment.[59] A series of abstract diagrams made scant reference to road building and the political scars of the past were manifest in the prose: 'it will be to no avail if it takes so long to come about and creates such utter chaos and confusion during the period of construction that by the time it becomes available, the City Centre has declined even further'.[60] This pessimistic tone reflected the continued depressed state of the economy and tensions between the city and county councils. Nonetheless, prior to the abolition of the GMC in 1986, work had commenced on the construction of the Inner Relief Route.[61] Part of the ring

---

59 Manchester City Council (1984) *Manchester City Centre Local Plan* (Manchester: Manchester City Council), p. 10.
60 Ibid., p. 11.
61 In 1986, the GMC was abolished following the Local Government Act (1985), with its powers devolved to the ten district councils of Greater Manchester.

road utilised Mancunian Way, an elevated motorway constructed in two main phases during the 1960s and 1970s. The remaining route was formed primarily from existing roads and dual carriageway sections, but also included a new section of carriageway to the north of the River Irwell. Though not the final route of the road, it was best visually represented by a Ben Kelly inspired graphic published in a brochure titled *The Ring* in 1987 [Figure 6.28]. Finally completed in 2004, the ring road adopted the catchy moniker of the *Manchester and Salford Inner Relief Route*.

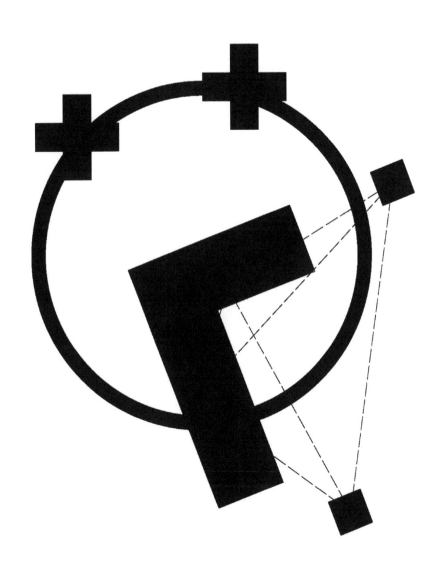

Conclusion

The state, in its many forms, is ever present in this particular account of Manchester. Following recent scholarship on post-war reconstruction, this book has eschewed a broad nationwide survey in favour of detailed and specific case studies of one city, focusing on the buildings and the individual planners and architects involved in its renewal. The use of the terms 'welfare state', 'warfare state' and 'nation state' all point to the idea that some form of centralised force touched most production in the renewal and modernisation of cities and society after 1945. In each chapter here, the magnitude of state influence on architectural production varied and moved generally from Whitehall to Manchester, dependent upon the context. At the National Computing Centre and Market Place, the arms of the state via local government planning officers showed a palpable relation between policy, plan and architecture; in the cases of UMIST and Central Station, more complex outside forces informed siting, mass and form; in other case studies, such as Ferranti's Wythenshawe factory and ICL in West Gorton, the architecture was much more in the hands of the architect, but the sponsorship and funding were bound up with central government administration.

There were two key political conditions that engendered this level of control. First were the surviving regional government structures, created to disperse political power during war. Second was the sweeping nationalisation of huge sectors of British industry and services. The creation of policy, not exclusively that used to inform the built environment, touched every architectural case study here in some way.

Like the structure of the chapters, conclusions about both the role and impact of the state, and conclusions about the shape of the city, should be drawn at different scales, as well as being drawn together. Such an interdependency, between state influences and morphology, was also signalled by the momentum towards regional government and the creation of the metropolitan counties. As the 1960s came to a close, a vast amount of planning work by Millar's department was concluded. The political landscape was shifting too. Twenty-seven authorities were asked under the terms of the 1968 amendments to the Town and Country Planning Act to prepare structure plans. This included the County Borough of Manchester.[1] Implicit in the direction was the demand to take broader account of the ways in which urban agglomerations, rather than demarcated townships, were planned at a regional scale. The pending 1969 Redcliffe-Maud Report would recommend the establishment of unitary authorities to govern city regions, and among these was SELNEC.

In its report of 1962, the SELNEC transportation committee, characteristic of the continuing importance of transportation in shaping the city and its governance, crystallised the composition of what would become Greater Manchester. The transport needs of the conurbation were telling the politicians what shape of governance was required – the city of Manchester was indisputably the regional hub and was served by satellite towns which were subservient to the economic centre. Derek Senior, a specialist freelance journalist trained as a planner and a member of the Royal Commission on Local Government, made public calls for the creation of a new county authority in the mid-1960s. He believed that the dreams and ambitions of the *1945 Plan* called for such and that without it the city would struggle to realise the comprehensive development set out.[2] Leslie Green's book, *Provincial Metropolis* had established what Senior considered an irrefutable argument for the creation of a city region authority.[3]

Such calls were not new; as early as 1915, Patrick Geddes made reference to 'Greater Manchester'.[4] In April 1935, the *Manchester Evening Chronicle* brought to the fore the issue of 'regional unity' under the headline 'Greater Manchester – The Ratepayers' Salvation'. It reported on the 'increasing demands for the exploration of the possibilities of a greater merger of public services throughout Manchester and the surrounding municipalities'.[5] Following the Local Government Act (1972) the wheels were set in motion for the inauguration of the new county and subsequently a new set of municipal structures that would be forced to re-imagine the city in a transformed political and economic climate. The formal switch to a new joint planning committee headed by Millar was

---

1 Town and Country Planning Act, 1968 (Structure Plans). HC Deb 11 November 1968 vol 773 cc52–3W, http://hansard.millbanksystems.com/written_answers/1968/nov/11/town-and-country-planning-act-1968#S5CV0773P0_19681111_CWA_268 [Accessed 20 August 2010].

2 'New Heart for Manchester'. *The Manchester Guardian*, 15 June 1960, p. 18.

3 Green, L.P. (1959) *Provincial Metropolis: The Future of Local Government in South-East Lancashire; A Study in Metropolitan Analysis* (London: Allen & Unwin).

4 Geddes, P. (1915) *Cities in Evolution* (London: Association for Planning and Regional Reconstruction) New and revised edition, 1949, p. 15.

5 Frangopulo, Nicholas Joseph (1977) *Tradition in Action: The Historical Evolution of the Greater Manchester County* (Wakefield: EP Publishing), p. 227. Cited in *The Manchester Evening Chronicle*, 25 April 1935.

CONCLUSION

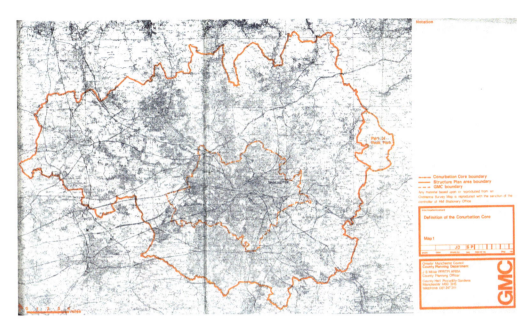

Figure 7.01   Greater Manchester.

made in February 1973 and Greater Manchester formally constituted in April 1974 [Figure 7.01]. The fact that the majority of the boroughs of Manchester were Labour governed meant that the operability of the GMC was not hindered by inter-party squabbles. After eighteen months' work the assembled team of planners from each of the boroughs of the new county had 'satisfied the Secretary for the Environment that it [was] capable of producing a plan setting out policies for providing houses, jobs, shops, transport systems, amenities and recreation areas'.[6] This shift, contrary to Derek Senior's forecast, brought to a close the detailed physical planning for the city seen in the *1945 Plan* and in the work of the planners in the 1960s: for this reason, and amidst difficult economic circumstances, renewal was over.

Urban renewal in Britain involved complex scenarios, where ideas were instituted in legislation, were alive in a population and required architectural mediation to achieve material form. In post-war Britain, planning and architecture were subject to increasing forms of legislation. The awarding of new powers for local authorities to determine their own physical shape paralleled increasingly centralised legislation, administered by the surviving regional offices of government. Amidst this political realignment was a bigger apolitical

---

6 'Planners Go to Public on Ideas for 30 Year Strategy', *The Manchester Guardian*, 22 February 1973, p. 5.

force – that of finance – which fed and helped to create the commercial property market. The work of planners and architects was interwoven through the growth of statute and guidance concerning the built environment. The state exerted forms of control in overt ways, such as the pursuit of rearmament and the race for technological supremacy, and in latent situations via the mechanisms of the planning machinery. To understand such complexities requires this reading, of central government policy filtered through a local lens, influenced and informed by other external forces, often beyond the control of any sole party. The actors and networks in these relations had varying degrees of agency and certain situations favoured the demands of a particular organisation or individual – central government, local government, architect, public, developer etc. – but the local interpretation and materialisation of ideas and words into form was an inevitable act of these relations.

There are obvious cultural contexts and architectural precedents that inform design generally and traditional forms of critique provide access to these influences. However, in schemes at all scales political, economic and legislative forces are at play too. One of the core aims of this book has been to explore, in depth, the range of forces acting on renewal cities during a very specific period in British history. In the introduction a series of questions established the themes of this exploration: the status of private practice and its relation to the state; the capacity to usefully critique mainstream modernism; the effects of statutory instruments on form and material; the role of the architect in commercial development and the locally nuanced states of each of these.

An extended study of a building's commission and creation, through an examination of its social, political, cultural and economic contexts also provides the means to look outward and reveal the broader conditions involved in renewal. The impact of the Cold War, for example, was instrumental in the sponsorship of new technologies and technological education. In analogous fashion, the shrinking Empire created some of the conditions for speculation around the massive development of Central Station. Such an approach can also turn inward and show how policy played out in detail in one particular city and among one particular group of actors. Renewal is important here as a historical term and as one that describes a certain group of cities with quite distinct characteristics. The periodisation of this term, between the loosening of building restrictions in the mid-1950s to the local government reform and economic collapse of the mid-1970s, is one that is particularly meaningful to the planning and architecture of cities that became centres of the new metropolitan counties in 1974. It is no accident that the majority of construction discussed across these pages falls within these limits.

Mainstream modern architecture cannot be usefully judged stylistically, nor read as art. It can, however, reveal much about the external forces that help to shape a city. In the case of building for new technologies, central government objectives effectively overrode any powers of the local authority. In terms of technological education, the joint interests of Whitehall and Manchester created significant interplay between these tiers of government in the creation of UMIST. The story of Central Station revealed how international finance usurped local ambitions and showed a certain ambivalence of central government towards the commercial renewal of centres. At Market Place a lack of financial support via the War Damage Commission meant that the local Labour Government formed public–private partnerships to deliver reconstruction. This was demonstrative of the political consensus towards renewal and typical of how other renewal cities rebuilt their centres.

This spatially informed inquiry has deliberately obviated political binaries and has acknowledged consensual policy objectives. Such an approach, enabled by mainstream modernism, is useful for studying a period that is often viewed through the lens of the welfare state, typically viewed as a socialist undertaking. As demonstrated in the case studies of the architecture of the technology, higher education and commercial sectors, there was an overarching political consensus in reconstruction, renewal and rearmament during the post-war period. The detailed case studies here support this notion and challenge the generalised view of the time. Whether legislation was designed to construct new social ideals or to dismantle existing statute by alternative administrations is not critical – nor is the political orientation of its authors. Legislation for the built environment emerged in the early twentieth century, as construction engaged with policy regulation. The eventual impact on architectural form was most palpable in the visual, three-dimensional planning and architectural proposals of 1960s renewal. This is extremely evident in the cases of Central Station and Market Place. As this type of planning faded from view in the mid-1970s – the local architect-planner ceded to the regional economic and strategic-planner – the qualitative properties of design were less visible in the reports and guidance of the state, either nationally or locally. The impact of planning upon architecture was less visually discernible, but the interplay between local and national legislative conditions continued, albeit more focused on quantifiable statistical measures – employment, traffic, investment returns and so on. These changes to statute and guidance in the planning sphere effectively mirrored those in society generally and those heralded by the rise of neo-liberal approaches to planning and development.

As we read in the opening chapter, the shape of the city of Manchester was founded first on its geography and then rapidly configured by its infrastructure. Within these limits, the major planning visions of the mid-twentieth century also left their palimpsestic traces. That these mid-twentieth century layers of the city are visible, but partial, attests to the difficulties of enacting total visions on existing cities. Expansion of the city during the industrial revolution gave little in the way of public space and was almost entirely unplanned. Manchester's rapid growth at the hands of wealthy industrialists occurred unchecked before the creation of any form of municipal authority. In many respects, the free-market or laissez-faire approach to development may be seen as the salvation of the Victorian city, but it was also the frustration of the many modern visions laid out through the course of the twentieth century. The Corporation did not own most of the land within its jurisdiction, which created difficult conditions for land assembly.

Only after the Town and Country Planning Act (1947) did local authorities have the necessary powers to design and affect change in the interests of the municipality. The *1945 Plan* and the work of the 1960s constituted the most creative period of planning in the city. Yet the role of the architect-planner soon faded from the public sector in much the same way as the role of the City Surveyor had given way to the Chief Planner before. As the political structure expanded to regional governance in the creation of the GMC, so planning followed suit. The defined formal visions of the 1960s faded, as strategic diagrams superseded traditional representation in the canon of the planner [Figure 7.02]. Nonetheless, whilst the visions of Millar's team in the 1960s were bold, influential and assertive, they were not necessarily autonomous and not as authoritative as they might appear. Planning is as reactive as it is proactive. In Manchester's case, this is best understood through the genesis of the CDAs and their dedication through the statutory approvals of 1967 and 1968.

The sixteen-year gap between the publication of the *1945 Plan* and the approval of its proceeding statutory counterpart meant that most buildings, up to 1961, were realised outside of any legal development framework or master plan. Fortunately, there was relatively little new central development in the 1950s and certainly nothing that would overtly prejudice the main features of Rowland Nicholas's vision. However, as the Development Plan was ratified in 1961 the economy began to boom and an overwhelmed department did all it could to cope with the influx of planning applications.[7] The predominant architectural production of the 1960s was actually realised within planning parameters defined in 1945 and the preceding decades. The fact that the shape of the city in 2021 can be directly attributed to the CDAs established through the mid-1960s demonstrates a similar cycle of policy implementation and a clear layering of ideas. Similarly, the sequences of ideas and their eventual realisation can be seen to be fragmented, rather than comprehensive, and bound to economics as opposed to planning. Often the seeds were sown generations earlier, and not always by professionals in the employment of the City Surveyor's office or the Planning Department.

Provisions were made within the Town and Country Planning Act in 1947 for the creation of CDAs, but it was not until 1964 that Manchester began to designate such zones. The fledgling Civic Trust was faster than the local authority to suggest the powers of the CDA, when they proposed and designed a plan for the area around Knott Mill in 1963.[8] As well as being overwhelmed by pressing

---

7   Turner, *The North Country*, pp. 69–70.
8   'Vision of How Central Area Could be Renewed', *The Manchester Guardian*, 14 December 1963, p. 4.

CONCLUSION

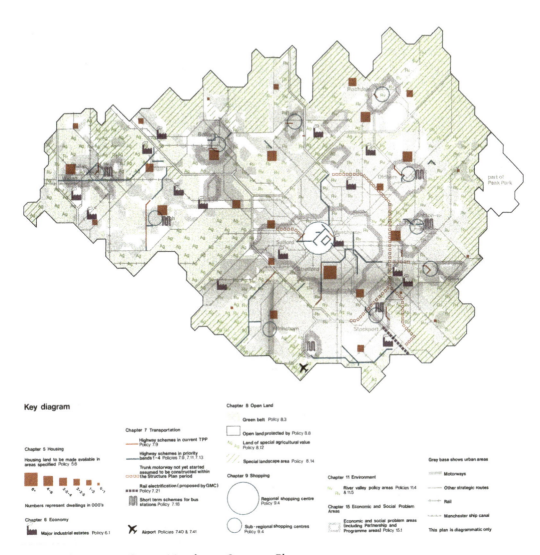

Figure 7.02   Greater Manchester Structure Plan, 1975.

private sector development, Millar's new planning department was behind the pace of campaign groups. In fact, all six of Manchester's CDAs were effectively constructed by external agents, prior to their designation by the local authority. Piccadilly Plaza and St Andrew's Tower were already under construction in the Mosley Street Area before it was named as the cultural and entertainment quarter. In 1961 private developers began negotiations for a comprehensive scheme for the area between Cross Street and Deansgate and W.S. Hattrell proposed a scheme for the Corn Exchange (Cathedral Area) in 1962; both of these were reflected in the formal characteristics of the Planning Department's subsequent

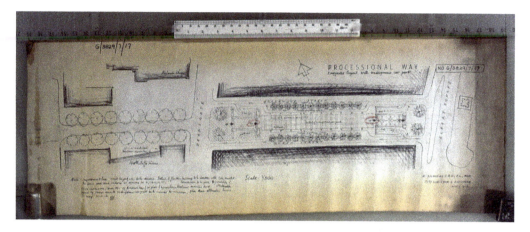

Figure 7.03 Designs for the beaux-arts boulevard of Manchester's processional way from the Town Hall to Deansgate. It was intended to continue to Crown Square, where the axis would be terminated by the symmetry of the Crown Court (L.C. Howitt, 1962).

framework.[9] The Civic Area was a legacy of the *1945 Plan* and was subject to redesign at the demands of the developer of Brazennose House; the 'processional way' [Figure 7.03] was dropped in favour of the passages and squares model.[10]

Such acquiescence is one indicator of the lack of financial resources of the local authority and their need to enable the private sector to develop. The relationship of the lead party in the development of the Arndale Centre (Market Street Area) is distinctly unclear. Informal discussion to ensure 'conformity' with the city's development plans took place as early as 1964, though Phase 1 of the development did not commence construction until 1972.[11] The Education Precinct was proceeding apace, driven by the institutions themselves in response to national policy, not the design of the Planning Department. Central Station was created by circumstances beyond the control of the local authority and its major elements were again driven by private sector interests, albeit never realised.

---

9 'Plans to Transform Deansgate Area', *The Manchester Guardian*, 4 May 1961, p. 18.

10 'Courts and Gardens for City Centre. No "processional way" Now?', *The Manchester Guardian*, 7 March 1962, p. 20. The Metropolitan Railways Surplus Land Company were pursuant to realise an office block along the line of Brazennose Street and this called into question the 'processional way' as drawn in 1945 and still adhered to in 1961/62. The proposal forced a redesign of the link between Albert Square and Deansgate.

11 '£15m Redevelopment Plan for City Centre', *The Manchester Guardian*, 14 January 1965, p. 18. The article suggests that proposals will be submitted within a month from the date of publication, which implies that the discussions referred to had taken place some time earlier.

CONCLUSION

Most evident, through the 1960s, was the relationship between economic conditions and the production of architecture. Whilst the expansion of the universities may be directly attributable to policy shifts in the post-war years, the city centre and its form continued to be dictated to by the commercial sector. Civic projects were rare. The reconstruction of the Free Trade Hall in the 1950s [Figure 7.04] was important to the pride and recovery of the public psyche, but

Figure 7.04   The Free Trade Hall. Rebuilt to designs by L.C. Howitt in the 1950s.

not emblematic of wider civic and cultural provision. Precious little cultural content was to be found in the schemes developed in the city centre during the 1960s and 1970s. The only civic aspect of the Corporation's plans actually built was the Crown Court – Mosley Street never witnessed the promised transformation into a vibrant cultural quarter.

Private enterprise flourished and a considerable amount of commercial and retail space was developed – between 1943 and 1964 there was a 62 per cent increase in available office space.[12] This was visualised in the telling diagram shown in the last chapter [Figure 6.22] illustrating new and pending commercial development in relation to the traditional core and the route of the city centre ring road. The diagram revealed is a citadel pattern with the largest and tallest buildings developing at the edge of the centre: this is due to the path of the proposed carriageway. This was not, however, about building near to the new road to attract greater revenue potential; it was attributable to the authority's focus on the delivery of the ring roads. Without the wholesale delivery of the ring road that would connect and service the CDAs, all of the mid-century plans appeared piecemeal. Each development had its own cut-off bridge link, anomalous blank facade or unfeasibly long stair – places where the total vision was arrested and never recommenced.

Such urban oddities, as we have read, attest to the complexities of urban renewal and the networks influencing manifold aspects of their conception, design and creation. Moreover, at different scales, these case studies show outward and inward influences. Manchester's role in the Cold War, for example, is an example of both. The race for rearmament drove the development of the computer, of new weaponry and the buildings associated with them. Subsequently, the technological innovations realised inside these buildings had global impact. This study of the renewal of Manchester has enabled discussion of a range of political, geographical and architectural scales and exposed their interrelation across an extended time period. Inwardly, it has permitted a close scrutiny of the effects of state policy and provided one way of answering the question: '[h]ow are we to address the differences between the exceptional and the everyday productions of the welfare state?'[13] This, and other questions, emerged from symposia and conferences that ran parallel to this research. Others include: 'Are there advantages in concentrating upon one scale of activity rather than another? Is it more productive to attend to the "territory", the region, the city, the dwelling or to the very smallest artefacts?'[14] Again, throughout this book I have provided a framework within which to

---

12 'Out of Centre', *The Manchester Guardian*, 12 July 1963, p. 12.
13 Forty, A. (2015) 'Appendix: Outcomes from the Liverpool Workshop 2012', in Swenarton, M., Avermaete, T. and van den Heuvel, D. (eds) *Architecture and the Welfare State* (London: Routledge), pp. 321–323.
14 Ibid.

consider this range of scales and what they have to say about the built environment more broadly.

Through the assembled case studies, I have shown the qualities of certain networks and accounted for cultural influences and the impact of assembled expertise – the mutually constitutive power of territory and networks in the coproduction of space. I have demonstrated how global and political forces shaped our built environment and shown local action as reacting to the invisible powers of globalisation *and* the legislative layering of shifting political structures regionally, nationally and internationally. The planner, the architect and the state were among many agents influencing the shape of renewal cities like Manchester. In viewing the architectural project as a continuum, architecture as negotiated practice and using mainstream modernism as a device, the complexities of urban renewal are revealed.

Bibliography

Books

Allmendinger, P., and Tewdwr-Jones, M. (eds) (2006) *Territory, Identity and Spatial Planning: Spatial Governance in a Fragmented Nation* (London: Routledge)

Ashworth, W. (1954) *The Genesis of Modern British Town Planning: A Study in Economic and Social History of the Nineteenth and Twentieth Centuries* (London: Routledge & Kegan Paul)

Auge, M. (1995) *Non-Places: Introduction to an Anthropology of Supermodernity* (London: Verso). Trans. J. Howe

Bacon, M. (2003) *Le Corbusier in America: Travels in the Land of the Timid* (Cambridge, MA: MIT Press)

Banham, M., and Hillier, B. (1976) *A Tonic to the Nation: The Festival of Britain in 1951* (London: Thames & Hudson)

Banham, R. (1966) *The New Brutalism: Ethic or Aesthetic* (London: Architectural Press)

Baudrillard, J. (1987) *Forget Foucault* (New York: Columbia University Press)

Birks, T (1972) *Building the New Universities* (Newton Abbot: David & Charles)

Bonavia, M.R. (1979) *The Birth of British Rail* (London: Allen & Unwin)

Borden, I., et al. (eds) (1996) *Strangely Familiar: Narratives of Architecture in the City* (London: Routledge)

Boudon, P. (1972) *Lived in Architecture* (London: Lund Humphries). Trans. G. Onn

Bowden, B.V. (ed.) (1953) *Faster Than Thought: A Symposium on Digital Computing Machines* (London: Sir Isaac Pitman & Sons)

Bowden, B.V. (1956) *Proposals for the Development of the Manchester College of Science and Technology* (Manchester: Manchester College of Science and Technology)

Boyd White, I. (ed.) (2006) *Man-Made Future: Planning, Education and Design in Mid-20th Century Britain* (London: Routledge)

Brown, N. et al. (1988) *Lyons Israel Ellis Gray: Buildings and Projects 1932–1983* (London: Architectural Association)

Bullock, N. (2002) *Building the Post-War World* (London: Routledge)

Cain, P.J., and Hopkins, A.G. (1993) *British Imperialism: Innovation and Expansion, 1688–1914* (Vol. 1) (Boston, MA: Addison-Wesley Longman)

Campbell-Kelly, M. (1989) *ICL: A Business and Technical History* (Oxford University Press: Oxford)
Campbell-Kelly, M. and Aspray, W. (1996) *Computer: A History of the Information Machine* (New York: Basic Books)
Canizaro, V.B. (ed.) (2007) *Architectural Regionalism: Collected Writings on Place, Identity, Modernity and Tradition* (New York: Princeton Architectural Press)
Cardwell, D.S.L. (ed.) (1974) *Artisan to Graduate: Essays to Commemorate the Foundation in 1824 of the Manchester Mechanics' Institution, now in 1974 the University of Manchester Institute of Science and Technology* (Manchester: Manchester University Press)
Carroll, R. (2009) *Ryder and Yates: Twentieth Century Architects* (London: RIBA, English Heritage)
Cherry, G.E. (1974) *The Evolution of British Town Planning* (London: Leonard Hill)
Cherry, G.E. (1988) *Cities and Plans: The Shaping of Urban Britain in the Nineteenth and Twentieth Centuries* (London: Edward Arnold)
Cherry, G.E. (1996) *Town Planning in Britain Since 1900: The Rise and Fall of the Planning Ideal* (Oxford: Wiley-Blackwell)
Chester, D.N. (1975) *The Nationalisation of British Industry, 1945–51* (London: HMSO)
Clawley, A. (2011) *John Madin* (London: RIBA, English Heritage)
Cohen, J.-L. (2011) *Architecture in Uniform Designing and Building for the Second World War* (New Haven: Yale University Press)
Conekin, B. (2003) *The Autobiography of a Nation: The 1951 Exhibition of Britain, Representing Britain in the Post-War World* (Manchester: Manchester University Press)
Le Corbusier (1947) *When the Cathedrals Were White: A Journey to the Country of Timid People* (New York: Reynal and Hitchcock). Trans. F.E. Hyslop
Crinson, M., and Lubbock, J. (1994) *Architecture – Art or Profession?: Three Hundred Years of Architectural Education in Britain* (Manchester: Manchester University Press)
Cullen, G. (1961) *The Concise Townscape* (London: Architectural Press)
Cullingworth, J.B. (1979) *Town and Country Planning in Britain* (London: Harper Collins)
Curtis, W.J.R. (1994) *Denys Lasdun: Architecture, City, Landscape* (London: Phaidon)
Damesick P.J., and Wood, P.A. (eds) (1987) *Regional Problems, Problem Regions and Public Policy in the United Kingdom* (Oxford: Clarendon Press)
Daunton, M. (2001) *The Cambridge Urban History of Britain* (Cambridge: Cambridge University Press)
Davidson, A.W., and Leonard, J.E. (eds) (1972) *Urban Renewal* (London: Centre For Advanced Land Use Studies)
Deakin, D. (1989) *Wythenshawe: The Story of a Garden City* (Chichester: Phillimore & Co.)
Delanda, M. (2002) *Intensive Science and Virtual Philosophy* (Chippenham: Continuum)
Denzin, N.K. (1989) *Interpretive Interactionism* (Newbury Park: Sage)
Dickinson, R.E. (1964) *The City and Region in Western Europe: A Geographical Interpretation* (London: Routledge & Kegan Paul)
Dobraszczyk, P. (2014) *Iron, Ornament and Architecture in Victorian Britain: Myth and Modernity* (Farnham: Ashgate)
Donaldson, B. (ed.) (1991) *Exterior Wall Systems: Glass and Concrete Technology, Design and Construction* (Philadelphia, PA: American Society for Testing and Materials)
Doucet, I. (2015) *The Practice Turn in Architecture: Brussels after 1968* (Farnham: Ashgate)
Dunkerley, D., Chalkley, B., and Gripaios, P. (eds) (1991) *Plymouth: Maritime City in Transition* (Newton Abbot: David & Charles)

Dunleavy, P. (1981) *The Politics of Mass Housing in Britain, 1945–1975: A Study of Corporate Power and Professional Influence in the Welfare State* (Oxford: Oxford University Press)

Dutta, A. (2013) *A Second Modernism: MIT, Architecture and the 'Techno-Social Movement'* (Cambridge, MA: MIT Press)

Dychoff, T. (ed.) (2000) *Journal 4: Post War Houses* (London: Twentieth Century Society)

Edgerton, D. (2006) *Warfare State: Britain, 1920–1970* (Cambridge: Cambridge University Press)

Esher, L. (1981) *A Broken Wave: The Rebuilding of England 1940–1980* (London: Viking)

Fairbairn, W. (1836) *Observations and Improvements of the Town of Manchester, particularly as regards the importance of blending in those improvements, the chaste and beautiful with the ornamental and useful* (Manchester: Robert Robinson)

Farías, I., and Bender, T. (eds) (2012) *Urban Assemblages: How Actor–Network Theory Changes Urban Studies* (London: Routledge)

Flamm, K. (1988) *Creating the Computer: Government, Industry and High Technology* (Washington DC: The Brookings Institution)

Fourastié, J. (1979) *Les Trentes Glorieuses: ou La Révolution invisible de 1946 a 1975* (Paris: Fayard)

Frampton, K. (1989) *Modern Architecture: A Critical History* (London: Thames & Hudson)

Friedmann, J., and Alonso, W. (eds) (1964) *Regional Development and Planning* (Cambridge, MA: MIT Press)

Gartman, D. (2009) *From Autos to Architecture: Fordism and Architectural Aesthetics in the Twentieth Century* (New York: Princeton Architectural Press)

Geddes, P. (1915) *Cities in Evolution* (London: Association for Planning and Regional Reconstruction) New and revised edition, 1949

Geertz, C. (1973) *The Interpretation of Cultures: Selected Essays* (New York: Basic Books)

Giedion, S. (1941) *Space, Time and Architecture: The Growth of a New Tradition* (Cambridge, MA: Harvard University Press)

Giedion, S. (1958) *Architecture You and Me: The Diary of a Development* (Cambridge, MA: Harvard University Press)

Glendinning, M. (2008) *Modern Architect: The Life and Times of Robert Matthew* (London: RIBA Publishing)

Glendinning, M., and Muthesius, S. (1994) *Tower Block: Modern Public Housing in England, Scotland, Wales, and Northern Ireland* (London: Paul Mellon Centre for Studies in British Art)

Gold, J.R. (2007) *The Practice of Modernism: Modern Architects and Urban Transformation, 1954–1972* (London: Routledge)

Goodden, H. (2011) *The Lion and the Unicorn: Symbolic Architecture for the Festival of Britain* (Norwich: Unicorn Press)

Grant, M. (2009) *After The Bomb: Civil Defence and Nuclear War in Cold War Britain, 1945–68* (London: Palgrave Macmillan)

Green, L.P. (1959) *Provincial Metropolis: The Future of Local Government in South-East Lancashire; a study in metropolitan analysis* (London: Allen & Unwin)

GUST (eds) *Post ex sub dis: urban fragmentations and constructions* (Rotterdam: 010 Publishers)

Hague, D.C. (1983) *The IRC: An Experiment in Industrial Intervention: A History of the Industrial Reorganisation Corporation* (London: Unwin Hyman)

Hall, P. (1988) *Cities of Tomorrow* (Oxford: Blackwell)

Hall, P., Thomas, R., Gracey, H., and Drewett, R. (1973) *The Containment of Urban England. Volume One: Urban and Metropolitan Growth Processes or Megalopolis Denied* (London: George Allen & Unwin)
Harper, C. (1947) *Manchester – City of Achievement* (London: Thomas Skinner)
Harris, S., and Berke, D. (eds) (1997) *The Architecture of the Everyday* (New York: Princeton Architectural Press)
Harrison, B. (2009) *Seeking a Role: The United Kingdom 1951–1970 (New Oxford History of England)* (Oxford: Oxford University Press)
Hart, T. (1968) *The Comprehensive Development Area: A Study of the legal and administrative problems of comprehensive land development with special reference to Glasgow. University of Glasgow Social and Economic Studies Occasional Papers No. 9* (Edinburgh and London: Oliver & Boyd)
Hartwell, C. (2001) *Manchester* (London: Penguin Books)
Harwood, E., and Powers, A. (eds) (2008) *Journal 9: Housing the Twentieth Century Nation.* (London: The Twentieth Century Society)
Harwood, E., and Powers, A. (eds) (2015) *Journal 12: Houses: Regional Practice and Local Character* (London: Twentieth Century Society)
Hasegawa, J. (1992) *Replanning the Blitzed City Centre: A Comparative Study of Bristol, Coventry and Southampton 1941–50* (Berkshire: Open University Press)
Hawkes J., and Whyte, W. (eds) (2014) *Architectural History after Colvin: the Society of Architectural Historians of Great Britain Symposium 2011* (Donington: Paul Watkins Publishing)
Hecht, G. (1998) *The Radiance of France: Nuclear Power and National Identity after World War II* (Cambridge, MA: MIT Press)
Hendry, J. (1989) *Innovating for Failure: Government Policy and the Early British Computer Industry* (Cambridge, MA: MIT Press)
Herrle, P., and Wegerhoff, E. (2008) *Architecture and Identity* (Munster: LIT Verlag)
Hill, J. (ed.) (1998) *Occupying Architecture: Between the Architect and the User* (London: Routledge)
Hitchcock, H.R., and Johnson, P. (1932) *The International Style: Architecture since 1922* (New York: W.W. Norton, Incorporated)
Holliday, J.C. (ed.) (1974) *City Centre Redevelopment: A Study of British City Centre Planning and Case Studies of Five English City Centres* (London: Charles Knight)
Hughes, J., and Sadler, S. (eds) (2013) *Non-Plan: Essays on Freedom, Participation and Change in Modern Architecture and Urbanism* (London: Routledge)
Jackson, A. (1970) *The Politics of Architecture: A History of Modern Architecture in Britain* (London: Architectural Press)
Jackson, I. and Holland, J. (2014) *The Architecture of Edwin Maxwell Fry and Jane Drew: Twentieth Century Architecture, Pioneer Modernism and the Tropics* (Farnham: Ashgate)
Jacobs, J. (1961) *The Death and Life of Great American Cities* (New York: Random House)
Jeremiah, D. (1980) *A Hundred Years and More* (Manchester: Manchester Polytechnic)
Johnson, P. (ed.) (1998) *Philip Johnson and the Museum of Modern Art* (New York: MoMA)
Keil, C.G. (1960) 'Supersonic Wind Tunnels: Details of the Two New High-Speed Tunnels Operated by English Electric Aviation Ltd. at Wharton', *Aircraft Engineering and Aerospace Technology*, Vol. 32, No. 11
Kelf-Cohen, R. (1973). *British Nationalisation 1945–1973* (London: Springer)

Kelly, S. (2002) *The Myth of Mr. Butskell: The Politics of British Economic Policy, 1950–55* (London: Ashgate)

Kidder Smith, G.E. (1950a) *Sweden Builds: Its Modern Architecture and Land Policy Background Development and Contribution* (London: The Architectural Press)

Kidder Smith G.E. (1950b) *Switzerland Builds: Its Native and Modern Architecture* (London: The Architectural Press)

Landau, R. (1968) *New Directions in British Architecture* (London: Studio Vista)

Larkham, P. (ed.) (2016) *The Blitz and its Legacy: Wartime Destruction to Post-War Reconstruction* (London: Routledge)

Larkham, P.J., and Lilley, K.D. (2001) *Planning the 'City of Tomorrow': British Reconstruction Planning, 1939–1952: An Annotated Bibliography* (Pickering: Inch's Books)

Latour B. (1996) *Aramis, or the Love of Technology* (Cambridge, MA: Harvard University Press). Trans. C. Porter

Latour, B. (2005) *Reassembling the Social: An Introduction to Actor–Network-Theory* (Oxford: Oxford University Press)

Lavington, S. (1975) *A History of Manchester Computers* (Manchester: The National Computing Centre)

Lavington, S. (1980) *Early British Computers: The Story of Vintage Computers and the People Who Built Them* (Manchester: Manchester University Press)

Lavington, S. (2000) *The Pegasus Story: A History of a Vintage British Computer* (London: The Science Museum)

Lavington, S. (2011) *Moving Targets – Elliott-Automation and the Dawn of the Computer Age in Britain, 1947–67* (London: Springer-Verlag)

Lefaivre, L., and Tzonis, A. (2012) *Architecture of Regionalism in the Age of Globalization: Peaks and Valleys in the Flat World* (London: Routledge)

Lejeune, J.-F. (2009) *Modern Architecture and the Mediterranean: Vernacular Dialogues and Contested Identities* (London: Taylor & Francis)

Lichtenstein, C., and Schregenberger, T. (2001) *As Found: The Discovery of the Ordinary* (Baden: Mueller Publishers)

Lingard, J., and Lingard, T. (2007) *Bradshaw Gass and Hope: The Story of an Architectural Practice – the First One Hundred Years 1862–1962* (London: Gallery Lingard)

Luccarelli, M. (1997) *Lewis Mumford and the Ecological Region: The Politics of Planning* (New York: Guilford Press)

Lynch, K. (1960) *The Image of the City* (Cambridge, MA: MIT Press)

MacEwen, M. (1974) *Crisis in Architecture* (London: RIBA Publications)

Mallgrave, H.F., and Goodman, D. (2011) *An Introduction to Architectural Theory: 1968 to the Present* (London: John Wiley & Sons)

Marriott, O. (1967) *The Property Boom* (London: Pan Books)

Martin, R. (2003) *The Organizational Complex: Architecture, Media and Corporate Space* (Cambridge, MA: MIT Press)

Martins, M.R. (1986) *An Organisational Approach to Regional Planning* (Aldershot: Gower)

Matthews, S. (2007) *From Agit-Prop to Free Space: The Architecture of Cedric Price* (London: Black Dog Publishing)

Miles, M. (2000) *The Uses of Decoration: Essays in the Architectural Everyday* (Chichester: Wiley)

Milligan, J. (ed.) (1986) *Strathclyde Papers on Planning: City Planners and the Glasgow City Centre* (Glasgow: University of Strathclyde, Department of Urban and Regional Planning)

Millward, R., and Singleton, J. (2002) *The Political Economy of Nationalisation in Britain, 1920–1950* (Cambridge: Cambridge University Press)
Moraes Zarzar, K., and Guney, A. (eds) (2008) *Understanding Meaningful Environments: Architectural Precedents and the Question of Identity in Creative Design* (Amsterdam: IOS Press)
Mosley, S. (2001) *The Chimney of the World: A History of Smoke Pollution in Victorian and Edwardian Manchester* (Cambridge: White Horse Press)
Mumford, E.P. (2002) *The CIAM Discourse on Urbanism, 1928–1960* (Cambridge, MA: MIT Press)
Mumford, L. (1934) *Technics and Civilisation* (New York: Harcourt)
Mumford, L. (1943) *The Social Foundations of Post-War Building: Rebuilding Britain Series, No. 9* (London: Faber & Faber)
Muthesius, S. (2000) *The Postwar University – Utopian Campus and College* (London: Yale University Press)
Ovendale, R. (1994) *British Defence Policy Since 1945* (Manchester: Manchester University Press)
Parkinson-Bailey, J.J. (2000) *Manchester: An Architectural History* (Manchester: Manchester University Press)
Powell, K. (2009) *Powell & Moya* (London: RIBA Publishing)
Powers, A. (2007) *Britain: Modern Architectures in History* (London: Reaktion Books)
Price, C. (1984) *The Square Book* (London: Wiley Academy; 2003 edition)
Rabinow, P. (1989) *French Modern: Norms and Forms of the Social Environment* (Cambridge, MA: MIT Press)
Ravetz, A. (2013) *The Government of Space: Town Planning in Modern Society* (London: Routledge)
Rees, G., and Lambert, J. (1985) *Cities in Crisis* (London: Edward Arnold)
Reeves, E.A. (ed.) (1992) *Newnes Electrical Pocket Book* (Oxford: Butterworth-Heinemann)
Reith, J.C.W. (1949) *Into the Wind* (London: Hodder & Stoughton)
Rhodes, M. (ed.) (1995) *The Regions and the New Europe: Patterns in Core and Periphery Development* (Manchester: Manchester University Press)
Rodger J. (ed.) (2007) *Gillespie, Kidd & Coia: Architecture 1956–1987* (Glasgow: Lighthouse)
Ruscha, E. (1963) *Twentysix Gasoline Stations* (Los Angeles: Edward Ruscha)
Saint, A. (1987) *Towards a Social Architecture: The Role of School-building in Post-war England* (London: Yale University Press)
Salter, B., and Tapper, T. (1994) *The State and Higher Education* (Ilford: The Woburn Press)
Sharp, T. (1940) *Town Planning* (London: Penguin)
Sharples, J., Powers, A., and Shippobottom, M. (1996) *Charles Reilly and the Liverpool School of Architecture, 1904–33* (Liverpool: Liverpool University Press)
Sharr, A. (ed.) (2012) *Reading Architecture and Culture: Researching Buildings, Spaces and Documents* (London: Routledge)
Shattock, M. (1994) *The UGC and the Management of British Universities* (Buckingham: SRHE and Open University Press)
Short, J.R. (1982) *Housing in Britain: The Post-war Experience* (York: Methuen)
Simon, E.D., and Inman, J. (1935) *The Rebuilding of Manchester* (London: Longman)
Smith, B.C. (1964) *Regionalism in England* (London: Acton Society Trust)
Stanek, Ł. (2011) *Henri Lefebvre on Space: Architecture, Urban Research and the Production of Theory* (Minneapolis, MN: University of Minnesota Press)

Stewart, C. (1954) *Art In Adversity: A short history of the Regional College of Art, Manchester* (Manchester: Council of the Royal Manchester Institution)
Stewart, C. (1956) *The Stones of Manchester* (London: Edward Arnold)
Stocker, J. (2004) *Britain and Ballistic Missile Defence, 1942–2002* (Abingdon: Psychology Press)
Sudjic, D. (2010) *Norman Foster: A Life in Architecture* (London: Weidenfeld & Nicolson)
Sunderland, D. (2007) *Managing British Colonial and Post-Colonial Development: The Crown Agents, 1914–74* (Woodbridge: The Boydell Press)
Sutcliffe, A. (1981) *The History of Urban and Regional Planning: An Annotated Bibliography* (London: Mansell Publishing)
Swenarton, M., Avermarte, T., and van den Heuval, D. (eds) (2015) *Architecture and the Welfare State* (London: Routledge)
Tiratsoo, N. (1990) *Reconstruction, Affluence and Labour Politics: Coventry, 1945–60* (London: Routledge)
Treib, M. (ed.) (1995) *An Everyday Modernism: The Houses of William Wurster* (Berkeley, CA: University of California Press)
Tripp, A. (1942) *Town Planning and Road Traffic* (London: Edward Arnold)
Turner, G. (1967) *The North Country* (London: Eyre & Spottiswoode)
Venables, P. (1978) *Higher Education Developments: the Technological Universities 1956–76* (London: Faber & Faber)
Venturi, R., Brown, D.S., and Izenour, S. (1972) *Learning from Las Vegas* (Cambridge, MA: MIT Press)
Vesely, D. (2004) *Architecture in the Age of Divided Representation* (Cambridge MA: MIT Press)
Vidler, A. (2008) *Histories of the Immediate Present: Inventing Architectural Modernism* (Cambridge, MA: MIT Press)
Wannop, U.A. (1995) *The Regional Imperative: Regional Planning and Governance in Britain, Europe and the United States* (London: Routledge)
Ward, S.V. (1994) *Planning and Urban Change* (London: Paul Chapman Publishing)
Whittam, W. (1986) *Fairhursts Architects: The History of a Manchester Practice* (Manchester: Department of History of Art and Design, Manchester Polytechnic)
Williams, G. (2003) *The Enterprising City Centre: Manchester's development challenge* (London: Routledge)
Wilson, H. (1971) *The Labour Government 1964–1979* (London: Weidenfeld & Nicolson and Michael Joseph)
Wilson, J.F. (1999) *Ferranti: A History. Building a Family Business, 1882–1975* (Lancaster: Carnegie Publishing)
Wright, J. (2003) *The Regionalist Movement in France 1890–1914: Jean Charles-Brun and French Political Thought* (Oxford: Oxford University Press)

Journal articles

Agar, J. (1996) 'The Provision of Digital Computers to British Universities up to the Flowers Report (1966)', *The Computer Journal*, Vol. 39, No. 7
Allan, J. (2010) 'Twentieth-Century Architects', *The Journal of Architecture*, Vol. 15, No. 6
Allen, P. (2011) 'The End of Modernism', *Journal of the Society of Architectural Historians*, Vol. 70, No. 3

Aylen, J. (2012) 'Bloodhound on my Trail: Building the Ferranti Argus Process Control Computer', *International Journal for the History of Engineering & Technology*, Vol. 82, No. 1

Banham, R. (1955) 'The New Brutalism', *The Architectural Review*, No. 118

Barr, A.H. Jr, Hitchcock, H.-R. Gropius, W. et al. (1948) 'What Is Happening to Modern Architecture?', *The Bulletin of the Museum of Modern Art*, Vol. 15, No. 3

Blomfield, R. (1933) 'Is Modern Architecture on the Right Track?' *The Listener*, X

Bocock, J., and Taylor, R. (2003) 'The Labour Party and Higher Education: 1945–51', *Higher Education Quarterly*, Vol. 57, No. 3

Bor, W., and Shankland, G. (1965) 'Renaissance of a City: A study of the redevelopment of Liverpool', *The Journal of the Town Planning Institute*, January, Vol. 51, No. 1

Bowden, B.V. (1960) 'Too Few Academic Eggs', *Higher Education Quarterly*, Volume 14, Issue 1, November

Brook, R. (2011) 'Manchester Chapels', *C20 The Magazine of the Twentieth Century Society*, Spring

Brook, R., and Jarvis, M. (2013) *Trying to Close the Loop: Post-war Ring Roads in Manchester* (Birmingham City University, Centre for Environment and Society Research, Working Paper Series, no. 24)

Bud, R. (1998) 'Penicillin and the new Elizabethans', *The British Journal for the History of Science*, Vol. 31, No. 3

Burch, M., and Holliday, I. (1993) 'Institutional Emergence: The Case of the North West Region of England', *Regional Politics and Policy*, Vol. 3, No. 2

Calder, B. (2013) 'Representing Science: the Architecture of the New Museums Site, Cambridge, 1952–71', *Twentieth Century Architecture*, No. 11 (London: The Twentieth Century Society)

Chase, S (1925) 'Coals to Newcastle', *Survey*, No. 54

Craggs, R., Geoghegan, H., and Neate, H. (2013) 'Architectural Enthusiasm: Visiting Buildings with the Twentieth Century Society', *Environment and Planning D: Society and Space*, Vol. 31, No. 5

Crinson, M. (2006) 'The Uses of Nostalgia: Stirling and Gowan's Preston Housing', *Journal of the Society of Architectural Historians*, Vol. 65, No. 2

Crompton, A. (2012) 'Manchester Black and Blue', *Bulletin of the John Rylands Library*, Volume 89, Number 1, Autumn

Delafons, J. (1998) 'Reforming the British Planning System 1964–5: The Planning Advisory Group and the genesis of the Planning Act of 1968', *Planning Perspectives*, Vol. 13, No. 4

Duncan, R.A. (1932) 'Modern Architectural Design', *Architects Journal*, LXXII

Edwards, E.P.J. (1994) 'Ben Lockspeiser. 9 March 1891–18 October 1990', *Biographical Memoirs of the Fellows of the Royal Society*, 1 February, No. 39

Fawcett, C.B. (1917) 'Natural Divisions of England', *The Geographical Journal*, Vol. 49, No. 2

Forgan, S. (1998) 'Festivals of Science and the Two Cultures: Science, Design and Display in the Festival of Britain, 1951', *British Journal for the History of Science*, Vol. 31, No. 2

Gardner-Medwin, R. (1956) 'The Decline of Architecture', *Higher Education Quarterly*, Vol. 10, No. 2

Giedion, S. (1950) 'Alvar Aalto', *Architectural Review*, February

Giedion, S. (1954) 'The State of Contemporary Architecture I: The Regional Approach', *Architectural Record*, January

Glendinning, M. (2003) 'Teamwork or Masterwork? The Design and Reception of the Royal Festival Hall', *Architectural History*, Vol. 46

Glendinning, M. (2005) 'The Royal Festival Hall: A Postscript', *Architectural History*, Vol. 48

Gold, J.R. (2006) 'The Making of a Megastructure: Architectural Modernism, Town Planning and Cumbernauld's Central Area, 1955–75', *Planning Perspectives*, Vol. 21, No. 2

Goldhagen, S.W. (2005) 'Something to Talk about: Modernism, Discourse, Style', *Journal of the Society of Architectural Historians*, Vol. 64, No. 2

Gough, T. (2015) 'Architecture is Always in the Middle ...', *Footprint*, Vol. 9, No. 2

Gunn, S. (2010) 'The Rise and Fall of British Urban Modernism: Planning Bradford, circa 1945–1970', *The Journal of British Studies*, Vol. 49, No. 4

Hartley, O.A. (1971) 'The Relationship Between Central and Local Authorities', *Public Administration*, No. 49

Hubbard, P., Faire, L., and Lilley, K. (2003) 'Contesting the Modern City: Reconstruction and Everyday Life in Post-war Coventry', *Planning Perspectives*, Vol. 18, No. 4

Imrie, R. (2007) 'The Interrelationships Between Building Regulations and Architects' Practices', *Environment and Planning B: Planning and Design*, Vol. 34, No. 5

Jacobs, J.M. (2006) 'A Geography of Big Things', *Cultural Geographies*, No. 13, January

Jackson, I. (2011) 'Post-War Modernism: Maxwell Fry's Buildings at the University of Liverpool', *The Journal of Architecture*, Vol. 16, No. 5

Kirby, M.W. (1999) 'Blackett in the "White Heat" of the Scientific Revolution: Industrial Modernisation under the Labour Governments, 1964–1970', *The Journal of the Operational Research Society*, Vol. 50, No. 10

Kitchen, T. (1996) 'The Future of Development Plans: Reflections on Manchester's Experiences 1945–1995', *Town Planning Review*, Vol. 67, No. 3

Kite, S., and Menin, S. (2005) 'Towards a New Cathedral: Mechanolatry and Metaphysics in the Milieu of Colin St John Wilson', *Architectural Research Quarterly*, Vol. 9, No. 1

Koolhaas, R., and Mau, B. (1994) 'The Generic City', *Theory, Culture & Society*, Vol. 16, No. 4

Latour, B. (1996) 'On Actor–Network Theory: A Few Clarifications', *Soziale welt*

Laver, M. (1999) 'ICL – The Ministry of Technology (Ministry of Technology) and the Merger', *Contemporary British History*, Vol. 13, No. 1

Lefebvre, H., and Levich, C. (1987) 'The Everyday and Everydayness', *Yale French Studies*, No. 73

Leventhal, F.M. (1995) '"A Tonic to the Nation": The Festival of Britain, 1951', *Albion: A Quarterly Journal Concerned with British Studies*, Vol. 27, No. 3

Lubbock, J (2002) 'The Counter-Modernist Sublime: the Campus of the University of Essex', *Twentieth Century Architecture*, No. 6, *The Sixties: Life: Style: Architecture* (London: The Twentieth Century Society)

MacArthur, J. (2005) 'The Nomenclature of Style: Brutalism, Minimalism, Art History and Visual Style in Architecture Journals', *Architectural Theory Review*, Vol. 10, No. 2

Maudling, C. (2016) '"Be Bold, Courageous and Wise": POST-war Reconstruction in the City of Exeter', *International Planning History Society Proceedings*, Vol. 17, No. 2

Mohr, P.D. (1998) 'Dr Catherine Chisholm and the Manchester Babies Hospital', *Trans. Lancashire & Cheshire Antiquarian Society*, Vol. 94

Murray, J. (1949) 'Halls of Residence in Universities', *Higher Education Quarterly* Vol. 3, Issue 2

Oliphant, M.L. (1949) 'University or Institute of Technology', *Higher Education Quarterly*, Vol. 4, No. 1
Panos, L. (2014) *Lez Cooke, A Sense of Place: Regional British Television Drama 1956–82* (Manchester: Manchester University Press)
Passanti, F. (1997) 'The Vernacular, Modernism, and Le Corbusier', *Journal of the Society of Architectural Historians*, Vol. 56, No. 4
Pfaffenberger, B. (1992) 'Technological Dramas', *Science, Technology and Human Values*, Vol. 17, No. 3
Philo, C. (1992) 'Foucault's Geography', *Environment and Planning D: Society and Space*, No. 10
Ponterotto, J.G. (2006) 'Brief Note on the Origins, Evolution and Meaning of the Qualitative Research Concept "Thick Description"', *The Qualitative Report*, Vol. 11, No. 3
Poxon, J. (2000) 'Solving the Development Plan Puzzle in Britain: Learning Lessons from History', *Planning Perspectives*, Vol. 15, No. 1
Proctor, R. (2006) 'The Architect's Intention: Interpreting Post-War Modernism through the Architect Interview', *Journal of Design History*, Vol. 19, No. 4
Rabinow, P. (1992) 'France in Morocco: Technocosmopolitanism and Middling Modernism', *Assemblage*, No. 17
Robertson, D.J. (1965) 'A Nation of Regions?', *Urban Studies*, Vol. 2, No. 2
Rutherford, E., and Bowden, B.V. (1932) 'The Gamma Rays from Actinium Emanation and their Origin', *Proc. Roy. Soc. A*, Vol. 136
Rutherford, E., Lewis, W.B., and Bowden, B.V. (1933) 'Analysis of the Long Range Alpha Particles from Radium C' by the Magnetic Focussing Method', *Proc. Roy. Soc. A*, Vol. 142
Rutherford, E., Wynn-Williams, C.E., Lewis, W.B., and Bowden, B.V. (1933) 'Analysis of Alpha Rays by an Annular Magnetic Field', *Proc. Roy. Soc. A*, Vol. 139
Salmon, F. (2002) 'R.W. Brunskill and the Study of Vernacular Buildings at the University of Manchester School of Architecture', *Transactions of the Ancient Monuments Society*, Vol. 46
Shankland, G. (1964) 'The Central Area of Liverpool', *Town Planning Review*, Vol. 35, No. 2
Shapely, P. (2011) 'The Entrepreneurial City: The Role of Local Government and City-Centre Redevelopment in Post-War Industrial English Cities', *Twentieth Century British History*, Vol. 22, No. 4
Shapely, P. (2013) 'Governance in the Post-War City: Historical Reflections on Public–Private Partnerships in the UK', *International Journal of Urban and Regional Research*, Vol. 37, No. 4
Smith, O.S. (2014) 'Graeme Shankland: A Sixties Architect-planner and the Political Culture of the British left', *Architectural History*, Vol. 57
Smith, O.S. (2015) 'Central Government and Town-Centre Redevelopment in Britain, 1959–1966', *The Historical Journal*, Vol. 58, No. 1
Smith, R.B.L., and Merchant, W. (1956) 'Critical Loads of Tall Building Frames', *The Structural Engineer*, No. 34
Smithson, R. (1967) 'The Monuments of Passaic', *Artforum*, No. 49 (December)
Stalder, L. (2008). '"New Brutalism", "Topology" and "Image": Some Remarks on the Architectural Debates in England Around 1950', *The Journal of Architecture*, Vol. 13, No. 3

Sumner, J. (2014) 'Defiance to Compliance: Visions of the Computer in Postwar Britain', *History and Technology*, Vol. 30, No. 4

Tweedale, G. (1992) 'Marketing in the Second Industrial Revolution: A Case Study of the Ferranti Computer Group, 1949–63', *Business History*, Vol. 34, No. 1

Todd, S. (2015) 'Phoenix Rising: Working-Class Life and Urban Reconstruction, c.1945–1967', *Journal of British Studies*, Vol. 54, No. 3

Whyte, W. (2013) 'Introduction: "A Pastiche or a Packing Case" Building in Twentieth-Century Oxford', *Twentieth Century Architecture*, No. 11 (London: The Twentieth Century Society)

Wildman, C. (2012) '*A City Speaks*: The Projection of Civic Identity in Manchester', *20th Century British History*, Vol. 23, No. 1

Williams, G. (1996) 'City Profile: Manchester', *Cities*, Vol. 13, No. 3

Williams, G. (2000) 'Rebuilding the Entrepreneurial City: The Master Planning Response to the Bombing of Manchester City Centre', *Environment and Planning B: Planning and Design*, No. 27 (August)

Williams, G., Batho, S., and Russell, L. (2000) 'Responding to Urban Crisis: The Emergency Planning Response to the Bombing of Manchester City Centre', *Cities*, Vol. 17, No. 4

Wilson, J.F. (1991) *Government and the Electronic Components Industry: The Case of Ferranti, 1953–1973* (Manchester: University of Manchester, Department of History) Working paper No. 7

Wood, G.C. (1993), 'Conference Introductory Paper why Manchester?', *Corrosion Science*, Vol. 35, Issues 1–4

Reports and planning bulletins

Barlow Report, Lord President of the Council (1946) *Scientific Manpower* (London: HMSO)

British Railways Board (1963) *The Reshaping of British Railways* (London: HMSO)

Brook, R. (2012) *Manchester Modern: The Shape of City* (Research Award Report)

Buchanan, C. (1963) *Traffic in Towns: A Study of the Long-term Problems of Traffic in Urban Areas* (London: HMSO)

Burns, W. (1967) *Newcastle-upon-Tyne: A Study in Replanning at Newcastle-upon-Tyne* (London: Leonard Hill)

Committee on Higher Education (1963) *Higher Education. Report of the Committee appointed by the Prime Minister under the Chairmanship of Lord Robbins 1961–63* (London: HMSO)

Coventry City Council (1951) *Coventry: The Development Plan*

De Leuw, Cather & Partners, Hennessey, Chadwick, O hEocha & Partners, Manchester City Transport (1967) Manchester Rapid Transit Study. Vols 1–3

Hankey, Lord (1945) *Higher Appointments: Report of the Committee appointed by the Minister of Labour and National Service in July 1943 (Chairman Lord Hankey)* (London: HMSO)

Hayes, J., City Engineer (1968) *Manchester City Centre Road* (Manchester: City of Manchester Corporation)

Heath, P.M., Manchester and District Joint Town Planning Advisory Committee, Manchester Society of Architects (1922) *A Record of the Town Planning Exhibition, held in the Town Hall, Manchester, Oct. 9th to 17th, 1922* (Manchester: Joint Town Planning Advisory Committee)

Higher Technological Education: Statement of Government Policy (1951) (London: HMSO)

Holford, W.G. (1949) *Proposals for the Development of a Site for the University of Liverpool* (Liverpool: Liverpool University Press)

Holford, W.G. (1955) *The Report of the Development Committee to the Council and Senate of the University on Building Progress 1949–1954* (The First Quinquennial Review of the Post-War development plan) (Liverpool: Liverpool University Press)

Manchester Area Council for Clean Air and Noise Control (1984) *Twenty Five Year Review: A Review of Some Aspects of Air Pollution and Noise Control in the Area of the Council 25 Years after the Clean Air Act, 1956*

Manchester Corporation (1967) *Joint Report on Car Parking in Central Manchester* (Manchester: City of Manchester)

Manchester and District Joint Town Planning Advisory Committee (1924) *Constitution And Functions* (Manchester: Manchester and District Joint Town Planning Advisory Committee)

Manchester Housing Development Group (1967) *Urban Renewal Manchester* (Manchester: Manchester Corporation Housing Committee)

Manchester Joint Research Council (1954) *Industry and Science: A Study of their Relationship Based on a Survey of Firms in the Greater Manchester Area Carried out by the Manchester Joint Research Council, 1950–1953* (Manchester: Manchester University Press)

Millar, J.S. (1965) *Manchester Corporation: City Planning Department 1964–65* (Manchester: City of Manchester)

Millar, J.S. (1967) *Manchester Corporation: City Planning Department 1965–67* (Manchester: City of Manchester)

Millar, J.S. (1968) *City and County Borough of Manchester: City Centre Map, 1967* (Manchester: City Planning Department).

Ministry of Education (1956) *Technical Education (White Paper)* (London: HMSO)

Ministry of Housing and Local Government (1947) *Town and Country Planning Act, 1947: Explanatory Memorandum* (London: HMSO)

Ministry of Housing and Local Government, *Planning Bulletin No. 1, Town Centres: Approach to Renewal* (London, 1962)

Ministry of War Transport (1946) *Design and Layout of Roads in Built-up Areas: Report of the Departmental Committee set up by the Minister of War Transport* (London: HMSO)

Niblett, W.R. University Grants Committee (1957) *Report of the Sub-Committee on Halls of Residence* (London: HMSO)

Nicholas, R.J. (1945a) *City of Manchester Plan 1945* (Norwich: Jarrold & Sons)

Nicholas, R. (1945b) *The Manchester and District Regional Planning Committee Report on the Tentative Regional Planning Proposals* (Norwich: Jarrold & Sons)

Nicholas, R., and Dingle, P.B. (1951) *Manchester Development Plan* (Manchester: City and County Borough of Manchester)

Nicholas, R., and Hellier, M.J. (1947) *South Lancashire and North Cheshire Advisory Planning Committee: An Advisory Plan* (Manchester: Advisory Planning Committee)

Percy Report (1945) Ministry of Education, *Higher Technological Education: Report of a Special Committee* (London: HMSO)

Planning Advisory Group (1962) *Planning Bulletin No. 1. Town Centres – Approach to Renewal* (London: HMSO)

Planning Advisory Group (1965) *The Future of Development Plans* (London: HMSO)

Report by the Committee of Inquiry appointed by the Minister of Overseas Development into the circumstances which led to the Crown Agents requesting financial assistance from the Government in 1974 (London: HMSO) 1977

Reproduction of Survey and Development Plan Maps, Town and Country Planning Act 1947 Circular No. 92 (London: 1951)

SELNEC (1962) *S.E.L.N.E.C. A Highway Plan* (Manchester: South-East Lancashire and North-East Cheshire Area Highway Engineering Committee)

Shankland, G. (1965) *Liverpool City Centre Plan* (Liverpool: City and County Borough of Liverpool)

Smigielski, K.R. (1968) *Leicester Today and Tomorrow* (London: Pyramid Press)

Taylor Woodrow Group (1968) *Manchester Central Station* (Report)

University Grants Committee (1948) *University Development 1935 to 1946* (London: HMSO)

University of Manchester and the Manchester College of Science and Technology (1960) *Joint Submission to Manchester Corporation Respecting Future Development*

Wilson, H., and Womersley, L. (1967) *Manchester Education Precinct: The Final Report of the Planning Consultants 1967* (Manchester: Corporation of Manchester)

Theses

Drath, P. (1973) *The Relationship Between Science and Technology: University Research and the Computer Industry 1945–1962* (Doctoral thesis, University of Manchester)

Lewis, A. (2006) 'A History of Sheffield's Central Area Planning Schemes, 1936–1952' (PhD thesis, University of Sheffield)

Lichtenstein, S. (1990) 'Editing Architecture: Architectural Record and the Growth of Modern Architecture, 1928–1938' (PhD thesis, Cornell University)

Parker, M. (2016) 'Making the City Mobile: The Place of the Motor Car in the Planning of Post-War Birmingham, c.1945–1973' (PhD thesis, School of Historical Studies, University of Leicester)

Steele, M. (2014) 'The Making of Manchester's Technical Colleges (1954 1964)' (MRes thesis, MMU)

Ephemera

Civic Trust, *Rebuilding City Centres – Report of the Conference*, 1960

Southport Technical College (1935) *Opening of New Building 1935: Programme*

The University of Manchester Institute of Science and Technology (1974) *1824–1974, 150 Years of Progress at UMIST* (Manchester: University of Manchester/UMIST)

Town Planning Institute, *Memorandum on Central Area Development*, 1960

Town Planning Institute, *Further Memorandum on Comprehensive Development*, 1961

Film

A City Speaks (Film) Producer: Films of Fact Ltd/Paul Rotha for Manchester City Council, 1946

Utopia London (DVD) Director: Tom Cordell, 2010

Illustrations

Chapter 1

1.01	**Plan showing the proposed improvements.** Source: Sir William Fairbairn's *Observations and Improvements of the Town of Manchester* (1836).	13
1.02	**Designs for a new exchange and quadrant.** Source: Sir William Fairbairn's *Observations and Improvements of the Town of Manchester* (1836).	14
1.03	**Manchester's railways.** Source: *Manchester Made Over* (1936).	17
1.04	**Manchester Central Reference Library and Town Hall extension.** Source: Author's own.	24
1.05	**Bootle Street Police Station.** Source: Author's own.	25
1.06	**Map III. A replanning scheme for the centre of Manchester.** Source: *Rebuilding Manchester*.	26
1.07	**The cover of the *City of Manchester Plan, 1945*.** Source: *City of Manchester Plan*, 1945.	29
1.08	**William Morrison and Rowland Nicholas.** Source: *Manchester Guardian*, 21 July 1945, p. 3.	30
1.09	**Cover of leaflet for planning exhibition, 1945.** Source: Author's scan from private collection.	32
1.10	**City of Manchester. Central Area.** Source: Nicholas, R. (1945) *City of Manchester Plan 1945*.	34

LIST OF ILLUSTRATIONS

1.11 Endpiece of the *1945 Plan*. 36
Source: Nicholas, R. (1945) *City of Manchester Plan 1945*.

1.12 Major highways, parks and parkways. 38
Source: Nicholas, R. (1945) *City of Manchester Plan 1945*.

1.13 Manchester Reform Synagogue. 40
Source: Author's own.

1.14 Postcard view of the new Crown Courts, Crown Square. 44
Source: Author's scan from private collection.

1.15 Peter House. 46
Source: Author's own.

1.16 Diagram of the City Architect's Department. 48
Source: *The Builder*, 28 May 1965, p. 1187.

1.17 Drawings by David Gosling of designs for the Civic Area. 49
Source: *Architectural Review*, August 1962.

1.18 Model showing the comprehensive redevelopment of the city centre. 51
Source: Manchester Town Hall Photographer's Collection.

1.19 Map showing the full extents of areas being planned under John Millar's direction. 52
Source: *Urban Renewal Manchester*.

1.20 Lego models of mass housing schemes. 53
Source: *Urban Renewal Manchester*.

1.21 The 'brutalist playground' in front of Charles Barry Crescent. 54
Source: Manchester Metropolitan University Special Collections. Ref: UGM5-132.

1.22 The central Comprehensive Development Areas. 56
Source: *City Centre Map, 1967*.

1.23 Viewed from Quay Street, the white gridded exoskeleton of Magistrates' Court. 58
Source: Manchester Metropolitan University Special Collections. Ref: ZX-308.

1.24 Cover of the fundraising publication *Our Blitz*. 59
Source: Author's scan from private collection.

Chapter 2

2.01 Nimrod at the Festival of Britain. 72
Source: Courtesy Malcolm Shifrin.

2.02 Architect's drawing of the scheme for a computing laboratory. 75
Source: Courtesy University of Manchester Estates.

LIST OF ILLUSTRATIONS

2.03 **Photograph showing the Electrical Engineering (Zochonis) Building and the Chemistry Building.** 76
Source: University of Manchester Library.

2.04 **Municipal advert.** 80
Source: *Manchester – City of Achievement* (1947).

2.05 **Scheme B. Preliminary plan for the Ferranti missile factory.** 83
Source: Author's edited photograph of drawing among 'Cost Estimate Reports (Wythenshawe Project)', Ferranti Collection, MSI Archive. Ref: YA1996 10/2/4/903.

2.06 **Renold Chain Company headquarters.** 85
Source: Cruickshank & Seward Archive. Courtesy Manchester Metropolitan University Special Collections.

2.07 **Entrance canopy to the Ferranti facility.** 86
Source: Cruickshank & Seward Archive. Courtesy Manchester Metropolitan University Special Collections.

2.08 **Ferranti gatehouse.** 87
Source: Cruickshank & Seward Archive. Courtesy Manchester Metropolitan University Special Collections.

2.09 **Option studies for extension to missile testing facility at Wythenshawe.** 88
Source: Author's photographs from drawings held at National Archives and Ferranti Collection at MSI Archive.

2.10 **Diagram to show British computer mergers.** 90
Source: Brian M. Russell, former engineer with ICL.

2.11 **Production of the Pegasus computer.** 94
Source: Author's photo from glass slide held at MOSI Archive. Ref. 1996.10/3/3/5951–5976.

2.12 **Plan of the West Gorton site.** 95
Source: Author's photograph from drawing in Ferranti Collection held at MOSI Archive. Ref. YA.1996.10/2/4/883.

2.13 **Gorton, ICT Offices, Thomas Street, from Hoyland Street, facing south, 1964. Minimal intervention on the part of ICT to alter the fabric of the existing site.** 96
Source: Manchester Local Image Collection, ref. m24294. Photographer: T. Brooks.

2.14 **Rebranded 'factory gate' to the ICT site. 'Gorton, Kelsall Street from Thomas Street, facing South', 1964.** 97
Source: Manchester Local Image Collection, ref. m23687. Photographer: T. Brooks.

LIST OF ILLUSTRATIONS

2.15　Watercolour perspective by Peter Sainsbury of the proposed tower for ICT.   99
Source: Cruickshank & Seward Archive. Courtesy Manchester Metropolitan University Special Collections.

2.16　The research building.   100
Source: Author's own.

2.17　Internal screening within the research building.   101
Source: Author's own.

2.18　Drawing showing the elevations of the research building.   102
Source: Author's photograph of drawing held on site. Lost to demolition.

2.19　New homes next to new industry.   103
Source: Manchester Local Image Collection, ref. m24426. Photographer: H. Milligan.

2.20　Drawing to show the familial nature of the satellite buildings.   104
Source: Author's photograph of drawing held on site. Lost to demolition.

2.21　ICL West Gorton. Proposed site plan October 1979.   105
Source: Author's photograph of drawing held on site. Lost to demolition.

2.22　Plan showing 'Area G'.   107
Source: Planning and Development Committee Minutes. UoMA: TGB/2/5/3.

2.23　The spartan grey box of the first incarnation of the National Computing Centre.   110
Source: Visual Resource Centre (35mm slide). Manchester Metropolitan University Special Collections. Ref: ZX-035.

2.24　Photograph from between the new BBC North HQ and the NCC.   111
Source: Visual Resource Centre (35 mm slide). Manchester Metropolitan University Special Collections. Ref: ZX-283.

2.25　Early drawings by BDP for the BBC North HQ.   112
Source: Courtesy BDP. Archive.

2.26　Extract from the Education Precinct plan.   113
Source: Extract from Wilson & Womersley's *Manchester Education Precinct* (1967).

2.27　Model by BDP.   114
Source: Courtesy BDP. Archive.

LIST OF ILLUSTRATIONS

2.28 **Perspective painting by Peter Sainsbury of the proposed NCC building.** 115
Source: Cruickshank & Seward Archive. Courtesy Manchester Metropolitan University Special Collections.

2.29 **Early iteration of the ground floor plan for the NCC, 1967.** 116
Source: Cruickshank & Seward Archive. Courtesy Manchester Metropolitan University Special Collections.

2.30 **Photograph of model with SW aspect.** 117
Source: Cruickshank & Seward Archive. Courtesy Manchester Metropolitan University Special Collections.

2.31 **Landscape plan (redrawn by author).** 118
Source: Author's photograph based on Archives+, Building control plans. Ref: 78018.

2.32 **NCC under construction.** 119
Source: Cruickshank & Seward Archive. Courtesy Manchester Metropolitan University Special Collections.

2.33 **Hard landscape at the NCC.** 119
Source: Author's own.

2.34 **Promotional brochure for the NCC.** 120
Source: Author's scan from private collection.

Chapter 3

3.01 **The Maths Tower viewed from the head of the ramp to the Precinct Centre.** 126
Source: Author's scan from private collection.

3.02 **Hubert Worthington's plan for the Centre of Education, Culture and Medicine.** 128
Source: Nicholas, R. (1945) *City of Manchester Plan*, Plate 30.

3.03 **The Sackville Street Building.** 129
Source: Author's own.

3.04 **Aerial view of the UMIST campus c.1973.** 131
Source: University of Manchester, Digital Collections. Ref: UPC/2/527.

3.05 **Development areas allocated to the expansion of the College by Manchester Corporation in 1955.** 139
Source: Bowden, B.V. (1956) *Proposals for the Development of the Manchester College of Science and Technology* (Manchester: Manchester College of Science and Technology), p. 140.

LIST OF ILLUSTRATIONS

3.06 **A survey of the anticipated lifespan of existing buildings around Temple Street and the River Medlock.** 140
Source: City Engineers slide collection. Uncatalogued, but listed by street. Ref: 3412/41.

3.07 **Tom Warburton.** 143
Source: University of Manchester, Digital Collections. Ref: UPC/1/200.

3.08 **Scheme Two.** 144
Source: Redrawn by author based on drawing in the Minutes of the Planning and Development Committee. UoMA: TGB/2/5/1.

3.09 **Scheme Three.** 147
Source: Redrawn by author based on drawing in the Minutes of the Planning and Development Committee. UoMA: TGB/2/5/1.

3.10 **Perspective painting by Peter Sainsbury for Cruickshank & Seward of the new campus.** 151
Source: Cruickshank & Seward Archive. Courtesy Manchester Metropolitan University Special Collections.

3.11 **Staff House, Hubert Worthington, 1960.** 154
Source: Author's own.

3.12 **Scheme Five.** 155
Source: Redrawn by author based on drawing in the Minutes of the Planning and Development Committee. UoMA: TGB/2/5/1.

3.13 **Perspective painting of the design for the Renold Building.** 157
Source: Cruickshank & Seward Archive. Courtesy Manchester Metropolitan University Special Collections.

3.14 *Metamorphosis*, **Victor Pasmore** 158
Source: Author's own.

3.15 **Bird's-mouth beams and open staircase.** 159
Source: Author's own.

3.16 **Chandos Hall.** 162
Source: Cruickshank & Seward Archive. Courtesy Manchester Metropolitan University Special Collections.

3.17 **Student-shared kitchen in Chandos Hall.** 162
Source: Cruickshank & Seward Archive. Courtesy Manchester Metropolitan University Special Collections.

3.18 **Interior of main hall with sculptural lighting units by Anthony Yeomans.** 165
Source: Cruickshank & Seward Archive. Courtesy Manchester Metropolitan University Special Collections.

LIST OF ILLUSTRATIONS

3.19 **The stair and lift tower of Wright Robinson Hall.** 165
Source: Cruickshank & Seward Archive. Courtesy Manchester Metropolitan University Special Collections.

3.20 **Expressive volumes on the roofscape of the Barnes Wallis Building.** 166
Source: Cruickshank & Seward Archive. Courtesy Manchester Metropolitan University Special Collections.

3.21 **The Faraday Building.** 168
Source: Author's own.

3.22 **Maths and Social Sciences Building.** 170
Source: Cruickshank & Seward Archive. Courtesy Manchester Metropolitan University Special Collections.

3.23 **Chemical Engineering Pilot Plant.** 171
Source: Visual Resource Centre (35mm slide). Manchester Metropolitan University Special Collections. Ref: ZW-2L-65.

3.24 **The Renold Building viewed from beneath the Sir Hubert Worthington Stair.** 172
Source: University of Manchester, Digital Collections. Ref: UPC/2/474.

3.25 **Cruickshank & Seward proposals for the Student Village.** 174
Source: Cruickshank & Seward Archive. Courtesy Manchester Metropolitan University Special Collections.

3.26 **Preliminary drawing for the Maths Tower.** 179
Source: Extract from Wilson, H., and Womersley, L. (1964) *Manchester Education Precinct. The Interim Report of the Planning Consultants* (Manchester).

3.27 **Preliminary sketch for the Maths Tower from Scherrer & Hicks.** 180
Source: Author's scan from private collection.

3.28 **Aerial walkways throughout the whole Education Precinct.** 181
Source: Extract from Wilson & Womersley's *Manchester Education Precinct* (1967).

3.29 **Ramped approach to the entrance of the Maths Tower.** 182
Source: Visual Resource Centre (35 mm slide). Manchester Metropolitan University Special Collections. Ref: ZX-071.

3.30 **The upper-level entrance to the Kilburn Building.** 184
Source: Courtesy Eddy Rhead.

3.31 **Inside the upper level of the Precinct Centre.** 186
Source: Courtesy Eddy Rhead.

LIST OF ILLUSTRATIONS

3.32 **Bridge connecting the Precinct Centre to the RNCM.** 186
Source: Visual Resource Centre (35 mm slide). Manchester Metropolitan University Special Collections. No ref.

3.33 **Medical School.** 187
Source: Author's scan from *Manchester Medical School* (1973) (Manchester: Alan Ward PR Services).

3.34 **Wilson & Womersley's scheme for a Sports Centre (unbuilt).** 187
Source: Author's scan from Wilson, H., and Womersley, L. (1974) *The Sports Centre, Oxford Road, Manchester: Final Design Scheme Report*.

3.35 **University of Manchester Business School.** 189
Source: Author's own.

3.36 **Loxford Tower.** 190
Source: Visual Resource Centre (35 mm slide). Manchester Metropolitan University Special Collections. Ref: ZX-264.

Chapter 4

4.01 **Rodwell House.** 200
Source: Author's scan of uncatalogued slides held at Chetham's Library.

4.02 **Illustrations by David Gosling of designs for the Civic Area.** 202
Source: *Architectural Review*, August 1962.

4.03 **Central Station.** 204
Source: Visual Resource Centre (35 mm slide). Manchester Metropolitan University Special Collections. Ref: ZGK-5-24.

4.04 **Proposal for new underground station at St Peter's Square.** 205
Source: Scan courtesy Capes Dunn Auctioneers.

4.05 **Model of the Advisory Scheme for the Central Station CDA.** 207
Source: Cruickshank & Seward Archive. Courtesy Manchester Metropolitan University Special Collections.

4.06 **Taylor Woodrow Group sponsored proposals for Central Station.** 209
Source: Courtesy BDP.

4.07 **Landscaped courtyard at ICL.** 215
Source: Cruickshank & Seward Archive. Courtesy Manchester Metropolitan University Special Collections.

4.08 **Model 01.** 216
Source: Cruickshank & Seward Archive. Courtesy Manchester Metropolitan University Special Collections.

LIST OF ILLUSTRATIONS

4.09 **Model 02.** 216
Source: Cruickshank & Seward Archive. Courtesy Manchester Metropolitan University Special Collections.

4.10 **Model 03.** 217
Source: Cruickshank & Seward Archive. Courtesy Manchester Metropolitan University Special Collections.

4.11 **Perspective painting by Peter Sainsbury.** 218
Source: Cruickshank & Seward Archive. Courtesy Manchester Metropolitan University Special Collections.

4.12 **Model 04.** 219
Source: Cruickshank & Seward Archive. Courtesy Manchester Metropolitan University Special Collections.

4.13 **Model 05.** 220
Source: Cruickshank & Seward Archive. Courtesy Manchester Metropolitan University Special Collections.

4.14 **Model 06.** 221
Source: Cruickshank & Seward Archive. Courtesy Manchester Metropolitan University Special Collections.

4.15 **Model 07.** 222
Source: Cruickshank & Seward Archive. Courtesy Manchester Metropolitan University Special Collections.

4.16 **Illustrative sketch of the Advisory Scheme for Central Station.** 224
Source: Millar, J.S. (1967) *Manchester City Centre Map 1967*.

4.17 **Approved outline planning scheme.** 226
Source: Cruickshank & Seward Archive. Courtesy Manchester Metropolitan University Special Collections.

4.18 **Essex Goodman Suggitt proposals for the Great Northern Warehouse.** 230
Source: Author's scan from private collection. *Central Station. Proposals for Regeneration*, Central Manchester Joint Venture Study.

Chapter 5

5.01 **Cross Street Manchester, 15 June 1996.** 236
Source: M&S Company Archives, University of Leeds.

5.02 **Extracts from Rowland Nicholas's plan of 1945 and John Millar's plan of 1967.** 238
Source: L: Nicholas, R. (1945) *City of Manchester Plan*, Plate 78. R: Millar, J.S. (1967) *Manchester Corporation. City Planning Department 1965–67*, p. 18.

LIST OF ILLUSTRATIONS

5.03 **Exterior of Kendal, Milne & Co.'s department store in Manchester, c.1950.** 240
Source: Design Council Slide Collection.

5.04 **Extract from bomb damage maps to show area around Market Place.** 240
Source: Archives+: GB127.MISC/1192/1.

5.05 **Drawing by J.D.M. Harvey showing the new Town Hall.** 241
Source: Nicholas, R. (1945) *City of Manchester Plan*, Plate 81.

5.06 **Extract from central area plan (1945).** 243
Source: Nicholas, R. (1945) *City of Manchester Plan*, Plate 78.

5.07 **Drawing by P.D. Hepworth of the Cathedral Precinct.** 244
Source: Nicholas, R. (1945) *City of Manchester Plan*, Plate 80.

5.08 **Longridge House, H.S. Fairhurst & Son, 1959.** 248
Source: Manchester Local Image Collection, ref. m01102.
Photographer: W. Higham.

5.09 **Extracts from government publications on highways and junction design.** 249
Sources: L – *Layout of Roads in Built-Up Areas* (1946); R – *Town Planning and Road Traffic* (1942).

5.10 **Entrance to the Corporation's underground car park.** 251
Source: Town Hall Photographers collection.

5.11 **Early drawings of development for Unicos Property Corporation.** 252
Source: Archives+, City Engineer's Microcard Library, 5281 Unicos Market Street.

5.12 **Michael House and Marks & Spencer.** 253
Source: Margaret Newbold Collection, Chetham's Library.

5.13 **Rowland Nicholas's second scheme for the area around Market Place.** 255
Source: *Interbuild*, February 1963, pp. 40–41.

5.14 **Accompanying sketches, by David Gosling, to Nicholas's 1962/3 Scheme.** 256
Source: *Interbuild*, February 1963, pp. 40–41.

5.15 **Proposals for the demolition and replacement of Manchester's Corn Exchange.** 257
Source: *The Builder*, 19 October 1962, pp. 773–775.

5.16 **The Shambles Being Lifted Up.** 259
Source: Margaret Newbold Collection, Chetham's Library.

LIST OF ILLUSTRATIONS

5.17 **Extract from Map 9 showing 'Comprehensive Planning Proposals' for the central area.** 261
Source: Millar, J.S. (1967) *Manchester City Centre Map 1967*.

5.18 **Advisory Scheme drawing.** 262
Source: National Archives ref: HLG/79/407.

5.19 **Advisory Scheme drawing.** 263
Source: National Archives ref: HLG/79/407.

5.20 **Advisory Scheme model.** 264
Source: National Archives ref: HLG/79/407.

5.21 **Urban Structure Map.** 265
Source: Planning Advisory Group (1965) Appendix C, Figure 1.

5.22 **Artist's impression of Market Place development.** 266
Source: Edited photograph from the Margaret Newbold Collection, Chetham's Library.

5.23 **Section BB, extract from C&S drawing no. 1655/133 rev. A.** 269
Source: National Archives ref: HLG/79/407.

5.24 **View eastwards along St Mary's Gate from Deansgate, 1980.** 269
Source: Author's scan of uncatalogued slides held at Chetham's Library.

5.25 **Elizabeth House, St Peter's Square. Cruickshank & Seward, 1971.** 271
Source: Cruickshank & Seward Archive. Courtesy Manchester Metropolitan University Special Collections.

5.26 **Master plan, October 1966.** 272
Source: National Archives ref: HLG/79/407.

5.27 **Artist's impression by Peter Sainsbury of Phase II of Market Place development.** 274
Source: *Environment North West*, March 1972, p. 2. LSE Library Store newspapers: N 547.

5.28 **Footbridge connecting St Michael House to the Arndale Centre.** 274
Source: Visual Resource Centre (35 mm slide). Manchester Metropolitan University Special Collections. No ref.

5.29 **Shambles Square in 1983.** 275
Source: Visual Resource Centre (35 mm slide). Manchester Metropolitan University Special Collections. No ref.

5.30 **The Arndale Centre, Wilson & Womersley, 1977.** 276
Source: Visual Resource Centre (35 mm slide). Manchester Metropolitan University Special Collections. No ref.

Chapter 6

6.01 **Drawing to illustrate proposed approximate radius of ring roads.** 281
Source: *Manchester Guardian*. 11 July 1929, p. 13.

6.02 **Drawings to illustrate two possible routes for a city centre ring road.** 282
Source: *Manchester Guardian*. 26 Oct. 1932, p. 11, and 4 July 1938, p. 13.

6.03 **Extract from *Manchester Regional Plan 1945*.** 283
Source: Nicholas, R.J. (1945) *Manchester and District. Regional planning proposals*.

6.04 **Extract from *SELNEC, A Highway Plan*.** 284
Source: South-East Lancashire and North-East Cheshire Area Highway Engineering Committee (1962) *SELNEC A Highway Plan*.

6.05 **Illustration by Kenneth Browne from *Traffic in Towns*.** 286
Source: Buchanan, C. (1963) *Traffic in Towns: A Study of the Long Term Problems of Traffic in Urban Areas*.

6.06 **Map to accompany *Manchester City Centre Road*, 1968.** 288
Source: Hayes, J. (1968) *Manchester: City Centre Road*.

6.07 **Extract from 1965–67 Report of the Planning Department.** 289
Source: Millar, J.S. (1967) *Manchester Corporation. City Planning Department 1965–67*, p. 18.

6.08 **Central Area Replanning, Sites Available for Development.** 290
Source: Author's scan from City Engineer's microcards held at Manchester Archives+.

6.09 **Granada TV photographed in February 1980.** 291
Source: Courtesy Phil Griffin.

6.10 **Courts of Justice, Crown Square (Leonard Cecil Howitt, City Architect, 1962).** 292
Source: Courtesy MMU Special Collections. Ref: ZX-207.

6.11 **The covered River Irwell.** 293
Source: *Manchester Guardian*, 1 February 1924, p. 10.

6.12 **Extract from drawing showing proposed Trinity Railway Station, c.1947.** 294
Source: Archives+. Ref: GB127.M507/5664.

6.13 **Sketch of Highland House (Leach Rhodes Walker, 1966).** 294
Source: Author's scan. *Architecture North West*, No. 22, p. 16.

LIST OF ILLUSTRATIONS

6.14 Cannon Street and the Arndale Centre, 2001. 295
    Source: flickr.
6.15 CWS and CIS Towers. 296
    Source: Author's own.
6.16 Model showing proposed canyon and multi-level traffic engineering along Portland Street. 298
    Source: Millar, J.S. (1967) *Manchester City Centre Map 1967*.
6.17 Portland Street. 299
    Source: Author's own.
6.18 Piccadilly Plaza under construction. 299
    Source: Visual Resource Centre (35 mm slide). Manchester Metropolitan University Special Collections. Ref: Piccadilly-02.
6.19 The roof garden of Williams Deacon Bank. 300
    Source: *Architecture North West*, No. 11.
6.20 Model showing the proposed bridge link across Mosley Street. 301
    Source: Cruickshank & Seward Archive. Courtesy Manchester Metropolitan University Special Collections.
6.21 Extract from *City Centre Map, 1967*. 302
    Source: Millar, J.S. (1967) *Manchester City Centre Map 1967*.
6.22 New construction in and around the city of Manchester in 1963. 303
    Source: *The Guardian*, 12 July 1963, p. 12.
6.23 John Dalton Street. 304
    Source: Author's photograph.
6.24 The unbuilt Portland Tower. 305
    Source: Author's scan from private collection. *Leach Rhodes Walker. Architects and Town Planning Consultants* (Brochure).
6.25 York House. 306
    Source: Town Hall Photographer's Collection – GB127.M850. Negative No: 1968–0718 – Negatives Book Entry: 01–04–1968_TP_York House City (Centre)_TP Inquiry.
6.26 The proposed network from the 1980 report. 308
    Source: *Manchester city centre local plan: report of survey / issues and choices: consultation document* (1980).
6.27 The diagram of the proposed network from the 1984 report. 309
    Source: Manchester City Centre Local Plan (1984).
6.28 The Ring. 310
    Source: *The Ring: The Manchester and Salford Ring Road: A Relief Route for the Regional Centre* (1987).

Chapter 7

7.01 Greater Manchester. 317
Source: Greater Manchester County Council (1975) *County Structure Plan: Report of Survey.*

7.02 Greater Manchester Structure Plan, 1975. 321
Source: Greater Manchester County Council (1975) *County Structure Plan: Report of Survey.*

7.03 Designs for the beaux-arts boulevard of Manchester's processional way from the Town Hall to Deansgate. 322
Source: City Engineer's microcards. Ref: 3829-7-17.

7.04 The Free Trade Hall. Rebuilt to designs by L.C. Howitt in the 1950s. 323
Source: *Manchester Free Trade Hall: commemorative brochure,* Manchester Municipal Information Bureau, 1951.

Index

1945 Plan 20–21, 27–37, 44–45, 60, 125–127, 178, 197, 242–245, 280–283, 320

Amsell & Bailey 45
Architecture North West 50
Arndale Centre 6, 23, 56, 177, 236, 246, 265, 273, 276, 295, 322
Atlas (computer) 108

Baby (computer) 70, 71, 90
Barnes Wallis Building 163–166
BBC 110–112, 116, 119, 175
Beaumont, J.W. & Sons 45, 74–76, 239
Besant-Roberts, Sidney G. 42, 57, 58
Blackett, (Sir) Patrick 73, 90
Bowden, (Lord) Bertram Vivian 69–70, 71, 73, 93, 108, 115, 120, 122, 125, 127, 130, 135, 136, 137, 146, 149, 152, 160–161, 163, 173, 175, 190
Brazennose House 57, 322
Brocklesby, R.S. 109–110
Buchanan, Colin 55, 178, 207, 238, 256, 262, 273, 285–287
Building Design Partnership 43, 58, 60, 111–112, 114, 185, 209–210, 300

canal 2, 12, 16, 18, 200, 215, 221, 227, 279
Cathedral Area 48, 50, 57, 201, 242, 255, 321
Central Station 59–60, 195–232, 318–319

Chandos Hall 161–163
Chemical Engineering Pilot Plant 170–171
Chippindale, Sam 246
City Architect 44, 45, 47, 48, 57, 58, 111, 282, 292
City Architect's Department 5, 47, 48, 185, 190
Civic Area 48–49, 57, 201, 202, 285, 322
Cold War 65, 67, 69, 71, 92, 293, 318, 324
Comprehensive Development Area 6, 47–60, 125, 195–203, 287
Compulsory Purchase Order 6, 39, 54, 145, 180, 197, 229, 266
computing 4, 65–122, 135, 184
Cousins, Frank 98, 106
Corn Exchange 50, 255–257, 264, 321
Crown Agents 60, 195–232
Crown Court 44, 57, 202, 322, 324
Cruickshank & Seward 5, 40, 43, 80–120, 130–175, 185, 189, 213–232, 235–275, 300–301
Cummings & Levy 40

Deansgate 16, 23, 57, 218, 219, 225, 239, 258, 266, 269, 272–274, 293, 321–322
Development Plan 6, 27–28, 39–45, 54–55, 196–199, 211, 265
Dingle, Philip B. 39, 175n.164, 177, 183, 259n.56

353

exhibition 30–32, 36, 50, 56, 72
  hall 206, 208–210, 224–225, 228, 291

Fairbairn (Sir) William 11–15, 43
Fairhurst, Harry S. & Sons 5, 75, 76, 130, 138, 139, 142, 146, 151, 160, 161, 166–168, 170, 173, 187, 188, 235, 242, 248, 300
Ferranti 66, 68–71, 72, 73, 78–94, 95–100, 106, 108, 122, 136, 149, 169, 315
  Building 169–170
Ferranti, Basil de 97
Ferranti, (Sir) Vincent de 92, 97
Festival of Britain 71–72, 176, 291
Free Trade Hall 44, 205, 323
Fry & Drew 6, 189, 298

Geddes, (Sir) Patrick 18, 316
Gibbon, Arthur 43, 84–85, 114, 115, 118, 141, 146, 148–151, 154, 158, 160, 161, 163, 164, 167–168, 169–170, 171–172, 175, 176, 190, 214, 248, 251–252, 268, 270–272
Granada TV Studios 40, 41, 290–292
Greater Manchester 3, 18, 61, 223, 307–310, 316–317, 320–321

Hagenbach, Arnold 246
Hall, Peter 70, 97, 98, 102, 108, 115, 122
Higher Education Precinct 107, 122, 125–192
Hodkinson, Gordon 85, 154, 158, 160
Hollaway, Antony 168, 170
Howitt, Leonard Cecil 33n.66, 43–44, 292, 323
Hulme 53, 54, 177, 221

International Computers and Tabulators (ICT) 89, 90, 95–100, 104, 108
International Computers Limited (ICL) 66, 89, 90–91, 96–106

Kilburn, Tom 70–71, 73, 92, 120

Leach Rhodes Walker 5, 57, 58, 200, 292, 293, 294, 295, 297

local government 2, 3, 4, 15, 18, 20, 27, 33, 51, 57, 117, 121, 136, 145, 195, 223, 235, 236, 237, 315, 316, 318
Local Government Act 27, 223, 307, 316

mainstream modernism 4, 5, 164, 173, 195, 214, 228, 236, 239, 249–254, 268, 273, 318, 319, 325
Manchester and District Joint Town Planning Advisory Committee 19
Manchester Corporation 1, 11, 28, 31, 37, 39, 40, 45, 52, 54, 59, 60, 79, 80, 81, 100, 103, 108–110, 112, 114, 117, 122, 130–132, 135–136, 137, 139, 145, 150, 151, 153, 166, 189, 192, 200, 201, 203, 205, 206, 208, 210, 211, 235, 237, 239, 246, 250, 266, 291, 296–298, 320
Manchester Education Precinct 56, 125, 172–192
Manchester, South Junction and Altrincham railway 138
Mancunian Way 107, 110, 111, 114, 116, 119, 168, 173, 188, 311
Market Place 4, 6, 232, 235–276, 290, 315, 319
Market Street Area 56–57, 200, 256, 322
Maths and Social Science Building 167, 169–170
military industrial network 65, 67, 78
Millar, John 27, 28, 41–47, 50–55, 60, 111, 125, 177, 198–199, 201, 206, 211, 223, 225, 227, 237, 242, 248, 254, 260–261, 262, 273–275, 282, 285, 307, 315–316, 320–321
Ministry of Civil Aviation 82
Ministry
  of Defence 71
  of Education 131, 133, 185
  of Health 26, 185, 198
  of Housing and Local Government 39, 185
  of Supply 67, 69, 70, 71, 74, 81, 84, 88, 92, 198
  of Technology 90n.92, 98–99, 105–106, 107, 108, 112, 114–115, 117, 120

of Town and Country Planning 27, 198, 243, 258
of Transport 42
of Works 26, 58, 198, 243, 245, 258
    and Buildings 26, 27
    and Planning 27
morphology 1, 11, 280, 315
Mosley Street 13, 25, 26, 57, 58, 59, 206, 300–302, 321, 324
motorway 107, 110, 116, 121, 130, 184, 192, 247, 254, 279, 281, 285, 311

National Computing Centre 4, 66, 78, 106–121, 271, 315
nationalisation 15, 315
National Research Development Corporation 71, 92, 93, 98
negotiated practice 6, 7, 325
Newman, Max 70–71, 73–74, 120
Nicholas, Rowland 27, 30–34, 42, 45, 142, 166–167, 173, 175, 177, 254, 280

oil crisis 3, 306
Old Wellington Inn 57, 241, 244–264, 267, 275
organizational complex 67
Oxford Road 4, 107, 110–113, 127, 151, 178–190, 205

Pariser, (Sir) Maurice 127, 136, 146
Pegasus (computer) 93, 94, 108
periodisation 3, 27, 318
Peter House 45–46
Planning Advisory Group 42, 55, 211, 260, 261, 267
Powell & Moya 6

Rapid Transit Study 205
railways 16–17, 203
Reform Synagogue 40
regional 227, 228, 230
    capital 2, 7, 28
    centre 16, 18, 24, 28, 56
    committee 198
    context 279

convergence 84
development 276
dynamics 24
economic planning 42, 61, 319
government 224, 258, 315, 320
hub 280, 316
interests 235
ministry 2, 38, 145, 250, 259, 317
network 65, 78, 93, 121, 122
objectives 135
planning 19, 20, 28, 33, 35, 42, 55, 280
policy 250
role 4
scale 33, 41, 122, 132, 316
setting 23
status 41
structures 120, 306, 325
system 281
regionalist 149
Renold Chain Company 84, 85
Renold Building 114, 129, 154, 155–160, 162, 163, 172, 190
Renold, (Sir) Charles 127, 146, 157, 177
RIBA Conference 43–45
ring road 4, 23–24, 33, 37, 41, 45, 55–57, 203, 217–219, 247, 255–256, 264–265, 279–311, 324
River Irwell 16, 23, 242, 255, 266, 282, 293, 294, 311
River Medlock 129, 137–140, 145
Robbins Report 142, 176
Rochdale Canal 16, 200
Rodwell Tower 150, 200, 214
Rutherford, Ernest 69, 73

Sainsbury, Peter 98–99, 115, 150–151, 218, 274
SELNEC 178, 282–285, 316
Senior, Derek 31n.64, 45, 316–317
Seward, John 43, 98, 100, 115, 118, 214, 217n.90, 223n.101, 225, 228
Simon, Alfred P. 21, 22–26
Simon, Ernest D. 20–22, 79
St. Augustine's Church 6
Stewart, Cecil 44

technical colleges 132
Telecommunications Research Establishment 69, 70–71, 73–74, 108, 120
Town and Country Planning Act 20, 27, 28, 37, 39, 42, 45, 54–55, 196, 243, 246, 316
Town Hall 19, 26, 31, 33, 50, 57, 202, 220, 241, 245, 260, 322
    Extension 23, 24, 241
townscape 19, 49, 237, 238, 256, 285
Traffic in Towns 55, 178, 207, 237, 238, 258, 285, 286
Treasury 112, 114, 131–133, 185
Trinity Station 35, 293–294
Tubbs (Sir) Ralph 40, 291–292
Turing, Alan 70

UMIST 69, 107–108, 125–172, 189–190
United Kingdom Atomic Energy Authority 69, 78, 79, 108, 109, 110, 112, 114, 116
University Grants Committee 109, 126, 131–138, 140, 141, 145, 146, 148, 153, 160, 161, 163, 164, 169, 175, 182, 191–192
University of Manchester 47, 66, 70, 74–75, 78, 125, 127, 131, 132, 175–192
Upper Brook Street 125, 178, 188
urban renewal 3, 43, 122, 237, 268, 273, 317

warfare state 3, 65, 121, 315
welfare state 3, 66, 315, 319, 324
West Gorton 81, 89–106, 108, 122, 214, 315
Whitehall 2, 27, 42, 61, 78, 122, 145, 175, 185, 192, 196, 203, 211, 259, 275, 315, 318
Williams, Desmond 6
Williams, Freddie 91–93, 108, 120
Williams, (Sir) Owen 171, 271
Wilson & Womersley 5, 23, 43, 53, 56, 111–112, 125, 177–178, 182, 187, 191, 270, 276
Wilson, Harold 70, 98, 114, 121
Wilson, Hugh L. 43, 53, 56, 111–112, 125, 177–178, 188, 270, 276
Womersley, Lewis 177, 182, 188
Worthington, (Sir) Hubert 34n.67, 35, 74–76, 126, 127, 128, 130, 138–173, 175, 183
Wurster, William 149–150
Wythenshawe 21, 31, 53, 78–89, 106, 108, 122, 149, 159, 315

Yorke Rosenberg Mardell 57, 58, 176

zoning 14, 15, 20, 21, 36, 60, 175, 201, 238, 239, 241, 242, 265

EU authorised representative for GPSR:
Easy Access System Europe, Mustamäe tee 50,
10621 Tallinn, Estonia
gpsr.requests@easproject.com

www.ingramcontent.com/pod-product-compliance
Lightning Source LLC
LaVergne TN
LVHW062117190525
811683LV00011B/147